Security Guide

SUSE Linux Enterprise Server 12 SP3

Security Guide

SUSE Linux Enterprise Server 12 SP3

Introduces basic concepts of system security, covering both local and network security aspects. Shows how to use the product inherent security software like AppArmor or the auditing system that reliably collects information about any security-relevant events.

Publication Date: January 08, 2018

SUSE LLC

10 Canal Park Drive

Suite 200

Cambridge MA 02141

USA

https://www.suse.com/documentation ↗

Changes to original document: page numbers added to top right corner of book.

Contents

About This Guide

This manual introduces the basic concepts of system security on SUSE Linux Enterprise Server. It covers extensive documentation about the authentication mechanisms available on Linux, such as NIS or LDAP. It deals with aspects of local security like access control lists, encryption and intrusion detection. In the network security part you learn how to secure computers with firewalls and masquerading, and how to set up virtual private networks (VPN). This manual shows how to use security software like AppArmor (which lets you specify per program which files the program may read, write, and execute) or the auditing system that collects information about security-relevant events.

1   Available Documentation

 Note: Online Documentation and Latest Updates

Documentation for our products is available at http://www.suse.com/documentation/ ⌐, where you can also find the latest updates, and browse or download the documentation in various formats.

In addition, the product documentation is usually available in your installed system under `/usr/share/doc/manual`.

The following documentation is available for this product:

Article "Installation Quick Start"

Lists the system requirements and guides you step-by-step through the installation of SUSE Linux Enterprise Server from DVD, or from an ISO image.

Book "Deployment Guide"

Shows how to install single or multiple systems and how to exploit the product inherent capabilities for a deployment infrastructure. Choose from various approaches, ranging from a local installation or a network installation server to a mass deployment using a remote-controlled, highly-customized, and automated installation technique.

Book "Administration Guide"

Covers system administration tasks like maintaining, monitoring and customizing an initially installed system.

Book "Virtualization Guide"

Describes virtualization technology in general, and introduces libvirt—the unified interface to virtualization—and detailed information on specific hypervisors.

Book "Storage Administration Guide"

Provides information about how to manage storage devices on a SUSE Linux Enterprise Server.

Book "AutoYaST"

AutoYaST is a system for unattended mass deployment SUSE Linux Enterprise Server systems using an AutoYaST profile containing installation and configuration data. The manual guides you through the basic steps of auto-installation: preparation, installation, and configuration.

Security Guide

Introduces basic concepts of system security, covering both local and network security aspects. Shows how to use the product inherent security software like AppArmor or the auditing system that reliably collects information about any security-relevant events.

Book "Security and Hardening Guide"

Deals with the particulars of installing and setting up a secure SUSE Linux Enterprise Server, and additional post-installation processes required to further secure and harden that installation. Supports the administrator with security-related choices and decisions.

Book "System Analysis and Tuning Guide"

An administrator's guide for problem detection, resolution and optimization. Find how to inspect and optimize your system by means of monitoring tools and how to efficiently manage resources. Also contains an overview of common problems and solutions and of additional help and documentation resources.

Book "Subscription Management Tool for SLES 12 SP3"

An administrator's guide to Subscription Management Tool—a proxy system for SUSE Customer Center with repository and registration targets. Learn how to install and configure a local SMT server, mirror and manage repositories, manage client machines, and configure clients to use SMT.

Book "GNOME User Guide"

Introduces the GNOME desktop of SUSE Linux Enterprise Server. It guides you through using and configuring the desktop and helps you perform key tasks. It is intended mainly for end users who want to make efficient use of GNOME as their default desktop.

2 Feedback

Several feedback channels are available:

Bugs and Enhancement Requests

For services and support options available for your product, refer to http://www.suse.com/support/ ↗.

Help for openSUSE is provided by the community. Refer to https://en.opensuse.org/Portal:Support ↗ for more information.

To report bugs for a product component, go to https://scc.suse.com/support/requests ↗, log in, and click *Create New*.

User Comments

We want to hear your comments about and suggestions for this manual and the other documentation included with this product. Use the User Comments feature at the bottom of each page in the online documentation or go to http://www.suse.com/documentation/feedback.html ↗ and enter your comments there.

Mail

For feedback on the documentation of this product, you can also send a mail to doc-team@suse.com. Make sure to include the document title, the product version and the publication date of the documentation. To report errors or suggest enhancements, provide a concise description of the problem and refer to the respective section number and page (or URL).

3 Documentation Conventions

The following notices and typographical conventions are used in this documentation:

- /etc/passwd: directory names and file names

- *PLACEHOLDER*: replace *PLACEHOLDER* with the actual value

- PATH: the environment variable PATH

- ls, --help: commands, options, and parameters

- user: users or groups

- `package name` : name of a package

- [Alt], [Alt]-[F1]: a key to press or a key combination; keys are shown in uppercase as on a keyboard

- *File*, *File* › *Save As*: menu items, buttons

- [x86_64] This paragraph is only relevant for the AMD64/Intel 64 architecture. The arrows mark the beginning and the end of the text block. ◁
  [System z, POWER] This paragraph is only relevant for the architectures `z Systems` and `POWER`. The arrows mark the beginning and the end of the text block. ◁

- *Dancing Penguins* (Chapter *Penguins*, ↑Another Manual): This is a reference to a chapter in another manual.

- Commands that must be run with `root` privileges. Often you can also prefix these commands with the **sudo** command to run them as non-privileged user.

  ```
  root # command
  tux > sudo command
  ```

- Commands that can be run by non-privileged users.

  ```
  tux > command
  ```

- Notices

Warning: Warning Notice

Vital information you must be aware of before proceeding. Warns you about security issues, potential loss of data, damage to hardware, or physical hazards.

Important: Important Notice

Important information you should be aware of before proceeding.

Note: Note Notice

Additional information, for example about differences in software versions.

Tip: Tip Notice

Helpful information, like a guideline or a piece of practical advice.

1 Security and Confidentiality

One of the main characteristics of a Linux or Unix system is its ability to handle several users at the same time (multiuser) and to allow these users to perform several tasks (multitasking) on the same computer simultaneously. Moreover, the operating system is network transparent. The users often do not know whether the data and applications they are using are provided locally from their machine or made available over the network.

With the multiuser capability, the data of different users must be stored separately, and security and privacy need to be guaranteed. Data security was already an important issue, even before computers could be linked through networks. Like today, the most important concern was the ability to keep data available in spite of a lost or otherwise damaged data medium (usually a hard disk).

This section is primarily focused on confidentiality issues and on ways to protect the privacy of users. But it cannot be stressed enough that a comprehensive security concept should always include procedures to have a regularly updated, workable, and tested backup in place. Without this, you could have a very hard time getting your data back—not only in the case of some hardware defect, but also in the case that someone has gained unauthorized access and tampered with files.

1.1 Local Security and Network Security

There are several ways of accessing data:

- personal communication with people who have the desired information or access to the data on a computer

- directly through physical access from the console of a computer

- over a serial line

- using a network link

In all these cases, a user should be authenticated before accessing the resources or data in question. A Web server might be less restrictive in this respect, but you still would not want it to disclose your personal data to an anonymous user.

In the list above, the first case is the one where the highest amount of human interaction is involved (such as when you are contacting a bank employee and are required to prove that you are the person owning that bank account). Then, you are asked to provide a signature, a PIN, or a password to prove that you are the person you claim to be. In some cases, it might be possible to elicit some intelligence from an informed person by mentioning known bits and pieces to win the confidence of that person. The victim could be led to reveal gradually more information, maybe without even being aware of it. Among hackers, this is called *social engineering*. You can only guard against this by educating people and by dealing with language and information in a conscious way. Before breaking into computer systems, attackers often try to target receptionists, service people working with the company, or even family members. Often such an attack based on social engineering is only discovered at a much later time.

A person wanting to obtain unauthorized access to your data could also use the traditional way and try to get at your hardware directly. Therefore, the machine should be protected against any tampering so that no one can remove, replace, or cripple its components. This also applies to backups and even any network cables or power cords. Also secure the boot procedure, because there are some well-known key combinations that might provoke unusual behavior. Protect yourself against this by setting passwords for the BIOS and the boot loader.

Serial terminals connected to serial ports are still used in many places. Unlike network interfaces, they do not rely on network protocols to communicate with the host. A simple cable or an infrared port is used to send plain characters back and forth between the devices. The cable itself is the weakest point of such a system: with an older printer connected to it, it is easy to record any data being transferred that way. What can be achieved with a printer can also be accomplished in other ways, depending on the effort that goes into the attack.

Reading a file locally on a host requires additional access rules than opening a network connection with a server on a different host. There is a distinction between local security and network security. The line is drawn where data must be put into packets to be sent somewhere else.

1.1.1 Local Security

Local security starts with the physical environment at the location in which computer is running. Set up your machine in a place where security is in line with your expectations and needs. The main goal of local security is to keep users separate from each other, so no user can assume the permissions or the identity of another. This is a general rule to be observed, but it is especially true for the user `root`, who holds system administration privileges. `root` can take on the identity of any other local user and read any locally-stored file without being prompted for the password.

1.1.1.1 Passwords

On a Linux system, passwords are not stored as plain text and the entered text string is not simply matched with the saved pattern. If this were the case, all accounts on your system would be compromised when someone got access to the corresponding file. Instead, the stored password is encrypted and, each time it is entered, is encrypted again and the two encrypted strings are compared. This only provides more security if the encrypted password cannot be reverse-computed into the original text string.

This is achieved by a special kind of algorithm, also called *trapdoor algorithm*, because it only works in one direction. An attacker who has obtained the encrypted string is not able to get your password by simply applying the same algorithm again. Instead, it would be necessary to test all the possible character combinations until a combination is found that looks like your password when encrypted. With passwords eight characters long, there are many combinations to calculate.

In the seventies, it was argued that this method would be more secure than others because of the relative slowness of the algorithm used which took a few seconds to encrypt one password. In the meantime, PCs have become powerful enough to do several hundred thousand or even millions of encryptions per second. Because of this, encrypted passwords should not be visible to regular users (`/etc/shadow` cannot be read by normal users). It is even more important that passwords are not easy to guess, in case the password file becomes visible because of an error. Consequently, it is not really useful to "translate" a password like "tantalize" into "t@nt@1lz3".

Replacing some letters of a word with similar looking numbers (like writing the password "tantalize" as "t@nt@1lz3") is not sufficient. Password cracking programs that use dictionaries to guess words also play with substitutions like that. A better way is to make up a word that only makes sense to you personally, like the first letters of the words of a sentence or the title of a book, such as "The Name of the Rose" by Umberto Eco. This would give the following safe password: "TNotRbUE9". In contrast, passwords like "beerbuddy" or "jasmine76" are easily guessed even by someone who has only some casual knowledge about you.

1.1.1.2   The Boot Procedure

Configure your system so it cannot be booted from a removable device, either by removing the drives entirely or by setting a BIOS password and configuring the BIOS to allow booting from a hard disk only. Normally, a Linux system is started by a boot loader, allowing you to pass additional options to the booted kernel. Prevent others from using such parameters during boot by setting an additional password for the boot loader (see *Book "Administration Guide", Chapter 12 "The Boot Loader GRUB 2", Section 12.2.6 "Setting a Boot Password"* for instructions). This is crucial to your system's security. Not only does the kernel itself run with `root` permissions, but it is also the first authority to grant `root` permissions at system start-up.

1.1.1.3   File Permissions

As a general rule, always work with the most restrictive privileges possible for a given task. For example, it is definitely not necessary to be `root` to read or write e-mail. If the mail program has a bug, this bug could be exploited for an attack that acts with exactly the permissions of the program when it was started. By following the above rule, minimize the possible damage.

The permissions of all files included in the SUSE Linux Enterprise Server distribution are carefully chosen. A system administrator who installs additional software or other files should take great care when doing so, especially when setting the permission bits. Experienced and security-conscious system administrators always use the `-l` option with the command `ls` to get an extensive file list, which allows them to detect any incorrect file permissions immediately. An incorrect file attribute does not only mean that files could be changed or deleted. These modified files could be executed by `root` or, in the case of configuration files, programs could use such files with the permissions of `root`. This significantly increases the possibilities of an attack. Attacks like these are called cuckoo eggs, because the program (the egg) is executed (hatched) by a different user (bird), similar to how a cuckoo tricks other birds into hatching its eggs.

An SUSE® Linux Enterprise Server system includes the files `permissions`, `permissions.easy`, `permissions.secure`, and `permissions.paranoid`, all in the directory `/etc`. The purpose of these files is to define special permissions, such as world-writable directories or, for files, the setuser ID bit (programs with the setuser ID bit set do not run with the permissions of the user that has launched it, but with the permissions of the file owner, usually `root`). An administrator can use the file `/etc/permissions.local` to add his own settings.

To define which of the above files is used by SUSE Linux Enterprise Server's configuration programs to set permissions, select *Local Security* in the *Security and Users* section of YaST. To learn more about the topic, read the comments in `/etc/permissions` or consult the manual page of **chmod** (**man** `chmod`).

1.1.1.4 Buffer Overflows and Format String Bugs

Special care must be taken whenever a program needs to process data that could be changed by a user, but this is more of an issue for the programmer of an application than for regular users. The programmer must make sure that his application interprets data in the correct way, without writing it into memory areas that are too small to hold it. Also, the program should hand over data in a consistent manner, using interfaces defined for that purpose.

A *buffer overflow* can happen if the actual size of a memory buffer is not taken into account when writing to that buffer. There are cases where this data (as generated by the user) uses up more space than what is available in the buffer. As a result, data is written beyond the end of that buffer area, which, under certain circumstances, makes it possible for a program to execute program sequences influenced by the user (and not by the programmer), rather than processing user data only. A bug of this kind may have serious consequences, especially if the program is being executed with special privileges (see Section 1.1.1.3, "File Permissions").

Format string bugs work in a slightly different way, but again it is the user input that could lead the program astray. Usually, these programming errors are exploited with programs executed with special permissions—setuid and setgid programs—which also means that you can protect your data and your system from such bugs by removing the corresponding execution privileges from programs. Again, the best way is to apply a policy of using the lowest possible privileges (see Section 1.1.1.3, "File Permissions").

Given that buffer overflows and format string bugs are related to the handling of user data, they are only exploitable if access has been given to a local account. Many of the bugs that have been reported can also be exploited over a network link. Accordingly, buffer overflows and format string bugs should be classified as being relevant for both local and network security.

1.1.1.5 Viruses

Contrary to popular opinion, there are viruses that run on Linux. However, the viruses that are known were released by their authors as a *proof of concept* that the technique works as intended. None of these viruses have been spotted *in the wild* so far.

Viruses cannot survive and spread without a host on which to live. In this case, the host would be a program or an important storage area of the system (for example, the master boot record) that needs to be writable for the program code of the virus. Because of its multiuser capability, Linux can restrict write access to certain files (this is especially important with system files). Therefore, if you did your normal work with `root` permissions, you would increase the chance of the system being infected by a virus. In contrast, if you follow the principle of using the lowest possible privileges as mentioned above, chances of getting a virus are slim.

Apart from that, you should never rush into executing a program from some Internet site that you do not really know. SUSE Linux Enterprise Server's RPM packages carry a cryptographic signature, as a digital label that the necessary care was taken to build them. Viruses are a typical sign that the administrator or the user lacks the required security awareness, putting at risk even a system that should be highly secure by its very design.

Viruses should not be confused with worms, which belong entirely to the world of networks. Worms do not need a host to spread.

1.1.2 Network Security

Network security is important for protecting from an attack that is started outside the network. The typical login procedure requiring a user name and a password for user authentication is still a local security issue. In the particular case of logging in over a network, differentiate between the two security aspects. What happens until the actual authentication is network security and anything that happens afterward is local security.

1.1.2.1 X Window System and X Authentication

As mentioned at the beginning, network transparency is one of the central characteristics of a Unix system. X, the windowing system of Unix operating systems, can use this feature in an impressive way. With X, it is no problem to log in to a remote host and start a graphical program that is then sent over the network to be displayed on your computer.

When an X client needs to be displayed remotely using an X server, the latter should protect the resource managed by it (the display) from unauthorized access. In more concrete terms, certain permissions must be given to the client program. With the X Window System, there are two ways to do this, called host-based access control and cookie-based access control. The former relies on the IP address of the host where the client should run. The program to control this is xhost. xhost enters the IP address of a legitimate client into a database belonging to the X server. However, relying on IP addresses for authentication is not very secure. For example, if there were a second user working on the host sending the client program, that user would have access to the X server as well—like someone stealing the IP address. Because of these shortcomings, this authentication method is not described in more detail here, but you can learn about it with **man** xhost.

In the case of cookie-based access control, a character string is generated that is only known to the X server and to the legitimate user, like an ID card of some kind. This cookie is stored on login in the file .Xauthority in the user's home directory and is available to any X client wanting to use the X server to display a window. The file .Xauthority can be examined by the user with the tool **xauth**. If you rename .Xauthority, or if you delete the file from your home directory by accident, you would not be able to open any new windows or X clients.

SSH (secure shell) can be used to encrypt a network connection and forward it to an X server transparently. This is also called X forwarding. X forwarding is achieved by simulating an X server on the server side and setting a DISPLAY variable for the shell on the remote host. Further details about SSH can be found in *Chapter 14, SSH: Secure Network Operations*.

 Warning: X Forwarding Can Be Insecure

> If you do not consider the host where you log in to be a secure host, do not use X forwarding. If X forwarding is enabled, an attacker could authenticate via your SSH connection. The attacker could then intrude on your X server and, for example, read your keyboard input.

1.1.2.2 Buffer Overflows and Format String Bugs

As discussed in *Section 1.1.1.4, "Buffer Overflows and Format String Bugs"*, buffer overflows and format string bugs should be classified as issues applying to both local and network security. As with the local variants of such bugs, buffer overflows in network programs, when successfully exploited, are mostly used to obtain `root` permissions. Even if that is not the case, an attacker could use the bug to gain access to an unprivileged local account to exploit other vulnerabilities that might exist on the system.

Buffer overflows and format string bugs exploitable over a network link are certainly the most frequent form of remote attacks, in general. Exploits for these—programs to exploit these newly-found security holes—are often posted on security mailing lists. They can be used to target the vulnerability without knowing the details of the code.

Experience has shown that the availability of exploit codes has contributed to more secure operating systems, as they force operating system makers to fix problems in their software. With free software, anyone has access to the source code (SUSE Linux Enterprise Server comes with complete source code) and anyone who finds a vulnerability and its exploit code can submit a patch to fix the corresponding bug.

1.1.2.3 Denial of Service

The purpose of a denial of service (DoS) attack is to block a server program or even an entire system. This can be achieved in several ways: overloading the server, keeping it busy with garbage packets, or exploiting a remote buffer overflow. Often, a DoS attack is made with the sole purpose of making the service disappear. However, when a given service has become unavailable, communications could become vulnerable to *man-in-the-middle attacks* (sniffing, TCP connection hijacking, spoofing) and DNS poisoning.

1.1.2.4 Man in the Middle: Sniffing, Hijacking, Spoofing

In general, any remote attack performed by an attacker who puts himself between the communicating hosts is called a *man-in-the-middle attack*. What almost all types of man-in-the-middle attacks have in common is that the victim is usually not aware that there is something happening. There are many variants. For example, the attacker could pick up a connection request and forward that to the target machine. Now the victim has unwittingly established a connection with the wrong host, because the other end is posing as the legitimate destination machine.

The simplest form of a man-in-the-middle attack is called *sniffer* (the attacker is "only" listening to the network traffic passing by). As a more complex attack, the "man in the middle" could try to take over an already established connection (hijacking). To do so, the attacker would need to analyze the packets for some time to be able to predict the TCP sequence numbers belonging to the connection. When the attacker finally seizes the role of the target host, the victims notice this, because they get an error message saying the connection was terminated because of a failure. That there are protocols not secured against hijacking through encryption (which only perform a simple authentication procedure upon establishing the connection) makes it easier for attackers.

Spoofing is an attack where packets are modified to contain counterfeit source data, usually the IP address. Most active forms of attack rely on sending out such fake packets (something that, on a Linux machine, can only be done by the superuser (root)).

Many of the attacks mentioned are carried out in combination with a DoS. If an attacker sees an opportunity to bring down a certain host abruptly, even if only for a short time, it makes it easier for him to push the active attack, because the host cannot interfere with the attack for some time.

1.1.2.5   DNS Poisoning

DNS poisoning means that the attacker corrupts the cache of a DNS server by replying to it with spoofed DNS reply packets, trying to get the server to send certain data to a victim who is requesting information from that server. Many servers maintain a trust relationship with other hosts, based on IP addresses or host names. The attacker needs a good understanding of the actual structure of the trust relationships among hosts to disguise itself as one of the trusted hosts. Usually, the attacker analyzes some packets received from the server to get the necessary information. The attacker often needs to target a well-timed DoS attack at the name server as well. Protect yourself by using encrypted connections that can verify the identity of the hosts to which to connect.

1.1.2.6   Worms

Worms are often confused with viruses, but there is a clear difference between the two. Unlike viruses, worms do not need to infect a host program to live. Instead, they are specialized to spread as quickly as possible on network structures. The worms that appeared in the past, such as Ramen, Lion, or Adore, used well-known security holes in server programs like bind8. Protection against worms is relatively easy. Given that some time elapses between the discovery of a security hole and the moment the worm hits your server, there is a good chance that an updated version of the affected program is available on time. That is only useful if the administrator actually installs the security updates on the systems in question.

1.2 Some General Security Tips and Tricks

To handle security competently, it is important to observe some recommendations. You may find the following list of rules useful in dealing with basic security concerns:

- Get and install the updated packages recommended by security announcements as quickly as possible.

- Stay informed about the latest security issues:

  - http://lists.opensuse.org/opensuse-security-announce/ ↗ is the SUSE mailing list for security announcements. It is a first-hand source of information regarding updated packages and includes members of SUSE's security team among its active contributors. You can subscribe to this list on page http://en.opensuse.org/openSUSE:Mailing_lists ↗.

  - Find SUSE security advisories at http://www.suse.com/support/update/ ↗.

  - bugtraq@securityfocus.com is one of the best-known security mailing lists worldwide. Reading this list, which receives between 15 and 20 postings per day, is recommended. More information can be found at http://www.securityfocus.com ↗.

- Discuss any security issues of interest on our mailing list opensuse-security@opensuse.org.

- According to the rule of using the most restrictive set of permissions possible for every job, avoid doing your regular jobs as root. This reduces the risk of getting a cuckoo egg or a virus and protects you from your own mistakes.

- If possible, always try to use encrypted connections to work on a remote machine. Using **ssh** (secure shell) to replace **telnet**, **ftp**, **rsh**, and **rlogin** should be standard practice.

- Avoid using authentication methods based solely on IP addresses.

- Try to keep the most important network-related packages up-to-date and subscribe to the corresponding mailing lists to receive announcements on new versions of such programs (`bind`, `postfix`, `ssh`, etc.). The same should apply to software relevant to local security.

- Change the `/etc/permissions` file to optimize the permissions of files crucial to your system's security. If you remove the setuid bit from a program, it might well be that it cannot do its job anymore in the intended way. On the other hand, the program will usually have ceased to be a potential security risk. You might take a similar approach with world-writable directories and files.

- Disable any network services you do not absolutely require for your server to work properly. This makes your system safer. Open ports, with the socket state LISTEN, can be found with the program `netstat`. As for the options, it is recommended to use `netstat` `-ap` or `netstat` `-anp`. The `-p` option allows you to see which process is occupying a port under which name.

  Compare the `netstat` results with those of a thorough port scan done from outside your host. An excellent program for this job is `nmap`, which not only checks out the ports of your machine, but also draws some conclusions as to which services are waiting behind them. However, port scanning may be interpreted as an aggressive act, so do not do this on a host without the explicit approval of the administrator. Finally, remember that it is important not only to scan TCP ports, but also UDP ports (options `-sS` and `-sU`).

- To monitor the integrity of the files of your system in a reliable way, use the program `AIDE` (Advanced Intrusion Detection Environment), available on SUSE Linux Enterprise Server. Encrypt the database created by AIDE to prevent someone from tampering with it. Furthermore, keep a backup of this database available outside your machine, stored on an external data medium not connected to it by a network link.

- Take proper care when installing any third-party software. There have been cases where a hacker had built a Trojan horse into the TAR archive of a security software package, which was fortunately discovered very quickly. If you install a binary package, have no doubts about the site from which you downloaded it.

  SUSE's RPM packages are gpg-signed. The key used by SUSE for signing is:

```
ID:9C800ACA 2000-10-19 SUSE Package Signing Key <build@suse.de>
    Key fingerprint = 79C1 79B2 E1C8 20C1 890F 9994 A84E DAE8 9C80 0ACA
```

The command **rpm** `--checksig package.rpm` shows whether the checksum and the signature of an uninstalled package are correct. Find the key on the first CD of the distribution and on most key servers worldwide.

- Check backups of user and system files regularly. Consider that if you do not test whether the backup works, it might actually be worthless.

- Check your log files. Whenever possible, write a small script to search for suspicious entries. Admittedly, this is not exactly a trivial task. In the end, only you can know which entries are unusual and which are not.

- Use `tcp_wrapper` to restrict access to the individual services running on your machine, so you have explicit control over which IP addresses can connect to a service. For further information regarding `tcp_wrapper`, consult the manual pages of tcpd and hosts_access (**man** `8 tcpd`, **man** `hosts_access`).

- Use SuSEfirewall to enhance the security provided by `tcpd` (`tcp_wrapper`).

- Design your security measures to be redundant: a message seen twice is much better than no message.

- If you use suspend to disk, consider configuring the suspend image encryption using the **configure-suspend-encryption.sh** script. The program creates the key, copies it to `/etc/suspend.key`, and modifies `/etc/suspend.conf` to use encryption for suspend images.

1.3 Using the Central Security Reporting Address

If you discover a security-related problem (check the available update packages first), write an e-mail to `security@suse.de`. Include a detailed description of the problem and the version number of the package concerned. SUSE will try to send a reply when possible. You are encouraged to pgp-encrypt your e-mail messages. SUSE's PGP key is:

```
ID:3D25D3D9 1999-03-06 SUSE Security Team <security@suse.de>
Key fingerprint = 73 5F 2E 99 DF DB 94 C4 8F 5A A3 AE AF 22 F2 D5
```

This key is also available for download from http://www.suse.com/support/security/contact.html ↗.

I Authentication

2 Authentication with PAM

Linux uses PAM (pluggable authentication modules) in the authentication process as a layer that mediates between user and application. PAM modules are available on a systemwide basis, so they can be requested by any application. This chapter describes how the modular authentication mechanism works and how it is configured.

2.1 What is PAM?

System administrators and programmers often want to restrict access to certain parts of the system or to limit the use of certain functions of an application. Without PAM, applications must be adapted every time a new authentication mechanism, such as LDAP, Samba, or Kerberos, is introduced. However, this process is time-consuming and error-prone. One way to avoid these drawbacks is to separate applications from the authentication mechanism and delegate authentication to centrally managed modules. Whenever a newly required authentication scheme is needed, it is sufficient to adapt or write a suitable *PAM module* for use by the program in question.

The PAM concept consists of:

- *PAM modules*, which are a set of shared libraries for a specific authentication mechanism.

- A *module stack* with of one or more PAM modules.

- A PAM-aware *service* which needs authentication by using a module stack or PAM modules. Usually a service is a familiar name of the corresponding application, like `login` or `su`. The service name `other` is a reserved word for default rules.

- *Module arguments*, with which the execution of a single PAM module can be influenced.

- A mechanism evaluating each *result* of a single PAM module execution. A positive value executes the next PAM module. The way a negative value is dealt with depends on the configuration: "no influence, proceed" up to "terminate immediately" and anything in between are valid options.

2.2 Structure of a PAM Configuration File

PAM can be configured in two ways:

File based configuration (`/etc/pam.conf`)

The configuration of each service is stored in `/etc/pam.conf`. However, for maintenance and usability reasons, this configuration scheme is not used in SUSE Linux Enterprise Server.

Directory based configuration (`/etc/pam.d/`)

Every service (or program) that relies on the PAM mechanism has its own configuration file in the `/etc/pam.d/` directory. For example, the service for `sshd` can be found in the `/etc/pam.d/sshd` file.

The files under `/etc/pam.d/` define the PAM modules used for authentication. Each file consists of lines, which define a service, and each line consists of a maximum of four components:

```
TYPE   CONTROL
 MODULE_PATH  MODULE_ARGS
```

The components have the following meaning:

TYPE

Declares the type of the service. PAM modules are processed as stacks. Different types of modules have different purposes. For example, one module checks the password, another verifies the location from which the system is accessed, and yet another reads user-specific settings. PAM knows about four different types of modules:

`auth`

Check the user's authenticity, traditionally by querying a password. However, this can also be achieved with a chip card or through biometrics (for example, fingerprints or iris scan).

`account`

Modules of this type check if the user has general permission to use the requested service. As an example, such a check should be performed to ensure that no one can log in with the user name of an expired account.

`password`

The purpose of this type of module is to enable the change of an authentication token. Usually this is a password.

`session`

> Modules of this type are responsible for managing and configuring user sessions. They are started before and after authentication to log login attempts and configure the user's specific environment (mail accounts, home directory, system limits, etc.).

CONTROL

> Indicates the behavior of a PAM module. Each module can have the following control flags:

`required`

> A module with this flag must be successfully processed before the authentication may proceed. After the failure of a module with the `required` flag, all other modules with the same flag are processed before the user receives a message about the failure of the authentication attempt.

`requisite`

> Modules having this flag must also be processed successfully, in much the same way as a module with the `required` flag. However, in case of failure a module with this flag gives immediate feedback to the user and no further modules are processed. In case of success, other modules are subsequently processed, like any modules with the `required` flag. The `requisite` flag can be used as a basic filter checking for the existence of certain conditions that are essential for a correct authentication.

`sufficient`

> After a module with this flag has been successfully processed, the requesting application receives an immediate message about the success and no further modules are processed, provided there was no preceding failure of a module with the `required` flag. The failure of a module with the `sufficient` flag has no direct consequences, in the sense that any subsequent modules are processed in their respective order.

`optional`

> The failure or success of a module with this flag does not have any direct consequences. This can be useful for modules that are only intended to display a message (for example, to tell the user that mail has arrived) without taking any further action.

`include`

> If this flag is given, the file specified as argument is inserted at this place.

MODULE_PATH

> Contains a full file name of a PAM module. It does not need to be specified explicitly, as long as the module is located in the default directory `/lib/security` (for all 64-bit platforms supported by SUSE® Linux Enterprise Server, the directory is `/lib64/security`).

MODULE_ARGS

> Contains a space-separated list of options to influence the behavior of a PAM module, such as `debug` (enables debugging) or `nullok` (allows the use of empty passwords).

In addition, there are global configuration files for PAM modules under `/etc/security`, which define the exact behavior of these modules (examples include `pam_env.conf` and `time.conf`). Every application that uses a PAM module actually calls a set of PAM functions, which then process the information in the various configuration files and return the result to the requesting application.

To simplify the creation and maintenance of PAM modules, common default configuration files for the types `auth`, `account`, `password`, and `session` modules have been introduced. These are retrieved from every application's PAM configuration. Updates to the global PAM configuration modules in `common-*` are thus propagated across all PAM configuration files without requiring the administrator to update every single PAM configuration file.

The global PAM configuration files are maintained using the **pam-config** tool. This tool automatically adds new modules to the configuration, changes the configuration of existing ones or deletes modules (or options) from the configurations. Manual intervention in maintaining PAM configurations is minimized or no longer required.

 Note: 64-Bit and 32-Bit Mixed Installations

> When using a 64-bit operating system, it is possible to also include a runtime environment for 32-bit applications. In this case, make sure that you also install the 32-bit version of the PAM modules.

2.3 The PAM Configuration of sshd

Consider the PAM configuration of sshd as an example:

EXAMPLE 2.1: PAM CONFIGURATION FOR SSHD (`/etc/pam.d/sshd`)

```
#%PAM-1.0 ●
```

```
auth      requisite    pam_nologin.so                              ➋
auth      include      common-auth                                 ➌
account   requisite    pam_nologin.so                              ➋
account   include      common-account                              ➌
password  include      common-password                             ➌
session   required     pam_loginuid.so                             ➍
session   include      common-session                              ➌
session   optional     pam_lastlog.so   silent noupdate showfailed ➎
```

➊ Declares the version of this configuration file for PAM 1.0. This is merely a convention, but could be used in the future to check the version.

➋ Checks, if /etc/nologin exists. If it does, no user other than root may log in.

➌ Refers to the configuration files of four module types: common-auth, common-account, common-password, and common-session. These four files hold the default configuration for each module type.

➍ Sets the login uid process attribute for the process that was authenticated.

➎ Displays information about the last login of a user.

By including the configuration files instead of adding each module separately to the respective PAM configuration, you automatically get an updated PAM configuration when an administrator changes the defaults. Formerly, you needed to adjust all configuration files manually for all applications when changes to PAM occurred or a new application was installed. Now the PAM configuration is made with central configuration files and all changes are automatically inherited by the PAM configuration of each service.

The first include file (common-auth) calls three modules of the auth type: pam_env.so, pam_gnome_keyring.so and pam_unix.so. See *Example 2.2, "Default Configuration for the auth Section (common-auth)"*.

EXAMPLE 2.2: DEFAULT CONFIGURATION FOR THE auth SECTION (common-auth)

```
auth   required   pam_env.so                        ➊
auth   optional   pam_gnome_keyring.so              ➋
auth   required   pam_unix.so   try_first_pass      ➌
```

➊ pam_env.so loads /etc/security/pam_env.conf to set the environment variables as specified in this file. It can be used to set the DISPLAY variable to the correct value, because the pam_env module knows about the location from which the login is taking place.

➋ pam_gnome_keyring.so checks the user's login and password against the GNOME key ring

3 `pam_unix` checks the user's login and password against `/etc/passwd` and `/etc/shadow`.

The whole stack of `auth` modules is processed before `sshd` gets any feedback about whether the login has succeeded. All modules of the stack having the `required` control flag must be processed successfully before `sshd` receives a message about the positive result. If one of the modules is not successful, the entire module stack is still processed and only then is `sshd` notified about the negative result.

When all modules of the `auth` type have been successfully processed, another include statement is processed, in this case, that in *Example 2.3, "Default Configuration for the* `account` *Section (common-account)"*. `common-account` contains only one module, `pam_unix`. If `pam_unix` returns the result that the user exists, sshd receives a message announcing this success and the next stack of modules (`password`) is processed, shown in *Example 2.4, "Default Configuration for the* `password` *Section (common-password)"*.

EXAMPLE 2.3: DEFAULT CONFIGURATION FOR THE account SECTION (common-account)

```
account   required   pam_unix.so  try_first_pass
```

EXAMPLE 2.4: DEFAULT CONFIGURATION FOR THE password SECTION (common-password)

```
password   requisite   pam_cracklib.so
password   optional    pam_gnome_keyring.so   use_authtok
password   required    pam_unix.so   use_authtok nullok shadow try_first_pass
```

Again, the PAM configuration of `sshd` involves only an include statement referring to the default configuration for `password` modules located in `common-password`. These modules must successfully be completed (control flags `requisite` and `required`) whenever the application requests the change of an authentication token.

Changing a password or another authentication token requires a security check. This is achieved with the `pam_cracklib` module. The `pam_unix` module used afterward carries over any old and new passwords from `pam_cracklib`, so the user does not need to authenticate again after changing the password. This procedure makes it impossible to circumvent the checks carried out by `pam_cracklib`. Whenever the `account` or the `auth` type are configured to complain about expired passwords, the `password` modules should also be used.

EXAMPLE 2.5: DEFAULT CONFIGURATION FOR THE session SECTION (common-session)

```
session   required   pam_limits.so
session   required   pam_unix.so  try_first_pass
```

```
session  optional  pam_umask.so
session  optional  pam_systemd.so
session  optional  pam_gnome_keyring.so auto_start only_if=gdm,gdm-password,lxdm,lightdm
session  optional  pam_env.so
```

As the final step, the modules of the `session` type (bundled in the `common-session` file) are called to configure the session according to the settings for the user in question. The `pam_limits` module loads the file `/etc/security/limits.conf`, which may define limits on the use of certain system resources. The `pam_unix` module is processed again. The `pam_umask` module can be used to set the file mode creation mask. Since this module carries the `optional` flag, a failure of this module would not affect the successful completion of the entire session module stack. The `session` modules are called a second time when the user logs out.

2.4 Configuration of PAM Modules

Some PAM modules are configurable. The configuration files are located in `/etc/security`. This section briefly describes the configuration files relevant to the sshd example— `pam_env.conf` and `limits.conf`.

2.4.1 pam_env.conf

`pam_env.conf` can be used to define a standardized environment for users that is set whenever the `pam_env` module is called. With it, preset environment variables using the following syntax:

```
VARIABLE   [DEFAULT=VALUE]   [OVERRIDE=VALUE]
```

VARIABLE

Name of the environment variable to set.

`[DEFAULT=<value>]`

Default *VALUE* the administrator wants to set.

`[OVERRIDE=<value>]`

Values that may be queried and set by `pam_env`, overriding the default value.

A typical example of how `pam_env` can be used is the adaptation of the `DISPLAY` variable, which is changed whenever a remote login takes place. This is shown in *Example 2.6, "pam_env.conf"*.

```
REMOTEHOST   DEFAULT=localhost          OVERRIDE=@{PAM_RHOST}
DISPLAY      DEFAULT=${REMOTEHOST}:0.0  OVERRIDE=${DISPLAY}
```

The first line sets the value of the `REMOTEHOST` variable to `localhost`, which is used whenever `pam_env` cannot determine any other value. The `DISPLAY` variable in turn contains the value of `REMOTEHOST`. Find more information in the comments in `/etc/security/pam_env.conf`.

2.4.2   pam_mount.conf.xml

The purpose of `pam_mount` is to mount user home directories during the login process, and to unmount them during logout in an environment where a central file server keeps all the home directories of users. With this method, it is not necessary to mount a complete `/home` directory where all the user home directories would be accessible. Instead, only the home directory of the user who is about to log in, is mounted.

After installing `pam_mount`, a template for `pam_mount.conf.xml` is available in `/etc/security`. The description of the various elements can be found in the manual page **man 5 pam_mount.conf**.

A basic configuration of this feature can be done with YaST. Select *Network Settings* › *Windows Domain Membership* › *Expert Settings* to add the file server; see *Book "Administration Guide", Chapter 28 "Samba", Section 28.5 "Configuring Clients"*.

2.4.3   limits.conf

System limits can be set on a user or group basis in `limits.conf`, which is read by the `pam_limits` module. The file allows you to set hard limits, which may not be exceeded, and soft limits, which may be exceeded temporarily. For more information about the syntax and the options, see the comments in `/etc/security/limits.conf`.

2.5   Configuring PAM Using pam-config

The **pam-config** tool helps you configure the global PAM configuration files (`/etc/pam.d/common-*`) and several selected application configurations. For a list of supported modules, use the **pam-config --list-modules** command. Use the **pam-config** command to maintain your

PAM configuration files. Add new modules to your PAM configurations, delete other modules or modify options to these modules. When changing global PAM configuration files, no manual tweaking of the PAM setup for individual applications is required.

A simple use case for `pam-config` involves the following:

1. **Auto-generate a fresh Unix-style PAM configuration.** Let pam-config create the simplest possible setup which you can extend later on. The `pam-config --create` command creates a simple Unix authentication configuration. Pre-existing configuration files not maintained by pam-config are overwritten, but backup copies are kept as `*.pam-config-backup`.

2. **Add a new authentication method.** Adding a new authentication method (for example, LDAP) to your stack of PAM modules comes down to a simple `pam-config --add --ldap` command. LDAP is added wherever appropriate across all `common-*-pc` PAM configuration files.

3. **Add debugging for test purposes.** To make sure the new authentication procedure works as planned, turn on debugging for all PAM-related operations. The `pam-config --add --ldap-debug` turns on debugging for LDAP-related PAM operations. Find the debugging output in the `systemd` journal (see *Book "Administration Guide", Chapter 15 "***journalctl**: *Query the* `systemd` *Journal"*).

4. **Query your setup.** Before you finally apply your new PAM setup, check if it contains all the options you wanted to add. The `pam-config --query --` *MODULE* lists both the type and the options for the queried PAM module.

5. **Remove the debug options.** Finally, remove the debug option from your setup when you are entirely satisfied with the performance of it. The `pam-config --delete --ldap-debug` command turns off debugging for LDAP authentication. In case you had debugging options added for other modules, use similar commands to turn these off.

For more information on the `pam-config` command and the options available, refer to the manual page of `pam-config(8)`.

2.6 Manually Configuring PAM

If you prefer to manually create or maintain your PAM configuration files, make sure to disable `pam-config` for these files.

When you create your PAM configuration files from scratch using the **pam-config --create** command, it creates symbolic links from the `common-*` to the `common-*-pc` files. **pam-config** only modifies the `common-*-pc` configuration files. Removing these symbolic links effectively disables pam-config, because pam-config only operates on the `common-*-pc` files and these files are not put into effect without the symbolic links.

2.7   For More Information

In the `/usr/share/doc/packages/pam` directory after installing the `pam-doc` package, find the following additional documentation:

READMEs

In the top level of this directory, there is the `modules` subdirectory holding README files about the available PAM modules.

The Linux-PAM System Administrators' Guide

This document comprises everything that the system administrator should know about PAM. It discusses a range of topics, from the syntax of configuration files to the security aspects of PAM.

The Linux-PAM Module Writers' Manual

This document summarizes the topic from the developer's point of view, with information about how to write standard-compliant PAM modules.

The Linux-PAM Application Developers' Guide

This document comprises everything needed by an application developer who wants to use the PAM libraries.

The PAM Manual Pages

PAM in general and the individual modules come with manual pages that provide a good overview of the functionality of all the components.

3 Using NIS

When multiple Unix systems in a network access common resources, it becomes imperative that all user and group identities are the same for all machines in that network. The network should be transparent to users: their environments should not vary, regardless of which machine they are actually using. This can be done by means of NIS and NFS services. NFS distributes file systems over a network and is discussed in Book *"Administration Guide", Chapter 27 "Sharing File Systems with NFS"*.

NIS (Network Information Service) can be described as a database-like service that provides access to the contents of `/etc/passwd`, `/etc/shadow`, and `/etc/group` across networks. NIS can also be used for other purposes (making the contents of files like `/etc/hosts` or `/etc/services` available, for example), but this is beyond the scope of this introduction. People often refer to NIS as *YP*, because it works like the network's "yellow pages."

3.1 Configuring NIS Servers

To distribute NIS information across networks, either install one single server (a *master*) that serves all clients, or NIS slave servers requesting this information from the master and relaying it to their respective clients.

- To configure just one NIS server for your network, proceed with *Section 3.1.1, "Configuring a NIS Master Server"*.

- If your NIS master server needs to export its data to slave servers, set up the master server as described in *Section 3.1.1, "Configuring a NIS Master Server"* and set up slave servers in the subnets as described in *Section 3.1.2, "Configuring a NIS Slave Server"*.

3.1.1 Configuring a NIS Master Server

To manage the NIS Server functionality with YaST, install the `yast2-nis-server` package by running the **`zypper in yast2-nis-server`** command as root. To configure a NIS master server for your network, proceed as follows:

1. Start *YaST* › *Network Services* › *NIS Server*.

2. If you need just one NIS server in your network or if this server is to act as the master for further NIS slave servers, select *Install and Set Up NIS Master Server*. YaST installs the required packages.

    Tip: Already Installed NIS Server Software

   > If NIS server software is already installed on your machine, initiate the creation of a NIS master server by clicking *Create NIS Master Server*.

FIGURE 3.1: NIS SERVER SETUP

3. Determine basic NIS setup options:

   a. Enter the NIS domain name.

b. Define whether the host should also be a NIS client (enabling users to log in and access data from the NIS server) by selecting *This Host is also a NIS Client*.

c. If your NIS server needs to act as a master server to NIS slave servers in other subnets, select *Active Slave NIS Server Exists*.
The option *Fast Map Distribution* is only useful with *Active Slave NIS Servers Exist*. It speeds up the transfer of maps to the slaves.

d. Select *Allow Changes to Passwords* to allow users in your network (both local users and those managed through the NIS server) to change their passwords on the NIS server (with the command `yppasswd`). This makes the options *Allow Changes to GECOS Field* and *Allow Changes to Login Shell* available. "GECOS" means that the users can also change their names and address settings with the command `ypchfn`. "Shell" allows users to change their default shell with the command `ypchsh` (for example, to switch from Bash to sh). The new shell must be one of the predefined entries in `/etc/shells`.

e. Select *Open Port in Firewall* to have YaST adapt the firewall settings for the NIS server.

FIGURE 3.2: MASTER SERVER SETUP

f. Leave this dialog with *Next* or click *Other Global Settings* to make additional settings.

Other Global Settings include changing the source directory of the NIS server (`/etc` by default). In addition, passwords can be merged here. The setting should be *Yes* to create the user database from the system authentication files `/etc/passwd`, `/etc/shadow`, and `/etc/group`. Also, determine the smallest user and group ID that should be offered by NIS. Click *OK* to confirm your settings and return to the previous screen.

FIGURE 3.3: CHANGING THE DIRECTORY AND SYNCHRONIZING FILES FOR A NIS SERVER

4. If you previously enabled *Active Slave NIS Server Exists*, enter the host names used as slaves and click *Next*. If no slave servers exist, this configuration step is skipped.

5. Continue to the dialog for the database configuration. Specify the *NIS Server Maps*, the partial databases to transfer from the NIS server to the client. The default settings are usually adequate. Leave this dialog with *Next*.

6. Check which maps should be available and click *Next* to continue.

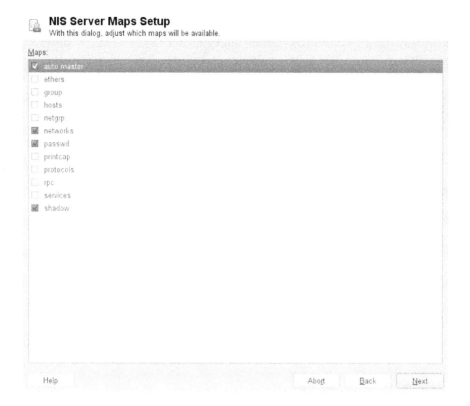

FIGURE 3.4: NIS SERVER MAPS SETUP

7. Determine which hosts are allowed to query the NIS server. You can add, edit, or delete hosts by clicking the appropriate button. Specify from which networks requests can be sent to the NIS server. Normally, this is your internal network. In this case, there should be the following two entries:

```
255.0.0.0     127.0.0.0
0.0.0.0       0.0.0.0
```

The first entry enables connections from your own host, which is the NIS server. The second one allows all hosts to send requests to the server.

NIS Server Query Hosts Setup
Please enter which hosts are allowed to query the NIS server. _more_

Netmask	Network
255.0.0.0	127.0.0.0

Add   Edit   Delete

Help   Abort   Back   Finish

FIGURE 3.5: SETTING REQUEST PERMISSIONS FOR A NIS SERVER

8. Click *Finish* to save your changes and exit the setup.

3.1.2 Configuring a NIS Slave Server

To configure additional NIS *slave servers* in your network, proceed as follows:

1. Start *YaST* › *Network Services* › *NIS Server*.

2. Select *Install and Set Up NIS Slave Server* and click *Next*.

    Tip

   If NIS server software is already installed on your machine, initiate the creation of a NIS slave server by clicking *Create NIS Slave Server*.

3. Complete the basic setup of your NIS slave server:

   a. Enter the NIS domain.

b. Enter host name or IP address of the master server.

c. Set *This Host is also a NIS Client* if you want to enable user logins on this server.

d. Adapt the firewall settings with *Open Ports in Firewall*.

e. Click *Next*.

4. Enter the hosts that are allowed to query the NIS server. You can add, edit, or delete hosts by clicking the appropriate button. Specify all networks from which requests can be sent to the NIS server. If it applies to all networks, use the following configuration:

```
255.0.0.0    127.0.0.0
0.0.0.0      0.0.0.0
```

The first entry enables connections from your own host, which is the NIS server. The second one allows all hosts with access to the same network to send requests to the server.

5. Click *Finish* to save changes and exit the setup.

3.2   Configuring NIS Clients

To use NIS on a workstation, do the following:

1. Start *YaST* > *Network Services* > *NIS Client*.

2. Activate the *Use NIS* button.

3. Enter the NIS domain. This is usually a domain name given by your administrator or a static IP address received by DHCP. For information about DHCP, see *Book* "Administration Guide", *Chapter 26 "DHCP"*.

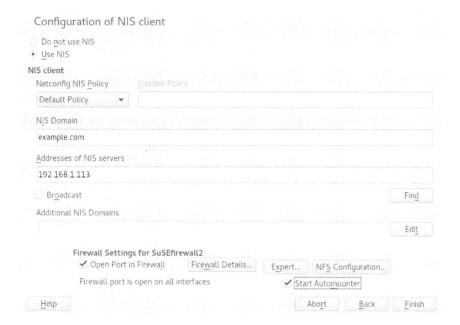

FIGURE 3.6: SETTING DOMAIN AND ADDRESS OF A NIS SERVER

4. Enter your NIS servers and separate their addresses by spaces. If you do not know your NIS server, click *Find* to let YaST search for any NIS servers in your domain. Depending on the size of your local network, this may be a time-consuming process. *Broadcast* asks for a NIS server in the local network after the specified servers fail to respond.

5. Depending on your local installation, you may also want to activate the automounter. This option also installs additional software if required.

6. If you do not want other hosts to be able to query which server your client is using, go to the *Expert* settings and disable *Answer Remote Hosts*. By checking *Broken Server*, the client is enabled to receive replies from a server communicating through an unprivileged port. For further information, see **man** ypbind.

7. Click *Finish* to save them and return to the YaST control center. Your client is now configured with NIS.

4 Setting Up Authentication Servers and Clients Using YaST

The Authentication Server is based on LDAP and optionally Kerberos. On SUSE Linux Enterprise Server you can configure it with a YaST wizard.

For more information about LDAP, see *Chapter 5, LDAP—A Directory Service*, and about Kerberos, see *Chapter 6, Network Authentication with Kerberos*.

4.1 Configuring an Authentication Server with YaST

4.1.1 Initial Configuration of an Authentication Server

To set up an authentication server for user account data, make sure the `yast2-auth-server`, `openldap2`, `krb5-server`, and `krb5-client` packages are installed; YaST will remind you and install them if one of these packages is missing. For Kerberos support, the `krb5-plugin-kdb-ldap` package is required.

The first part of the Authentication Server configuration with YaST is setting up an LDAP server, then you can enable Kerberos.

PROCEDURE 4.1: AUTHENTICATION SERVER CONFIGURATION WITH YAST

1. Start YaST as `root` and select *Network Services* > *Authentication Server* to invoke the configuration wizard.

2. Configure the *Global Settings* of your LDAP server (you can change these settings later)—see *Figure 4.1, "YaST Authentication Server Configuration"*:

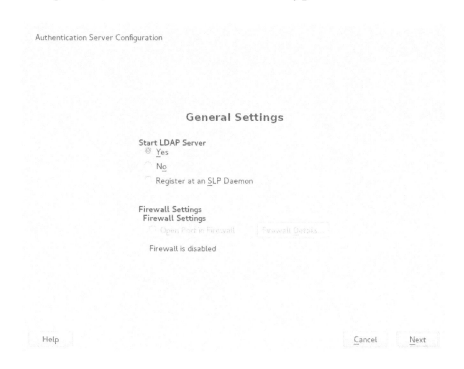

FIGURE 4.1: YAST AUTHENTICATION SERVER CONFIGURATION

a. Set LDAP to be started.

b. If the LDAP server should announce its services via SLP, check *Register at an SLP Daemon*.

c. Configure *Firewall Settings*.

d. Click *Next*.

3. Select the server type: *Stand-alone server*, *Master server in a replication setup*, or *Replica (slave) server*.

4. Select security options (*TLS Settings*).
It is strongly recommended to *Enable TLS*. For more information, see *Procedure 4.2, "Editing Authentication Server Configuration"*, *Step 4*.

 Warning: Authentication Without Encryption

When using authentication without enabling transport encryption using TLS, the password will be transmitted in the clear.

Also consider using LDAP over SSL with certificates.

5. Confirm *Basic Database Settings* with entering an *LDAP Administrator Password* and then clicking *Next*—see *Figure 4.2, "YaST LDAP Server—New Database"*.

FIGURE 4.2: YAST LDAP SERVER—NEW DATABASE

6. In the *Kerberos Authentication* dialog, decide whether to enable Kerberos authentication or not (you can change these settings later)—see *Figure 4.3, "YaST Kerberos Authentication"*.

FIGURE 4.3: YAST KERBEROS AUTHENTICATION

7. Choose whether Kerberos support is needed or not. If you enable it, also specify your *Realm*. Then confirm with *Next*.

   - The *Advanced Configuration* allows you to specify various aspects such as *Maximum ticket life time* or ports to use.

8. Finally, check the *Authentication Server Configuration Summary* and click *Finish* to exit the configuration wizard.

4.1.2 Editing an Authentication Server Configuration with YaST

For changes or additional configuration start the Authentication Server module again and in the left pane expand *Global Settings* to make subentries visible—see *Figure 4.4, "YaST Editing Authentication Server Configuration"*:

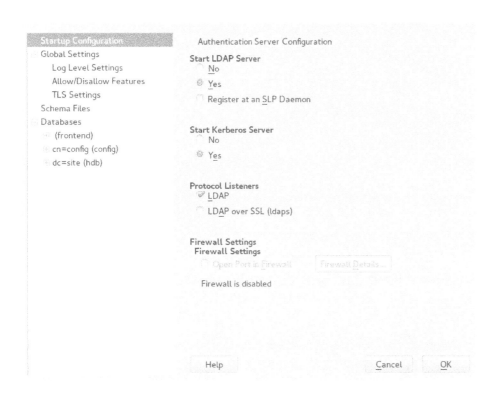

FIGURE 4.4: YAST EDITING AUTHENTICATION SERVER CONFIGURATION

PROCEDURE 4.2: EDITING AUTHENTICATION SERVER CONFIGURATION

1. With *Log Level Settings*, configure the degree of logging activity (verbosity) of the LDAP server. From the predefined list, select or deselect logging options according to your needs. The more options are enabled, the larger your log files grow.

2. Configure which connection types the server should offer under *Allow/Disallow Features*. Choose from:

   LDAPv2 Bind Requests

   This option enables connection requests (bind requests) from clients using the previous version of the protocol (LDAPv2).

Anonymous Bind When Credentials Not Empty

Normally, the LDAP server denies any authentication attempts with empty credentials, that is, a distinguished name (DN) or a password. However, enabling this option makes it possible to connect with a password and no DN to establish an anonymous connection.

Unauthenticated Bind When DN Not Empty

Enabling this option makes it possible to connect without authentication (anonymously) using a distinguished name (DN) but no password.

Unauthenticated Update Options to Process

Enabling this option allows non-authenticated (anonymous) update operations. Access is restricted according to ACLs and other rules.

3. *Allow/Disallow Features* also lets you configure the server flags. Choose from:

Disable Acceptance of Anonymous Bind Requests

The server will no longer accept anonymous bind requests. Note, that this does not generally prohibit anonymous directory access.

Disable Simple Bind Authentication

Completely disable Simple Bind authentication.

Disable Forcing Session to Anonymous Status upon StartTLS Operation Receipt

The server will no longer force an authenticated connection back to the anonymous state when receiving the StartTLS operation.

Disallow the StartTLS Operation if Authenticated

The server will disallow the StartTLS operation on already authenticated connections.

4. To configure secure communication between client and server, proceed with *TLS Settings*:

a. Activate *Enable TLS* to enable TLS and SSL encryption of the client/server communication.

b. Either *Import Certificate* by specifying the exact path to its location or enable the *Use Common Server Certificate*. If the *Use Common Server Certificate* is not available, because it has not been created during installation, go for *Launch CA Management Module* first—for more information, see *Section 17.2, "YaST Modules for CA Management"*.

38

Add Schema files to be included in the server's configuration by selecting *Schema Files* in the left part of the dialog. The default selection of schema files applies to the server providing a source of YaST user account data.

YaST allows to add traditional Schema files (usually with a name ending in `.schema`) or LDIF files containing Schema definitions in OpenLDAP's LDIF Schema format.

FIGURE 4.5: YAST AUTHENTICATION SERVER DATABASE CONFIGURATION

To configure the databases managed by your LDAP server, proceed as follows:

1. Select the *Databases* item in the left part of the dialog.

2. Click *Add Database* to add a new database.

3. Specify the requested data:

   Base DN

   Enter the base DN (distinguished name) of your LDAP server.

   Administrator DN

   Enter the DN of the administrator in charge of the server. If you check *Append Base DN*, only provide the `cn` of the administrator and the system fills in the rest automatically.

LDAP Administrator Password

Enter the password for the database administrator.

Use This Database as the Default for OpenLDAP Clients

For convenience, check this option if wanted.

4. In the next dialog, configure replication settings.

5. In the next dialog, enable enforcement of password policies to provide extra security to your LDAP server:

   a. Check *Enable Password Policies* to be able to specify a password policy.

   b. Activate *Hash Clear Text Passwords* to have clear text passwords be hashed before they are written to the database whenever they are added or modified.

   c. *Disclose "Account Locked" Status* provides a relevant error message for bind requests to locked accounts.

    Warning: Locked Accounts in Security Sensitive Environments

   Do not use the *Disclose "Account Locked" Status* option if your environment is sensitive to security issues, because the "Locked Account" error message provides security-sensitive information that can be exploited by a potential attacker.

   d. Enter the DN of the default policy object. To use a DN other than the one suggested by YaST, enter your choice. Otherwise, accept the default settings.

6. Complete the database configuration by clicking *Finish*.

If you have not opted for password policies, your server is ready to run at this point. If you have chosen to enable password policies, proceed with the configuration of the password policy in detail. If you have chosen a password policy object that does not yet exist, YaST creates one:

1. Enter the LDAP server password. In the navigation tree below *Databases* expand your database object and activate the *Password Policy Configuration* item.

2. Make sure *Enable Password Policies* is activated. Then click *Edit Policy*.

3. Configure the password change policies:

    a. Determine the number of passwords stored in the password history. Saved passwords may not be reused by the user.

    b. Determine if users can change their passwords and if they will need to change their passwords after a reset by the administrator. Require the old password for password changes (optional).

    c. Determine whether and to what extent passwords should be subject to quality checking. Set the minimum password length that must be met before a password is valid. If you select *Accept Uncheckable Passwords*, users are allowed to use encrypted passwords, even though the quality checks cannot be performed. If you opt for *Only Accept Checked Passwords* only those passwords that pass the quality tests are accepted as valid.

4. Configure the password time-limit policies:

    a. Determine the minimum password time-limit (the time that needs to pass between two valid password changes) and the maximum password time limit.

    b. Determine the time between a password expiration warning and the actual password expiration.

    c. Set the number of postponement uses of an expired password before the password expires permanently.

5. Configure the lockout policies:

    a. Enable password locking.

    b. Determine the number of bind failures that trigger a password lock.

    c. Determine the duration of the password lock.

    d. Determine the length of time that password failures are kept in the cache before they are purged.

6. Apply your password policy settings with *OK*.

To edit a previously created database, select its base DN in the tree to the left. In the right part of the window, YaST displays a dialog similar to the one used for the creation of a new database (with the main difference that the base DN entry is grayed out and cannot be changed).

After leaving the Authentication Server configuration by selecting *Finish*, you are ready to go with a basic working configuration for your Authentication Server. To fine-tune this setup, use OpenLDAP's dynamic configuration back-end.

The OpenLDAP's dynamic configuration back-end stores the configuration in an LDAP database. That database consists of a set of `.ldif` files in `/etc/openldap/slapd.d`. There is no need to access these files directly. To access the settings you can either use the YaST Authentication Server module (the `yast2-auth-server` package) or an LDAP client such as **ldapmodify** or **ldapsearch**. For more information on the dynamic configuration of OpenLDAP, see the "OpenLDAP Administration Guide".

4.1.3   Editing LDAP Users and Groups

For editing LDAP users and groups with YaST, see *Section 5.4, "Configuring LDAP Users and Groups in YaST"*.

4.2   Configuring an Authentication Client with YaST

YaST allows setting up authentication to clients using different modules:

- *User Logon Management.*   Use both an identity service (usually LDAP) and a user authentication service (usually Kerberos). This option is based on SSSD and in the majority of cases is best suited for joining Active Directory domains.
  This module is described in *Section 7.3.2, "Joining Active Directory Using User Logon Management"*.

- *Windows Domain Membership.*   Join an Active Directory (which entails use of Kerberos and LDAP). This option is based on **winbind** and is best suited for joining an Active Directory domain if support for NTLM or cross-forest trusts is necessary.
  This module is described in *Section 7.3.3, "Joining Active Directory Using Windows Domain Membership"*.

- *LDAP and Kerberos Authentication.*   Allows setting up LDAP identities and Kerberos authentication independently from each other and provides fewer options. While this module also uses SSSD, it is not as well suited for connecting to Active Directory as the previous two options.

This module is described in:

- **LDAP:** *Section 5.3, "Configuring an LDAP Client with YaST"*

- **Kerberos:** *Section 6.5, "Setting up Kerberos using LDAP and Kerberos Client"*

4.3   SSSD

Two of the YaST modules are based on SSSD: *User Logon Management* and *LDAP and Kerberos Authentication.*

SSSD stands for System Security Services Daemon. SSSD talks to remote directory services that provide user data and provides various authentication methods, such as LDAP, Kerberos, or Active Directory (AD). It also provides an NSS (Name Service Switch) and PAM (Pluggable Authentication Module) interface.

SSSD can locally cache user data and then allow users to use the data, even if the real directory service is (temporarily) unreachable.

4.3.1   Checking the Status

After running one of the YaST authentication modules, you can check whether SSSD is running with:

```
systemctl status sssd
sssd.service - System Security Services Daemon
   Loaded: loaded (/usr/lib/systemd/system/sssd.service; enabled)
   Active: active (running) since Thu 2015-10-23 11:03:43 CEST; 5s ago
   [...]
```

4.3.2   Caching

To allow logging in when the authentication back-end is unavailable, SSSD will use its cache even if it was invalidated. This happens until the back-end is available again.

To invalidate the cache, run **sss_cache -E** (the command **sss_cache** is part of the package `sssd-tools`).

To completely remove the SSSD cache, run:

```
systemctl stop sssd
```

```
rm -f /var/lib/sss/db/*
systemctl start sssd
```

4.3.3   For More Information

For more information, see the SSSD man pages `sssd.conf` (**man sssd.conf**) and `sssd` (**man sssd**). There are also man pages for most SSSD modules.

5 LDAP—A Directory Service

The Lightweight Directory Access Protocol (LDAP) is a set of protocols designed to access and maintain information directories. LDAP can be used for user and group management, system configuration management, address management, and more. This chapter provides a basic understanding of how OpenLDAP works.

In a network environment, it is crucial to keep important information structured and to serve it quickly. A directory service keeps information available in a well-structured and searchable form.

Ideally, a central server stores the data in a directory and distributes it to all clients using a well-defined protocol. The structured data allow a wide range of applications to access them. A central repository reduces the necessary administrative effort. The use of an open and standardized protocol like LDAP ensures that as many client applications as possible can access such information.

A directory in this context is a type of database optimized for quick and effective reading and searching:

- To make multiple concurrent reading accesses possible, the number of updates is usually very low. The number of read and write accesses is often limited to a few users with administrative privileges. In contrast, conventional databases are optimized for accepting the largest possible data volume in a short time.

- When static data is administered, updates of the existing data sets are very rare. When working with dynamic data, especially when data sets like bank accounts or accounting are concerned, the consistency of the data is of primary importance. If an amount should be subtracted from one place to be added to another, both operations must happen concurrently, within one *transaction*, to ensure balance over the data stock. Traditional relational databases usually have a very strong focus on data consistency, such as the referential integrity support of transactions. Conversely, short-term inconsistencies are usually acceptable in LDAP directories. LDAP directories often do not have the same strong consistency requirements as relational databases.

The design of a directory service like LDAP is not laid out to support complex update or query mechanisms. All applications are guaranteed to access this service quickly and easily.

5.1 LDAP versus NIS

Unix system administrators traditionally use NIS (Network Information Service) for name resolution and data distribution in a network. The configuration data contained in the files `group`, `hosts`, `mail`, `netgroup`, `networks`, `passwd`, `printcap`, `protocols`, `rpc`, and `services` in the `/etc` directory is distributed to clients all over the network. These files can be maintained without major effort because they are simple text files. The handling of larger amounts of data, however, becomes increasingly difficult because of nonexistent structuring. NIS is only designed for Unix platforms, and is not suitable as a centralized data administration tool in heterogeneous networks.

Unlike NIS, the LDAP service is not restricted to pure Unix networks. Windows™ servers (starting with Windows 2000) support LDAP as a directory service. The application tasks mentioned above are additionally supported in non-Unix systems.

The LDAP principle can be applied to any data structure that needs to be centrally administered. A few application examples are:

  * Replacement for the NIS service

  * Mail routing (postfix)

  * Address books for mail clients, like Mozilla Thunderbird, Evolution, and Outlook

  * Administration of zone descriptions for a BIND 9 name server

  * User authentication with Samba in heterogeneous networks

This list can be extended because LDAP is extensible, unlike NIS. The clearly-defined hierarchical structure of the data simplifies the administration of large amounts of data, as it can be searched more easily.

5.2 Structure of an LDAP Directory Tree

To get background knowledge on how an LDAP server works and how the data is stored, it is vital to understand the way the data is organized on the server and how this structure enables LDAP to provide fast access to the data. To successfully operate an LDAP setup, you also need to be familiar with some basic LDAP terminology. This section introduces the basic layout of an LDAP directory tree and provides the basic terminology used with regard to LDAP. Skip this introductory section if you already have some LDAP background knowledge and only want to learn how to set up an LDAP environment in SUSE Linux Enterprise Server. Read on at *Section 5.5, "Manually Configuring an LDAP Server"*.

An LDAP directory has a tree structure. All entries (called objects) of the directory have a defined position within this hierarchy. This hierarchy is called the *directory information tree* (DIT). The complete path to the desired entry, which unambiguously identifies it, is called the *distinguished name* or DN. A single node along the path to this entry is called *relative distinguished name* or RDN.

The relations within an LDAP directory tree become more evident in the following example, shown in *Figure 5.1, "Structure of an LDAP Directory"*.

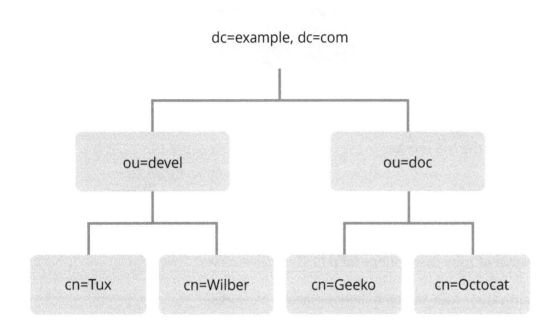

FIGURE 5.1: STRUCTURE OF AN LDAP DIRECTORY

The complete diagram is a fictional directory information tree. The entries on three levels are depicted. Each entry corresponds to one box in the image. The complete, valid *distinguished name* for the fictional employee `Geeko Linux`, in this case, is `cn=Geeko Linux,ou=doc,dc=example,dc=com`. It is composed by adding the RDN `cn=Geeko Linux` to the DN of the preceding entry `ou=doc,dc=example,dc=com`.

The types of objects that can be stored in the DIT are globally determined following a *Schema*. The type of an object is determined by the *object class*. The object class determines what attributes the relevant object must or can be assigned. The Schema, therefore, must contain definitions of all object classes and attributes used in the desired application scenario. There are a few common Schemas (see RFC 2252 and 2256). The LDAP RFC defines a few commonly used Schemas (see for example, RFC4519). Additionally, Schemas are available for many other use cases (for example, Samba or NIS replacement). It is, however, possible to create custom Schemas or to use multiple Schemas complementing each other (if this is required by the environment in which the LDAP server should operate).

Table 5.1, "Commonly Used Object Classes and Attributes" offers a small overview of the object classes from `core.schema` and `inetorgperson.schema` used in the example, including required attributes (Req. Attr.) and valid attribute values.

TABLE 5.1: COMMONLY USED OBJECT CLASSES AND ATTRIBUTES

Object Class	Meaning	Example Entry	Req. Attr.
`dcObject`	*domainComponent* (name components of the domain)	example	dc
`organizationalUnit`	*organizationalUnit* (organizational unit)	doc	ou
`inetOrgPerson`	*inetOrgPerson* (person-related data for the intranet or Internet)	Geeko Linux	sn and cn

Example 5.1, "Excerpt from schema.core" shows an excerpt from a Schema directive with explanations.

EXAMPLE 5.1: EXCERPT FROM SCHEMA.CORE

```
attributetype (2.5.4.11 NAME ( 'ou' 'organizationalUnitName') ①
      DESC 'RFC2256: organizational unit this object belongs to' ②
      SUP name ) ③

objectclass ( 2.5.6.5 NAME 'organizationalUnit' ④
      DESC 'RFC2256: an organizational unit' ⑤
      SUP top STRUCTURAL ⑥
      MUST ou ⑦
MAY (userPassword $ searchGuide $ seeAlso $ businessCategory ⑧
  $ x121Address $ registeredAddress $ destinationIndicator
  $ preferredDeliveryMethod $ telexNumber
  $ teletexTerminalIdentifier $ telephoneNumber
  $ internationaliSDNNumber $ facsimileTelephoneNumber
  $ street $ postOfficeBox $ postalCode $ postalAddress
```

```
$ physicalDeliveryOfficeName
$ st $ l $ description) )
...
```

The attribute type `organizationalUnitName` and the corresponding object class `organizationalUnit` serve as an example here.

① The name of the attribute, its unique OID (*object identifier*) (numerical), and the abbreviation of the attribute.

② A brief description of the attribute with `DESC`. The corresponding RFC, on which the definition is based, is also mentioned here.

③ `SUP` indicates a superordinate attribute type to which this attribute belongs.

④ The definition of the object class `organizationalUnit` begins—the same as in the definition of the attribute—with an OID and the name of the object class.

⑤ A brief description of the object class.

⑥ The `SUP top` entry indicates that this object class is not subordinate to another object class.

⑦ With `MUST` list all attribute types that must be used with an object of the type `organizationalUnit`.

⑧ With `MAY` list all attribute types that are permitted with this object class.

A very good introduction to the use of Schemas can be found in the OpenLDAP documentation (`openldap2-doc`). When installed, find it in `/usr/share/doc/packages/openldap2/admin-guide/guide.html`.

5.3   Configuring an LDAP Client with YaST

YaST includes the module *LDAP and Kerberos Client* that helps define authentication scenarios involving either LDAP or Kerberos.

It can also be used to join Kerberos and LDAP separately. However, in many such cases, using this module may not be the first choice, such as for joining Active Directory (which uses a combination of LDAP and Kerberos). For more information, see *Section 4.2, "Configuring an Authentication Client with YaST"*.

Start the module by selecting *Network Services* › *LDAP and Kerberos Client*.

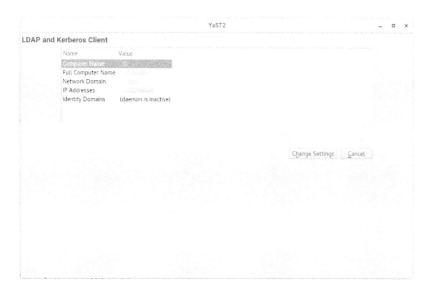

FIGURE 5.2: *LDAP AND KERBEROS CLIENT* WINDOW

To configure an LDAP client, follow the procedure below:

1. In the window *LDAP and Kerberos Client*, click *Change Settings*.
   Make sure that the tab *Use a Directory as Identity Provider (LDAP)* is chosen.

2. Specify one or more LDAP server URLs, host names, or IP addresses under *Enter LDAP server locations*. When specifying multiple addresses, separate them with spaces.

3. Specify the appropriate LDAP distinguished name (DN) under *DN of Search Base*. For example, a valid entry could be `dc=example,dc=com`.

4. If your LDAP server supports TLS encryption, choose the appropriate security option under *Secure LDAP Connection*.

To first ask the server whether it supports TLS encryption and be able to downgrade to an unencrypted connection if it does not, use *Secure Communication via StartTLS*.

5. Activate other options as necessary:

   • You can *Allow users to authenticate via LDAP* and *Automatically Create Home Directories* on the local computer for them.

   • Use *Cache LDAP Entries For Faster Response* to cache LDAP entries locally. However, this bears the danger that entries can be slightly out of date.

   • Specify the types of data that should be used from the LDAP source, such as *Users* and *Groups, Super-User Commands*, and *Network Disk Locations* (network-shared drives that can be automatically mounted on request).

   • Specify the distinguished name (DN) and password of the user under whose name you want to bind to the LDAP directory in *DN of Bind User* and *Password of the Bind User*.
     Otherwise, if the server supports it, you can also leave both text boxes empty to bind anonymously to the server.

    Warning: Authentication Without Encryption

   When using authentication without enabling transport encryption using TLS or StartTLS, the password will be transmitted in the clear.

   Under *Extended Options*, you can additionally configure timeouts for BIND operations.

6. To check whether the LDAP connection works, click *Test Connection*.

7. To leave the dialog, click *OK*. Then wait for the setup to complete.
   Finally, click *Finish*.

5.4   Configuring LDAP Users and Groups in YaST

The actual registration of user and group data differs only slightly from the procedure when not using LDAP. The following instructions relate to the administration of users. The procedure for administering groups is analogous.

1. Access the YaST user administration with *Security and Users > User and Group Management*.

2. Use *Set Filter* to limit the view of users to the LDAP users and enter the password for Root DN.

3. Click *Add* to enter the user configuration. A dialog with four tabs opens:

   a. Specify the user's name, login name, and password in the *User Data* tab.

   b. Check the *Details* tab for the group membership, login shell, and home directory of the new user. If necessary, change the default to values that better suit your needs.

   c. Modify or accept the default *Password Settings*.

   d. Enter the *Plug-Ins* tab, select the LDAP plug-in, and click *Launch* to configure additional LDAP attributes assigned to the new user.

4. Click *OK* to apply your settings and leave the user configuration.

The initial input form of user administration offers *LDAP Options*. This allows you to apply LDAP search filters to the set of available users. Alternatively open the module for configuring LDAP users and groups by selecting *LDAP User and Group Configuration*.

5.5   Manually Configuring an LDAP Server

YaST uses OpenLDAP's dynamic configuration database (`back-config`) to store the LDAP server's configuration. For details about the dynamic configuration back-end, see the `slapd-config(5)` man page or the OpenLDAP Software 2.4 Administrator's Guide located at `/usr/share/doc/packages/openldap2/guide/admin/guide.html` on your system if the `openldap2` package is installed.

 Tip: Upgrading an Old OpenLDAP Installation

YaST does not use `/etc/openldap/slapd.conf` to store the OpenLDAP configuration anymore. In case of a system upgrade, a copy of the original `/etc/openldap/slapd.conf` file will get created as `/etc/openldap/slapd.conf.YaSTsave`.

To conveniently access the configuration back-end, you use SASL external authentication. For example, the following **ldapsearch** command executed as root can show the complete **slapd** configuration:

```
ldapsearch -Y external -H ldapi:/// -b cn=config
```

 Note: LDAP Server Is Part of the Authentication Server

Basic LDAP Server initialization and configuration can be done within the Authentication Server YaST module. For more information, see *Section 4.1, "Configuring an Authentication Server with YaST"*.

When the LDAP server is fully configured and all desired entries have been made according to the pattern described in *Section 5.6, "Manually Administering LDAP Data"*, start the LDAP server as root by entering **sudo systemctl start slapd**. To stop the server manually, enter the command **sudo systemctl stop slapd**. Query the status of the running LDAP server with **sudo systemctl status slapd**.

Use the YaST *Services Manager*, described in *Book "Administration Guide", Chapter 13 "The systemd Daemon", Section 13.4 "Managing Services with YaST"*, to have the server started and stopped automatically on system bootup and shutdown. You can also create the corresponding links to the start and stop scripts with the **systemctl** commands as described in *Book "Administration Guide", Chapter 13 "The systemd Daemon", Section 13.2.1 "Managing Services in a Running System"*.

5.6 Manually Administering LDAP Data

OpenLDAP offers a series of tools for the administration of data in the LDAP directory. The four most important tools for adding to, deleting from, searching through and modifying the data stock are explained in this section.

5.6.1 Inserting Data into an LDAP Directory

Once your LDAP server is correctly configured (it features appropriate entries for suffix, directory, rootdn, rootpw and index), proceed to entering records. OpenLDAP offers the **ldapadd** command for this task. If possible, add the objects to the database in bundles (for practical reasons). LDAP can process the LDIF format (LDAP data interchange format) for this.

An LDIF file is a simple text file that can contain an arbitrary number of attribute and value pairs. The LDIF file for creating a rough framework for the example in *Figure 5.1, "Structure of an LDAP Directory"* would look like the one in *Example 5.2, "An LDIF File"*.

 Important: Encoding of LDIF Files

LDAP works with UTF-8 (Unicode). Umlauts must be encoded correctly. Otherwise, avoid umlauts and other special characters or use **iconv** to convert the input to UTF-8.

EXAMPLE 5.2: AN LDIF FILE

```
# The Organization
dn: dc=example,dc=com
objectClass: dcObject
objectClass: organization
o: Example dc: example

# The organizational unit development (devel)
dn: ou=devel,dc=example,dc=com
objectClass: organizationalUnit
ou: devel

# The organizational unit documentation (doc)
dn: ou=doc,dc=example,dc=com
objectClass: organizationalUnit
ou: doc

# The organizational unit internal IT (it)
dn: ou=it,dc=example,dc=com
objectClass: organizationalUnit
ou: it
```

Save the file with the `.ldif` suffix then pass it to the server with the following command:

```
ldapadd -x -D DN_OF_THE_ADMINISTRATOR -W -f FILE.ldif
```

`-x` switches off the authentication with SASL in this case. `-D` declares the user that calls the operation. The valid DN of the administrator is entered here, as it has been configured in `slapd.conf`. In the current example, this is `cn=Administrator,dc=example,dc=com`. `-W` circumvents entering the password on the command line (in clear text) and activates a separate password prompt. The `-f` option passes the file name. See the details of running **ldapadd** in *Example 5.3, "ldapadd with example.ldif"*.

```
ldapadd -x -D cn=Administrator,dc=example,dc=com -W -f example.ldif

Enter LDAP password:
adding new entry "dc=example,dc=com"
adding new entry "ou=devel,dc=example,dc=com"
adding new entry "ou=doc,dc=example,dc=com"
adding new entry "ou=it,dc=example,dc=com"
```

The user data of individuals can be prepared in separate LDIF files. *Example 5.4, "LDIF Data for Tux"* adds Tux to the new LDAP directory.

EXAMPLE 5.4: LDIF DATA FOR TUX

```
# coworker Tux
dn: cn=Tux Linux,ou=devel,dc=example,dc=com
objectClass: inetOrgPerson
cn: Tux Linux
givenName: Tux
sn: Linux
mail: tux@example.com
uid: tux
telephoneNumber: +49 1234 567-8
```

An LDIF file can contain an arbitrary number of objects. It is possible to pass directory branches (entirely or in part) to the server in one go, as shown in the example of individual objects. If it is necessary to modify some data relatively often, a fine subdivision of single objects is recommended.

5.6.2 Modifying Data in the LDAP Directory

The tool **ldapmodify** is provided for modifying the data stock. The easiest way to do this is to modify the corresponding LDIF file and pass the modified file to the LDAP server. To change the telephone number of colleague Tux from +49 1234 567-8 to +49 1234 567-10, edit the LDIF file like in *Example 5.5, "Modified LDIF File tux.ldif"*.

EXAMPLE 5.5: MODIFIED LDIF FILE TUX.LDIF

```
# coworker Tux
dn: cn=Tux Linux,ou=devel,dc=example,dc=com
```

```
changetype: modify
replace: telephoneNumber
telephoneNumber: +49 1234 567-10
```

Import the modified file into the LDAP directory with the following command:

```
ldapmodify -x -D cn=Administrator,dc=example,dc=com -W -f tux.ldif
```

Alternatively, pass the attributes to change directly to **ldapmodify** as follows:

1. Start **ldapmodify** and enter your password:

   ```
   ldapmodify -x -D cn=Administrator,dc=example,dc=com -W
   Enter LDAP password:
   ```

2. Enter the changes while carefully complying with the syntax in the order presented below:

   ```
   dn: cn=Tux Linux,ou=devel,dc=example,dc=com
   changetype: modify
   replace: telephoneNumber
   telephoneNumber: +49 1234 567-10
   ```

For more information about **ldapmodify** and its syntax, see the **ldapmodify** man page.

5.6.3 Searching or Reading Data from an LDAP Directory

OpenLDAP provides, with **ldapsearch**, a command line tool for searching data within an LDAP directory and reading data from it. This is a simple query:

```
ldapsearch -x -b dc=example,dc=com "(objectClass=*)"
```

The `-b` option determines the search base (the section of the tree within which the search should be performed). In the current case, this is `dc=example,dc=com`. To perform a more finely-grained search in specific subsections of the LDAP directory (for example, only within the `devel` department), pass this section to **ldapsearch** with `-b`. `-x` requests activation of simple authentication. `(objectClass=*)` declares that all objects contained in the directory should be read. This command option can be used after the creation of a new directory tree to verify that all entries have been recorded correctly and the server responds as desired. For more information about the use of **ldapsearch**, see the `ldapsearch(1)` man page.

5.6.4 Deleting Data from an LDAP Directory

Delete unwanted entries with **ldapdelete**. The syntax is similar to that of the other commands. To delete, for example, the complete entry for Tux Linux, issue the following command:

```
ldapdelete -x -D cn=Administrator,dc=example,dc=com -W cn=Tux \
Linux,ou=devel,dc=example,dc=com
```

5.7 For More Information

More complex subjects (like SASL configuration or establishment of a replicating LDAP server that distributes the workload among multiple slaves) were omitted from this chapter. Find detailed information about both subjects in the *OpenLDAP 2.4 Administrator's Guide*—see at *OpenLDAP 2.4 Administrator's Guide*.

The Web site of the OpenLDAP project offers exhaustive documentation for beginner and advanced LDAP users:

OpenLDAP Faq-O-Matic

A detailed question and answer collection applying to the installation, configuration, and use of OpenLDAP. Find it at http://www.openldap.org/faq/data/cache/1.html ↗.

Quick Start Guide

Brief step-by-step instructions for installing your first LDAP server. Find it at http://www.openldap.org/doc/admin24/quickstart.html ↗ or on an installed system in Section 2 of /usr/share/doc/packages/openldap2/guide/admin/guide.html.

OpenLDAP 2.4 Administrator's Guide

A detailed introduction to all important aspects of LDAP configuration, including access controls and encryption. See http://www.openldap.org/doc/admin24/ ↗ or, on an installed system, /usr/share/doc/packages/openldap2/guide/admin/guide.html.

Understanding LDAP

A detailed general introduction to the basic principles of LDAP: http://www.redbooks.ibm.com/redbooks/pdfs/sg244986.pdf ↗.

Printed literature about LDAP:

- *LDAP System Administration* by Gerald Carter (ISBN 1-56592-491-6)

- *Understanding and Deploying LDAP Directory Services* by Howes, Smith, and Good (ISBN 0-672-32316-8)

The ultimate reference material for the subject of LDAP are the corresponding RFCs (request for comments), 2251 to 2256.

6 Network Authentication with Kerberos

An open network provides no means of ensuring that a workstation can identify its users properly, except through the usual password mechanisms. In common installations, the user must enter the password each time a service inside the network is accessed. Kerberos provides an authentication method with which a user registers only once and is trusted in the complete network for the rest of the session. To have a secure network, the following requirements must be met:

- Have all users prove their identity for each desired service and make sure that no one can take the identity of someone else.

- Make sure that each network server also proves its identity. Otherwise an attacker might be able to impersonate the server and obtain sensitive information transmitted to the server. This concept is called *mutual authentication*, because the client authenticates to the server and vice versa.

Kerberos helps you meet these requirements by providing strongly encrypted authentication. Only the basic principles of Kerberos are discussed here. For detailed technical instruction, refer to the Kerberos documentation.

6.1 Kerberos Terminology

The following glossary defines some Kerberos terminology.

credential

Users or clients need to present some kind of credentials that authorize them to request services. Kerberos knows two kinds of credentials—tickets and authenticators.

ticket

A ticket is a per-server credential used by a client to authenticate at a server from which it is requesting a service. It contains the name of the server, the client's name, the client's Internet address, a time stamp, a lifetime, and a random session key. All this data is encrypted using the server's key.

authenticator

Combined with the ticket, an authenticator is used to prove that the client presenting a ticket is really the one it claims to be. An authenticator is built using the client's name, the workstation's IP address, and the current workstation's time, all encrypted with the session key known only to the client and the relevant server. An authenticator can only be used once, unlike a ticket. A client can build an authenticator itself.

principal

A Kerberos principal is a unique entity (a user or service) to which it can assign a ticket. A principal consists of the following components:

```
USER/INSTANCE@REALM
```

- **primary:** The first part of the principal. In the case of users, this is usually the same as the user name.

- **instance** *(optional)*: Additional information characterizing the *primary*. This string is separated from the *primary* by a `/`.
  `tux@example.org` and `tux/admin@example.org` can both exist on the same Kerberos system and are treated as different principals.

- **realm:** Specifies the Kerberos realm. Normally, your realm is your domain name in uppercase letters.

mutual authentication

Kerberos ensures that both client and server can be sure of each other's identity. They share a session key, which they can use to communicate securely.

session key

Session keys are temporary private keys generated by Kerberos. They are known to the client and used to encrypt the communication between the client and the server for which it requested and received a ticket.

replay

Almost all messages sent in a network can be eavesdropped, stolen, and resent. In the Kerberos context, this would be most dangerous if an attacker manages to obtain your request for a service containing your ticket and authenticator. The attacker could then try to resend it (*replay*) to impersonate you. However, Kerberos implements several mechanisms to deal with this problem.

server or service

> *Service* is used to refer to a specific action to perform. The process behind this action is called a *server*.

6.2 How Kerberos Works

Kerberos is often called a third-party trusted authentication service, which means all its clients trust Kerberos's judgment of another client's identity. Kerberos keeps a database of all its users and their private keys.

To ensure Kerberos is working correctly, run both the authentication and ticket-granting server on a dedicated machine. Make sure that only the administrator can access this machine physically and over the network. Reduce the (networking) services running on it to the absolute minimum—do not even run `sshd`.

6.2.1 First Contact

Your first contact with Kerberos is quite similar to any login procedure at a normal networking system. Enter your user name. This piece of information and the name of the ticket-granting service are sent to the authentication server (Kerberos). If the authentication server knows you, it generates a random session key for further use between your client and the ticket-granting server. Now the authentication server prepares a ticket for the ticket-granting server. The ticket contains the following information—all encrypted with a session key only the authentication server and the ticket-granting server know:

- The names of both, the client and the ticket-granting server

- The current time

- A lifetime assigned to this ticket

- The client's IP address

- The newly-generated session key

This ticket is then sent back to the client together with the session key, again in encrypted form, but this time the private key of the client is used. This private key is only known to Kerberos and the client, because it is derived from your user password. Now that the client has received this response, you are prompted for your password. This password is converted into the key that can decrypt the package sent by the authentication server. The package is "unwrapped" and password and key are erased from the workstation's memory. As long as the lifetime given to the ticket used to obtain other tickets does not expire, your workstation can prove your identity.

6.2.2   Requesting a Service

To request a service from any server in the network, the client application needs to prove its identity to the server. Therefore, the application generates an authenticator. An authenticator consists of the following components:

* The client's principal

* The client's IP address

* The current time

* A checksum (chosen by the client)

All this information is encrypted using the session key that the client has already received for this special server. The authenticator and the ticket for the server are sent to the server. The server uses its copy of the session key to decrypt the authenticator, which gives it all the information needed about the client requesting its service, to compare it to that contained in the ticket. The server checks if the ticket and the authenticator originate from the same client.

Without any security measures implemented on the server side, this stage of the process would be an ideal target for replay attacks. Someone could try to resend a request stolen off the net some time before. To prevent this, the server does not accept any request with a time stamp and ticket received previously. In addition to that, a request with a time stamp differing too much from the time the request is received is ignored.

6.2.3   Mutual Authentication

Kerberos authentication can be used in both directions. It is not only a question of the client being the one it claims to be. The server should also be able to authenticate itself to the client requesting its service. Therefore, it sends an authenticator itself. It adds one to the checksum it received in the client's authenticator and encrypts it with the session key, which is shared between it and the client. The client takes this response as a proof of the server's authenticity and they both start cooperating.

6.2.4 Ticket Granting—Contacting All Servers

Tickets are designed to be used for one server at a time. Therefore, you need to get a new ticket each time you request another service. Kerberos implements a mechanism to obtain tickets for individual servers. This service is called the "ticket-granting service". The ticket-granting service is a service (like any other service mentioned before) and uses the same access protocols that have already been outlined. Any time an application needs a ticket that has not already been requested, it contacts the ticket-granting server. This request consists of the following components:

- The requested principal

- The ticket-granting ticket

- An authenticator

Like any other server, the ticket-granting server now checks the ticket-granting ticket and the authenticator. If they are considered valid, the ticket-granting server builds a new session key to be used between the original client and the new server. Then the ticket for the new server is built, containing the following information:

- The client's principal

- The server's principal

- The current time

- The client's IP address

- The newly-generated session key

The new ticket has a lifetime, which is either the remaining lifetime of the ticket-granting ticket or the default for the service. The lesser of both values is assigned. The client receives this ticket and the session key, which are sent by the ticket-granting service. But this time the answer is encrypted with the session key that came with the original ticket-granting ticket. The client can decrypt the response without requiring the user's password when a new service is contacted. Kerberos can thus acquire ticket after ticket for the client without bothering the user.

6.3 User View of Kerberos

Ideally, a user only contact with Kerberos happens during login at the workstation. The login process includes obtaining a ticket-granting ticket. At logout, a user's Kerberos tickets are automatically destroyed, which makes it difficult for anyone else to impersonate this user.

The automatic expiration of tickets can lead to a situation when a user's login session lasts longer than the maximum lifespan given to the ticket-granting ticket (a reasonable setting is 10 hours). However, the user can get a new ticket-granting ticket by running `kinit`. Enter the password again and Kerberos obtains access to desired services without additional authentication. To get a list of all the tickets silently acquired for you by Kerberos, run `klist`.

Here is a short list of applications that use Kerberos authentication. These applications can be found under `/usr/lib/mit/bin` or `/usr/lib/mit/sbin` after installing the package `krb5-apps-clients`. They all have the full functionality of their common Unix and Linux brothers plus the additional bonus of transparent authentication managed by Kerberos:

- **telnet**, telnetd

- **rlogin**

- **rsh**, **rcp**, rshd

- **ftp**, ftpd

- **ksu**

You no longer need to enter your password for using these applications because Kerberos has already proven your identity. **ssh**, if compiled with Kerberos support, can even forward all the tickets acquired for one workstation to another one. If you use **ssh** to log in to another workstation, **ssh** makes sure that the encrypted contents of the tickets are adjusted to the new situation. Simply copying tickets between workstations is not sufficient because the ticket contains workstation-specific information (the IP address). XDM and GDM offer Kerberos support, too. Read more about the Kerberos network applications in *Kerberos V5 UNIX User's Guide* at http://web.mit.edu/kerberos .

6.4 Installing and Administering Kerberos

A Kerberos environment consists of several components. A key distribution center (KDC) holds the central database with all Kerberos-relevant data. All clients rely on the KDC for proper authentication across the network. Both the KDC and the clients need to be configured to match your setup:

General Preparations

Check your network setup and make sure it meets the minimum requirements outlined in *Section 6.4.1, "Kerberos Network Topology"*. Choose an appropriate realm for your Kerberos setup, see *Section 6.4.2, "Choosing the Kerberos Realms"*. Carefully set up the machine that is to serve as the KDC and apply tight security, see *Section 6.4.3, "Setting Up the KDC Hardware"*. Set up a reliable time source in your network to make sure all tickets contain valid time stamps, see *Section 6.4.4, "Configuring Time Synchronization"*.

Basic Configuration

Configure the KDC and the clients, see *Section 6.4.5, "Configuring the KDC"* and *Section 6.4.6, "Configuring Kerberos Clients"*. Enable remote administration for your Kerberos service, so you do not need physical access to your KDC machine, see *Section 6.4.7, "Configuring Remote Kerberos Administration"*. Create service principals for every service in your realm, see *Section 6.4.8, "Creating Kerberos Service Principals"*.

Enabling Kerberos Authentication

Various services in your network can use Kerberos. To add Kerberos password-checking to applications using PAM, proceed as outlined in *Section 6.4.9, "Enabling PAM Support for Kerberos"*. To configure SSH or LDAP with Kerberos authentication, proceed as outlined in *Section 6.4.10, "Configuring SSH for Kerberos Authentication"* and *Section 6.4.11, "Using LDAP and Kerberos"*.

6.4.1   Kerberos Network Topology

Any Kerberos environment must meet the following requirements to be fully functional:

- Provide a DNS server for name resolution across your network, so clients and servers can locate each other. Refer to *Book "Administration Guide", Chapter 25 "The Domain Name System"* for information on DNS setup.

- Provide a time server in your network. Using exact time stamps is crucial to a Kerberos setup, because valid Kerberos tickets must contain correct time stamps. Refer to *Book "Administration Guide", Chapter 24 "Time Synchronization with NTP"* for information on NTP setup.

- Provide a key distribution center (KDC) as the center piece of the Kerberos architecture. It holds the Kerberos database. Use the tightest possible security policy on this machine to prevent any attacks on this machine compromising your entire infrastructure.

- Configure the client machines to use Kerberos authentication.

The following figure depicts a simple example network with only the minimum components needed to build a Kerberos infrastructure. Depending on the size and topology of your deployment, your setup may vary.

FIGURE 6.1: KERBEROS NETWORK TOPOLOGY

Tip: Configuring Subnet Routing

For a setup similar to the one in *Figure 6.1, "Kerberos Network Topology"*, configure routing between the two subnets (192.168.1.0/24 and 192.168.2.0/24). Refer to *Book "Administration Guide", Chapter 16 "Basic Networking", Section 16.4.1.5 "Configuring Routing"* for more information on configuring routing with YaST.

6.4.2 Choosing the Kerberos Realms

The domain of a Kerberos installation is called a realm and is identified by a name, such as `EXAMPLE.COM` or simply `ACCOUNTING`. Kerberos is case-sensitive, so `example.com` is actually a different realm than `EXAMPLE.COM`. Use the case you prefer. It is common practice, however, to use uppercase realm names.

It is also a good idea to use your DNS domain name (or a subdomain, such as `ACCOUNTING.EX-AMPLE.COM`). As shown below, your life as an administrator can be much easier if you configure your Kerberos clients to locate the KDC and other Kerberos services via DNS. To do so, it is helpful if your realm name is a subdomain of your DNS domain name.

Unlike the DNS name space, Kerberos is not hierarchical. So if you have a realm named `EXAMPLE.COM` with two "subrealms" named `DEVELOPMENT` and `ACCOUNTING`, and these subordinate realms do not inherit principals from `EXAMPLE.COM`. Instead, you would have three separate realms, and you would need to configure cross-realm authentication for each realm, so that users from one realm to interact with servers or other users from another realm.

For the sake of simplicity, let us assume you are setting up just one realm for your entire organization. For the remainder of this section, the realm name `EXAMPLE.COM` is used in all examples.

6.4.3 Setting Up the KDC Hardware

The first thing required to use Kerberos is a machine that acts as the key distribution center, or KDC for short. This machine holds the entire Kerberos user database with passwords and all information.

The KDC is the most important part of your security infrastructure—if someone breaks into it, all user accounts and all of your infrastructure protected by Kerberos is compromised. An attacker with access to the Kerberos database can impersonate any principal in the database. Tighten security for this machine as much as possible:

1. Put the server machine into a physically secured location, such as a locked server room to which only a very few people have access.

2. Do not run any network applications on it except the KDC. This includes servers and clients —for example, the KDC should not import any file systems via NFS or use DHCP to retrieve its network configuration.

3. Install a minimal system first then check the list of installed packages and remove any unneeded packages. This includes servers, such as `inetd`, `portmap`, and CUPS, plus anything X-based. Even installing an SSH server should be considered a potential security risk.

4. No graphical login is provided on this machine as an X server is a potential security risk. Kerberos provides its own administration interface.

5. Configure `/etc/nsswitch.conf` to use only local files for user and group lookup. Change the lines for `passwd` and `group` to look like this:

```
passwd:        files
group:         files
```

Edit the `passwd`, `group`, and `shadow` files in `/etc` and remove the lines that start with a `+` character (these are for NIS lookups).

6. Disable all user accounts except `root`'s account by editing `/etc/shadow` and replacing the hashed passwords with `*` or `!` characters.

6.4.4   Configuring Time Synchronization

To use Kerberos successfully, make sure that all system clocks within your organization are synchronized within a certain range. This is important because Kerberos protects against replayed credentials. An attacker might be able to observe Kerberos credentials on the network and reuse them to attack the server. Kerberos employs several defenses to prevent this. One of them is that it puts time stamps into its tickets. A server receiving a ticket with a time stamp that differs from the current time rejects the ticket.

Kerberos allows a certain leeway when comparing time stamps. However, computer clocks can be very inaccurate in keeping time—it is not unheard of for PC clocks to lose or gain half an hour during a week. For this reason, configure all hosts on the network to synchronize their clocks with a central time source.

A simple way to do so is by installing an NTP time server on one machine and having all clients synchronize their clocks with this server. Do this either by running an NTP daemon in client mode on all these machines or by running **ntpdate** once a day from all clients (this solution probably works for a few clients only). The KDC itself needs to be synchronized to the common time source as well. Because running an NTP daemon on this machine would be a security risk, it is probably a good idea to do this by running ntpdate via a cron job. To configure your machine as an NTP client, proceed as outlined in *Book "Administration Guide", Chapter 24 "Time Synchronization with NTP", Section 24.1 "Configuring an NTP Client with YaST"*.

A different way to secure the time service and still use the NTP daemon is to attach a hardware reference clock to a dedicated NTP server and an additional hardware reference clock to the KDC.

It is also possible to adjust the maximum deviation Kerberos allows when checking time stamps. This value (called *clock skew*) can be set in the `krb5.conf` file as described in *Section 6.4.6.3, "Adjusting the Clock Skew"*.

6.4.5   Configuring the KDC

This section covers the initial configuration and installation of the KDC, including the creation of an administrative principal. This procedure consists of several steps:

1. **Install the RPMs.**   On a machine designated as the KDC, install the following software packages: `krb5`, `krb5-server` and `krb5-client` packages.

2. **Adjust the Configuration Files.**   The `/etc/krb5.conf` and `/var/lib/kerberos/krb5kdc/kdc.conf` configuration files must be adjusted for your scenario. These files contain all information on the KDC.

3. **Create the Kerberos Database.**   Kerberos keeps a database of all principal identifiers and the secret keys of all principals that need to be authenticated. Refer to *Section 6.4.5.1, "Setting Up the Database"* for details.

4. **Adjust the ACL Files: Add Administrators.** The Kerberos database on the KDC can be managed remotely. To prevent unauthorized principals from tampering with the database, Kerberos uses access control lists. You must explicitly enable remote access for the administrator principal to enable them to manage the database. The Kerberos ACL file is located under `/var/lib/kerberos/krb5kdc/kadm5.acl`. Refer to *Section 6.4.7, "Configuring Remote Kerberos Administration"* for details.

5. **Adjust the Kerberos Database: Add Administrators.** You need at least one administrative principal to run and administer Kerberos. This principal must be added before starting the KDC. Refer to *Section 6.4.5.2, "Creating a Principal"* for details.

6. **Start the Kerberos Daemon.** After the KDC software is installed and properly configured, start the Kerberos daemon to provide Kerberos service for your realm. Refer to *Section 6.4.5.3, "Starting the KDC"* for details.

7. **Create a Principal for Yourself.** You need a principal for yourself. Refer to *Section 6.4.5.2, "Creating a Principal"* for details.

6.4.5.1 Setting Up the Database

Your next step is to initialize the database where Kerberos keeps all information about principals. Set up the database master key, which is used to protect the database from accidental disclosure (in particular if it is backed up to tape). The master key is derived from a pass phrase and is stored in a file called the stash file. This is so you do not need to enter the password every time the KDC is restarted. Make sure that you choose a good pass phrase, such as a sentence from a book opened to a random page.

When you make tape backups of the Kerberos database (`/var/lib/kerberos/krb5kdc/principal`), do not back up the stash file (which is in `/var/lib/kerberos/krb5kdc/.k5.EXAMPLE.COM`). Otherwise, everyone able to read the tape could also decrypt the database. Therefore, keep a copy of the pass phrase in a safe or some other secure location, because you will need it to restore your database from backup tape after a crash.

To create the stash file and the database, run:

```
kdb5_util create -r EXAMPLE.COM -s
```

You will see the following output:

```
Initializing database '/var/lib/kerberos/krb5kdc/principal' for realm 'EXAMPLE.COM',
master key name 'K/M@EXAMPLE.COM'
```

```
You will be prompted for the database Master Password.
It is important that you NOT FORGET this password.
Enter KDC database master key:    ❶
Re-enter KDC database master key to verify:    ❷
```

❶   Type the master password.

❷   Type the password again.

To verify, use the list command:

```
kadmin.local

kadmin> listprincs
```

You will see several principals in the database, which are for internal use by Kerberos:

```
K/M@EXAMPLE.COM
kadmin/admin@EXAMPLE.COM
kadmin/changepw@EXAMPLE.COM
krbtgt/EXAMPLE.COM@EXAMPLE.COM
```

6.4.5.2   Creating a Principal

Create two Kerberos principals for yourself: one normal principal for everyday work and one for administrative tasks relating to Kerberos. Assuming your login name is exampleuserIII_plain, proceed as follows:

```
kadmin.local

kadmin> ank geeko
```

You will see the following output:

```
geeko@EXAMPLE.COM's Password:    ❶
Verifying password:    ❷
```

❶   Type exampleuserIII_plain's password.

❶   Type exampleuserIII_plain's password again.

Next, create another principal named geeko/admin by typing **ank** geeko/admin at the **kadmin** prompt. The admin suffixed to your user name is a *role*. Later, use this role when administering the Kerberos database. A user can have several roles for different purposes. Roles act like completely different accounts that have similar names.

6.4.5.3 Starting the KDC

Start the KDC daemon and the kadmin daemon. To start the daemons manually, enter:

```
sudo systemctl start krb5kdc
sudo systemctl start kadmind
```

Also make sure that the services KDC (`krb5kdc`) and kadmind (`kadmind`) are started by default when the server machine is rebooted. Enable them by entering:

```
sudo systemctl enable krb5kdc kadmind
```

or by using the YaST *Services Manager*.

6.4.6 Configuring Kerberos Clients

When the supporting infrastructure is in place (DNS, NTP) and the KDC has been properly configured and started, configure the client machines. To configure a Kerberos client, use one of the two manual approaches described below.

When configuring Kerberos, there are two approaches you can take—static configuration in the `/etc/krb5.conf` file or dynamic configuration with DNS. With DNS configuration, Kerberos applications try to locate the KDC services using DNS records. With static configuration, add the host names of your KDC server to `krb5.conf` (and update the file whenever you move the KDC or reconfigure your realm in other ways).

DNS-based configuration is generally a lot more flexible and the amount of configuration work per machine is a lot less. However, it requires that your realm name is either the same as your DNS domain or a subdomain of it. Configuring Kerberos via DNS also creates a security issue: an attacker can seriously disrupt your infrastructure through your DNS (by shooting down the name server, spoofing DNS records, etc.). However, this amounts to a denial of service at worst. A similar scenario applies to the static configuration case unless you enter IP addresses in `krb5.conf` instead of host names.

6.4.6.1 Static Configuration

One way to configure Kerberos is to edit `/etc/krb5.conf`. The file installed by default contains various sample entries. Erase all of these entries before starting. `krb5.conf` is made up of several sections (stanzas), each introduced by the section name in brackets like `[this]`.

To configure your Kerberos clients, add the following stanza to `krb5.conf` (where `kdc.example.com` is the host name of the KDC):

```
[libdefaults]
        default_realm = EXAMPLE.COM

[realms]
        EXAMPLE.COM = {
                kdc = kdc.example.com
                admin_server = kdc.example.com
        }
```

The `default_realm` line sets the default realm for Kerberos applications. If you have several realms, add additional statements to the `[realms]` section.

Also add a statement to this file that tells applications how to map host names to a realm. For example, when connecting to a remote host, the Kerberos library needs to know in which realm this host is located. This must be configured in the `[domain_realms]` section:

```
[domain_realm]
.example.com = EXAMPLE.COM
www.example.org = EXAMPLE.COM
```

This tells the library that all hosts in the `example.com` DNS domains are in the `EXAMPLE.COM` Kerberos realm. In addition, one external host named `www.example.org` should also be considered a member of the `EXAMPLE.COM` realm.

6.4.6.2 DNS-Based Configuration

DNS-based Kerberos configuration makes heavy use of SRV records. See *(RFC2052) A DNS RR for specifying the location of services* at http://www.ietf.org ↗.

The name of an SRV record, as far as Kerberos is concerned, is always in the format `_service._proto.realm`, where realm is the Kerberos realm. Domain names in DNS are case-insensitive, so case-sensitive Kerberos realms would break when using this configuration method. `_service` is a service name (different names are used when trying to contact the KDC or the password service, for example). `_proto` can be either `_udp` or `_tcp`, but not all services support both protocols.

The data portion of SRV resource records consists of a priority value, a weight, a port number, and a host name. The priority defines the order in which hosts should be tried (lower values indicate a higher priority). The weight value is there to support some sort of load balancing among servers of equal priority. You probably do not need any of this, so it is okay to set these to zero.

MIT Kerberos currently looks up the following names when looking for services:

_kerberos

> This defines the location of the KDC daemon (the authentication and ticket granting server). Typical records look like this:

```
_kerberos._udp.EXAMPLE.COM.  IN  SRV    0 0 88 kdc.example.com.
_kerberos._tcp.EXAMPLE.COM.  IN  SRV    0 0 88 kdc.example.com.
```

_kerberos-adm

> This describes the location of the remote administration service. Typical records look like this:

```
_kerberos-adm._tcp.EXAMPLE.COM. IN   SRV    0 0 749 kdc.example.com.
```

> Because kadmind does not support UDP, there should be no _udp record.

As with the static configuration file, there is a mechanism to inform clients that a specific host is in the EXAMPLE.COM realm, even if it is not part of the example.com DNS domain. This can be done by attaching a TXT record to _kerberos.host_name, as shown here:

```
_kerberos.www.example.org.  IN TXT "EXAMPLE.COM"
```

6.4.6.3 Adjusting the Clock Skew

The *clock skew* is the tolerance for accepting tickets with time stamps that do not exactly match the host's system clock. Usually, the clock skew is set to 300 seconds (five minutes). This means a ticket can have a time stamp somewhere between five minutes behind and five minutes ahead of the server's clock.

When using NTP to synchronize all hosts, you can reduce this value to about one minute. The clock skew value can be set in /etc/krb5.conf like this:

```
[libdefaults]
```

```
        clockskew = 60
```

6.4.7 Configuring Remote Kerberos Administration

To be able to add and remove principals from the Kerberos database without accessing the KDC's console directly, tell the Kerberos administration server which principals are allowed to do what by editing `/var/lib/kerberos/krb5kdc/kadm5.acl`. The ACL (access control list) file allows you to specify privileges with a precise degree of control. For details, refer to the manual page with **man** 8 kadmind.

For now, grant yourself the privilege to administer the database by putting the following line into the file:

```
geeko/admin                    *
```

Replace the user name `exampleuserIII_plain` with your own. Restart `kadmind` for the change to take effect.

You should now be able to perform Kerberos administration tasks remotely using the kadmin tool. First, obtain a ticket for your admin role and use that ticket when connecting to the kadmin server:

```
kadmin -p geeko/admin
Authenticating as principal geeko/admin@EXAMPLE.COM with password.
Password for geeko/admin@EXAMPLE.COM:
kadmin:  getprivs
current privileges: GET ADD MODIFY DELETE
kadmin:
```

Using the **getprivs** command, verify which privileges you have. The list shown above is the full set of privileges.

As an example, modify the principal `exampleuserIII_plain`:

```
kadmin -p geeko/admin
Authenticating as principal geeko/admin@EXAMPLE.COM with password.
Password for geeko/admin@EXAMPLE.COM:

kadmin:  getprinc geeko
Principal: geeko@EXAMPLE.COM
Expiration date: [never]
Last password change: Wed Jan 12 17:28:46 CET 2005
Password expiration date: [none]
Maximum ticket life: 0 days 10:00:00
Maximum renewable life: 7 days 00:00:00
```

```
Last modified: Wed Jan 12 17:47:17 CET 2005 (admin/admin@EXAMPLE.COM)
Last successful authentication: [never]
Last failed authentication: [never]
Failed password attempts: 0
Number of keys: 2
Key: vno 1, Triple DES cbc mode with HMAC/sha1, no salt
Key: vno 1, DES cbc mode with CRC-32, no salt
Attributes:
Policy: [none]

kadmin:  modify_principal -maxlife "8 hours" geeko
Principal "geeko@EXAMPLE.COM" modified.
kadmin:  getprinc geeko
Principal: geeko@EXAMPLE.COM
Expiration date: [never]
Last password change: Wed Jan 12 17:28:46 CET 2005
Password expiration date: [none]
Maximum ticket life: 0 days 08:00:00
Maximum renewable life: 7 days 00:00:00
Last modified: Wed Jan 12 17:59:49 CET 2005 (geeko/admin@EXAMPLE.COM)
Last successful authentication: [never]
Last failed authentication: [never]
Failed password attempts: 0
Number of keys: 2
Key: vno 1, Triple DES cbc mode with HMAC/sha1, no salt
Key: vno 1, DES cbc mode with CRC-32, no salt
Attributes:
Policy: [none]
kadmin:
```

This changes the maximum ticket life time to eight hours. For more information about the **kadmin** command and the options available, see the `krb5-doc` package or refer to the **man 8 kadmin** manual page.

6.4.8   Creating Kerberos Service Principals

So far, only user credentials have been discussed. However, Kerberos-compatible services usually need to authenticate themselves to the client user, too. Therefore, special service principals must be in the Kerberos database for each service offered in the realm. For example, if ldap.example.com offers an LDAP service, you need a service principal, `ldap/ldap.example.com@EXAMPLE.COM`, to authenticate this service to all clients.

The naming convention for service principals is *SERVICE/HOSTNAME@REALM*, where *HOSTNAME* is the host's fully qualified host name.

Valid service descriptors are:

Service Descriptor	Service
host	Telnet, RSH, SSH
nfs	NFSv4 (with Kerberos support)
HTTP	HTTP (with Kerberos authentication)
imap	IMAP
pop	POP3
ldap	LDAP

Service principals are similar to user principals, but have significant differences. The main difference between a user principal and a service principal is that the key of the former is protected by a password. When a user obtains a ticket-granting ticket from the KDC, they needs to type their password, so Kerberos can decrypt the ticket. It would be inconvenient for system administrators to obtain new tickets for the SSH daemon every eight hours or so.

Instead, the key required to decrypt the initial ticket for the service principal is extracted by the administrator from the KDC only once and stored in a local file called the *keytab*. Services such as the SSH daemon read this key and use it to obtain new tickets automatically, when needed. The default keytab file resides in /etc/krb5.keytab.

To create a host service principal for jupiter.example.com enter the following commands during your kadmin session:

```
kadmin -p geeko/admin
Authenticating as principal geeko/admin@EXAMPLE.COM with password.
Password for geeko/admin@EXAMPLE.COM:
kadmin:  addprinc -randkey host/jupiter.example.com
WARNING: no policy specified for host/jupiter.example.com@EXAMPLE.COM;
defaulting to no policy
Principal "host/jupiter.example.com@EXAMPLE.COM" created.
```

Instead of setting a password for the new principal, the -randkey flag tells **kadmin** to generate a random key. This is used here because no user interaction is wanted for this principal. It is a server account for the machine.

Finally, extract the key and store it in the local keytab file `/etc/krb5.keytab`. This file is owned by the superuser, so you must be `root` to execute the next command in the kadmin shell:

```
kadmin:  ktadd host/jupiter.example.com
Entry for principal host/jupiter.example.com with kvno 3, encryption type Triple
DES cbc mode with HMAC/sha1 added to keytab WRFILE:/etc/krb5.keytab.
Entry for principal host/jupiter.example.com with kvno 3, encryption type DES
cbc mode with CRC-32 added to keytab WRFILE:/etc/krb5.keytab.
kadmin:
```

When completed, make sure that you destroy the admin ticket obtained with kinit above with **kdestroy**.

6.4.9 Enabling PAM Support for Kerberos

SUSE® Linux Enterprise Server comes with a PAM module named `pam_krb5`, which supports Kerberos login and password update. This module can be used by applications such as console login, **su**, and graphical login applications like GDM. That is, it can be used in all cases where the user enters a password and expects the authenticating application to obtain an initial Kerberos ticket on their behalf. To configure PAM support for Kerberos, use the following command:

```
pam-config --add --krb5
```

The above command adds the `pam_krb5` module to the existing PAM configuration files and makes sure it is called in the right order. To make precise adjustments to the way in which `pam_krb5` is used, edit the file `/etc/krb5.conf` and add default applications to `pam`. For details, refer to the manual page with **man** `5 pam_krb5`.

The `pam_krb5` module was specifically not designed for network services that accept Kerberos tickets as part of user authentication. This is an entirely different matter, and is discussed below.

6.4.10 Configuring SSH for Kerberos Authentication

OpenSSH supports Kerberos authentication in both protocol version 1 and 2. In version 1, there are special protocol messages to transmit Kerberos tickets. Version 2 does not use Kerberos directly anymore, but relies on GSSAPI, the General Security Services API. This is a programming interface that is not specific to Kerberos—it was designed to hide the peculiarities of the underlying authentication system, be it Kerberos, a public-key authentication system like SPKM, or others. However, the included GSSAPI library only supports Kerberos.

To use sshd with Kerberos authentication, edit `/etc/ssh/sshd_config` and set the following options:

```
# These are for protocol version 1
#
# KerberosAuthentication yes
# KerberosTicketCleanup yes


# These are for version 2 - better to use this
GSSAPIAuthentication yes
GSSAPICleanupCredentials yes
```

Then restart your SSH daemon using **sudo systemctl restart sshd**.

To use Kerberos authentication with protocol version 2, enable it on the client side as well. Do this either in the systemwide configuration file `/etc/ssh/ssh_config` or on a per-user level by editing `~/.ssh/config`. In both cases, add the option `GSSAPIAuthentication yes`.

You should now be able to connect using Kerberos authentication. Use **klist** to verify that you have a valid ticket, then connect to the SSH server. To force SSH protocol version 1, specify the `-1` option on the command line.

Tip: Additional Information

The file `/usr/share/doc/packages/openssh/README.kerberos` discusses the interaction of OpenSSH and Kerberos in more detail.

Tip: Additional Directives for Protocol Version 2

The `GSSAPIKeyExchange` mechanism (RFC 4462) is supported. This directive specifies how host keys are exchanged. For more information, see the sshd_config manual page (**man sshd_config**).

6.4.11 Using LDAP and Kerberos

When using Kerberos, one way to distribute the user information (such as user ID, groups, and home directory) in your local network is to use LDAP. This requires a strong authentication mechanism that prevents packet spoofing and other attacks. One solution is to use Kerberos for LDAP communication, too.

OpenLDAP implements most authentication flavors through SASL, the simple authentication session layer. SASL is a network protocol designed for authentication. The SASL implementation is cyrus-sasl, which supports several authentication flavors. Kerberos authentication is performed through GSSAPI (General Security Services API). By default, the SASL plug-in for GSSAPI is not installed. Install the `cyrus-sasl-gssapi` with YaST.

To enable Kerberos to bind to the OpenLDAP server, create a principal `ldap/ldap.example.com` and add that to the keytab.

By default, the LDAP server slapd runs as user and group `ldap`, while the keytab file is readable by `root` only. Therefore, either change the LDAP configuration so the server runs as `root` or make the keytab file readable by the group `ldap`. The latter is done automatically by the OpenLDAP start script (`/usr/lib/openldap/start`) if the keytab file has been specified in the `OPENLDAP_KRB5_KEYTAB` variable in `/etc/sysconfig/openldap` and the `OPENLDAP_CHOWN_DIRS` variable is set to `yes`, which is the default setting. If `OPENLDAP_KRB5_KEYTAB` is left empty, the default keytab under `/etc/krb5.keytab` is used and you must adjust the privileges yourself as described below.

To run slapd as `root`, edit `/etc/sysconfig/openldap`. Disable the `OPENLDAP_USER` and `OPENLDAP_GROUP` variables by putting a comment character in front of them.

To make the keytab file readable by group LDAP, execute

```
chgrp ldap /etc/krb5.keytab
chmod 640 /etc/krb5.keytab
```

A third (and maybe the best) solution is to tell OpenLDAP to use a special keytab file. To do this, start kadmin, and enter the following command after you have added the principal ldap/ldap.example.com:

```
ktadd -k /etc/openldap/ldap.keytab ldap/ldap.example.com@EXAMPLE.COM
```

Then in the shell run:

```
chown ldap.ldap /etc/openldap/ldap.keytab
chmod 600 /etc/openldap/ldap.keytab
```

To tell OpenLDAP to use a different keytab file, change the following variable in `/etc/sysconfig/openldap`:

```
OPENLDAP_KRB5_KEYTAB="/etc/openldap/ldap.keytab"
```

Finally, restart the LDAP server using **sudo systemctl restart slapd**.

6.4.11.1 Using Kerberos Authentication with LDAP

You are now able to automatically use tools such as ldapsearch with Kerberos authentication.

```
ldapsearch -b ou=people,dc=example,dc=com '(uid=geeko)'

SASL/GSSAPI authentication started
SASL SSF: 56
SASL installing layers
[...]

# geeko, people, example.com
dn: uid=geeko,ou=people,dc=example,dc=com
uid: geeko
cn: Suzanne Geeko
[...]
```

As you can see, **ldapsearch** prints a message that it started GSSAPI authentication. The next message is very cryptic, but it shows that the *security strength factor* (SSF for short) is 56 (The value 56 is somewhat arbitrary. Most likely it was chosen because this is the number of bits in a DES encryption key). This means that GSSAPI authentication was successful and that encryption is being used to protect integrity and provide confidentiality for the LDAP connection.

In Kerberos, authentication is always mutual. This means that not only have you authenticated yourself to the LDAP server, but also the LDAP server has authenticated itself to you. In particular, this means communication is with the desired LDAP server, rather than some bogus service set up by an attacker.

6.4.11.2 Kerberos Authentication and LDAP Access Control

There is one minor piece of the puzzle missing—how the LDAP server can find out that the Kerberos user tux@EXAMPLE.COM corresponds to the LDAP distinguished name uid=tux,ou=people,dc=example,dc=com. This sort of mapping must be configured manually using the saslExpr directive. In this example, the "authz-regexp" change in LDIF would look as follows:

```
dn: cn=config
add: olcAuthzRegexp
olcAuthzRegexp: uid=(.*),cn=GSSAPI,cn=auth uid=$1,ou=people,dc=example,dc=com
```

All these changes can be applied via **ldapmodify** on the command line.

When SASL authenticates a user, OpenLDAP forms a distinguished name from the name given to it by SASL (such as tux) and the name of the SASL flavor (GSSAPI). The result would be uid=tux,cn=GSSAPI,cn=auth.

If a `authz-regexp` has been configured, it checks the DN formed from the SASL information using the first argument as a regular expression. If this regular expression matches, the name is replaced with the second argument of the `authz-regexp` statement. The placeholder `$1` is replaced with the substring matched by the `(.*)` expression.

More complicated match expressions are possible. If you have a more complicated directory structure or a schema in which the user name is not part of the DN, you can even use search expressions to map the SASL DN to the user DN.

For more information, see the `slapd-config` man page.

6.5 Setting up Kerberos using *LDAP and Kerberos Client*

YaST includes the module *LDAP and Kerberos Client* that helps define authentication scenarios involving either LDAP or Kerberos.

It can also be used to join Kerberos and LDAP separately. However, in many such cases, using this module may not be the first choice, such as for joining Active Directory (which uses a combination of LDAP and Kerberos). For more information, see *Section 4.2, "Configuring an Authentication Client with YaST"*.

Start the module by selecting *Network Services* › *LDAP and Kerberos Client*.

FIGURE 6.2: *LDAP AND KERBEROS CLIENT* WINDOW

To configure a Kerberos client, follow the procedure below:

1. In the window *LDAP and Kerberos Client*, click *Change Settings*.
   Choose the tab *Authentication via Kerberos*.

2. Click *Add Realm*.

3. In the appearing dialog, specify the correct *Realm name*. Usually, the realm name is an uppercase version of the domain name. Additionally, you can specify the following:

   - To apply mappings from the realm name to the domain name, activate *Map Domain Name to the Realm* and/or *Map Wildcard Domain Name to the Realm*.

   - You can specify the *Host Name of Administration Server*, the *Host Name of Master Key Distribution Server* and additional *Key Distribution Centers*.
     All of these items are optional if they can be automatically discovered via the SRV and TXT records in DNS.

   - To manually map Principals to local user names, use *Custom Mappings of Principal Names to User Names*.
     You can also use `auth_to_local` rules to supply such mappings using *Custom Rules for Mapping Principal Names to User Names*. For more information about using such rules, see the official documentation at https://web.mit.edu/kerberos/krb5-current/doc/admin/conf_files/krb5_conf.html#realms ↗.

   Continue with *OK*.

4. To add more realms, repeat from *Step 2*.

5. Enable Kerberos users logging in and creation of home directories by activating *Allow Kerberos Users to Authenticate* and *Automatically Create Home Directory*.

6. If you left empty the optional text boxes in *Step 3*, make sure to enable automatic discovery of realms and key distribution centers by activating *Use DNS TXT Record to Discover Realms* and *Use DNS SRV Record to Discover KDC Servers*.

7. You can additionally activate the following:

   - *Allow Insecure Encryption (for Windows NT)* allows the encryption types listed as weak at http://web.mit.edu/kerberos/krb5-current/doc/admin/conf_files/kdc_conf.html#encryption-types ↗.

   - *Allow KDC on Other Networks to Issue Authentication Tickets* allows forwarding of tickets.

   - *Allow Kerberos-Enabled Services to Take on The Identity Of a User* allows the use of proxies between the computer of the user and the key distribution center.

   - *Issue Address-Less Tickets for Computers Behind NAT* allows granting tickets to users behind networks using network address translation.

8. To set up allowed encryption types and define the name of the keytab file which lists the names of principals and their encrypted keys, use the *Extended Options*.

9. Finish with *OK* and *Finish*.
   YaST may now install extra packages.

6.6   For More Information

The official site of MIT Kerberos is http://web.mit.edu/kerberos ↗. There, find links to any other relevant resource concerning Kerberos, including Kerberos installation, user, and administration guides.

The book *Kerberos—A Network Authentication System* by Brian Tung (ISBN 0-201-37924-4) offers extensive information.

7 Active Directory Support

Active Directory* (AD) is a directory-service based on LDAP, Kerberos, and other services. It is used by Microsoft* Windows* to manage resources, services, and people. In a Microsoft Windows network, Active Directory provides information about these objects, restricts access to them, and enforces policies. SUSE® Linux Enterprise Server lets you join existing Active Directory domains and integrate your Linux machine into a Windows environment.

7.1 Integrating Linux and Active Directory Environments

With a Linux client (configured as an Active Directory client) that is joined to an existing Active Directory domain, benefit from various features not available on a pure SUSE Linux Enterprise Server Linux client:

Browsing Shared Files and Directories with SMB

GNOME Files (previously called Nautilus) supports browsing shared resources through SMB.

Sharing Files and Directories with SMB

GNOME Files supports sharing directories and files as in Windows.

Accessing and Manipulating User Data on the Windows Server

Through GNOME Files, users can access their Windows user data and can edit, create, and delete files and directories on the Windows server. Users can access their data without having to enter their password multiple times.

Offline Authentication

Users can log in and access their local data on the Linux machine even if they are offline or the Active Directory server is unavailable for other reasons.

Windows Password Change

This port of Active Directory support in Linux enforces corporate password policies stored in Active Directory. The display managers and console support password change messages and accept your input. You can even use the Linux `passwd` command to set Windows passwords.

Single-Sign-On through Kerberized Applications

> Many desktop applications are Kerberos-enabled (*kerberized*), which means they can transparently handle authentication for the user without the need for password reentry at Web servers, proxies, groupware applications, or other locations.

 Note: Managing Unix Attributes from Windows Server* 2016 and Later

> In Windows Server 2016 and later, Microsoft has removed the role *IDMU/NIS Server* and along with it the *Unix Attributes* plug-in for the *Active Directory Users and Computers* MMC snap-in.
>
> However, Unix attributes can still be managed manually when *Advanced Options* are enabled in the *Active Directory Users and Computers* MMC snap-in. For more information, see https://blogs.technet.microsoft.com/activedirectoryua/2016/02/09/identity-management-for-unix-idmu-is-deprecated-in-windows-server/ ↗.
>
> Alternatively, use the method described in *Procedure 7.1, "Joining an Active Directory Domain Using User Logon Management "* to complete attributes on the client side (in particular, see *Step 6.c*).

The following section contains technical background for most of the previously named features.

7.2 Background Information for Linux Active Directory Support

Many system components need to interact flawlessly to integrate a Linux client into an existing Windows Active Directory domain. The following sections focus on the underlying processes of the key events in Active Directory server and client interaction.

To communicate with the directory service, the client needs to share at least two protocols with the server:

LDAP

> LDAP is a protocol optimized for managing directory information. A Windows domain controller with Active Directory can use the LDAP protocol to exchange directory information with the clients. To learn more about LDAP in general and about the open source port of it, OpenLDAP, refer to *Chapter 5, LDAP—A Directory Service*.

Kerberos

Kerberos is a third-party trusted authentication service. All its clients trust Kerberos's authorization of another client's identity, enabling kerberized single-sign-on (SSO) solutions. Windows supports a Kerberos implementation, making Kerberos SSO possible even with Linux clients. To learn more about Kerberos in Linux, refer to *Chapter 6, Network Authentication with Kerberos*.

Depending on which YaST module you use to set up Kerberos authentication, different client components process account and authentication data:

Solutions Based on SSSD

- The `sssd` daemon is the central part of this solution. It handles all communication with the Active Directory server.

- To gather name service information, `sssd_nss` is used.

- To authenticate users, the `pam_sss` module for PAM is used. The creation of user homes for the Active Directory users on the Linux client is handled by `pam_mkhomedir`.
  For more information about PAM, see *Chapter 2, Authentication with PAM*.

Solution Based On Winbind (Samba)

- The `winbindd` daemon is the central part of this solution. It handles all communication with the Active Directory server.

- To gather name service information, `nss_winbind` is used.

- To authenticate users, the `pam_winbind` module for PAM is used. The creation of user homes for the Active Directory users on the Linux client is handled by `pam_mkhomedir`.
  For more information about PAM, see *Chapter 2, Authentication with PAM*.

Figure 7.1, "Schema of Winbind-based Active Directory Authentication" highlights the most prominent components of Winbind-based Active Directory authentication.

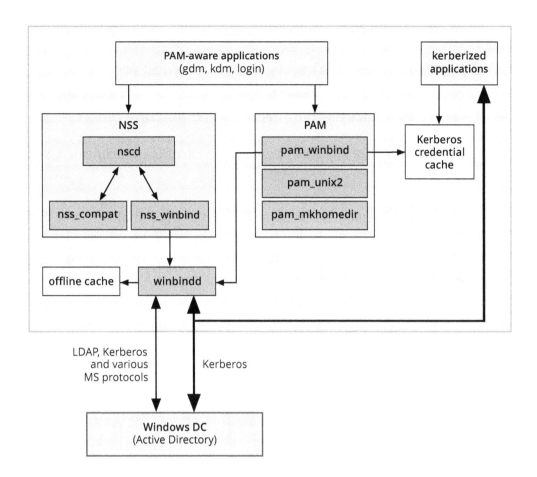

FIGURE 7.1: SCHEMA OF WINBIND-BASED ACTIVE DIRECTORY AUTHENTICATION

Applications that are PAM-aware, like the login routines and the GNOME display manager, interact with the PAM and NSS layer to authenticate against the Windows server. Applications supporting Kerberos authentication (such as file managers, Web browsers, or e-mail clients) use the Kerberos credential cache to access user's Kerberos tickets, making them part of the SSO framework.

7.2.1   Domain Join

During domain join, the server and the client establish a secure relation. On the client, the following tasks need to be performed to join the existing LDAP and Kerberos SSO environment provided by the Windows domain controller. The entire join process is handled by the YaST Domain Membership module, which can be run during installation or in the installed system:

1. The Windows domain controller providing both LDAP and KDC (Key Distribution Center) services is located.

2. A machine account for the joining client is created in the directory service.

3. An initial ticket granting ticket (TGT) is obtained for the client and stored in its local Kerberos credential cache. The client needs this TGT to get further tickets allowing it to contact other services, like contacting the directory server for LDAP queries.

4. NSS and PAM configurations are adjusted to enable the client to authenticate against the domain controller.

During client boot, the winbind daemon is started and retrieves the initial Kerberos ticket for the machine account. winbindd automatically refreshes the machine's ticket to keep it valid. To keep track of the current account policies, winbindd periodically queries the domain controller.

7.2.2 Domain Login and User Homes

The login manager of GNOME (GDM) has been extended to allow the handling of Active Directory domain login. Users can choose to log in to the primary domain the machine has joined or to one of the trusted domains with which the domain controller of the primary domain has established a trust relationship.

User authentication is mediated by several PAM modules as described in *Section 7.2, "Background Information for Linux Active Directory Support"*. If there are errors, the error codes are translated into user-readable error messages that PAM gives at login through any of the supported methods (GDM, console, and SSH):

`Password has expired`

The user sees a message stating that the password has expired and needs to be changed. The system prompts for a new password and informs the user if the new password does not comply with corporate password policies (for example the password is too short, too simple, or already in the history). If a user's password change fails, the reason is shown and a new password prompt is given.

`Account disabled`

The user sees an error message stating that the account has been disabled and to contact the system administrator.

`Account locked out`

The user sees an error message stating that the account has been locked and to contact the system administrator.

Password has to be changed

The user can log in but receives a warning that the password needs to be changed soon. This warning is sent three days before that password expires. After expiration, the user cannot log in.

Invalid workstation

When a user is restricted to specific workstations and the current SUSE Linux Enterprise Server machine is not among them, a message appears that this user cannot log in from this workstation.

Invalid logon hours

When a user is only allowed to log in during working hours and tries to log in outside working hours, a message informs the user that logging in is not possible at that time.

Account expired

An administrator can set an expiration time for a specific user account. If that user tries to log in after expiration, the user gets a message that the account has expired and cannot be used to log in.

During a successful authentication, the client acquires a ticket granting ticket (TGT) from the Kerberos server of Active Directory and stores it in the user's credential cache. It also renews the TGT in the background, requiring no user interaction.

SUSE Linux Enterprise Server supports local home directories for Active Directory users. If configured through YaST as described in *Section 7.3, "Configuring a Linux Client for Active Directory"*, user home directories are created when a Windows/Active Directory user first logs in to the Linux client. These home directories look and feel identical to standard Linux user home directories and work independently of the Active Directory Domain Controller.

Using a local user home, it is possible to access a user's data on this machine (even when the Active Directory server is disconnected) as long as the Linux client has been configured to perform offline authentication.

7.2.3   Offline Service and Policy Support

Users in a corporate environment must have the ability to become roaming users (for example, to switch networks or even work disconnected for some time). To enable users to log in to a disconnected machine, extensive caching was integrated into the winbind daemon. The winbind daemon enforces password policies even in the offline state. It tracks the number of failed login attempts and reacts according to the policies configured in Active Directory. Offline support is disabled by default and must be explicitly enabled in the YaST Domain Membership module.

When the domain controller has become unavailable, the user can still access network resources (other than the Active Directory server itself) with valid Kerberos tickets that have been acquired before losing the connection (as in Windows). Password changes cannot be processed unless the domain controller is online. While disconnected from the Active Directory server, a user cannot access any data stored on this server. When a workstation has become disconnected from the network entirely and connects to the corporate network again later, SUSE Linux Enterprise Server acquires a new Kerberos ticket when the user has locked and unlocked the desktop (for example, using a desktop screen saver).

7.3 Configuring a Linux Client for Active Directory

Before your client can join an Active Directory domain, some adjustments must be made to your network setup to ensure the flawless interaction of client and server.

DNS

Configure your client machine to use a DNS server that can forward DNS requests to the Active Directory DNS server. Alternatively, configure your machine to use the Active Directory DNS server as the name service data source.

NTP

To succeed with Kerberos authentication, the client must have its time set accurately. It is highly recommended to use a central NTP time server for this purpose (this can be also the NTP server running on your Active Directory domain controller). If the clock skew between your Linux host and the domain controller exceeds a certain limit, Kerberos authentication fails and the client is logged in using the weaker NTLM (NT LAN Manager) authentication. For more details about using Active Directory for time synchronization, see *Procedure 7.2, "Joining an Active Directory Domain Using Windows Domain Membership"*.

Firewall

To browse your network neighborhood, either disable the firewall entirely or mark the interface used for browsing as part of the internal zone.

To change the firewall settings on your client, log in as `root` and start the YaST firewall module. Select *Interfaces*. Select your network interface from the list of interfaces and click *Change*. Select *Internal Zone* and apply your settings with *OK*. Leave the firewall settings with *Next > Finish*. To disable the firewall, check the *Disable Firewall Automatic Starting* option, and leave the firewall module with *Next > Finish*.

Active Directory Account

You cannot log in to an Active Directory domain unless the Active Directory administrator has provided you with a valid user account for that domain. Use the Active Directory user name and password to log in to the Active Directory domain from your Linux client.

7.3.1   Choosing Which YaST Module to Use for Connecting to Active Directory

YaST contains multiple modules that allow connecting to an Active Directory:

- *User Logon Management.* Use both an identity service (usually LDAP) and a user authentication service (usually Kerberos). This option is based on SSSD and in the majority of cases is best suited for joining Active Directory domains.
  This module is described in *Section 7.3.2, "Joining Active Directory Using User Logon Management ".*

- *Windows Domain Membership.* Join an Active Directory (which entails use of Kerberos and LDAP). This option is based on `winbind` and is best suited for joining an Active Directory domain if support for NTLM or cross-forest trusts is necessary.
  This module is described in *Section 7.3.3, "Joining Active Directory Using Windows Domain Membership ".*

- *LDAP and Kerberos Authentication.* Allows setting up LDAP identities and Kerberos authentication independently from each other and provides fewer options. While this module also uses SSSD, it is not as well suited for connecting to Active Directory as the previous two options.
  This module is described in:

  - LDAP: *Section 5.3, "Configuring an LDAP Client with YaST"*

  - Kerberos: *Section 6.5, "Setting up Kerberos using LDAP and Kerberos Client"*

7.3.2 Joining Active Directory Using *User Logon Management*

The YaST module *User Logon Management* supports authentication at an Active Directory. Additionally, it also supports the following related authentication and identification providers:

Identification Providers

- *Delegate to third-party software library.* Support for legacy NSS providers via a proxy.

- *FreeIPA.* FreeIPA and Red Hat Enterprise Identity Management provider.

- *Generic directory service (LDAP).* An LDAP provider. For more information about configuring LDAP, see `man 5 sssd-ldap`.

- *Local SSSD file database.* An SSSD-internal provider for local users.

Authentication Providers

- *Delegate to third-party software library.* Relay authentication to another PAM target via a proxy.

- *FreeIPA.* FreeIPA and Red Hat Enterprise Identity Management provider.

- *Generic Kerberos service.* An LDAP provider.

- *Generic directory service (LDAP).* Kerberos authentication.

- *Local SSSD file database.* An SSSD-internal provider for local users.

- *This domain does not provide authentication service.* Disables authentication explicitly.

To join an Active Directory domain using SSSD and the *User Logon Management* module of YaST, proceed as follows:

PROCEDURE 7.1: JOINING AN ACTIVE DIRECTORY DOMAIN USING *USER LOGON MANAGEMENT*

1. Open YaST.

2. To be able to use DNS auto-discovery later, set up the Active Directory Domain Controller (the Active Directory server) as the name server for your client.

   a. In YaST, click *Network Settings*.

   b. Select *Hostname/DNS*, then enter the IP address of the Active Directory Domain Controller into the text box *Name Server 1*.

Save the setting with *OK*.

3. From the YaST main window, start the module *User Logon Management.*
The module opens with an overview showing different network properties of your computer and the authentication method currently in use.

FIGURE 7.2: MAIN WINDOW OF *USER LOGON MANAGEMENT*

4. To start editing, click *Change Settings*.

5. Now join the domain.

   a. Click *Join Domain.*

   b. In the appearing dialog, specify the correct *Domain name.* Then specify the services to use for identity data and authentication: Select *Microsoft Active Directory* for both. Ensure that *Enable the domain* is activated.
   Click *OK*.

   c. *(Optional)* Usually, you can keep the default settings in the following dialog. However, there are reasons to make changes:

      • **If the Local Host Name Does Not Match the Host Name Set on the Domain Controller.** Find out if the host name of your computer matches what the name your computer is known as to the Active Directory Domain Controller. In a terminal, run the command `hostname`, then compare its output to the configuration of the Active Directory Domain Controller.

If the values differ, specify the host name from the Active Directory configuration under *AD hostname*. Otherwise, leave the appropriate text box empty.

- **If You Do Not Want to Use DNS Auto-Discovery.** Specify the *Host names of Active Directory servers* that you want to use. If there are multiple Domain Controllers, separate their host names with commas.

d. To continue, click *OK*.

If not all software is installed already, the computer will now install missing software. It will then check whether the configured Active Directory Domain Controller is available.

e. If everything is correct, the following dialog should now show that it has discovered an *Active Directory Server* but that you are *Not yet enrolled*.

In the dialog, specify the *Username* and *Password* of the Active Directory administrator account (usually `Administrator`).

To make sure that the current domain is enabled for Samba, activate *Overwrite Samba configuration to work with this AD*.

To enroll, click *OK*.

FIGURE 7.3: ENROLLING INTO A DOMAIN

f. You should now see a message confirming that you have enrolled successfully. Finish with *OK*.

6. After enrolling, configure the client using the window *Manage Domain User Logon*.

a. To allow logging in to the computer using login data provided by Active Directory, activate *Allow Domain User Logon*.

b. *(Optional)* Optionally, under *Enable domain data source*, activate additional data sources such as information on which users are allowed to use **sudo** or which network drives are available.

c. To allow Active Directory users to have home directories, activate *Create Home Directories*. The path for home directories can be set in multiple ways—on the client, on the server, or both ways:

   - To configure the home directory paths on the Domain Controller, set an appropriate value for the attribute `UnixHomeDirectory` for each user. Additionally, make sure that this attribute replicated to the global catalog. For information on achieving that under Windows, see https://support.microsoft.com/en-us/kb/248717 ↗ .

   - To configure home directory paths on the client in such a way that precedence will be given to the path set on the domain controller, use the option `fallback_homedir`.

   - To configure home directory paths on the client in such a way that the client setting will override the server setting, use `override_homedir`.

As settings on the Domain Controller are outside of the scope of this documentation, only the configuration of the client-side options will be described in the following. From the side bar, select *Service Options* › *Name switch*, then click *Extended Options*. From that window, select either `fallback_homedir` or `override_homedir`, then click *Add*.

Specify a value. To have home directories follow the format `/home/USER_NAME`, use `/home/%u`. For more information about possible variables, see the man page `sssd.conf` (**man 5 sssd.conf**), section *override_homedir*.
Click *OK*.

7. Save the changes by clicking *OK*. Then make sure that the values displayed now are correct. To leave the dialog, click *Cancel*.

7.3.3   Joining Active Directory Using *Windows Domain Membership*

To join an Active Directory domain using **winbind** and the *Windows Domain Membership* module of YaST, proceed as follows:

PROCEDURE 7.2: JOINING AN ACTIVE DIRECTORY DOMAIN USING *WINDOWS DOMAIN MEMBERSHIP*

1. Log in as `root` and start YaST.

2. Start *Network Services* › *Windows Domain Membership*.

3. Enter the domain to join at *Domain or Workgroup* in the *Windows Domain Membership* screen (see *Figure 7.5, "Determining Windows Domain Membership"*). If the DNS settings on your host are properly integrated with the Windows DNS server, enter the Active Directory domain name in its DNS format (`mydomain.mycompany.com`). If you enter the short name of your domain (also known as the pre–Windows 2000 domain name), YaST must rely on NetBIOS name resolution instead of DNS to find the correct domain controller.

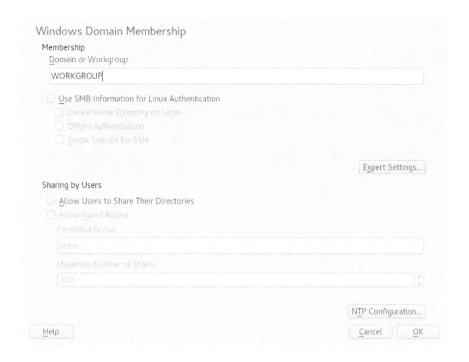

FIGURE 7.5: DETERMINING WINDOWS DOMAIN MEMBERSHIP

4. To use the SMB source for Linux authentication, activate *Also Use SMB Information for Linux Authentication.*

5. To automatically create a local home directory for Active Directory users on the Linux machine, activate *Create Home Directory on Login.*

6. Check *Offline Authentication* to allow your domain users to log in even if the Active Directory server is temporarily unavailable, or if you do not have a network connection.

7. To change the UID and GID ranges for the Samba users and groups, select *Expert Settings.* Let DHCP retrieve the WINS server only if you need it. This is the case when some machines are resolved only by the WINS system.

8. Configure NTP time synchronization for your Active Directory environment by selecting *NTP Configuration* and entering an appropriate server name or IP address. This step is obsolete if you have already entered the appropriate settings in the stand-alone YaST NTP configuration module.

9. Click *OK* and confirm the domain join when prompted for it.

10. Provide the password for the Windows administrator on the Active Directory server and click *OK* (see *Figure 7.6, "Providing Administrator Credentials"*).

Enter the username and the password
for joining the domain sbs-test.site.

To join the domain anonymously, leave the
text entries empty.

Username

Administrator

Password

OK   Cancel

FIGURE 7.6: PROVIDING ADMINISTRATOR CREDENTIALS

After you have joined the Active Directory domain, you can log in to it from your workstation using the display manager of your desktop or the console.

Important: Domain Name

Joining a domain may not succeed if the domain name ends with `.local`. Names ending in `.local` cause conflicts with Multicast DNS (MDNS) where `.local` is reserved for link-local host names.

Note: Only Administrators Can Enroll a Computer

Only a domain administrator account, such as `Administrator`, can join SUSE Linux Enterprise Server into Active Directory.

7.3.4   Checking Active Directory Connection Status

To check whether you are successfully enrolled in an Active Directory domain, use the following commands:

* **klist** shows whether the current user has a valid Kerberos ticket.

* **getent passwd** shows published LDAP data for all users.

7.4 Logging In to an Active Directory Domain

Provided your machine has been configured to authenticate against Active Directory and you have a valid Windows user identity, you can log in to your machine using the Active Directory credentials. Login is supported for GNOME, the console, SSH, and any other PAM-aware application.

 Important: Offline Authentication

> SUSE Linux Enterprise Server supports offline authentication, allowing you to log in to your client machine even when it is offline. See *Section 7.2.3, "Offline Service and Policy Support"* for details.

7.4.1 GDM

To authenticate a GNOME client machine against an Active Directory server, proceed as follows:

1. Click *Not listed.*

2. In the text box *Username*, enter the domain name and the Windows user name in this form: `DOMAIN_NAME\USER_NAME` .

3. Enter your Windows password.

If configured to do so, SUSE Linux Enterprise Server creates a user home directory on the local machine on the first login of each user authenticated via Active Directory. This allows you to benefit from the Active Directory support of SUSE Linux Enterprise Server while still having a fully functional Linux machine at your disposal.

7.4.2 Console Login

Besides logging in to the Active Directory client machine using a graphical front-end, you can log in using the text-based console or even remotely using SSH.

To log in to your Active Directory client from a console, enter `DOMAIN_NAME\USER_NAME` at the `login:` prompt and provide the password.

To remotely log in to your Active Directory client machine using SSH, proceed as follows:

1. At the login prompt, enter:

   ```
   ssh DOMAIN_NAME\\USER_NAME@HOST_NAME
   ```

   The \ domain and login delimiter is escaped with another \ sign.

2. Provide the user's password.

7.5 Changing Passwords

SUSE Linux Enterprise Server helps the user choose a suitable new password that meets the corporate security policy. The underlying PAM module retrieves the current password policy settings from the domain controller, informing the user about the specific password quality requirements a user account typically has by means of a message on login. Like its Windows counterpart, SUSE Linux Enterprise Server presents a message describing:

- Password history settings

- Minimum password length requirements

- Minimum password age

- Password complexity

The password change process cannot succeed unless all requirements have been successfully met. Feedback about the password status is given both through the display managers and the console.

GDM provides feedback about password expiration and the prompt for new passwords in an interactive mode. To change passwords in the display managers, provide the password information when prompted.

To change your Windows password, you can use the standard Linux utility, **passwd**, instead of having to manipulate this data on the server. To change your Windows password, proceed as follows:

1. Log in at the console.

2. Enter passwd.

3. Enter your current password when prompted.

4. Enter the new password.

5. Reenter the new password for confirmation. If your new password does not comply with the policies on the Windows server, this feedback is given to you and you are prompted for another password.

To change your Windows password from the GNOME desktop, proceed as follows:

1. Click the *Computer* icon on the left edge of the panel.

2. Select *Control Center*.

3. From the *Personal* section, select *About Me* › *Change Password*.

4. Enter your old password.

5. Enter and confirm the new password.

6. Leave the dialog with *Close* to apply your settings.

II Local Security

8 Configuring Security Settings with YaST

The YaST module *Security Center and Hardening* offers a central clearinghouse to configure security-related settings for SUSE Linux Enterprise Server. Use it to configure security aspects such as settings for the login procedure and for password creation, for boot permissions, user creation or for default file permissions. Launch it from the YaST control center by *Security and Users* › *Security Center and Hardening*. The *Security Center* dialog always starts with the *Security Overview*, and other configuration dialogs are available from the right pane.

8.1 Security Overview

The *Security Overview* displays a comprehensive list of the most important security settings for your system. The security status of each entry in the list is clearly visible. A green check mark indicates a secure setting while a red cross indicates an entry as being insecure. Click *Help* to open an overview of the setting and information on how to make it secure. To change a setting, click the corresponding link in the Status column. Depending on the setting, the following entries are available:

Enabled/Disabled

Click this entry to toggle the status of the setting to either enabled or disabled.

Configure

Click this entry to launch another YaST module for configuration. You will return to the Security Overview when leaving the module.

Unknown

A setting's status is set to unknown when the associated service is not installed. Such a setting does not represent a potential security risk.

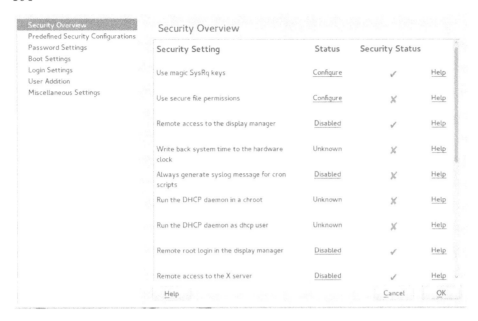

FIGURE 8.1: YAST SECURITY CENTER AND HARDENING: SECURITY OVERVIEW

8.2 Predefined Security Configurations

SUSE Linux Enterprise Server comes with three *Predefined Security Configurations*. These configurations affect all the settings available in the *Security Center* module. Each configuration can be modified to your needs using the dialogs available from the right pane changing its state to *Custom Settings*:

Workstation

A configuration for a workstation with any kind of network connection (including a connection to the Internet).

Roaming Device

This setting is designed for a laptop or tablet that connects to different networks.

Network Server

Security settings designed for a machine providing network services such as a Web server, file server, name server, etc. This set provides the most secure configuration of the predefined settings.

Custom Settings

> A pre-selected *Custom Settings* (when opening the *Predefined Security Configurations* dialog) indicates that one of the predefined sets has been modified. Actively choosing this option does not change the current configuration—you will need to change it using the *Security Overview*.

8.3 Password Settings

Passwords that are easy to guess are a major security issue. The *Password Settings* dialog provides the means to ensure that only secure passwords can be used.

Check New Passwords

> By activating this option, a warning will be issued if new passwords appear in a dictionary, or if they are proper names (proper nouns).

Minimum Acceptable Password Length

> If the user chooses a password with a length shorter than specified here, a warning will be issued.

Number of Passwords to Remember

> When password expiration is activated (via *Password Age*), this setting stores the given number of a user's previous passwords, preventing their reuse.

Password Encryption Method

> Choose a password encryption algorithm. Normally there is no need to change the default (Blowfish).

Password Age

> Activate password expiration by specifying a minimum and a maximum time limit (in days). By setting the minimum age to a value greater than 0 days, you can prevent users from immediately changing their passwords again (and in doing so circumventing the password expiration). Use the values 0 and 99999 to deactivate password expiration.

Days Before Password Expires Warning

> When a password expires, the user receives a warning in advance. Specify the number of days prior to the expiration date that the warning should be issued.

8.4 Boot Settings

Configure which users can shut down the machine via the graphical login manager in this dialog. You can also specify how `Ctrl`–`Alt`–`Del` will be interpreted and who can hibernate the system.

8.5 Login Settings

This dialog lets you configure security-related login settings:

Delay after Incorrect Login Attempt

To make it difficult to guess a user's password by repeatedly logging in, it is recommended to delay the display of the login prompt that follows an incorrect login. Specify the value in seconds. Make sure that users who have mistyped their passwords do not need to wait too long.

Allow Remote Graphical Login

When checked, the graphical login manager (GDM) can be accessed from the network. This is a potential security risk.

8.6 User Addition

Set minimum and maximum values for user and group IDs. These default settings would rarely need to be changed.

8.7 Miscellaneous Settings

Other security settings that do not fit the above-mentioned categories are listed here:

File Permissions

SUSE Linux Enterprise Server comes with three predefined sets of file permissions for system files. These permission sets define whether a regular user may read log files or start certain programs. *Easy* file permissions are suitable for stand-alone machines. These settings allow regular users to, for example, read most system files. See the file `/etc/permissions.easy` for the complete configuration. The *Secure* file permissions are designed for multiuser machines with network access. A thorough explanation of these settings can be found in `/etc/permissions.secure`. The *Paranoid* settings are the most restrictive ones and should be used with care. See `/etc/permissions.paranoid` for more information.

User Launching updatedb

The program **updatedb** scans the system and creates a database of all file locations which can be queried with the command **locate**. When **updatedb** is run as user nobody, only world-readable files will be added to the database. When run as user `root`, almost all files (except the ones root is not allowed to read) will be added.

Enable Magic SysRq Keys

The magic SysRq key is a key combination that enables you to have some control over the system even when it has crashed. The complete documentation can be found at https://www.kernel.org/doc/html/latest/admin-guide/sysrq.html ↗.

9 Authorization with PolKit

PolKit (formerly known as PolicyKit) is an application framework that acts as a negotiator between the unprivileged user session and the privileged system context. Whenever a process from the user session tries to carry out an action in the system context, PolKit is queried. Based on its configuration—specified in a so-called "policy"—the answer could be "yes", "no", or "needs authentication". Unlike classical privilege authorization programs such as sudo, PolKit does not grant `root` permissions to an entire session, but only to the action in question.

9.1 Conceptual Overview

PolKit works by limiting specific actions by users, by group, or by name. It then defines how those users are allowed to perform this action.

9.1.1 Available Authentication Agents

When a user starts a session (using the graphical environment or on the console), each session consists of the *authority* and an *authentication agent*. The authority is implemented as a service on the system message bus, whereas the authentication agent is used to authenticate the current user, which started the session. The current user needs to prove their authenticity, for example, using a passphrase.

Each desktop environment has its own authentication agent. Usually it is started automatically, whatever environment you choose.

9.1.2 Structure of PolKit

PolKit's configuration depends on *actions* and *authorization rules*:

Actions (file extension `*.policy`)
> Written as XML files and located in `/usr/share/polkit-1/actions`. Each file defines one or more actions, and each action contains descriptions and default permissions. Although a system administrator can write their own rules, PolKit's files must not be edited.

Authorization Rules (file extension `*.rules`)

Written as JavaScript files and located in two places: `/usr/share/polkit-1/rules.d` is used for third party packages and `/etc/polkit-1/rules.d` for local configurations. Each rule file refers to the action specified in the action file. A rule determines what restrictions are allowed to a subset of users. For example, a rule file could overrule a restrictive permission and allow some users to allow it.

9.1.3 Available Commands

PolKit contains several commands for specific tasks (see also the specific man page for further details):

pkaction

Get details about a defined action. See *Section 9.3, "Querying Privileges"* for more information.

pkcheck

Checks whether a process is authorized, specified by either `--process` or `--system-bus-name`.

pkexec

Allows an authorized user to execute the specific program as another user.

pkttyagent

Starts a textual authentication agent. This agent is used if a desktop environment does not have its own authentication agent.

9.1.4 Available Policies and Supported Applications

At the moment, not all applications requiring privileges use PolKit. Find the most important policies available on SUSE® Linux Enterprise Server below, sorted into the categories where they are used.

PulseAudio

Set scheduling priorities for the PulseAudio daemon

CUPS

Add, remove, edit, enable or disable printers

GNOME

Modify system and mandatory values with GConf

Change the system time

libvirt

Manage and monitor local virtualized systems

PolKit

Read and change privileges for other users

Modify defaults

PackageKit

Update and remove packages

Change and refresh repositories

Install local files

Rollback

Import repository keys

Accepting EULAs

Setting the network proxy

System

Wake on LAN

Mount or unmount fixed, hotpluggable and encrypted devices

Eject and decrypt removable media

Enable or disable WLAN

Enable or disable Bluetooth

Device access

Stop, suspend, hibernate and restart the system

Undock a docking station

Change power-management settings

YaST

Register product

Change the system time and language

9.2 Authorization Types

Every time a PolKit-enabled process carries out a privileged operation, PolKit is asked whether this process is entitled to do so. PolKit answers according to the policy defined for this process. The answers can be `yes`, `no`, or `authentication needed`. By default, a policy contains `implicit` privileges, which automatically apply to all users. It is also possible to specify `explicit` privileges which apply to a specific user.

9.2.1 Implicit Privileges

Implicit privileges can be defined for any active and inactive sessions. An active session is the one in which you are currently working. It becomes inactive when you switch to another console for example. When setting implicit privileges to "no", no user is authorized, whereas "yes" authorizes all users. However, usually it is useful to demand authentication.

A user can either authorize by authenticating as `root` or by authenticating as self. Both authentication methods exist in four variants:

Authentication

> The user always needs to authenticate.

One Shot Authentication

> The authentication is bound to the instance of the program currently running. After the program is restarted, the user is required to authenticate again.

Keep Session Authentication

> The authentication dialog offers a check button *Remember authorization for this session*. If checked, the authentication is valid until the user logs out.

Keep Indefinitely Authentication

> The authentication dialog offers a check button *Remember authorization*. If checked, the user needs to authenticate only once.

9.2.2 Explicit Privileges

Explicit privileges can be granted to specific users. They can either be granted without limitations, or, when using constraints, limited to an active session and/or a local console.

It is not only possible to grant privileges to a user, a user can also be blocked. Blocked users cannot carry out an action requiring authorization, even though the default implicit policy allows authorization by authentication.

9.2.3   Default Privileges

Each application supporting PolKit comes with a default set of implicit policies defined by the application's developers. Those policies are the so-called "upstream defaults". The privileges defined by the upstream defaults are not necessarily the ones that are activated by default on SUSE systems. SUSE Linux Enterprise Server comes with a predefined set of privileges that override the upstream defaults:

`/etc/polkit-default-privs.standard`
> Defines privileges suitable for most desktop systems

`/etc/polkit-default-privs.restrictive`
> Designed for machines administrated centrally. It is active by default.

To switch between the two sets of default privileges, adjust the value of `POLKIT_DEFAULT_PRIVS` to either `restrictive` or `standard` in `/etc/sysconfig/security`. Then run the command **`set_polkit_default_privs`** as `root`.

Do not modify the two files in the list above. To define your own custom set of privileges, use `/etc/polkit-default-privs.local`. For details, refer to *Section 9.4.3, "Modifying Configuration Files for Implicit Privileges"*.

9.3   Querying Privileges

To query privileges use the command **`pkaction`** included in PolKit.

PolKit comes with command line tools for changing privileges and executing commands as another user (see *Section 9.1.3, "Available Commands"* for a short overview). Each existing policy has a speaking, unique name with which it can be identified. List all available policies with the command **`pkaction`**.

When invoked with no parameters, the command **`pkaction`** lists all policies. By adding the `--show-overrides` option, you can list all policies that differ from the default values. To reset the privileges for a given action to the (upstream) defaults, use the option `--reset-defaults AC-TION`. See **`man pkaction`** for more information.

If you want to display the needed authorization for a given policy (for example, `org.freedesk-top.login1.reboot`) use **pkaction** as follows:

```
pkaction -v --action-id org.freedesktop.login1.reboot
org.freedesktop.login1.reboot:
  description:       Reboot the system
  message:          Authentication is required to allow rebooting the system
  vendor:           The systemd Project
  vendor_url:       http://www.freedesktop.org/wiki/Software/systemd
  icon:
  implicit any:     auth_admin_keep
  implicit inactive: auth_admin_keep
  implicit active:   yes
```

The keyword `auth_admin_keep` means that users need to enter a passphrase.

 Note: Restrictions of **pkaction** on SUSE Linux Enterprise Server

pkaction always operates on the upstream defaults. Therefore it cannot be used to list or restore the defaults shipped with SUSE Linux Enterprise Server. To do so, refer to *Section 9.5, "Restoring the Default Privileges"*.

9.4   Modifying Configuration Files

Adjusting privileges by modifying configuration files is useful when you want to deploy the same set of policies to different machines, for example to the computers of a specific team. It is possible to change implicit and explicit privileges by modifying configuration files.

9.4.1   Adding Action Rules

The available actions depend on what additional packages you have installed on your system. For a quick overview, use **pkaction** to list all defined rules.

To get an idea, the following example describes how the command **gparted** ("GNOME Partition Editor") is integrated into PolKit.

The file `/usr/share/polkit-1/actions/org.opensuse.policykit.gparted.policy` contains the following content:

```
<?xml version="1.0" encoding="UTF-8"?>
```

```
<!DOCTYPE policyconfig PUBLIC
 "-//freedesktop//DTD PolicyKit Policy Configuration 1.0//EN"
 "http://www.freedesktop.org/standards/PolicyKit/1.0/policyconfig.dtd">
<policyconfig> ➊

  <action id="org.opensuse.policykit.gparted"> ➋
    <message>Authentication is required to run the GParted Partition Editor</message>
    <icon_name>gparted</icon_name>
    <defaults> ➌
      <allow_any>auth_admin</allow_any>
      <allow_inactive>auth_admin</allow_inactive>
     < allow_active>auth_admin</allow_active>
    </defaults>
    <annotate ➍
      key="org.freedesktop.policykit.exec.path">/usr/sbin/gparted</annotate>
    <annotate ➍
      key="org.freedesktop.policykit.exec.allow_gui">true</annotate>
  </action>

</policyconfig>
```

➊ Root element of the policy file.

➋ Contains one single action.

➌ The `defaults` element contains several permissions used in remote sessions like SSH, VNC (element `allow_inactive`), when logged directly into the machine on a TTY or X display (element `allow_active`), or for both (element `allow_any`). The value `auth_admin` indicates authentication is required as an administrative user.

➍ The `annotate` element contains specific information regarding how PolKit performs an action. In this case, it contains the path to the executable and states whether a GUI is allowed to open a X display.

To add your own policy, create a `.policy` file with the structure above, add the appropriate value into the `id` attribute, and define the default permissions.

9.4.2 Adding Authorization Rules

Your own authorization rules overrule the default settings. To add your own settings, store your files under `/etc/polkit-1/rules.d/`.

The files in this directory start with a two-digit number, followed by a descriptive name, and end with `.rules`. Functions inside these files are executed in the order they have been sorted in. For example, `00-foo.rules` is sorted (and hence executed) before `60-bar.rules` or even `90-default-privs.rules`.

Inside the file, the script checks for the specified action ID, which is defined in the `.policy` file. For example, if you want to allow the command **gparted** to be executed by any member of the `admin` group, check for the action ID `org.opensuse.policykit.gparted`:

```
/* Allow users in admin group to run GParted without authentication */
polkit.addRule(function(action, subject) {
    if (action.id == "org.opensuse.policykit.gparted" &&
        subject.isInGroup("admin")) {
        return polkit.Result.YES;
    }
});
```

Find the description of all classes and methods of the functions in the PolKit API at http://www.freedesktop.org/software/polkit/docs/latest/ref-api.html ↗.

9.4.3   Modifying Configuration Files for Implicit Privileges

SUSE Linux Enterprise Server ships with two sets of default authorizations, located in `/etc/polkit-default-privs.standard` and `/etc/polkit-default-privs.restrictive`. For more information, refer to *Section 9.2.3, "Default Privileges"*.

Custom privileges are defined in `/etc/polkit-default-privs.local`. Privileges defined here will always take precedence over the ones defined in the other configuration files. To define your custom set of privileges, do the following:

1. Open `/etc/polkit-default-privs.local`. To define a privilege, add a line for each policy with the following format:

   ```
   <privilege_identifier>      <any session>:<inactive session>:<active session>
   ```

   For example:

   ```
   org.freedesktop.policykit.modify-defaults      auth_admin_keep_always
   ```

The following values are valid for the *SESSION* placeholders:

yes

> grant privilege

no

> block

auth_self

> user needs to authenticate with own password every time the privilege is requested

auth_self_keep_session

> user needs to authenticate with own password once per session, privilege is granted for the whole session

auth_self_keep_always

> user needs to authenticate with own password once, privilege is granted for the current and for future sessions

auth_admin

> user needs to authenticate with `root` password every time the privilege is requested

auth_admin_keep_session

> user needs to authenticate with `root` password once per session, privilege is granted for the whole session

auth_admin_keep_always

> user needs to authenticate with `root` password once, privilege is granted for the current and for future sessions

2. Run as `root` for changes to take effect:

```
# /sbin/set_polkit_default_privs
```

3. Optionally check the list of all privilege identifiers with the command **pkaction**.

9.5 Restoring the Default Privileges

SUSE Linux Enterprise Server comes with a predefined set of privileges that is activated by default and thus overrides the upstream defaults. For details, refer to *Section 9.2.3, "Default Privileges"*.

Since the graphical PolKit tools and the command line tools always operate on the upstream defaults, SUSE Linux Enterprise Server includes an additional command-line tool, **set_polkit_default_privs**. It resets privileges to the values defined in /etc/polkit-default-privs.*. However, the command **set_polkit_default_privs** will only reset policies that are set to the upstream defaults.

1. Make sure /etc/polkit-default-privs.local does not contain any overrides of the default policies.

   Important: Custom Policy Configuration

   Policies defined in /etc/polkit-default-privs.local will be applied on top of the defaults during the next step.

2. To reset all policies to the upstream defaults first and then apply the SUSE Linux Enterprise Server defaults:

```
rm -f /var/lib/polkit/* && set_polkit_default_privs
```

10 Access Control Lists in Linux

POSIX ACLs (access control lists) can be used as an expansion of the traditional permission concept for file system objects. With ACLs, permissions can be defined more flexibly than with the traditional permission concept.

The term *POSIX ACL* suggests that this is a true POSIX (*portable operating system interface*) standard. The respective draft standards POSIX 1003.1e and POSIX 1003.2c have been withdrawn for several reasons. Nevertheless, ACLs (as found on many systems belonging to the Unix family) are based on these drafts and the implementation of file system ACLs (as described in this chapter) follows these two standards.

10.1 Traditional File Permissions

Find detailed information about the traditional file permissions in the GNU Coreutils Info page, Node *File permissions* (**info coreutils "File permissions"**). More advanced features are the setuid, setgid, and sticky bit.

10.1.1 The setuid Bit

In certain situations, the access permissions may be too restrictive. Therefore, Linux has additional settings that enable the temporary change of the current user and group identity for a specific action. For example, the **passwd** program normally requires root permissions to access /etc/passwd. This file contains some important information, like the home directories of users and user and group IDs. Thus, a normal user would not be able to change passwd, because it would be too dangerous to grant all users direct access to this file. A possible solution to this problem is the *setuid* mechanism. setuid (set user ID) is a special file attribute that instructs the system to execute programs marked accordingly under a specific user ID. Consider the **passwd** command:

```
-rwsr-xr-x  1 root shadow 80036 2004-10-02 11:08 /usr/bin/passwd
```

You can see the s that denotes that the setuid bit is set for the user permission. By means of the setuid bit, all users starting the **passwd** command execute it as root.

10.1.2   The setgid Bit

The setuid bit applies to users. However, there is also an equivalent property for groups: the *setgid* bit. A program for which this bit was set runs under the group ID under which it was saved, no matter which user starts it. Therefore, in a directory with the setgid bit, all newly created files and subdirectories are assigned to the group to which the directory belongs. Consider the following example directory:

```
drwxrws--- 2 tux archive 48 Nov 19 17:12  backup
```

You can see the s that denotes that the setgid bit is set for the group permission. The owner of the directory and members of the group archive may access this directory. Users that are not members of this group are "mapped" to the respective group. The effective group ID of all written files will be archive. For example, a backup program that runs with the group ID archive can access this directory even without root privileges.

10.1.3   The Sticky Bit

There is also the *sticky bit*. It makes a difference whether it belongs to an executable program or a directory. If it belongs to a program, a file marked in this way is loaded to RAM to avoid needing to get it from the hard disk each time it is used. This attribute is used rarely, because modern hard disks are fast enough. If this bit is assigned to a directory, it prevents users from deleting each other's files. Typical examples include the /tmp and /var/tmp directories:

```
drwxrwxrwt 2 root root 1160 2002-11-19 17:15 /tmp
```

10.2   Advantages of ACLs

Traditionally, three permission sets are defined for each file object on a Linux system. These sets include the read (r), write (w), and execute (x) permissions for each of three types of users—the file owner, the group, and other users. In addition to that, it is possible to set the *set user id*, the *set group id*, and the *sticky* bit. This lean concept is fully adequate for most practical cases. However, for more complex scenarios or advanced applications, system administrators formerly needed to use several workarounds to circumvent the limitations of the traditional permission concept.

ACLs can be used as an extension of the traditional file permission concept. They allow the assignment of permissions to individual users or groups even if these do not correspond to the original owner or the owning group. Access control lists are a feature of the Linux kernel and are currently supported by ReiserFS, Ext2, Ext3, JFS, and XFS. Using ACLs, complex scenarios can be realized without implementing complex permission models on the application level.

The advantages of ACLs are evident if you want to replace a Windows server with a Linux server. Some connected workstations may continue to run under Windows even after the migration. The Linux system offers file and print services to the Windows clients with Samba. With Samba supporting access control lists, user permissions can be configured both on the Linux server and in Windows with a graphical user interface (only Windows NT and later). With **winbindd**, part of the Samba suite, it is even possible to assign permissions to users only existing in the Windows domain without any account on the Linux server.

10.3 Definitions

User Class

The conventional POSIX permission concept uses three *classes* of users for assigning permissions in the file system: the owner, the owning group, and other users. Three permission bits can be set for each user class, giving permission to read (r), write (w), and execute (x).

ACL

The user and group access permissions for all kinds of file system objects (files and directories) are determined by means of ACLs.

Default ACL

Default ACLs can only be applied to directories. They determine the permissions a file system object inherits from its parent directory when it is created.

ACL Entry

Each ACL consists of a set of ACL entries. An ACL entry contains a type, a qualifier for the user or group to which the entry refers, and a set of permissions. For some entry types, the qualifier for the group or users is undefined.

10.4 Handling ACLs

Table 10.1, "ACL Entry Types" summarizes the six possible types of ACL entries, each defining permissions for a user or a group of users. The *owner* entry defines the permissions of the user owning the file or directory. The *owning group* entry defines the permissions of the file's owning group. The superuser can change the owner or owning group with `chown` or `chgrp`, in which case the owner and owning group entries refer to the new owner and owning group. Each *named user* entry defines the permissions of the user specified in the entry's qualifier field. Each *named group* entry defines the permissions of the group specified in the entry's qualifier field. Only the named user and named group entries have a qualifier field that is not empty. The *other* entry defines the permissions of all other users.

The *mask* entry further limits the permissions granted by named user, named group, and owning group entries by defining which of the permissions in those entries are effective and which are masked. If permissions exist in one of the mentioned entries and in the mask, they are effective. Permissions contained only in the mask or only in the actual entry are not effective—meaning the permissions are not granted. All permissions defined in the owner and owning group entries are always effective. The example in *Table 10.2, "Masking Access Permissions"* demonstrates this mechanism.

There are two basic classes of ACLs: A *minimum* ACL contains only the entries for the types owner, owning group, and other, which correspond to the conventional permission bits for files and directories. An *extended* ACL goes beyond this. It must contain a mask entry and may contain several entries of the named user and named group types.

TABLE 10.1: ACL ENTRY TYPES

Type	Text Form
owner	`user::rwx`
named user	`user:name:rwx`
owning group	`group::rwx`
named group	`group:name:rwx`
mask	`mask::rwx`
other	`other::rwx`

TABLE 10.2: MASKING ACCESS PERMISSIONS

Entry Type	Text Form	Permissions
named user	`user:geeko:r-x`	`r-x`
mask	`mask::rw-`	`rw-`
	effective permissions:	`r--`

10.4.1 ACL Entries and File Mode Permission Bits

Figure 10.1, "Minimum ACL: ACL Entries Compared to Permission Bits" **and** *Figure 10.2, "Extended ACL: ACL Entries Compared to Permission Bits"* illustrate the two cases of a minimum ACL and an extended ACL. The figures are structured in three blocks—the left block shows the type specifications of the ACL entries, the center block displays an example ACL, and the right block shows the respective permission bits according to the conventional permission concept (for example, as displayed by `ls -l`). In both cases, the *owner class* permissions are mapped to the ACL entry owner. *Other class* permissions are mapped to the respective ACL entry. However, the mapping of the *group class* permissions is different in the two cases.

FIGURE 10.1: MINIMUM ACL: ACL ENTRIES COMPARED TO PERMISSION BITS

In the case of a minimum ACL—without mask—the group class permissions are mapped to the ACL entry owning group. This is shown in *Figure 10.1, "Minimum ACL: ACL Entries Compared to Permission Bits"*. In the case of an extended ACL—with mask—the group class permissions are mapped to the mask entry. This is shown in *Figure 10.2, "Extended ACL: ACL Entries Compared to Permission Bits"*.

owner	user : : rw-		rw-	owner class
named user	user : jane : rw-			
owning group	group : : r--			
mask	mask : : rw-		r--	group class
other	other : : ---		---	other class

FIGURE 10.2: EXTENDED ACL: ACL ENTRIES COMPARED TO PERMISSION BITS

This mapping approach ensures the smooth interaction of applications, regardless of whether they have ACL support. The access permissions that were assigned by means of the permission bits represent the upper limit for all other "fine adjustments" made with an ACL. Changes made to the permission bits are reflected by the ACL and vice versa.

10.4.2 A Directory with an ACL

With **getfacl** and **setfacl** on the command line, you can access ACLs. The usage of these commands is demonstrated in the following example.

Before creating the directory, use the **umask** command to define which access permissions should be masked each time a file object is created. The command **umask** 027 sets the default permissions by giving the owner the full range of permissions (0), denying the group write access (2), and giving other users no permissions (7). **umask** actually masks the corresponding permission bits or turns them off. For details, consult the **umask** man page.

mkdir mydir creates the mydir directory with the default permissions as set by **umask**. Use **ls** -dl mydir to check whether all permissions were assigned correctly. The output for this example is:

```
drwxr-x--- ... tux project3 ... mydir
```

With **getfacl** mydir, check the initial state of the ACL. This gives information like:

```
# file: mydir
# owner: tux
# group: project3
user::rwx
group::r-x
```

```
other::---
```

The first three output lines display the name, owner, and owning group of the directory. The next three lines contain the three ACL entries owner, owning group, and other. In fact, in the case of this minimum ACL, the **getfacl** command does not produce any information you could not have obtained with **ls**.

Modify the ACL to assign read, write, and execute permissions to an additional user geeko and an additional group mascots with:

```
setfacl -m user:geeko:rwx,group:mascots:rwx mydir
```

The option -m prompts **setfacl** to modify the existing ACL. The following argument indicates the ACL entries to modify (multiple entries are separated by commas). The final part specifies the name of the directory to which these modifications should be applied. Use the **getfacl** command to take a look at the resulting ACL.

```
# file: mydir
# owner: tux
# group: project3
user::rwx
user:geeko:rwx
group::r-x
group:mascots:rwx
mask::rwx
other::---
```

In addition to the entries initiated for the user geeko and the group mascots, a mask entry has been generated. This mask entry is set automatically so that all permissions are effective. **setfacl** automatically adapts existing mask entries to the settings modified, unless you deactivate this feature with -n. The mask entry defines the maximum effective access permissions for all entries in the group class. This includes named user, named group, and owning group. The group class permission bits displayed by **ls** -dl mydir now correspond to the mask entry.

```
drwxrwx---+ ... tux project3 ... mydir
```

The first column of the output contains an additional + to indicate that there is an *extended* ACL for this item.

According to the output of the **ls** command, the permissions for the mask entry include write access. Traditionally, such permission bits would mean that the owning group (here project3) also has write access to the directory mydir.

However, the effective access permissions for the owning group correspond to the overlapping portion of the permissions defined for the owning group and for the mask—which is `r-x` in our example (see *Table 10.2, "Masking Access Permissions"*). As far as the effective permissions of the owning group in this example are concerned, nothing has changed even after the addition of the ACL entries.

Edit the mask entry with **setfacl** or **chmod**. For example, use **chmod** `g-w mydir`. **ls** `-dl mydir` then shows:

```
drwxr-x---+ ... tux project3 ... mydir
```

getfacl `mydir` provides the following output:

```
# file: mydir
# owner: tux
# group: project3
user::rwx
user:geeko:rwx          # effective: r-x
group::r-x
group:mascots:rwx       # effective: r-x
mask::r-x
other::---
```

After executing **chmod** to remove the write permission from the group class bits, the output of **ls** is sufficient to see that the mask bits must have changed accordingly: write permission is again limited to the owner of `mydir`. The output of the **getfacl** confirms this. This output includes a comment for all those entries in which the effective permission bits do not correspond to the original permissions, because they are filtered according to the mask entry. The original permissions can be restored at any time with **chmod g+w mydir**.

10.4.3   A Directory with a Default ACL

Directories can have a default ACL, which is a special kind of ACL defining the access permissions that objects in the directory inherit when they are created. A default ACL affects both subdirectories and files.

10.4.3.1 Effects of a Default ACL

There are two ways in which the permissions of a directory's default ACL are passed to the files and subdirectories:

- A subdirectory inherits the default ACL of the parent directory both as its default ACL and as an ACL.

- A file inherits the default ACL as its ACL.

All system calls that create file system objects use a `mode` parameter that defines the access permissions for the newly created file system object. If the parent directory does not have a default ACL, the permission bits as defined by the `umask` are subtracted from the permissions as passed by the `mode` parameter, with the result being assigned to the new object. If a default ACL exists for the parent directory, the permission bits assigned to the new object correspond to the overlapping portion of the permissions of the `mode` parameter and those that are defined in the default ACL. The `umask` is disregarded in this case.

10.4.3.2 Application of Default ACLs

The following three examples show the main operations for directories and default ACLs:

1. Add a default ACL to the existing directory `mydir` with:

```
setfacl -d -m group:mascots:r-x mydir
```

The option `-d` of the **setfacl** command prompts **setfacl** to perform the following modifications (option `-m`) in the default ACL.
Take a closer look at the result of this command:

```
getfacl mydir

# file: mydir
# owner: tux
# group: project3
user::rwx
user:geeko:rwx
group::r-x
group:mascots:rwx
mask::rwx
other::---
```

```
default:user::rwx
default:group::r-x
default:group:mascots:r-x
default:mask::r-x
default:other::---
```

getfacl returns both the ACL and the default ACL. The default ACL is formed by all lines that start with default. Although you merely executed the **setfacl** command with an entry for the mascots group for the default ACL, **setfacl** automatically copied all other entries from the ACL to create a valid default ACL. Default ACLs do not have an immediate effect on access permissions. They only come into play when file system objects are created. These new objects inherit permissions only from the default ACL of their parent directory.

2. In the next example, use **mkdir** to create a subdirectory in mydir, which inherits the default ACL.

```
mkdir mydir/mysubdir

getfacl mydir/mysubdir

# file: mydir/mysubdir
# owner: tux
# group: project3
user::rwx
group::r-x
group:mascots:r-x
mask::r-x
other::---
default:user::rwx
default:group::r-x
default:group:mascots:r-x
default:mask::r-x
default:other::---
```

As expected, the newly-created subdirectory mysubdir has the permissions from the default ACL of the parent directory. The ACL of mysubdir is an exact reflection of the default ACL of mydir. The default ACL that this directory will hand down to its subordinate objects is also the same.

3. Use **touch** to create a file in the mydir directory, for example, **touch** mydir/myfile. **ls** -l mydir/myfile then shows:

```
-rw-r-----+ ... tux project3 ... mydir/myfile
```

The output of **getfacl** mydir/myfile is:

```
# file: mydir/myfile
# owner: tux
# group: project3
user::rw-
group::r-x              # effective:r--
group:mascots:r-x       # effective:r--
mask::r--
other::---
```

touch uses a mode with the value 0666 when creating new files, which means that the files are created with read and write permissions for all user classes, provided no other restrictions exist in **umask** or in the default ACL (see *Section 10.4.3.1, "Effects of a Default ACL"*). In effect, this means that all access permissions not contained in the mode value are removed from the respective ACL entries. Although no permissions were removed from the ACL entry of the group class, the mask entry was modified to mask permissions not set in mode.

This approach ensures the smooth interaction of applications (such as compilers) with ACLs. You can create files with restricted access permissions and subsequently mark them as executable. The **mask** mechanism guarantees that the right users and groups can execute them as desired.

10.4.4   The ACL Check Algorithm

A check algorithm is applied before any process or application is granted access to an ACL-protected file system object. As a basic rule, the ACL entries are examined in the following sequence: owner, named user, owning group or named group, and other. The access is handled in accordance with the entry that best suits the process. Permissions do not accumulate.

Things are more complicated if a process belongs to more than one group and would potentially suit several group entries. An entry is randomly selected from the suitable entries with the required permissions. It is irrelevant which of the entries triggers the final result "access granted". Likewise, if none of the suitable group entries contain the required permissions, a randomly selected entry triggers the final result "access denied".

10.5 ACL Support in Applications

ACLs can be used to implement very complex permission scenarios that meet the requirements of modern applications. The traditional permission concept and ACLs can be combined in a smart manner. The basic file commands (`cp`, `mv`, `ls`, etc.) support ACLs, as do Samba and Nautilus.

Unfortunately, many editors and file managers still lack ACL support. When copying files with Emacs, for example, the ACLs of these files are lost. When modifying files with an editor, the ACLs of files are sometimes preserved and sometimes not, depending on the backup mode of the editor used. If the editor writes the changes to the original file, the ACL is preserved. If the editor saves the updated contents to a new file that is subsequently renamed to the old file name, the ACLs may be lost, unless the editor supports ACLs. Except for the `star` archiver, there are currently no backup applications that preserve ACLs.

10.6 For More Information

For more information about ACLs, see the man pages for `getfacl(1)`, `acl(5)`, and `setfacl(1)`.

11 Encrypting Partitions and Files

Encrypting files, partitions, and entire disks prevents unauthorized access to your data and protects your confidential files and documents.

You can choose between the following encryption options:

Encrypting a Hard Disk Partition

It is possible to create an encrypted partition with YaST during installation or in an already installed system. For further info, see *Section 11.1.1, "Creating an Encrypted Partition during Installation"* and *Section 11.1.2, "Creating an Encrypted Partition on a Running System"*. This option can also be used for removable media, such as external hard disks, as described in *Section 11.1.4, "Encrypting the Content of Removable Media"*.

Creating an Encrypted Virtual Disk

You can create a file-based encrypted virtual disk on your hard disk or a removable medium with YaST. The encrypted virtual disk can then be used as a regular folder for storing files or directories. For more information, refer to *Section 11.1.3, "Creating an Encrypted Virtual Disk"*.

Encrypting Home Directories

With SUSE Linux Enterprise Server, you can also create encrypted user home directories. When the user logs in to the system, the encrypted home directory is mounted and the contents are made available to the user. Refer to *Section 11.2, "Using Encrypted Home Directories"* for more information.

Encrypting Single Files with GPG

To quickly encrypt one or several files, you can use the GPG tool. See *Section 11.3, "Encrypting Files with GPG"* for more information.

 ## Warning: Encryption Offers Limited Protection

Encryption methods described in this chapter cannot protect your running system from being compromised. After the encrypted volume is successfully mounted, everybody with appropriate permissions can access it. However, encrypted media are useful in case of loss or theft of your computer, or to prevent unauthorized individuals from reading your confidential data.

11.1   Setting Up an Encrypted File System with YaST

Use YaST to encrypt partitions or parts of your file system during installation or in an already installed system. However, encrypting a partition in an already-installed system is more difficult, because you need to resize and change existing partitions. In such cases, it may be more convenient to create an encrypted file of a defined size, in which to *store* other files or parts of your file system. To encrypt an entire partition, dedicate a partition for encryption in the partition layout. The standard partitioning proposal as suggested by YaST, does not include an encrypted partition by default. Add it manually in the partitioning dialog.

11.1.1   Creating an Encrypted Partition during Installation

 Warning: Password Input

> Make sure to memorize the password for your encrypted partitions well. Without that password, you cannot access or restore the encrypted data.

The YaST expert dialog for partitioning offers the options needed for creating an encrypted partition. To create a new encrypted partition proceed as follows:

1. Run the YaST Expert Partitioner with *System* › *Partitioner*.

2. Select a hard disk, click *Add*, and select a primary or an extended partition.

3. Select the partition size or the region to use on the disk.

4. Select the file system, and mount point of this partition.

5. Activate the *Encrypt device* check box.

    Note: Additional Software Required

   > After checking *Encrypt device*, a pop-up window asking for installing additional software may appear. Confirm to install all the required packages to ensure that the encrypted partition works well.

6. If the encrypted file system needs to be mounted only when necessary, enable *Do not mount partition* in the *Fstab Options*. otherwise enable *Mount partition* and enter the mount point.

7. Click *Next* and enter a password which is used to encrypt this partition. This password is not displayed. To prevent typing errors, you need to enter the password twice.

8. Complete the process by clicking *Finish*. The newly-encrypted partition is now created.

During the boot process, the operating system asks for the password before mounting any encrypted partition which is set to be auto-mounted in `/etc/fstab`. Such a partition is then available to all users when it has been mounted.

To skip mounting the encrypted partition during start-up, press `Enter` when prompted for the password. Then decline the offer to enter the password again. In this case, the encrypted file system is not mounted and the operating system continues booting, blocking access to your data.

To mount an encrypted partition which is not mounted during the boot process, open a file manager and click the partition entry in the pane listing common places on your file system. You will be prompted for a password and the partition will be mounted.

When you are installing your system on a machine where partitions already exist, you can also decide to encrypt an existing partition during installation. In this case follow the description in *Section 11.1.2, "Creating an Encrypted Partition on a Running System"* and be aware that this action destroys all data on the existing partition.

11.1.2   Creating an Encrypted Partition on a Running System

 Warning: Activating Encryption on a Running System

It is also possible to create encrypted partitions on a running system. However, encrypting an existing partition destroys all data on it, and requires re-sizing and restructuring of existing partitions.

On a running system, select *System › Partitioner* in the YaST control center. Click *Yes* to proceed. In the *Expert Partitioner*, select the partition to encrypt and click *Edit*. The rest of the procedure is the same as described in *Section 11.1.1, "Creating an Encrypted Partition during Installation"*.

11.1.3 Creating an Encrypted Virtual Disk

Instead of encrypting an entire disk or partition, you can use YaST to set up a file-based encrypted virtual disk. It will appear as a regular file in the file system, but can be mounted and used like a regular folder. Unlike encrypted partitions, encrypted virtual disks can be created without re-partitioning the hard disk.

To set up an encrypted virtual disk, you need to create an empty file first (this file is called loop file). In the terminal, switch to the desired directory and run the **touch** *FILE* command (where *FILE* is the desired name, for example: `secret`). It is also recommended to create an empty directory that will act as a mount point for the encrypted virtual disk. To do this, use the **mkdir** *DIR* command (replace *DIR* with the actual path and directory name, for example: `~/my_docs`).

To set up an encrypted virtual disk, launch YaST, switch to the *System* section, and start Partitioner. Switch to the *Crypt Files* section and press *Add Crypt File*. Enter the path to the created loop file into the *Path Name of Loop File* field. Enable the *Create Loop File* option, specify the desired size, and press *Next*. In the *Mount Point* field, enter the path to the directory that serves as a mount point (in this example, it is `~/my_docs`). Make sure that the *Encrypt Device* option is enabled and press *Next*. Provide the desired password and press *Finish*.

11.1.4 Encrypting the Content of Removable Media

YaST treats removable media (like external hard disks or flash disks) the same as any other storage device. Virtual disks or partitions on external media can be encrypted as described above. However, you should disable mounting at boot time, because removable media is usually connected only when the system is up and running.

If you encrypted your removable device with YaST, the GNOME desktop automatically recognizes the encrypted partition and prompts for the password when the device is detected. If you plug in a FAT-formatted removable device when running GNOME, the desktop user entering the password automatically becomes the owner of the device. For devices with a file system other than FAT, change the ownership explicitly for users other than `root` to give them read-write access to the device.

If you have created a virtual disk as described in *Section 11.1.3, "Creating an Encrypted Virtual Disk"* but with the loop file on a removable disk, then you need to mount the file manually as follows:

```
sudo cryptsetup luksOpen  FILE NAME
sudo mount /dev/mapper/NAME DIR
```

In the commands above, the *FILE* refers to the path to the loop file, *NAME* is a user-defined name, and *DIR* is the path to the mount point. For example:

```
sudo cryptsetup luksOpen /run/media/tux/usbstick/secret my_secret
sudo mount /dev/mapper/my_secret /home/tux/my_docs
```

11.2 Using Encrypted Home Directories

To protect data in home directories from unauthorized access, use the YaST user management module to encrypt home directories. You can create encrypted home directories for new or existing users. To encrypt or decrypt home directories of already existing users, you need to know their login password. See *Book "Deployment Guide", Chapter 16 "Managing Users with YaST", Section 16.3.3 "Managing Encrypted Home Directories"* for instructions.

Encrypted home partitions are created within a virtual disk as described in *Section 11.1.3, "Creating an Encrypted Virtual Disk"*. Two files are created under /home for each encrypted home directory:

LOGIN.img
> The image holding the directory

LOGIN.key
> The image key, protected with the user's login password.

On login, the home directory automatically gets decrypted. Internally, it works through the PAM module called *pam_mount*. If you need to add an additional login method that provides encrypted home directories, you need to add this module to the respective configuration file in /etc/pam.d/. For more information, see *Chapter 2, Authentication with PAM* and the man page of pam_mount.

 Warning: Security Restrictions

> Encrypting a user's home directory does not provide strong security from other users. If strong security is required, the system should not be shared physically.
>
> To enhance security, also encrypt the swap partition and the /tmp and /var/tmp directories, because these may contain temporary images of critical data. You can encrypt swap, /tmp, and /var/tmp with the YaST partitioner as described in *Section 11.1.1, "Creating an Encrypted Partition during Installation"* or *Section 11.1.3, "Creating an Encrypted Virtual Disk"*.

11.3 Encrypting Files with GPG

The GPG encryption software can be used to encrypt individual files and documents.

To encrypt a file with GPG, you need to generate a key pair first. To do this, run the **gpg --gen-key** and follow the on-screen instructions. When generating the key pair, GPG creates a user ID (UID) to identify the key based on your real name, comments, and email address. You need this UID (or just a part of it like your first name or email address) to specify the key you want to use to encrypt a file. To find the UID of an existing key, use the **gpg --list-keys** command. To encrypt a file use the following command:

```
gpg -e -r UID
  FILE
```

Replace *UID* with part of the UID (for example, your first name) and *FILE* with the file you want to encrypt. For example:

```
gpg -e -r Tux secret.txt
```

This command creates an encrypted version of the specified file recognizable by the `.gpg` file extension (in this example, it is `secret.txt.gpg`).

To decrypt an encrypted file, use the following command:

```
gpg -d -o DECRYPTED_FILE
  ENCRYPTED_FILE
```

Replace *DECRYPTED_FILE* with the desired name for the decrypted file and *ENCRYPTED_FILE* with the encrypted file you want to decrypt.

Keep that the encrypted file can be only decrypted using the same key that was used for encryption. If you want to share an encrypted file with another person, you have to use that person's public key to encrypt the file.

12 Certificate Store

Certificates play an important role in the authentication of companies and individuals. Usually certificates are administered by the application itself. In some cases, it makes sense to share certificates between applications. The certificate store is a common ground for Firefox, Evolution, and NetworkManager. This chapter explains some details.

The certificate store is a common database for Firefox, Evolution, and NetworkManager at the moment. Other applications that use certificates are not covered but may be in the future. If you have such an application, you can continue to use its private, separate configuration.

12.1 Activating Certificate Store

The configuration is mostly done in the background. To activate it, proceed as follows:

1. Decide if you want to activate the certificate store globally (for every user on your system) or specifically to a certain user:

   - **For every user.** Use the file `/etc/profile.local`

   - **For a specific user.** Use the file `~/.bashrc`

2. Open the file from the previous step and insert the following line:

   ```
   export NSS_USE_SHARED_DB=1
   ```

   Save the file

3. Log out of and log in to your desktop.

All the certificates are stored under `$HOME/.local/var/pki/nssdb/`.

12.2 Importing Certificates

To import a certificate into the certificate store, do the following:

1. Start Firefox.

2. Open the dialog from *Edit › Preferences*. Change to *Advanced › Encryption* and click *View Certificates*.

3. Import your certificate depending on your type: use *Servers* to import server certificate, *People* to identify other, and *Your Certificates* to identify yourself.

13 Intrusion Detection with AIDE

Securing your systems is a mandatory task for any mission-critical system administrator. Because it is impossible to always guarantee that the system is not compromised, it is very important to do extra checks regularly (for example with `cron`) to ensure that the system is still under your control. This is where AIDE, the *Advanced Intrusion Detection Environment*, comes into play.

13.1 Why Use AIDE?

An easy check that often can reveal unwanted changes can be done by means of RPM. The package manager has a built-in verify function that checks all the managed files in the system for changes. To verify of all files, run the command **`rpm -Va`**. However, this command will also display changes in configuration files and you will need to do some filtering to detect important changes.

An additional problem to the method with RPM is that an intelligent attacker will modify **`rpm`** itself to hide any changes that might have been done by some kind of root-kit which allows the attacker to mask its intrusion and gain root privilege. To solve this, you should implement a secondary check that can also be run completely independent of the installed system.

13.2 Setting Up an AIDE Database

> **Important: Initialize AIDE Database After Installation**
>
> Before you install your system, verify the checksum of your medium (see *Book "Administration Guide", Chapter 40 "Common Problems and Their Solutions", Section 40.2.1 "Checking Media"*) to make sure you do not use a compromised source. After you have installed the system, initialize the AIDE database. To make sure that all went well during and after the installation, do an installation directly on the console, without any network attached to the computer. Do not leave the computer unattended or connected to any network before AIDE creates its database.

AIDE is not installed by default on SUSE Linux Enterprise Server. To install it, either use *Computer › Install Software*, or enter `zypper install aide` on the command line as `root`.

To tell AIDE which attributes of which files should be checked, use the `/etc/aide.conf` configuration file. It must be modified to become the actual configuration. The first section handles general parameters like the location of the AIDE database file. More relevant for local configurations are the `Custom Rules` and the `Directories and Files` sections. A typical rule looks like the following:

```
Binlib     = p+i+n+u+g+s+b+m+c+md5+sha1
```

After defining the variable `Binlib`, the respective check boxes are used in the files section. Important options include the following:

TABLE 13.1: IMPORTANT AIDE CHECK BOXES

Option	Description
p	Check for the file permissions of the selected files or directories.
i	Check for the inode number. Every file name has a unique inode number that should not change.
n	Check for the number of links pointing to the relevant file.
u	Check if the owner of the file has changed.
g	Check if the group of the file has changed.
s	Check if the file size has changed.
b	Check if the block count used by the file has changed.
m	Check if the modification time of the file has changed.
c	Check if the files access time has changed.

Option	Description
md5	Check if the md5 checksum of the file has changed.
sha1	Check if the sha1 (160 Bit) checksum of the file has changed.

This is a configuration that checks for all files in /sbin with the options defined in Binlib but omits the /sbin/conf.d/ directory:

```
/sbin  Binlib
!/sbin/conf.d
```

To create the AIDE database, proceed as follows:

1. Open /etc/aide.conf.

2. Define which files should be checked with which check boxes. For a complete list of available check boxes, see /usr/share/doc/packages/aide/manual.html. The definition of the file selection needs some knowledge about regular expressions. Save your modifications.

3. To check whether the configuration file is valid, run:

   ```
   aide --config-check
   ```

   Any output of this command is a hint that the configuration is not valid. For example, if you get the following output:

   ```
   aide --config-check
   35:syntax error:!
   35:Error while reading configuration:!
   Configuration error
   ```

   The error is to be expected in line 36 of /etc/aide.conf. Note that the error message contains the last successfully read line of the configuration file.

4. Initialize the AIDE database. Run the command:

   ```
   aide -i
   ```

5. Copy the generated database to a save location like a CD-R or DVD-R, a remote server or a flash disk for later use.

 Important:

> This step is essential as it avoids compromising your database. It is recommended to use a medium which can be written only once to prevent the database being modified. *Never* leave the database on the computer which you want to monitor.

13.3 Local AIDE Checks

To perform a file system check, proceed as follows:

1. Rename the database:

```
mv /var/lib/aide/aide.db.new /var/lib/aide/aide.db
```

2. After any configuration change, you always need to re-initialize the AIDE database and subsequently move the newly generated database. It is also a good idea to make a backup of this database. See *Section 13.2, "Setting Up an AIDE Database"* for more information.

3. Perform the check with the following command:

```
aide --check
```

If the output is empty, everything is fine. If AIDE found changes, it displays a summary of changes, for example:

```
aide --check
AIDE found differences between database and filesystem!!

Summary:
  Total number of files:     1992
  Added files:               0
  Removed files:             0
  Changed files:             1
```

To learn about the actual changes, increase the verbose level of the check with the parameter -V. For the previous example, this could look like the following:

```
aide --check -V
```

```
AIDE found differences between database and filesystem!!
Start timestamp: 2009-02-18 15:14:10

Summary:
  Total number of files:        1992
  Added files:                  0
  Removed files:                0
  Changed files:                1


-------------------------------------------------
Changed files:
-------------------------------------------------

changed: /etc/passwd

-------------------------------------------------
Detailed information about changes:
-------------------------------------------------


File: /etc/passwd
  Mtime    : 2009-02-18 15:11:02              , 2009-02-18 15:11:47
  Ctime    : 2009-02-18 15:11:02              , 2009-02-18 15:11:47
```

In this example, the file `/etc/passwd` was touched to demonstrate the effect.

13.4 System Independent Checking

To avoid risk, it is advisable to also run the AIDE binary from a trusted source. This excludes the risk that some attacker also modified the aide binary to hide its traces.

To accomplish this task, AIDE must be run from a rescue system that is independent of the installed system. With SUSE Linux Enterprise Server it is relatively easy to extend the rescue system with arbitrary programs, and thus add the needed functionality.

Before you can start using the rescue system, you need to provide two packages to the system. These are included with the same syntax as you would add a driver update disk to the system. For a detailed description about the possibilities of linuxrc that are used for this purpose, see http://en.opensuse.org/SDB:Linuxrc ↗. In the following, one possible way to accomplish this task is discussed.

PROCEDURE 13.1: STARTING A RESCUE SYSTEM WITH AIDE

  1. Provide an FTP server as a second machine.

2. Copy the packages `aide` and `mhash` to the FTP server directory, in our case `/srv/ftp/`. Replace the placeholders *ARCH* and *VERSION* with the corresponding values:

```
cp DVD1/suse/ARCH/aideVERSION.ARCH.rpm /srv/ftp
cp DVD1/suse/ARCH/mhashVERSION.ARCH.rpm /srv/ftp
```

3. Create an info file `/srv/ftp/info.txt` that provides the needed boot parameters for the rescue system:

```
dud:ftp://ftp.example.com/aideVERSION.ARCH.rpm
dud:ftp://ftp.example.com/mhashVERSION.ARCH.rpm
```

Replace your FTP domain name, *VERSION* and *ARCH* with the values used on your system.

4. Restart the server that needs to go through an AIDE check with the Rescue system from your DVD. Add the following string to the boot parameters:

```
info=ftp://ftp.example.com/info.txt
```

This parameter tells **linuxrc** to also read in all information from the `info.txt` file.

After the rescue system has booted, the AIDE program is ready for use.

13.5   For More Information

Information about AIDE is available at the following places:

- The home page of AIDE: http://aide.sourceforge.net ↗
- In the documented template configuration `/etc/aide.conf`.
- In several files below `/usr/share/doc/packages/aide` after installing the `aide` package.
- On the AIDE user mailing list at https://mailman.cs.tut.fi/mailman/listinfo/aide ↗.

III   Network Security

14 SSH: Secure Network Operations

In networked environments, it is often necessary to access hosts from a remote location. If a user sends login and password strings for authentication purposes as plain text, they could be intercepted and misused to gain access to that user account. This would open all the user's files to an attacker and the illegal account could be used to obtain administrator or root access, or to penetrate other systems. In the past, remote connections were established with **telnet**, **rsh** or **rlogin**, which offered no guards against eavesdropping in the form of encryption or other security mechanisms. There are other unprotected communication channels, like the traditional FTP protocol and some remote copying programs like **rcp**.

The SSH suite provides the necessary protection by encrypting the authentication strings (usually a login name and a password) and all the other data exchanged between the hosts. With SSH, the data flow could still be recorded by a third party, but the contents are encrypted and cannot be reverted to plain text unless the encryption key is known. So SSH enables secure communication over insecure networks, such as the Internet. The SSH implementation coming with SUSE Linux Enterprise Server is OpenSSH.

SUSE Linux Enterprise Server installs the OpenSSH package by default providing the commands **ssh**, **scp**, and **sftp**. In the default configuration, remote access of a SUSE Linux Enterprise Server system is only possible with the OpenSSH utilities, and only if the sshd is running and the firewall permits access.

SSH on SUSE Linux Enterprise Server uses cryptographic hardware acceleration if available. As a result, the transfer of large quantities of data through an SSH connection is considerably faster than without cryptographic hardware. As an additional benefit, the CPU will see a significant reduction in load.

14.1 ssh—Secure Shell

With **ssh** it is possible to log in to remote systems and to work interactively. To log in to the host sun as user tux enter one of the following commands:

```
ssh tux@sun
ssh -l tux sun
```

If the user name is the same on both machines, you can omit it. Using `ssh sun` is sufficient. The remote host prompts for the remote user's password. After a successful authentication, you can work on the remote command line or use interactive applications, such as YaST in text mode.

Furthermore, `ssh` offers the possibility to run non-interactive commands on remote systems using `ssh HOST COMMAND`. `COMMAND` needs to be properly quoted. Multiple commands can be concatenated as on a local shell.

```
ssh root@sun "dmesg -T | tail -n 25"
ssh root@sun "cat /etc/issue && uptime"
```

14.1.1 Starting X Applications on a Remote Host

SSH also simplifies the use of remote X applications. If you run `ssh` with the `-X` option, the `DISPLAY` variable is automatically set on the remote machine and all X output is exported to the local machine over the existing SSH connection. At the same time, X applications started remotely cannot be intercepted by unauthorized individuals.

14.1.2 Agent Forwarding

By adding the `-A` option, the ssh-agent authentication mechanism is carried over to the next machine. This way, you can work from different machines without having to enter a password, but only if you have distributed your public key to the destination hosts and properly saved it there. Refer to *Section 14.5.2, "Copying an SSH Key"* for details.

This mechanism is deactivated in the default settings, but can be permanently activated at any time in the systemwide configuration file `/etc/ssh/sshd_config` by setting `AllowAgentForwarding yes`.

14.2 scp—Secure Copy

`scp` copies files to or from a remote machine. If the user name on jupiter is different than the user name on sun, specify the latter using the `USER_NAME@host` format. If the file should be copied into a directory other than the remote user's home directory, specify it as sun:`DIRECTORY`. The following examples show how to copy a file from a local to a remote machine and vice versa.

```
# local -> remote
```

```
scp ~/MyLetter.tex tux@sun:/tmp
# remote -> local
scp tux@sun:/tmp/MyLetter.tex ~
```

 Tip: The -l Option

> With the **ssh** command, the option -l can be used to specify a remote user (as an alternative to the *USER_NAME*@host format). With **scp** the option -l is used to limit the bandwidth consumed by **scp**.

After the correct password is entered, **scp** starts the data transfer. It displays a progress bar and the time remaining for each file that is copied. Suppress all output with the -q option.

scp also provides a recursive copying feature for entire directories. The command

```
scp -r src/ sun:backup/
```

copies the entire contents of the directory src including all subdirectories to the ~/backup directory on the host sun. If this subdirectory does not exist, it is created automatically.

The -p option tells **scp** to leave the time stamp of files unchanged. -C compresses the data transfer. This minimizes the data volume to transfer, but creates a heavier burden on the processors of both machines.

14.3   **sftp**—Secure File Transfer

14.3.1   Using **sftp**

If you want to copy several files from or to different locations, **sftp** is a convenient alternative to **scp**. It opens a shell with a set of commands similar to a regular FTP shell. Type **help** at the sftp-prompt to get a list of available commands. More details are available from the **sftp** man page.

```
sftp sun
Enter passphrase for key '/home/tux/.ssh/id_rsa':
Connected to sun.
sftp> help
Available commands:
bye                           Quit sftp
```

```
cd path                          Change remote directory to 'path'
[...]
```

14.3.2   Setting Permissions for File Uploads

As with a regular FTP server, a user cannot only download, but also upload files to a remote machine running an SFTP server by using the **put** command. By default the files will be uploaded to the remote host with the same permissions as on the local host. There are two options to automatically alter these permissions:

Setting a umask

A umask works as a filter against the permissions of the original file on the local host. It can only withdraw permissions:

TABLE 14.1:

permissions original	umask	permissions uploaded
0666	0002	0664
0600	0002	0600
0775	0025	0750

To apply a umask on an SFTP server, edit the file `/etc/ssh/sshd_configuration`. Search for the line beginning with `Subsystem sftp` and add the `-u` parameter with the desired setting, for example:

```
Subsystem sftp /usr/lib/ssh/sftp-server -u 0002
```

Explicitly Setting the Permissions

Explicitly setting the permissions sets the same permissions for all files uploaded via SFTP. Specify a three-digit pattern such as `600`, `644`, or `755` with `-u`. When both `-m` and `-u` are specified, `-u` is ignored.

To apply explicit permissions for uploaded files on an SFTP server, edit the file `/etc/ssh/sshd_configuration`. Search for the line beginning with `Subsystem sftp` and add the `-m` parameter with the desired setting, for example:

```
Subsystem sftp /usr/lib/ssh/sftp-server -m 600
```

14.4 The SSH Daemon (sshd)

To work with the SSH client programs **ssh** and **scp**, a server (the SSH daemon) must be running in the background, listening for connections on `TCP/IP port 22`. The daemon generates three key pairs when starting for the first time. Each key pair consists of a private and a public key. Therefore, this procedure is called public key-based. To guarantee the security of the communication via SSH, access to the private key files must be restricted to the system administrator. The file permissions are set accordingly by the default installation. The private keys are only required locally by the SSH daemon and must not be given to anyone else. The public key components (recognizable by the name extension `.pub`) are sent to the client requesting the connection. They are readable for all users.

A connection is initiated by the SSH client. The waiting SSH daemon and the requesting SSH client exchange identification data to compare the protocol and software versions, and to prevent connections through the wrong port. Because a child process of the original SSH daemon replies to the request, several SSH connections can be made simultaneously.

For the communication between SSH server and SSH client, OpenSSH supports versions 1 and 2 of the SSH protocol. Version 2 of the SSH protocol is used by default. Override this to use version 1 of protocol with the `-1` option.

When using version 1 of SSH, the server sends its public host key and a server key, which is regenerated by the SSH daemon every hour. Both allow the SSH client to encrypt a freely chosen session key, which is sent to the SSH server. The SSH client also tells the server which encryption method (cipher) to use. Version 2 of the SSH protocol does not require a server key. Both sides use an algorithm according to Diffie-Hellman to exchange their keys.

The private host and server keys are absolutely required to decrypt the session key and cannot be derived from the public parts. Only the contacted SSH daemon can decrypt the session key using its private keys. This initial connection phase can be watched closely by turning on verbose debugging using the `-v` option of the SSH client.

 Tip: Viewing the SSH Daemon Log File

To watch the log entries from the `sshd` use the following command:

```
tux > sudo journalctl -u sshd
```

14.4.1 Maintaining SSH Keys

It is recommended to back up the private and public keys stored in `/etc/ssh/` in a secure, external location. In this way, key modifications can be detected or the old ones can be used again after having installed a new system.

 Tip: Existing SSH Host Keys

If you install SUSE Linux Enterprise Server on a machine with existing Linux installations, the installation routine automatically imports the SSH host key with the most recent access time from an existing installation.

When establishing a secure connection with a remote host for the first time, the client stores all public host keys in `~/.ssh/known_hosts`. This prevents any man-in-the-middle attacks—attempts by foreign SSH servers to use spoofed names and IP addresses. Such attacks are detected either by a host key that is not included in `~/.ssh/known_hosts`, or by the server's inability to decrypt the session key in the absence of an appropriate private counterpart.

If the public keys of a host have changed (that needs to be verified before connecting to such a server), the offending keys can be removed with **ssh-keygen -r** *HOSTNAME*.

14.4.2 Rotating Host Keys

As of version 6.8, OpenSSH comes with a protocol extension that supports host key rotation. It makes sense to replace keys, if you are still using weak keys such as 1024-bit RSA keys. It is strongly recommended to replace such a key and go for 2048-bit DSA keys or something even better. The client will then use the "best" host key.

 Tip: Restarting sshd

After installing new host keys on the server, restart sshd.

This protocol extension can inform a client of all the new host keys on the server, if the user initiates a connection with **ssh**. Then, the software on the client updates `~/.ssh/known_hosts`, and the user is not required to accept new keys of previously known and trusted hosts manually. The local `known_hosts` file will contain all the host keys of the remote hosts, in addition to the one that authenticated the host during this session.

Once the administrator of the server knows that all the clients have fetched the new keys, they can remove the old keys. The protocol extension ensures that the obsolete keys will be removed from the client's configuration, too. The key removal occurs while initiating an **ssh** session.

For more information, see:

- http://blog.djm.net.au/2015/02/key-rotation-in-openssh-68.html ↗

- http://heise.de/-2540907 ↗ ("Endlich neue Schlüssel für SSH-Server", German only)

14.5 SSH Authentication Mechanisms

In its simplest form, authentication is done by entering the user's password just as if logging in locally. However, having to memorize passwords of several users on remote machines is inefficient. What is more, these passwords may change. On the other hand—when granting root access—an administrator needs to be able to quickly revoke such a permission without having to change the root password.

To accomplish a login that does not require to enter the remote user's password, SSH uses another key pair, which needs to be generated by the user. It consists of a public (id_rsa.pub or id_dsa.pub) and a private key (id_rsa or id_dsa).

To be able to log in without having to specify the remote user's password, the public key of the "SSH user" must be in ~/.ssh/authorized_keys. This approach also ensures that the remote user has got full control: adding the key requires the remote user's password and removing the key revokes the permission to log in from remote.

For maximum security such a key should be protected by a passphrase which needs to be entered every time you use **ssh**, **scp**, or **sftp**. Contrary to the simple authentication, this passphrase is independent from the remote user and therefore always the same.

An alternative to the key-based authentication described above, SSH also offers a host-based authentication. With host-based authentication, users on a trusted host can log in to another host on which this feature is enabled using the same user name. SUSE Linux Enterprise Server is set up for using key-based authentication, covering setting up host-based authentication on SUSE Linux Enterprise Server is beyond the scope of this manual.

Note: File Permissions for Host-Based Authentication

If the host-based authentication is to be used, the file `/usr/lib/ssh/ssh-keysign` (32-bit systems) or `/usr/lib64/ssh/ssh-keysign` (64-bit systems) should have the setuid bit set, which is not the default setting in SUSE Linux Enterprise Server. In such case, set the file permissions manually. You should use `/etc/permissions.local` for this purpose, to make sure that the setuid bit is preserved after security updates of `openssh`.

14.5.1 Generating an SSH Key

1. To generate a key with default parameters (RSA, 2048 bits), enter the command **ssh-keygen**.

2. Accept the default location to store the key (`~/.ssh/id_rsa`) by pressing [Enter] (strongly recommended) or enter an alternative location.

3. Enter a passphrase consisting of 10 to 30 characters. The same rules as for creating safe passwords apply. It is strongly advised to refrain from specifying no passphrase.

You should make absolutely sure that the private key is not accessible by anyone other than yourself (always set its permissions to `0600`). The private key must never fall into the hands of another person.

To change the password of an existing key pair, use the command **ssh-keygen -p**.

14.5.2 Copying an SSH Key

To copy a public SSH key to `~/.ssh/authorized_keys` of a user on a remote machine, use the command **ssh-copy-id**. To copy your personal key stored under `~/.ssh/id_rsa.pub` you may use the short form. To copy DSA keys or keys of other users, you need to specify the path:

```
# ~/.ssh/id_rsa.pub
ssh-copy-id -i tux@sun

# ~/.ssh/id_dsa.pub
ssh-copy-id -i ~/.ssh/id_dsa.pub   tux@sun

# ~notme/.ssh/id_rsa.pub
ssh-copy-id -i ~notme/.ssh/id_rsa.pub   tux@sun
```

To successfully copy the key, you need to enter the remote user's password. To remove an existing key, manually edit `~/.ssh/authorized_keys`.

14.5.3   Using the `ssh-agent`

When doing lots of secure shell operations it is cumbersome to type the SSH passphrase for each such operation. Therefore, the SSH package provides another tool, **ssh-agent**, which retains the private keys for the duration of an X or terminal session. All other windows or programs are started as clients to the **ssh-agent**. By starting the agent, a set of environment variables is set, which will be used by **ssh**, **scp**, or **sftp** to locate the agent for automatic login. See the **ssh-agent** man page for details.

After the **ssh-agent** is started, you need to add your keys by using **ssh-add**. It will prompt for the passphrase. After the password has been provided once, you can use the secure shell commands within the running session without having to authenticate again.

14.5.3.1   Using **ssh-agent** in an X Session

On SUSE Linux Enterprise Server, the **ssh-agent** is automatically started by the GNOME display manager. To also invoke **ssh-add** to add your keys to the agent at the beginning of an X session, do the following:

1. Log in as the desired user and check whether the file `~/.xinitrc` exists.

2. If it does not exist, use an existing template or copy it from `/etc/skel`:

   ```
   if [ -f ~/.xinitrc.template ]; then mv ~/.xinitrc.template ~/.xinitrc; \
   else cp /etc/skel/.xinitrc.template ~/.xinitrc; fi
   ```

3. If you have copied the template, search for the following lines and uncomment them. If `~/.xinitrc` already existed, add the following lines (without comment signs).

   ```
   # if test -S "$SSH_AUTH_SOCK" -a -x "$SSH_ASKPASS"; then
   #       ssh-add < /dev/null
   # fi
   ```

4. When starting a new X session, you will be prompted for your SSH passphrase.

14.5.3.2   Using **ssh-agent** in a Terminal Session

In a terminal session you need to manually start the **ssh-agent** and then call **ssh-add** afterward. There are two ways to start the agent. The first example given below starts a new Bash shell on top of your existing shell. The second example starts the agent in the existing shell and modifies the environment as needed.

```
ssh-agent -s /bin/bash
eval $(ssh-agent)
```

After the agent has been started, run **ssh-add** to provide the agent with your keys.

14.6   Port Forwarding

ssh can also be used to redirect TCP/IP connections. This feature, also called `SSH tunneling`, redirects TCP connections to a certain port to another machine via an encrypted channel.

With the following command, any connection directed to jupiter port 25 (SMTP) is redirected to the SMTP port on sun. This is especially useful for those using SMTP servers without SMTP-AUTH or POP-before-SMTP features. From any arbitrary location connected to a network, e-mail can be transferred to the "home" mail server for delivery.

```
ssh -L 25:sun:25 jupiter
```

Similarly, all POP3 requests (port 110) on jupiter can be forwarded to the POP3 port of sun with this command:

```
ssh -L 110:sun:110 jupiter
```

Both commands must be executed as `root`, because the connection is made to privileged local ports. E-mail is sent and retrieved by normal users in an existing SSH connection. The SMTP and POP3 host must be set to `localhost` for this to work. Additional information can be found in the manual pages for each of the programs described above and in the OpenSSH package documentation under `/usr/share/doc/packages/openssh`.

14.7   For More Information

http://www.openssh.com ↗

The home page of OpenSSH

http://en.wikibooks.org/wiki/OpenSSH ↗

The OpenSSH Wikibook

man sshd

The man page of the OpenSSH daemon

man ssh_config

The man page of the OpenSSH SSH client configuration files

man scp ,

man sftp ,

man slogin ,

man ssh ,

man ssh-add ,

man ssh-agent ,

man ssh-copy-id ,

man ssh-keyconvert ,

man ssh-keygen ,

man ssh-keyscan

Man pages of several binary files to securely copy files (**scp** , **sftp**), to log in (**slogin** , **ssh**), and to manage keys.

/usr/share/doc/packages/openssh/README.SUSE ,

/usr/share/doc/packages/openssh/README.FIPS

SUSE package specific documentation; changes in defaults with respect to upstream, notes on FIPS mode etc.

15 Masquerading and Firewalls

Whenever Linux is used in a network environment, you can use the kernel functions that allow the manipulation of network packets to maintain a separation between internal and external network areas. The Linux `netfilter` framework provides the means to establish an effective firewall that keeps different networks apart. Using iptables—a generic table structure for the definition of rule sets—precisely controls the packets allowed to pass a network interface. Such a packet filter can be set up using SuSEFirewall2 and the corresponding YaST module.

15.1 Packet Filtering with iptables

The components `netfilter` and `iptables` are responsible for the filtering and manipulation of network packets and for network address translation (NAT). The filtering criteria and any actions associated with them are stored in chains, which must be matched one after another by individual network packets as they arrive. The chains to match are stored in tables. The **iptables** command allows you to alter these tables and rule sets.

The Linux kernel maintains three tables, each for a particular category of functions of the packet filter:

filter

> This table holds the bulk of the filter rules, because it implements the *packet filtering* mechanism in the stricter sense, which determines whether packets are let through (`ACCEPT`) or discarded (`DROP`), for example.

nat

> This table defines any changes to the source and target addresses of packets. Using these functions also allows you to implement *masquerading*, which is a special case of NAT used to link a private network with the Internet.

mangle

> The rules held in this table make it possible to manipulate values stored in IP headers (such as the type of service).

These tables contain several predefined chains to match packets:

PREROUTING

> This chain is applied to incoming packets.

INPUT

This chain is applied to packets destined for the system's internal processes.

FORWARD

This chain is applied to packets that are only routed through the system.

OUTPUT

This chain is applied to packets originating from the system itself.

POSTROUTING

This chain is applied to all outgoing packets.

Figure 15.1, "iptables: A Packet's Possible Paths" illustrates the paths along which a network packet may travel on a given system. For the sake of simplicity, the figure lists tables as parts of chains, but in reality these chains are held within the tables themselves.

In the simplest case, an incoming packet destined for the system itself arrives at the `eth0` interface. The packet is first referred to the `PREROUTING` chain of the `mangle` table then to the `PREROUTING` chain of the `nat` table. The following step, concerning the routing of the packet, determines that the actual target of the packet is a process of the system itself. After passing the `INPUT` chains of the `mangle` and the `filter` table, the packet finally reaches its target, provided that the rules of the `filter` table are actually matched.

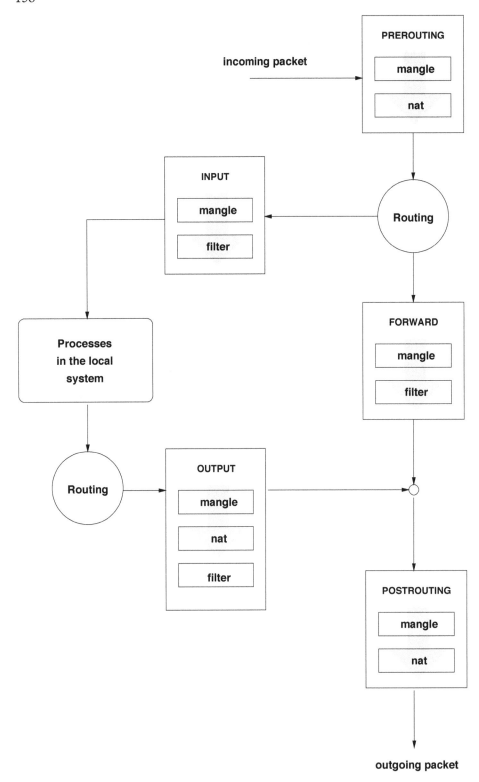

FIGURE 15.1: IPTABLES: A PACKET'S POSSIBLE PATHS

15.2 Masquerading Basics

Masquerading is the Linux-specific form of NAT (network address translation) and can be used to connect a small LAN with the Internet. LAN hosts use IP addresses from the private range (see *Book "Administration Guide", Chapter 16 "Basic Networking", Section 16.1.2 "Netmasks and Routing"*) and on the Internet official IP addresses are used. To be able to connect to the Internet, a LAN host's private address is translated to an official one. This is done on the router, which acts as the gateway between the LAN and the Internet. The underlying principle is a simple one: The router has more than one network interface, typically a network card and a separate interface connecting with the Internet. While the latter links the router with the outside world, one or several others link it with the LAN hosts. With these hosts in the local network connected to the network card (such as `eth0`) of the router, they can send any packets not destined for the local network to their default gateway or router.

> **Important: Using the Correct Network Mask**
>
> When configuring your network, make sure both the broadcast address and the netmask are the same for all local hosts. Failing to do so prevents packets from being routed properly.

As mentioned, whenever one of the LAN hosts sends a packet destined for an Internet address, it goes to the default router. However, the router must be configured before it can forward such packets. For security reasons, this is not enabled in a default installation. To enable it, set the variable `IP_FORWARD` in the file `/etc/sysconfig/sysctl` to `IP_FORWARD=yes`.

The target host of the connection can see your router, but knows nothing about the host in your internal network where the packets originated. This is why the technique is called masquerading. Because of the address translation, the router is the first destination of any reply packets. The router must identify these incoming packets and translate their target addresses, so packets can be forwarded to the correct host in the local network.

With the routing of inbound traffic depending on the masquerading table, there is no way to open a connection to an internal host from the outside. For such a connection, there would be no entry in the table. In addition, any connection already established has a status entry assigned to it in the table, so the entry cannot be used by another connection.

As a consequence of all this, you might experience some problems with several application protocols, such as ICQ, cucme, IRC (DCC, CTCP), and FTP (in PORT mode). Web browsers, the standard FTP program, and many other programs use the PASV mode. This passive mode is much less problematic as far as packet filtering and masquerading are concerned.

15.3 Firewalling Basics

Firewall is probably the term most widely used to describe a mechanism that provides and manages a link between networks while also controlling the data flow between them. Strictly speaking, the mechanism described in this section is called a *packet filter*. A packet filter regulates the data flow according to certain criteria, such as protocols, ports, and IP addresses. This allows you to block packets that, according to their addresses, are not supposed to reach your network. To allow public access to your Web server, for example, explicitly open the corresponding port. However, a packet filter does not scan the contents of packets with legitimate addresses, such as those directed to your Web server. For example, if incoming packets were intended to compromise a CGI program on your Web server, the packet filter would still let them through.

A more effective but more complex mechanism is the combination of several types of systems, such as a packet filter interacting with an application gateway or proxy. In this case, the packet filter rejects any packets destined for disabled ports. Only packets directed to the application gateway are accepted. This gateway or proxy pretends to be the actual client of the server. In a sense, such a proxy could be considered a masquerading host on the protocol level used by the application. One example for such a proxy is Squid, an HTTP and FTP proxy server. To use Squid, the browser must be configured to communicate via the proxy. Any HTTP pages or FTP files requested are served from the proxy cache and objects not found in the cache are fetched from the Internet by the proxy.

The following section focuses on the packet filter that comes with SUSE Linux Enterprise Server. For further information about packet filtering and firewalling, read the Firewall HOWTO (http://www.tldp.org/HOWTO/Firewall-HOWTO.html) ↗.

15.4   SuSEFirewall2

SuSEFirewall2 is a script that reads the variables set in `/etc/sysconfig/SuSEfirewall2` to generate a set of iptables rules. It defines three security zones, although only the first and the second one are considered in the following sample configuration:

External Zone

> Given that there is no way to control what is happening on the external network, the host needs to be protected from it. Usually, the external network is the Internet, but it could be another insecure network, such as a Wi-Fi.

Internal Zone

> This refers to the private network, usually the LAN. If the hosts on this network use IP addresses from the private range (see *Book "Administration Guide", Chapter 16 "Basic Networking", Section 16.1.2 "Netmasks and Routing"*), enable network address translation (NAT), so hosts on the internal network can access the external one. All ports are open in the internal zone. The main benefit of putting interfaces into the internal zone (rather than stopping the firewall) is that the firewall still runs, so when you add new interfaces, they will be put into the external zone by default. That way an interface is not accidentally "open" by default.

Demilitarized Zone (DMZ)

> While hosts located in this zone can be reached both from the external and the internal network, they cannot access the internal network themselves. This setup can be used to put an additional line of defense in front of the internal network, because the DMZ systems are isolated from the internal network.

 Note: No Zone Assigned Behavior

> By default, all network interfaces are set to `no zone assigned`. This mode behaves as the External Zone profile.

Any kind of network traffic not explicitly allowed by the filtering rule set is suppressed by iptables. Therefore, each of the interfaces with incoming traffic must be placed into one of the three zones. For each of the zones, define the services or protocols allowed. The rule set is only applied to packets originating from remote hosts. Locally generated packets are not captured by the firewall.

The configuration can be performed with YaST (see *Section 15.4.1, "Configuring the Firewall with YaST"*). It can also be made manually in the file `/etc/sysconfig/SuSEfirewall2`, which is well commented. Additionally, several example scenarios are available in `/usr/share/doc/packages/SuSEfirewall2/EXAMPLES`.

15.4.1 Configuring the Firewall with YaST

15.4.1.1 Basic Configuration

The YaST dialogs for the graphical configuration can be accessed from the YaST control center. Select *Security and Users* › *Firewall*. The configuration is divided into seven sections that can be accessed directly from the tree structure on the left side.

Start-Up

Set the start-up behavior in this dialog. In a default installation, SuSEFirewall2 is started automatically. You can also start and stop the firewall here. To implement your new settings in a running firewall, use *Save Settings and Restart Firewall Now*.

Interfaces

All known network interfaces are listed here. To remove an interface from a zone, select the interface, press *Change*, and choose *No Zone Assigned*. To add an interface to a zone, select the interface, press *Change* and choose any of the available zones. You may also create a special interface with your own settings by using *Custom*.

Allowed Services

You need this option to offer services from your system to a zone from which it is protected. By default, the system is only protected from external zones. Explicitly allow the services that should be available to external hosts. After selecting the desired zone in *Allowed Services for Selected Zone*, activate the services from the list.

Masquerading

Masquerading hides your internal network from external networks (such as the Internet) while enabling hosts in the internal network to access the external network transparently. Requests from the external network to the internal one are blocked and requests from the internal network seem to be issued by the masquerading server when seen externally. If special services of an internal machine need to be available to the external network, add special redirect rules for the service.

Broadcast

In this dialog, configure the UDP ports that allow broadcasts. Add the required port numbers or services to the appropriate zone, separated by spaces. See also the file `/etc/services`.

The logging of broadcasts that are not accepted can be enabled here. This may be problematic, because Windows hosts use broadcasts to know about each other and so generate many packets that are not accepted.

IPsec Support

Configure whether the IPsec service should be available to the external network in this dialog. Configure which packets are trusted under *Details*.

There is another functionality under *Details*: IPsec packets are packed in an encrypted format, so they need to be decrypted and you can configure the way the firewall will handle the decrypted packets. If you select *Internal Zone*, the decrypted IPsec packets will be trusted as if they came from the Internal Zone - although they could possibly come from the external one. Choose *Same Zone as Original Source Network* to avoid this situation.

Logging Level

There are two rules for logging: accepted and not accepted packets. Packets that are not accepted are DROPPED or REJECTED. Select from *Log All*, *Log Only Critical*, or *Do Not Log Any*.

Custom Rules

Here, set special firewall rules that allow connections, matching specified criteria such as source network, protocol, destination port, and source port. Configure such rules for external, internal, and demilitarized zones.

When finished with the firewall configuration, exit this dialog with *Next*. A zone-oriented summary of your firewall configuration then opens. In it, check all settings. All services, ports, and protocols that have been allowed and all custom rules are listed in this summary. To modify the configuration, use *Back*. Click *Finish* to save your configuration.

15.4.1.2 Opening Ports

In case your network interfaces are located in a firewall zone where network traffic is blocked on most ports, services that manage their network traffic via a blocked port, will not work. For example, SSH is a popular service that uses port 22. By default, this port is blocked on interfaces located in the external or demilitarized zone. To make SSH work, you need to open port 22 in the firewall configuration. This can be done with the YaST module *Firewall*.

FIGURE 15.2: FIREWALL CONFIGURATION: ALLOWED SERVICES

 Important: Automatic Firewall Configuration

After the installation, YaST automatically starts a firewall on all configured interfaces. If a server is configured and activated on the system, YaST can modify the automatically generated firewall configuration with the options *Open Ports on Selected Interface in Firewall* or *Open Ports on Firewall* in the server configuration modules. Some server module dialogs include a *Firewall Details* button for activating additional services and ports. The YaST firewall configuration module can be used to activate, deactivate, or reconfigure the firewall.

PROCEDURE 15.1: MANUALLY OPEN FIREWALL PORTS WITH YAST

1. Open *YaST › Security and Users › Firewall* and switch to the *Allowed Services* tab.

2. Select a zone at *Allow Services for Selected Zone* in which to open the port. It is not possible to open a port for several zones at once.

3. Select a service from *Service to Allow* and choose *Add* to add it to the list of *Allowed Services*. The port this service uses will be unblocked.

   In case your service is not listed, you need to manually specify the port(s) to unblock. Choose *Advanced* to open a dialog where you can specify TCP, UPD, RPC ports and IP protocols. Refer to the help section in this dialog for details.

4. Choose *Next* to display a summary of your changes. Modify them by choosing *Back* or apply them by choosing *Finish*.

15.4.2   Configuring Manually

The following paragraphs provide step-by-step instructions for a successful configuration. Each configuration item is marked whether it is relevant to firewalling or masquerading. Use port range (for example, `500:510`) whenever appropriate. Aspects related to the DMZ (demilitarized zone) as mentioned in the configuration file are not covered here. They are applicable only to a more complex network infrastructure found in larger organizations (corporate networks), which require extensive configuration and in-depth knowledge about the subject.

To enable SuSEFirewall2, use **sudo systemctl enable SuSEfirewall2** or use the YaST module Services Manager.

`FW_DEV_EXT` **(firewall, masquerading)**

> The device linked to the Internet. For a modem connection, enter `ppp0`. DSL connections use `dsl0`. Specify `auto` to use the interface that corresponds to the default route.

`FW_DEV_INT` **(firewall, masquerading)**

> The device linked to the internal, private network (such as `eth0`). Leave this blank if there is no internal network and the firewall protects only the host on which it runs.

`FW_ROUTE` **(firewall, masquerading)**

> If you need the masquerading function, set this to `yes`. Your internal hosts will not be visible to the outside, because their private network addresses (for example `192.168.x.x`) are ignored by Internet routers.

For a firewall without masquerading, set this to `yes` if you want to allow access to the internal network. Your internal hosts need to use officially registered IP addresses in this case. Normally, however, you should *not* allow access to your internal network from the outside.

FW_MASQUERADE (masquerading)

Set this to `yes` if you need the masquerading function. This provides a virtually direct connection to the Internet for the internal hosts. It is more secure to have a proxy server between the hosts of the internal network and the Internet. Masquerading is not needed for services that a proxy server provides.

FW_MASQ_NETS (masquerading)

Specify the hosts or networks to masquerade, leaving a space between the individual entries. For example:

```
FW_MASQ_NETS="192.168.0.0/24 192.168.10.1"
```

FW_PROTECT_FROM_INT (firewall)

Set this to `yes` to protect your firewall host from attacks originating in your internal network. Services are only available to the internal network if explicitly enabled. Also see `FW_SERVICES_INT_TCP` and `FW_SERVICES_INT_UDP`.

FW_SERVICES_EXT_TCP (firewall)

Enter the TCP ports that should be made available. Leave this blank for a normal workstation at home that should not offer any services.

FW_SERVICES_EXT_UDP (firewall)

Leave this blank unless you run a UDP service and want to make it available to the outside. The services that use UDP include DNS servers, IPsec, TFTP, DHCP and others. In that case, enter the UDP ports to use.

FW_SERVICES_ACCEPT_EXT (firewall)

List services to allow from the Internet. This is a more generic form of the `FW_SERVICES_EXT_TCP` and `FW_SERVICES_EXT_UDP` settings, and more specific than `FW_TRUSTED_NETS`. The notation is a space-separated list of *NET*,*PROTOCOL*[,*D-PORT*][,*SPORT*], for example `0/0,tcp,22` or `0/0,tcp,22,,hitcount=3,blockseconds=60,recentname=ssh`, which means: allow a maximum of three SSH connects per minute from one IP address.

FW_SERVICES_INT_TCP (firewall)

> With this variable, define the services available for the internal network. The notation is the same as for `FW_SERVICES_EXT_TCP`, but the settings are applied to the *internal* network. The variable only needs to be set if `FW_PROTECT_FROM_INT` is set to `yes`.

FW_SERVICES_INT_UDP (firewall)

> See `FW_SERVICES_INT_TCP`.

FW_SERVICES_ACCEPT_INT (firewall)

> List services to allow from internal hosts. See `FW_SERVICES_ACCEPT_EXT`.

FW_SERVICES_ACCEPT_RELATED_* (firewall)

> This is how the SuSEFirewall2 implementation considers packets `RELATED` by netfilter. For example, to allow finer grained filtering of Samba broadcast packets, `RELATED` packets are not accepted unconditionally. Variables starting with `FW_SERVICES_ACCEPT_RELATED_` allow restricting `RELATED` packets handling to certain networks, protocols and ports. This means that adding connection tracking modules (conntrack modules) to `FW_LOAD_MODULES` does not automatically result in accepting the packets tagged by those modules. Additionally, you must set variables starting with `FW_SERVICES_ACCEPT_RELATED_` to a suitable value.

FW_CUSTOMRULES (firewall)

> Uncomment this variable to install custom rules. Find examples in `/etc/sysconfig/scripts/SuSEfirewall2-custom`.

After configuring the firewall, test your setup. The firewall rule sets are created by entering **systemctl start SuSEfirewall2** as `root`. Then use **telnet**, for example, from an external host to see whether the connection is actually denied. After that, review the output of **journalctl** (see *Book "Administration Guide", Chapter 15 "**journalctl**: Query the* systemd *Journal"*), where you should see something like this:

```
Mar 15 13:21:38 linux kernel: SFW2-INext-DROP-DEFLT IN=eth0
OUT= MAC=00:80:c8:94:c3:e7:00:a0:c9:4d:27:56:08:00 SRC=192.168.10.0
DST=192.168.10.1 LEN=60 TOS=0x10 PREC=0x00 TTL=64 ID=15330 DF PROTO=TCP
SPT=48091 DPT=23 WINDOW=5840 RES=0x00 SYN URGP=0
OPT (020405B40402080A061AFEBC0000000001030300)
```

Other packages to test your firewall setup are Nmap (portscanner) or OpenVAS (Open Vulnerability Assessment System). The documentation of Nmap is found at `/usr/share/doc/packages/nmap` after installing the package and the documentation of openVAS resides at http://www.openvas.org ↗.

15.5 For More Information

The most up-to-date information and other documentation about the `SuSEFirewall2` package is found in `/usr/share/doc/packages/SuSEfirewall2`. The home page of the netfilter and iptables project, http://www.netfilter.org ↗, provides a large collection of documents in many languages.

16 Configuring a VPN Server

Today, Internet connections are cheap and available almost everywhere. However, not all connections are secure. Using a Virtual Private Network (VPN), you can create a secure network within an insecure network such as the Internet or Wi-Fi. It can be implemented in different ways and serves several purposes. In this chapter, we focus on the OpenVPN (http://www.openvpn.net) ↗ implementation to link branch offices via secure wide area networks (WANs).

16.1 Conceptual Overview

This section defines some terms regarding VPN and gives a brief overview of some scenarios.

16.1.1 Terminology

Endpoint

> The two "ends" of a tunnel, the source or destination client.

Tap Device

> A tap device simulates an Ethernet device (layer 2 packets in the OSI model, such as IP packets). A tap device is used for creating a network bridge. It works with Ethernet frames.

Tun Device

> A tun device simulates a point-to-point network (layer 3 packets in the OSI model, such as Ethernet frames). A tun device is used with routing and works with IP frames.

Tunnel

> Linking two locations through a primarily public network. From a more technical viewpoint, it is a connection between the client's device and the server's device. Usually a tunnel is encrypted, but it does need to be by definition.

16.1.2   VPN Scenarios

Whenever you set up a VPN connection, your IP packets are transferred over a secured *tunnel*. A tunnel can use either a *tun* or *tap* device. They are virtual network kernel drivers which implement the transmission of Ethernet frames or IP frames/packets.

Any user space program, such as OpenVPN, can attach itself to a tun or tap device to receive packets sent by your operating system. The program is also able to write packets to the device.

There are many solutions to set up and build a VPN connection. This section focuses on the OpenVPN package. Compared to other VPN software, OpenVPN can be operated in two modes:

Routed VPN

Routing is an easy solution to set up. It is more efficient and scales better than a bridged VPN. Furthermore, it allows the user to tune MTU (Maximum Transfer Unit) to raise efficiency. However, in a heterogeneous environment, if you do not have a Samba server on the gateway, NetBIOS broadcasts do not work. If you need IPv6, the drivers for the tun devices on both ends must support this protocol explicitly. This scenario is depicted in *Figure 16.1, "Routed VPN"*.

LAN 2 (192.168.2.1/24)

eth1

Switch/Router

eth0

Machine 2 (Client)

tun0 (192.168.0.2)

Internet

VPN Tunnel

tun0 (192.168.0.1)

Machine 1 (Server)

eth0

Switch/Router

eth1

LAN 1 (192.168.1.1/24)

FIGURE 16.1: ROUTED VPN

Bridged VPN

Bridging is a more complex solution. It is recommended when you need to browse Windows file shares across the VPN without setting up a Samba or WINS server. Bridged VPN is also needed to use non-IP protocols (such as IPX) or applications relying on network broadcasts. However, it is less efficient than routed VPN. Another disadvantage is that it does not scale well. This scenario is depicted in the following figures.

Machine 2 (Client)

tap0 (192.168.100.2/24)

VPN Bridge

tap0 (192.168.100.1/24)

Machine 1 (Server)

FIGURE 16.2: BRIDGED VPN - SCENARIO 1

FIGURE 16.3: BRIDGED VPN - SCENARIO 2

174

FIGURE 16.4: BRIDGED VPN - SCENARIO 3

The major difference between bridging and routing is that a routed VPN cannot IP-broadcast while a bridged VPN can.

16.2 Setting Up a Simple Test Scenario

In the following example, we will create a point-to-point VPN tunnel. The example demonstrates how to create a VPN tunnel between one client and a server. It is assumed that your VPN server will use private IP addresses like *IP_OF_SERVER* and your client will use the IP address *IP_OF_CLIENT*. Make sure you select addresses which do not conflict with other IP addresses.

Warning: Use Only for Testing

This following scenario is provided as an example meant for familiarizing yourself with VPN technology. *Do not* use this as a real world scenario, as it can compromise the security and safety of your IT infrastructure!

 Tip: Names for Configuration File

To simplify working with OpenVPN configuration files, we recommend the following:

- Place your OpenVPN configuration files in the directory /etc/openvpn.

- Name your configuration files *MY_CONFIGURATION*.conf.

- If there are multiple files that belong to the same configuration, place them in a subdirectory like /etc/openvpn/*MY_CONFIGURATION*.

16.2.1 Configuring the VPN Server

To configure a VPN server, proceed as follows:

PROCEDURE 16.1: VPN SERVER CONFIGURATION

1. Install the package openvpn on the machine that will later become your VPN server.

2. Open a shell, become root and create the VPN secret key:

```
root # openvpn --genkey --secret /etc/openvpn/secret.key
```

3. Copy the secret key to your client:

```
root # scp /etc/openvpn/secret.key root@IP_OF_CLIENT:/etc/openvpn/
```

4. Create the file /etc/openvpn/server.conf with the following content:

```
dev tun
ifconfig IP_OF_SERVER IP_OF_CLIENT
secret secret.key
```

5. Set up a tun device configuration by creating a file called `/etc/sysconfig/net-work/ifcfg-tun0` with the following content:

```
STARTMODE='manual'
BOOTPROTO='static'
TUNNEL='tun'
TUNNEL_SET_OWNER='nobody'
TUNNEL_SET_GROUP='nobody'
LINK_REQUIRED=no
PRE_UP_SCRIPT='systemd:openvpn@server'
PRE_DOWN_SCRIPT='systemd:openvpn@service'
```

The notation `openvpn@server` points to the OpenVPN server configuration file located at `/etc/openvpn/server.conf`. For more information, see `/usr/share/doc/pack-ages/openvpn/README.SUSE`.

6. If you use a firewall, start YaST and open UDP port 1194 (*Security and Users* › *Firewall* › *Allowed Services*).

7. Start the OpenVPN server service by setting the tun device to `up`:

```
tux > sudo wicked ifup tun0
```

You should see the confirmation:

```
tun0            up
```

16.2.2   Configuring the VPN Clients

To configure the VPN client, do the following:

PROCEDURE 16.2: VPN CLIENT CONFIGURATION

1. Install the package `openvpn` on your client VPN machine.

2. Create `/etc/openvpn/client.conf` with the following content:

```
remote DOMAIN_OR_PUBLIC_IP_OF_SERVER
dev tun
ifconfig IP_OF_CLIENT IP_OF_SERVER
secret secret.key
```

Replace the placeholder *IP_OF_CLIENT* in the first line with either the domain name, or the public IP address of your server.

3. Set up a tun device configuration by creating a file called `/etc/sysconfig/net-work/ifcfg-tun0` with the following content:

```
STARTMODE='manual'
BOOTPROTO='static'
TUNNEL='tun'
TUNNEL_SET_OWNER='nobody'
TUNNEL_SET_GROUP='nobody'
LINK_REQUIRED=no
PRE_UP_SCRIPT='systemd:openvpn@client'
PRE_DOWN_SCRIPT='systemd:openvpn@client'
```

4. If you use a firewall, start YaST and open UDP port 1194 as described in *Step 6* of *Procedure 16.1, "VPN Server Configuration"*.

5. Start the OpenVPN server service by setting the tun device to up:

```
tux > sudo wicked ifup tun0
```

You should see the confirmation:

```
tun0            up
```

16.2.3 Testing the VPN Example Scenario

After OpenVPN has successfully started, test the availability of the tun device with the following command:

```
ip addr show tun0
```

To verify the VPN connection, use **ping** on both client and server side to see if they can reach each other. Ping the server from the client:

```
ping -I tun0 IP_OF_SERVER
```

Ping the client from the server:

```
ping -I tun0 IP_OF_CLIENT
```

16.3   Setting Up Your VPN Server Using a Certificate Authority

The example in *Section 16.2* is useful for testing, but not for daily work. This section explains how to build a VPN server that allows more than one connection at the same time. This is done with a public key infrastructure (PKI). A PKI consists of a pair of public and private keys for the server and each client, and a master certificate authority (CA), which is used to sign every server and client certificate.

This setup involves the following basic steps:

1. *Section 16.3.1, "Creating Certificates"*

2. *Section 16.3.2, "Configuring the VPN Server"*

3. *Section 16.3.3, "Configuring the VPN Clients"*

16.3.1   Creating Certificates

Before a VPN connection can be established, the client must authenticate the server certificate. Conversely, the server must also authenticate the client certificate. This is called *mutual authentication*. To create such certificates, use the YaST CA module. See *Chapter 17, Managing X.509 Certification* for more details.

To create a VPN root, server, and client CA, proceed as follows:

PROCEDURE 16.3: CREATING A VPN SERVER CERTIFICATE

1. Prepare a common VPN Certificate Authority (CA):

   a. Start the YaST CA module.

   b. Click *Create Root CA*.

   c. Enter a *CA Name* and a *Common Name*, for example `VPN-Server-CA`.

   d. Fill out the other boxes like e-mail addresses, organization, etc. and proceed with *Next*.

   e. Enter your password twice and proceed with *Next*.

   f. Review the summary. YaST displays the current settings for confirmation. Click *Create*. The root CA is created and displayed in the overview.

2. Create a VPN server certificate:

    a. Select the root CA you created in *Step 1* and click *Enter CA*.

    b. When prompted, enter the *CA Password*.

    c. Click the *Certificate* tab and click *Add* › *Add Server Certificate*.

    d. Specify a *Common Name*, for example, `openvpn.example.com` and proceed with *Next*.

    e. Specify your password and confirm it. Then click *Advanced options*.
    Switch to the *Advanced Settings* › *Key Usage* list and check one of the following sets:

        ● `digitalSignature` and `keyEncipherment`, or,

        ● `digitalSignature` and `keyAgreement`

    Switch to the *Advanced Settings* › *extendedKeyUsage* and type `serverAuth` for a server certificate.

 Important: Avoiding Man-in-the-Middle Attacks

    If you are using the method `remote-cert-tls server` or `remote-cert-tls client` to verify certificates, limit the number of times a key can be used. This mitigates man-in-the-middle attacks.

    For more information, see http://openvpn.net/index.php/open-source/documentation/howto.html#mitm ↗.

    Finish with *Ok* and proceed with *Next*.

    f. Review the summary. YaST displays the current settings for confirmation. Click *Create*. When the VPN server certificate is created, it is displayed in the *Certificates* tab.

3. Create VPN client certificates:

    a. Make sure you are on the *Certificates* tab.

    b. Click *Add* › *Add Client Certificate*.

    c. Enter a *Common Name*, for example, `client1.example.com`.

d. Enter the e-mail addresses for your client, for example, `user1@client1.example.com`, and click *Add*. Proceed with *Next*.

e. Enter your password twice and click *Advanced options*.
Switch to *Advanced Settings* › *Key Usage* list and check one of the following flags:

  * `digitalSignature` or,

  * `keyAgreement` or,

  * `digitalSignature` and `keyAgreement`.

Switch to the *Advanced Settings* › *extendedKeyUsage* and type `clientAuth` for a server certificate.

f. Review the summary. YaST displays the current settings for confirmation. Click *Create*. The VPN client certificate is created and is displayed in the *Certificates* tab.

g. If you need certificates for more clients, repeat *Step 3*.

After you have successfully finished *Procedure 16.3, "Creating a VPN Server Certificate"* you have a VPN root CA, a VPN server CA, and one or more VPN client CAs. To finish the task, proceed with the following procedure:

1. Choose the *Certificates* tab.

2. Export the VPN server certificate in two formats: PEM and unencrypted key in PEM.

   a. Select your VPN server certificate (`openvpn.example.com` in our example) and choose *Export* › *Export to File*.

   b. Select *Only the Certificate in PEM Format*, enter your VPN server certificate password and save the file to `/etc/openvpn/server_crt.pem`.

   c. Repeat *Step 2.a* and *Step 2.b*, but choose the format *Only the Key Unencrypted in PEM Format*. Save the file to `/etc/openvpn/server_key.pem`.

3. Export the VPN client certificates and choose an export format, PEM or PKCS12 (preferred). For each client:

   a. Select your VPN client certificate (`client1.example.com` in our example) and choose *Export* › *Export to File*.

b. Select *Like PKCS12 and Include the CA Chain*, enter your VPN client certificate key password and provide a PKCS12 password. Enter a *File Name*, click *Browse* and save the file to `/etc/openvpn/client1.p12`.

4. Copy the files to your client (in our example, `client1.example.com`).

5. Export the VPN CA (in our example `VPN-Server-CA`):

   a. Switch to the *Description* tab.

   b. Select *Advanced > Export to File*.

   c. Mark *Only the Certificate in PEM Format* and save the file to `/etc/openvpn/vpn_ca.pem`.

If desired, the client PKCS12 file can be converted into the PEM format using this command:

```
openssl pkcs12 -in client1.p12 -out client1.pem
```

Enter your client password to create the `client1.pem` file. The PEM file contains the client certificate, client key, and the CA certificate. You can split this combined file using a text editor and create three separate files. The file names can be used for the `ca`, `cert`, and `key` options in the OpenVPN configuration file (see *Example 16.1, "VPN Server Configuration File"*).

16.3.2 Configuring the VPN Server

As the basis of your configuration file, copy `/usr/share/doc/packages/openvpn/sample-config-files/server.conf` to `/etc/openvpn/`. Then customize it to your needs.

EXAMPLE 16.1: VPN SERVER CONFIGURATION FILE

```
# /etc/openvpn/server.conf
port 1194 ①
proto udp ②
dev tun0 ③

# Security ④

ca     vpn_ca.pem
cert   server_crt.pem
key    server_key.pem

# ns-cert-type server
remote-cert-tls client ⑤
```

```
dh     server/dh2048.pem ⑥

server 192.168.1.0 255.255.255.0 ⑦
ifconfig-pool-persist /var/run/openvpn/ipp.txt ⑧

# Privileges ⑨
user nobody
group nobody

# Other configuration ⑩
keepalive 10 120
comp-lzo
persist-key
persist-tun
# status       /var/log/openvpn-status.tun0.log ⑪
# log-append   /var/log/openvpn-server.log ⑫
verb 4
```

① The TCP/UDP port on which OpenVPN listens. You need to open the port in the firewall, see *Chapter 15, Masquerading and Firewalls*. The standard port for VPN is 1194, so you can usually leave that as it is.

② The protocol, either UDP or TCP.

③ The tun or tap device. For the difference between these, see *Section 16.1.1, "Terminology"*.

④ The following lines contain the relative or absolute path to the root server CA certificate (ca), the root CA key (cert), and the private server key (key). These were generated in *Section 16.3.1, "Creating Certificates"*.

⑤ Require that peer certificates have been signed with an explicit key usage and extended key usage based on RFC3280 TLS rules. There is a description of how to make a server use this explicit key in *Procedure 16.3, "Creating a VPN Server Certificate"*.

⑥ The Diffie-Hellman parameters. Create the required file with the following command:

```
openssl dhparam -out /etc/openvpn/dh2048.pem 2048
```

⑦ Supplies a VPN subnet. The server can be reached by 192.168.1.1.

⑧ Records a mapping of clients and its virtual IP address in the given file. Useful when the server goes down and (after the restart) the clients get their previously assigned IP address.

⑨ For security reasons, run the OpenVPN daemon with reduced privileges. To do so, specify that it should use the group and user nobody.

⑩ Several other configuration options—see the comment in the example configuration file: /usr/share/doc/packages/openvpn/sample-config-files.

⑪ Enable this option to write short status updates with statistical data ("operational status dump") to the named file. By default, this is not enabled.

All output is written to syslog. If you have more than one configuration file (for example, one for home and another for work), it is recommended to include the device name into the file name. This avoids overwriting output files accidentally. In this case, it is `tun0`, taken from the `dev` directive—see ❸.

⑫ By default, log messages go to syslog. Overwrite this behavior by removing the hash character. In that case, all messages go to `/var/log/openvpn-server.log`. Do not forget to configure a logrotate service. See **man 8 logrotate** for further details.

After having completed this configuration, you can see log messages of your OpenVPN server under `/var/log/openvpn.log`. After having started it for the first time, it should finish with:

```
... Initialization Sequence Completed
```

If you do not see this message, check the log carefully for any hints of what is wrong in your configuration file.

16.3.3 Configuring the VPN Clients

As the basis of your configuration file, copy `/usr/share/doc/packages/openvpn/sample-config-files/client.conf` to `/etc/openvpn/`. Then customize it to your needs.

EXAMPLE 16.2: VPN CLIENT CONFIGURATION FILE

```
# /etc/openvpn/client.conf
client ❶
dev tun ❷
proto udp ❸
remote IP_OR_HOST_NAME 1194 ❹
resolv-retry infinite
nobind

remote-cert-tls server ❺

# Privileges ❻
user nobody
group nobody

# Try to preserve some state across restarts.
persist-key
```

```
persist-tun

# Security ⓖ
pkcs12 client1.p12

comp-lzo ⓗ
```

ⓐ   Specifies that this machine is a client.

ⓑ   The network device. Both clients and server must use the same device.

ⓒ   The protocol. Use the same settings as on the server.

ⓔ   This is security option for clients which ensures that the host they connect to is a designated server.

ⓓ   Replace the placeholder *IP_OR_HOST_NAME* with the respective host name or IP address of your VPN server. After the host name, the port of the server is given. You can have multiple lines of `remote` entries pointing to different VPN servers. This is useful for load balancing between different VPN servers.

ⓕ   For security reasons, run the OpenVPN daemon with reduced privileges. To do so, specify that it should use the group and user `nobody`.

ⓖ   Contains the client files. For security reasons, use a separate pair of files for each client.

ⓗ   Turn on compression. Only use this parameter if compression is enabled on the server as well.

16.4   Setting Up a VPN Server or Client Using YaST

You can also use YaST to set up a VPN server. However, the YaST module does not support OpenVPN. Instead, it provides support for the IPsec protocol (as implemented in the software StrongSwan). Like OpenVPN, IPsec is a widely supported VPN scheme.

PROCEDURE 16.4: SETTING UP AN IPSEC SERVER

1. To start the YaST VPN module, select *Applications* › *VPN Gateways and Clients*.

2. Under *Global Configuration*, activate *Enable VPN Daemon*.

3. To create a new VPN, click *New VPN*, then enter a name for the connection.

4. Under *Type*, select *Gateway (Server)*.

5. Then choose the scenario:

- The scenarios *Secure communication with a pre-shared key* and *Secure communication with a certificate* are best suited to Linux client setups.

- The scenario *Provide access to Android, iOS, Mac OS X clients* sets up a configuration that is natively supported by modern versions of Android, iOS, and macOS. It is based on a pre-shared key setup with an additional user name and password authentication.

- The scenario *Provide access to Windows 7, Windows 8 clients* is a configuration that is natively supported by Windows and BlackBerry devices. It is based on a certificate setup with an additional user name and password authentication.

For this example, choose *Secure communication with a pre-shared key*.

6. To specify the key, click *Edit Credentials*. Activate *Show key*, then type the secret key. Confirm with *OK*.

7. Choose whether and how to limit access within your VPN under *Provide VPN clients access to*. To enable only certain IP ranges, specify these in CIDR format, separated by commas in *Limited CIDRs*. For more information about the CIDR format, see https://en.wikipedia.org/wiki/Classless_Inter-Domain_Routing ↗.

8. Under *Clients' address pool*, specify the format of IP addresses your VPN should provide to its clients.

9. To finish, click *OK*. The YaST VPN module will now automatically add and enable firewall rules to allow clients to connect to the new VPN.
To view the connection status, in the following confirmation window, click *Yes*. You will then see the output of `systemctl status` for your VPN, which allows you to check if the VPN is running and configured correctly.

16.5   For More Information

For more information about VPN in general, see:

- http://www.openvpn.net ↗: the OpenVPN home page

- `man` openvpn

- `/usr/share/doc/packages/openvpn/sample-config-files/`: example configuration files for different scenarios.

- `/usr/src/linux/Documentation/networking/tuntap.txt`, to install the `kernel-source` package.

17 Managing X.509 Certification

An increasing number of authentication mechanisms are based on cryptographic procedures. Digital certificates that assign cryptographic keys to their owners play an important role in this context. These certificates are used for communication and can also be found, for example, on company ID cards. The generation and administration of certificates is mostly handled by official institutions that offer this as a commercial service. In some cases, however, it may make sense to carry out these tasks yourself. For example, if a company does not want to pass personal data to third parties.

YaST provides two modules for certification, which offer basic management functions for digital X.509 certificates. The following sections explain the basics of digital certification and how to use YaST to create and administer certificates of this type.

17.1 The Principles of Digital Certification

Digital certification uses cryptographic processes to encrypt and protect data from access by unauthorized people. The user data is encrypted using a second data record, or *key*. The key is applied to the user data in a mathematical process, producing an altered data record in which the original content can no longer be identified. Asymmetrical encryption is now in general use (*public key method*). Keys always occur in pairs:

Private Key

The private key must be kept safely by the key owner. Accidental publication of the private key compromises the key pair and renders it useless.

Public Key

The key owner circulates the public key for use by third parties.

17.1.1 Key Authenticity

Because the public key process is in widespread use, there are many public keys in circulation. Successful use of this system requires that every user be sure that a public key actually belongs to the assumed owner. The assignment of users to public keys is confirmed by trustworthy organizations with public key certificates. Such certificates contain the name of the key owner, the corresponding public key, and the electronic signature of the person issuing the certificate.

Trustworthy organizations that issue and sign public key certificates are usually part of a certification infrastructure. This is responsible for the other aspects of certificate management, such as publication, withdrawal, and renewal of certificates. An infrastructure of this kind is generally called a *public key infrastructure* or *PKI*. One familiar PKI is the *OpenPGP* standard in which users publish their certificates themselves without central authorization points. These certificates become trustworthy when signed by other parties in the "web of trust."

The *X.509 Public Key Infrastructure* (PKIX) is an alternative model defined by the *IETF* (Internet Engineering Task Force) that serves as a model for almost all publicly-used PKIs today. In this model, authentication is made by *certificate authorities* (CA) in a hierarchical tree structure. The root of the tree is the root CA, which certifies all sub-CAs. The lowest level of sub-CAs issue user certificates. The user certificates are trustworthy by certification that can be traced to the root CA.

The security of such a PKI depends on the trustworthiness of the CA certificates. To make certification practices clear to PKI customers, the PKI operator defines a *certification practice statement* (CPS) that defines the procedures for certificate management. This should ensure that the PKI only issues trustworthy certificates.

17.1.2 X.509 Certificates

An X.509 certificate is a data structure with several fixed fields and, optionally, additional extensions. The fixed fields mainly contain the name of the key owner, the public key, and the data relating to the issuing CA (name and signature). For security reasons, a certificate should only have a limited period of validity, so a field is also provided for this date. The CA guarantees the validity of the certificate in the specified period. The CPS usually requires the PKI (the issuing CA) to create and distribute a new certificate before expiration.

The extensions can contain any additional information. An application is only required to be able to evaluate an extension if it is identified as *critical*. If an application does not recognize a critical extension, it must reject the certificate. Some extensions are only useful for a specific application, such as signature or encryption.

Table 17.1 shows the fields of a basic X.509 certificate in version 3.

TABLE 17.1: X.509V3 CERTIFICATE

Field	Content
Version	The version of the certificate, for example, v3
Serial Number	Unique certificate ID (an integer)
Signature	The ID of the algorithm used to sign the certificate
Issuer	Unique name (DN) of the issuing authority (CA)
Validity	Period of validity
Subject	Unique name (DN) of the owner
Subject Public Key Info	Public key of the owner and the ID of the algorithm
Issuer Unique ID	Unique ID of the issuing CA (optional)
Subject Unique ID	Unique ID of the owner (optional)
Extensions	Optional additional information, such as "KeyUsage" or "BasicConstraints"

17.1.3   Blocking X.509 Certificates

If a certificate becomes untrustworthy before it has expired, it must be blocked immediately. This can become necessary if, for example, the private key has accidentally been made public. Blocking certificates is especially important if the private key belongs to a CA rather than a user certificate. In this case, all user certificates issued by the relevant CA must be blocked immediately. If a certificate is blocked, the PKI (the responsible CA) must make this information available to all those involved using a *certificate revocation list* (CRL).

These lists are supplied by the CA to public CRL distribution points (CDPs) at regular intervals. The CDP can optionally be named as an extension in the certificate, so a checker can fetch a current CRL for validation purposes. One way to do this is the *online certificate status protocol* (OCSP). The authenticity of the CRLs is ensured with the signature of the issuing CA. *Table 17.2* shows the basic parts of a X.509 CRL.

TABLE 17.2: X.509 CERTIFICATE REVOCATION LIST (CRL)

Field	Content
Version	The version of the CRL, such as v2
Signature	The ID of the algorithm used to sign the CRL
Issuer	Unique name (DN) of the publisher of the CRL (usually the issuing CA)
This Update	Time of publication (date, time) of this CRL
Next Update	Time of publication (date, time) of the next CRL
List of revoked certificates	Every entry contains the serial number of the certificate, the time of revocation, and optional extensions (CRL entry extensions)
Extensions	Optional CRL extensions

17.1.4   Repository for Certificates and CRLs

The certificates and CRLs for a CA must be made publicly accessible using a *repository*. Because the signature protects the certificates and CRLs from being forged, the repository itself does not need to be secured in a special way. Instead, it tries to grant the simplest and fastest access possible. For this reason, certificates are often provided on an LDAP or HTTP server. Find explanations about LDAP in *Chapter 5, LDAP—A Directory Service*. *Book "Administration Guide", Chapter 31 "The Apache HTTP Server"* contains information about the HTTP server.

17.1.5   Proprietary PKI

YaST contains modules for the basic management of X.509 certificates. This mainly involves the creation of CAs, sub-CAs, and their certificates. The services of a PKI go far beyond simply creating and distributing certificates and CRLs. The operation of a PKI requires a well-conceived administrative infrastructure allowing continuous update of certificates and CRLs. This infrastructure is provided by commercial PKI products and can also be partly automated. YaST provides tools for creating and distributing CAs and certificates, but cannot currently offer this background infrastructure. To set up a small PKI, you can use the available YaST modules. However, you should use commercial products to set up an "official" or commercial PKI.

17.2   YaST Modules for CA Management

YaST provides two modules for basic CA management. The primary management tasks with these modules are explained here.

17.2.1   Creating a Root CA

After a default installation, SUSE Linux Enterprise Server contains already a root CA named YaST_Default_CA. Use this module to create additional root CAs. The first step when setting up a PKI is to create a root CA. Do the following:

1. Start YaST and go to *Security and Users* › *CA Management*.

2. Click *Create Root CA*.

3. Enter the basic data for the CA in the first dialog, shown in *Figure 17.1*. The text boxes have the following meanings:

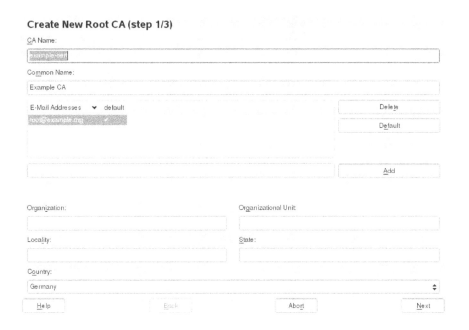

FIGURE 17.1: YAST CA MODULE—BASIC DATA FOR A ROOT CA

CA Name

Enter the technical name of the CA. Directory names, among other things, are derived from this name, which is why only the characters listed in the help can be used. The technical name is also displayed in the overview when the module is started.

Common Name

Enter the name for use in referring to the CA.

E-Mail Addresses

Several e-mail addresses can be entered that can be seen by the CA user. This can be helpful for inquiries.

Country

Select the country where the CA is operated.

Organization, Organizational Unit, Locality, State

Optional values

Proceed with *Next*.

4. Enter a password in the second dialog. This password is always required when using the CA—when creating a sub-CA or generating certificates. The text boxes have the following meaning:

Key Length

Key Length contains a meaningful default and does not generally need to be changed unless an application cannot deal with this key length. The higher the number the more secure your password is.

Valid Period (days)

The *Valid Period* in the case of a CA defaults to 3650 days (roughly ten years). This long period makes sense because the replacement of a deleted CA involves an enormous administrative effort.

Clicking *Advanced Options* opens a dialog for setting different attributes from the X.509 extensions (*Figure 17.4, "YaST CA Module—Extended Settings"*). These values have rational default settings and should only be changed if you are really sure of what you are doing. Proceed with *Next*.

5. Review the summary. YaST displays the current settings for confirmation. Click *Create*. The root CA is created then appears in the overview.

 Tip

In general, it is best not to allow user certificates to be issued by the root CA. It is better to create at least one sub-CA and create the user certificates from there. This has the advantage that the root CA can be kept isolated and secure, for example, on an isolated computer on secure premises. This makes it very difficult to attack the root CA.

17.2.2 Changing Password

If you need to change your password for your CA, proceed as follows:

1. Start YaST and open the CA module.

2. Select the required root CA and click *Enter CA*.

3. Enter the password if you entered a CA the first time. YaST displays the CA key information in the *Description* tab (see *Figure 17.2*).

4. Click *Advanced* and select *Change CA Password*. A dialog opens.

5. Enter the old and the new password.

6. Finish with *OK*

17.2.3   Creating or Revoking a Sub-CA

A sub-CA is created in the same way as a root CA.

 Note

The validity period for a sub-CA must be fully within the validity period of the "parent" CA. A sub-CA is always created after the "parent" CA, therefore, the default value leads to an error message. To avoid this, enter a permissible value for the period of validity.

Do the following:

1. Start YaST and open the CA module.

2. Select the required root CA and click *Enter CA*.

3. Enter the password if you are entering a CA for the first time. YaST displays the CA key information in the tab *Description* (see Figure 17.2).

Certificate Authority (CA)

CA Name: example-cert

Description	Certificates	CRL	Requests

Description for example-cert

Issued For:

```
Common Name:   Example CA
Organization:
Location:
State:
Country:       DE
EMAIL:         root@example.org
```

Issued By:

```
Common Name:   Example CA
Organization:
Location:
State:
Country:       DE
EMAIL:         root@example.org
```

Valid from: Oct 23 15:7:20 2008 GMT

Advanced... ▾

Help	Back	Abort	OK

FIGURE 17.2: YAST CA MODULE—USING A CA

4. Click *Advanced* and select *Create SubCA*. This opens the same dialog as for creating a root CA.

5. Proceed as described in *Section 17.2.1, "Creating a Root CA"*.
   It is possible to use one password for all your CAs. Enable *Use CA Password as Certificate Password* to give your sub-CAs the same password as your root CA. This helps to reduce the amount of passwords for your CAs.

 Note: Check your Valid Period

Take into account that the valid period must be lower than the valid period in the root CA.

6. Select the *Certificates* tab. Reset compromised or otherwise unwanted sub-CAs here, using *Revoke*. Revocation alone is not enough to deactivate a sub-CA. You must also publish revoked sub-CAs in a CRL. The creation of CRLs is described in *Section 17.2.6, "Creating Certificate Revocation Lists (CRLs)"*.

7. Finish with *OK*.

17.2.4 Creating or Revoking User Certificates

Creating client and server certificates is very similar to creating CAs in *Section 17.2.1, "Creating a Root CA"*. The same principles apply here. In certificates intended for e-mail signature, the e-mail address of the sender (the private key owner) should be contained in the certificate to enable the e-mail program to assign the correct certificate.

For certificate assignment during encryption, it is necessary for the e-mail address of the recipient (the public key owner) to be included in the certificate. In the case of server and client certificates, the host name of the server must be entered in the *Common Name* field. The default validity period for certificates is 365 days.

To create client and server certificates, do the following:

1. Start YaST and open the CA module.

2. Select the required root CA and click *Enter CA*.

3. Enter the password if you are entering a CA for the first time. YaST displays the CA key information in the *Description* tab.

4. Click *Certificates* (see *Figure 17.3*).

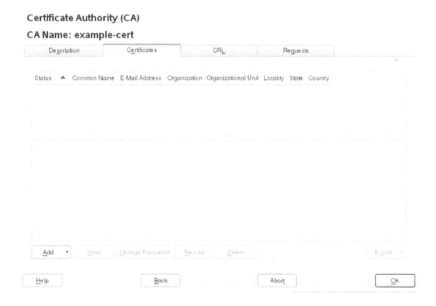

FIGURE 17.3: CERTIFICATES OF A CA

5. Click *Add > Add Server Certificate* and create a server certificate.

6. Click *Add > Add Client Certificate* and create a client certificate. Do not forget to enter an e-mail address.

7. Finish with *OK*

To revoke compromised or otherwise unwanted certificates, do the following:

1. Start YaST and open the CA module.

2. Select the required root CA and click *Enter CA*.

3. Enter the password if you are entering a CA for the first time. YaST displays the CA key information in the *Description* tab.

4. Click *Certificates* (see *Section 17.2.3, "Creating or Revoking a Sub-CA"*).

5. Select the certificate to revoke and click *Revoke*.

6. Choose a reason to revoke this certificate.

7. Finish with *OK*.

 Note

Revocation alone is not enough to deactivate a certificate. Also publish revoked certificates in a CRL. *Section 17.2.6, "Creating Certificate Revocation Lists (CRLs)"* explains how to create CRLs. Revoked certificates can be completely removed after publication in a CRL with *Delete*.

17.2.5   Changing Default Values

The previous sections explained how to create sub-CAs, client certificates, and server certificates. Special settings are used in the extensions of the X.509 certificate. These settings have been given rational defaults for every certificate type and do not normally need to be changed. However, it may be that you have special requirements for these extensions. In this case, it may make sense to adjust the defaults. Otherwise, start from scratch every time you create a certificate.

1. Start YaST and open the CA module.

2. Enter the required root CA, as described in *Section 17.2.3, "Creating or Revoking a Sub-CA"*.

3. Click *Advanced* › *Edit Default*.

4. Choose type of certificate to change and proceed with *Next*.

5. The dialog for changing the defaults as shown in *Figure 17.4, "YaST CA Module—Extended Settings"* opens.

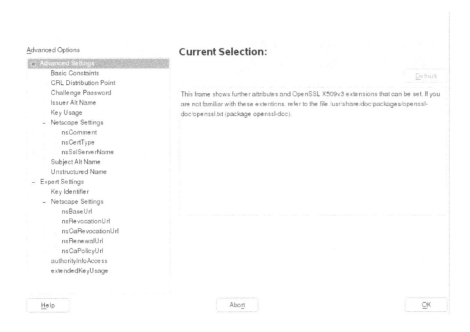

FIGURE 17.4: YAST CA MODULE—EXTENDED SETTINGS

6. Change the associated value on the right side and set or delete the critical setting with *critical*.

7. Click *Next* to see a short summary.

8. Finish your changes with *Save*.

 Note

All changes to the defaults only affect objects created after this point. Already-existing CAs and certificates remain unchanged.

17.2.6 Creating Certificate Revocation Lists (CRLs)

If compromised or otherwise unwanted certificates need to be excluded from further use, they must first be revoked. The procedure for this is explained in *Section 17.2.3, "Creating or Revoking a Sub-CA"* (for sub-CAs) and *Section 17.2.4, "Creating or Revoking User Certificates"* (for user certificates). After this, a CRL must be created and published with this information.

The system maintains only one CRL for each CA. To create or update this CRL, do the following:

1. Start YaST and open the CA module.

2. Enter the required CA, as described in *Section 17.2.3, "Creating or Revoking a Sub-CA"*.

3. Click *CRL*. The dialog that opens displays a summary of the last CRL of this CA.

4. Create a new CRL with *Generate CRL* if you have revoked new sub-CAs or certificates since its creation.

5. Specify the period of validity for the new CRL (default: 30 days).

6. Click *OK* to create and display the CRL. Afterward, you must publish this CRL.

 Note

Applications that evaluate CRLs reject every certificate if the CRL is not available or has expired. As a PKI provider, it is your duty always to create and publish a new CRL before the current CRL expires (period of validity). YaST does not provide a function for automating this procedure.

17.2.7 Exporting CA Objects to LDAP

The executing computer should be configured with the YaST LDAP client for LDAP export. This provides LDAP server information at runtime that can be used when completing dialog fields. Otherwise (although export may be possible), all LDAP data must be entered manually. You must always enter several passwords (see *Table 17.3, "Passwords during LDAP Export"*).

TABLE 17.3: PASSWORDS DURING LDAP EXPORT

Password	Meaning
LDAP Password	Authorizes the user to make entries in the LDAP tree.
Certificate Password	Authorizes the user to export the certificate.
New Certificate Password	The PKCS12 format is used during LDAP export. This format forces the assignment of a new password for the exported certificate.

Certificates, CAs, and CRLs can be exported to LDAP.

Exporting a CA to LDAP

To export a CA, enter the CA as described in *Section 17.2.3, "Creating or Revoking a Sub-CA"*. Select *Extended › Export to LDAP* in the subsequent dialog, which opens the dialog for entering LDAP data. If your system has been configured with the YaST LDAP client, the fields are already partly completed. Otherwise, enter all the data manually. Entries are made in LDAP in a separate tree with the attribute "caCertificate".

Exporting a Certificate to LDAP

Enter the CA containing the certificate to export then select *Certificates*. Select the required certificate from the certificate list in the upper part of the dialog and select *Export › Export to LDAP*. The LDAP data is entered here in the same way as for CAs. The certificate is saved with the corresponding user object in the LDAP tree with the attributes "userCertificate" (PEM format) and "userPKCS12" (PKCS12 format).

Exporting a CRL to LDAP

Enter the CA containing the CRL to export and select *CRL*. If desired, create a new CRL and click *Export*. The dialog that opens displays the export parameters. You can export the CRL for this CA either once or in periodical time intervals. Activate the export by selecting *Export to LDAP* and enter the respective LDAP data. To do this at regular intervals, select the *Repeated Recreation and Export* radio button and change the interval, if appropriate.

17.2.8 Exporting CA Objects as a File

If you have set up a repository on the computer for administering CAs, you can use this option to create the CA objects directly as a file at the correct location. Different output formats are available, such as PEM, DER, and PKCS12. In the case of PEM, it is also possible to choose whether a certificate should be exported with or without key and whether the key should be encrypted. In the case of PKCS12, it is also possible to export the certification path.

Export a file in the same way for certificates, CAs as with LDAP, described in *Section 17.2.7, "Exporting CA Objects to LDAP"*, except you should select *Export as File* instead of *Export to LDAP*. This then takes you to a dialog for selecting the required output format and entering the password and file name. The certificate is stored at the required location after clicking *OK*.

For CRLs click *Export*, select *Export to file*, choose the export format (PEM or DER) and enter the path. Proceed with *OK* to save it to the respective location.

Tip

You can select any storage location in the file system. This option can also be used to save CA objects on a transport medium, such as a flash disk. The `/media` directory generally holds any type of drive except the hard disk of your system.

17.2.9   Importing Common Server Certificates

If you have exported a server certificate with YaST to your media on an isolated CA management computer, you can import this certificate on a server as a *common server certificate*. Do this during installation or at a later point with YaST.

 Note

You need one of the PKCS12 formats to import your certificate successfully.

The general server certificate is stored in **/etc/ssl/servercerts** and can be used there by any CA-supported service. When this certificate expires, it can easily be replaced using the same mechanisms. To get things functioning with the replaced certificate, restart the participating services.

 Tip

If you select *Import* here, you can select the source in the file system. This option can also be used to import certificates from removable media, such as a flash disk.

To import a common server certificate, do the following:

1. Start YaST and open *Common Server Certificate* under *Security and Users*

2. View the data for the current certificate in the description field after YaST has been started.

3. Select *Import* and the certificate file.

4. Enter the password and click *Next*. The certificate is imported then displayed in the description field.

5. Close YaST with *Finish*.

IV Confining Privileges with AppArmor

18   Introducing AppArmor

Many security vulnerabilities result from bugs in *trusted* programs. A trusted program runs with privileges that attackers want to possess. The program fails to keep that trust if there is a bug in the program that allows the attacker to acquire said privilege.

AppArmor® is an application security solution designed specifically to apply privilege confinement to suspect programs. AppArmor allows the administrator to specify the domain of activities the program can perform by developing a security *profile*. A security profile is a listing of files that the program may access and the operations the program may perform. AppArmor secures applications by enforcing good application behavior without relying on attack signatures, so it can prevent attacks even if previously unknown vulnerabilities are being exploited.

18.1   AppArmor Components

AppArmor consists of:

- A library of AppArmor profiles for common Linux* applications, describing what files the program needs to access.

- A library of AppArmor profile foundation classes (profile building blocks) needed for common application activities, such as DNS lookup and user authentication.

- A tool suite for developing and enhancing AppArmor profiles, so that you can change the existing profiles to suit your needs and create new profiles for your own local and custom applications.

- Several specially modified applications that are AppArmor enabled to provide enhanced security in the form of unique subprocess confinement (including Apache).

- The AppArmor-related kernel code and associated control scripts to enforce AppArmor policies on your SUSE® Linux Enterprise Server system.

18.2 Background Information on AppArmor Profiling

For more information about the science and security of AppArmor, refer to the following papers:

SubDomain: Parsimonious Server Security by Crispin Cowan, Steve Beattie, Greg Kroah-Hartman, Calton Pu, Perry Wagle, and Virgil Gligor

> Describes the initial design and implementation of AppArmor. Published in the proceedings of the USENIX LISA Conference, December 2000, New Orleans, LA. This paper is now out of date, describing syntax and features that are different from the current AppArmor product. This paper should be used only for background, and not for technical documentation.

Defcon Capture the Flag: Defending Vulnerable Code from Intense Attack by Crispin Cowan, Seth Arnold, Steve Beattie, Chris Wright, and John Viega

> A good guide to strategic and tactical use of AppArmor to solve severe security problems in a very short period of time. Published in the Proceedings of the DARPA Information Survivability Conference and Expo (DISCEX III), April 2003, Washington, DC.

AppArmor for Geeks by Seth Arnold

> This document tries to convey a better understanding of the technical details of AppArmor. It is available at http://en.opensuse.org/SDB:AppArmor_geeks ↗.

19 Getting Started

Prepare a successful deployment of AppArmor on your system by carefully considering the following items:

1. Determine the applications to profile. Read more on this in *Section 19.3, "Choosing Applications to Profile"*.

2. Build the needed profiles as roughly outlined in *Section 19.4, "Building and Modifying Profiles"*. Check the results and adjust the profiles when necessary.

3. Update your profiles whenever your environment changes or you need to react to security events logged by the reporting tool of AppArmor. Refer to *Section 19.5, "Updating Your Profiles"*.

19.1 Installing AppArmor

AppArmor is installed and running on any installation of SUSE® Linux Enterprise Server by default, regardless of what patterns are installed. The packages listed below are needed for a fully-functional instance of AppArmor:

- `apparmor-docs`
- `apparmor-parser`
- `apparmor-profiles`
- `apparmor-utils`
- `audit`
- `libapparmor1`
- `perl-libapparmor`
- `yast2-apparmor`

 Tip

> If AppArmor is not installed on your system, install the pattern `apparmor` for a complete AppArmor installation. Either use the YaST Software Management module for installation, or use Zypper on the command line:
>
> ```
> zypper in -t pattern apparmor
> ```

19.2   Enabling and Disabling AppArmor

AppArmor is configured to run by default on any fresh installation of SUSE Linux Enterprise Server. There are two ways of toggling the status of AppArmor:

Using YaST Services Manager

Disable or enable AppArmor by removing or adding its boot script to the sequence of scripts executed on system boot. Status changes are applied on reboot.

Using AppArmor Configuration Window

Toggle the status of AppArmor in a running system by switching it off or on using the YaST AppArmor Control Panel. Changes made here are applied instantaneously. The Control Panel triggers a stop or start event for AppArmor and removes or adds its boot script in the system's boot sequence.

To disable AppArmor permanently (by removing it from the sequence of scripts executed on system boot) proceed as follows:

1. Start YaST.

2. Select *System* › *Services Manager*.

3. Mark `apparmor` by clicking its row in the list of services, then click *Enable/Disable* in the lower part of the window. Check that *Enabled* changed to *Disabled* in the `apparmor` row.

4. Confirm with *OK*.

AppArmor will not be initialized on reboot, and stays inactive until you re-enable it. Re-enabling a service using the YaST *Services Manager* tool is similar to disabling it.

Toggle the status of AppArmor in a running system by using the AppArmor Configuration window. These changes take effect when you apply them and survive a reboot of the system. To toggle the status of AppArmor, proceed as follows:

1. Start YaST, select *AppArmor Configuration*, and click *Settings* in the main window.

2. Enable AppArmor by checking *Enable AppArmor* or disable AppArmor by deselecting it.

3. Click *Done* in the *AppArmor Configuration* window.

19.3 Choosing Applications to Profile

You only need to protect the programs that are exposed to attacks in your particular setup, so only use profiles for those applications you actually run. Use the following list to determine the most likely candidates:

Network Agents

Web Applications

Cron Jobs

To find out which processes are currently running with open network ports and might need a profile to confine them, run **aa-unconfined** as `root`.

EXAMPLE 19.1: OUTPUT OF aa-unconfined

```
19848 /usr/sbin/cupsd not confined
19887 /usr/sbin/sshd not confined
19947 /usr/lib/postfix/master not confined
1328 /usr/sbin/ntpd confined by '/usr/sbin/ntpd (enforce)'
```

Each of the processes in the above example labeled `not confined` might need a custom profile to confine it. Those labeled `confined by` are already protected by AppArmor.

Tip: For More Information

For more information about choosing the right applications to profile, refer to *Section 20.2, "Determining Programs to Immunize"*.

19.4 Building and Modifying Profiles

AppArmor on SUSE Linux Enterprise Server ships with a preconfigured set of profiles for the most important applications. In addition, you can use AppArmor to create your own profiles for any application you want.

There are two ways of managing profiles. One is to use the graphical front-end provided by the YaST AppArmor modules and the other is to use the command line tools provided by the AppArmor suite itself. The main difference is that YaST supports only basic functionality for AppArmor profiles, while the command line tools let you update/tune the profiles in a more fine-grained way.

For each application, perform the following steps to create a profile:

1. As `root`, let AppArmor create a rough outline of the application's profile by running **aa-genprof** `PROGRAM_NAME`.

   or

   Outline the basic profile by running *YaST › Security and Users › AppArmor Configuration › Manually Add Profile* and specifying the complete path to the application you want to profile.

   A new basic profile is outlined and put into learning mode, which means that it logs any activity of the program you are executing, but does not yet restrict it.

2. Run the full range of the application's actions to let AppArmor get a very specific picture of its activities.

3. Let AppArmor analyze the log files generated in *Step 2* by typing ⌷s⌷ in aa-genprof. AppArmor scans the logs it recorded during the application's run and asks you to set the access rights for each event that was logged. Either set them for each file or use globbing.

4. Depending on the complexity of your application, it might be necessary to repeat *Step 2* and *Step 3*. Confine the application, exercise it under the confined conditions, and process any new log events. To properly confine the full range of an application's capabilities, you might be required to repeat this procedure often.

5. When you finish **aa-genprof**, your profile is set to enforce mode. The profile is applied and AppArmor restricts the application according to it.

   If you started **aa-genprof** on an application that had an existing profile that was in complain mode, this profile remains in learning mode upon exit of this learning cycle. For more information about changing the mode of a profile, refer to *Section 24.6.3.2, "aa-complain— Entering Complain or Learning Mode"* and *Section 24.6.3.6, "aa-enforce—Entering Enforce Mode"*.

Test your profile settings by performing every task you need with the application you confined. Normally, the confined program runs smoothly and you do not notice AppArmor activities. However, if you notice certain misbehavior with your application, check the system logs and see if AppArmor is too tightly confining your application. Depending on the log mechanism used on your system, there are several places to look for AppArmor log entries:

`/var/log/audit/audit.log`

The command **journalctl | grep -i apparmor**

The command **dmesg -T**

To adjust the profile, analyze the log messages relating to this application again as described in *Section 24.6.3.9, "aa-logprof—Scanning the System Log"*. Determine the access rights or restrictions when prompted.

 Tip: For More Information

> For more information about profile building and modification, refer to *Chapter 21, Profile Components and Syntax*, *Chapter 23, Building and Managing Profiles with YaST*, and *Chapter 24, Building Profiles from the Command Line*.

19.5   Updating Your Profiles

Software and system configurations change over time. As a result, your profile setup for AppArmor might need some fine-tuning from time to time. AppArmor checks your system log for policy violations or other AppArmor events and lets you adjust your profile set accordingly. Any application behavior that is outside of any profile definition can be addressed by `aa-logprof`. For more information, see *Section 24.6.3.9, "aa-logprof—Scanning the System Log"*.

20 Immunizing Programs

Effective hardening of a computer system requires minimizing the number of programs that mediate privilege, then securing the programs as much as possible. With AppArmor, you only need to profile the programs that are exposed to attack in your environment, which drastically reduces the amount of work required to harden your computer. AppArmor profiles enforce policies to make sure that programs do what they are supposed to do, but nothing else.

AppArmor provides immunization technologies that protect applications from the inherent vulnerabilities they possess. After installing AppArmor, setting up AppArmor profiles, and rebooting the computer, your system becomes immunized because it begins to enforce the AppArmor security policies. Protecting programs with AppArmor is called *immunizing*.

Administrators need only concern themselves with the applications that are vulnerable to attacks, and generate profiles for these. Hardening a system thus comes down to building and maintaining the AppArmor profile set and monitoring any policy violations or exceptions logged by AppArmor's reporting facility.

Users should not notice AppArmor. It runs "behind the scenes" and does not require any user interaction. Performance is not noticeably affected by AppArmor. If some activity of the application is not covered by an AppArmor profile or if some activity of the application is prevented by AppArmor, the administrator needs to adjust the profile of this application.

AppArmor sets up a collection of default application profiles to protect standard Linux services. To protect other applications, use the AppArmor tools to create profiles for the applications that you want protected. This chapter introduces the philosophy of immunizing programs. Proceed to *Chapter 21, Profile Components and Syntax*, *Chapter 23, Building and Managing Profiles with YaST*, or *Chapter 24, Building Profiles from the Command Line* if you are ready to build and manage AppArmor profiles.

AppArmor provides streamlined access control for network services by specifying which files each program is allowed to read, write, and execute, and which type of network it is allowed to access. This ensures that each program does what it is supposed to do, and nothing else. AppArmor quarantines programs to protect the rest of the system from being damaged by a compromised process.

AppArmor is a host intrusion prevention or mandatory access control scheme. Previously, access control schemes were centered around users because they were built for large timeshare systems. Alternatively, modern network servers largely do not permit users to log in, but instead provide a variety of network services for users (such as Web, mail, file, and print servers). AppArmor controls the access given to network services and other programs to prevent weaknesses from being exploited.

 Tip: Background Information for AppArmor

To get a more in-depth overview of AppArmor and the overall concept behind it, refer to *Section 18.2, "Background Information on AppArmor Profiling"*.

20.1 Introducing the AppArmor Framework

This section provides a very basic understanding of what is happening "behind the scenes" (and under the hood of the YaST interface) when you run AppArmor.

An AppArmor profile is a plain text file containing path entries and access permissions. See *Section 21.1, "Breaking an AppArmor Profile into Its Parts"* for a detailed reference profile. The directives contained in this text file are then enforced by the AppArmor routines to quarantine the process or program.

The following tools interact in the building and enforcement of AppArmor profiles and policies:

aa-status

> **aa-status** reports various aspects of the current state of the running AppArmor confinement.

aa-unconfined

> **aa-unconfined** detects any application running on your system that listens for network connections and is not protected by an AppArmor profile. Refer to *Section 24.6.3.12, "aa-unconfined—Identifying Unprotected Processes"* for detailed information about this tool.

aa-autodep

> **aa-autodep** creates a basic framework of a profile that needs to be fleshed out before it is put to use in production. The resulting profile is loaded and put into complain mode, reporting any behavior of the application that is not (yet) covered by AppArmor rules. Refer to *Section 24.6.3.1, "aa-autodep—Creating Approximate Profiles"* for detailed information about this tool.

`aa-genprof`

> `aa-genprof` generates a basic profile and asks you to refine this profile by executing the application and generating log events that need to be taken care of by AppArmor policies. You are guided through a series of questions to deal with the log events that have been triggered during the application's execution. After the profile has been generated, it is loaded and put into enforce mode. Refer to *Section 24.6.3.8, "aa-genprof—Generating Profiles"* for detailed information about this tool.

`aa-logprof`

> `aa-logprof` interactively scans and reviews the log entries generated by an application that is confined by an AppArmor profile in both complain and enforced modes. It assists you in generating new entries in the profile concerned. Refer to *Section 24.6.3.9, "aa-logprof— Scanning the System Log"* for detailed information about this tool.

`aa-easyprof`

> `aa-easyprof` provides an easy-to-use interface for AppArmor profile generation. `aa-easyprof` supports the use of templates and policy groups to quickly profile an application. Note that while this tool can help with policy generation, its utility is dependent on the quality of the templates, policy groups and abstractions used. `aa-easyprof` may create a profile that is less restricted than creating the profile with `aa-genprof` and `aa-logprof`.

`aa-complain`

> `aa-complain` toggles the mode of an AppArmor profile from enforce to complain. Violations to rules set in a profile are logged, but the profile is not enforced. Refer to *Section 24.6.3.2, "aa-complain—Entering Complain or Learning Mode"* for detailed information about this tool.

`aa-enforce`

> `aa-enforce` toggles the mode of an AppArmor profile from complain to enforce. Violations to rules set in a profile are logged and not permitted—the profile is enforced. Refer to *Section 24.6.3.6, "aa-enforce—Entering Enforce Mode"* for detailed information about this tool.

`aa-disable`

> `aa-disable` disables the enforcement mode for one or more AppArmor profiles. This command will unload the profile from the kernel and prevent it from being loaded on AppArmor start-up. The `aa-enforce` and `aa-complain` utilities may be used to change this behavior.

aa-exec

> **aa-exec** launches a program confined by the specified AppArmor profile and/or name-space. If both a profile and namespace are specified, the command will be confined by the profile in the new policy namespace. If only a namespace is specified, the profile name of the current confinement will be used. If neither a profile or namespace is specified, the command will be run using standard profile attachment—as if run without **aa-exec**.

aa-notify

> **aa-notify** is a handy utility that displays AppArmor notifications in your desktop environment. You can also configure it to display a summary of notifications for the specified number of recent days. For more information, see *Section 24.6.3.13, "aa-notify"*.

20.2   Determining Programs to Immunize

Now that you have familiarized yourself with AppArmor, start selecting the applications for which to build profiles. Programs that need profiling are those that mediate privilege. The following programs have access to resources that the person using the program does not have, so they grant the privilege to the user when used:

cron Jobs

> Programs that are run periodically by `cron`. Such programs read input from a variety of sources and can run with special privileges, sometimes with as much as `root` privilege. For example, `cron` can run `/usr/sbin/logrotate` daily to rotate, compress, or even mail system logs. For instructions for finding these types of programs, refer to *Section 20.3, "Immunizing cron Jobs"*.

Web Applications

> Programs that can be invoked through a Web browser, including CGI Perl scripts, PHP pages, and more complex Web applications. For instructions for finding these types of programs, refer to *Section 20.4.1, "Immunizing Web Applications"*.

Network Agents

> Programs (servers and clients) that have open network ports. User clients, such as mail clients and Web browsers mediate privilege. These programs run with the privilege to write to the user's home directory and they process input from potentially hostile remote sources, such as hostile Web sites and e-mailed malicious code. For instructions for finding these types of programs, refer to *Section 20.4.2, "Immunizing Network Agents"*.

Conversely, unprivileged programs do not need to be profiled. For example, a shell script might invoke the **cp** program to copy a file. Because **cp** does not by default have its own profile or subprofile, it inherits the profile of the parent shell script. Thus **cp** can copy any files that the parent shell script's profile can read and write.

20.3 Immunizing cron Jobs

To find programs that are run by cron, inspect your local cron configuration. Unfortunately, cron configuration is rather complex, so there are numerous files to inspect. Periodic cron jobs are run from these files:

```
/etc/crontab
/etc/cron.d/*
/etc/cron.daily/*
/etc/cron.hourly/*
/etc/cron.monthly/*
/etc/cron.weekly/*
```

The **crontab** command lists/edits the current user's crontab. To manipulate root 's cron jobs, first become root , and then edit the tasks with **crontab -e** or list them with **crontab -l**.

20.4 Immunizing Network Applications

An automated method for finding network server daemons that should be profiled is to use the **aa-unconfined** tool.

The **aa-unconfined** tool uses the command **netstat -nlp** to inspect open ports from inside your computer, detect the programs associated with those ports, and inspect the set of AppArmor profiles that you have loaded. **aa-unconfined** then reports these programs along with the AppArmor profile associated with each program, or reports "none" (if the program is not confined).

 Note

> If you create a new profile, you must restart the program that has been profiled to have it be effectively confined by AppArmor.

Below is a sample **aa-unconfined** output:

```
3702❶ /usr/sbin/sshd❷ confined
```

```
   by '/usr/sbin/sshd❸ (enforce)'
4040 /usr/sbin/ntpd confined by '/usr/sbin/ntpd (enforce)'
4373 /usr/lib/postfix/master confined by '/usr/lib/postfix/master (enforce)'
4505 /usr/sbin/httpd2-prefork confined by '/usr/sbin/httpd2-prefork (enforce)'
646 /usr/lib/wicked/bin/wickedd-dhcp4 not confined
647 /usr/lib/wicked/bin/wickedd-dhcp6 not confined
5592 /usr/bin/ssh not confined
7146 /usr/sbin/cupsd confined by '/usr/sbin/cupsd (complain)'
```

❶ The first portion is a number. This number is the process ID number (PID) of the listening program.

❷ The second portion is a string that represents the absolute path of the listening program

❸ The final portion indicates the profile confining the program, if any.

 Note

> `aa-unconfined` requires `root` privileges and should not be run from a shell that is confined by an AppArmor profile.

`aa-unconfined` does not distinguish between one network interface and another, so it reports all unconfined processes, even those that might be listening to an internal LAN interface.

Finding user network client applications is dependent on your user preferences. The `aa-unconfined` tool detects and reports network ports opened by client applications, but only those client applications that are running at the time the `aa-unconfined` analysis is performed. This is a problem because network services tend to be running all the time, while network client applications tend only to be running when the user is interested in them.

Applying AppArmor profiles to user network client applications is also dependent on user preferences. Therefore, we leave the profiling of user network client applications as an exercise for the user.

To aggressively confine desktop applications, the `aa-unconfined` command supports a `--paranoid` option, which reports all processes running and the corresponding AppArmor profiles that might or might not be associated with each process. The user can then decide whether each of these programs needs an AppArmor profile.

If you have new or modified profiles, you can submit them to the `apparmor@lists.ubuntu.com` mailing list along with a use case for the application behavior that you exercised. The AppArmor team reviews and may submit the work into SUSE Linux Enterprise Server. We cannot guarantee that every profile will be included, but we make a sincere effort to include as much as possible.

20.4.1 Immunizing Web Applications

To find Web applications, investigate your Web server configuration. The Apache Web server is highly configurable and Web applications can be stored in many directories, depending on your local configuration. SUSE Linux Enterprise Server, by default, stores Web applications in `/srv/www/cgi-bin/`. To the maximum extent possible, each Web application should have an AppArmor profile.

Once you find these programs, you can use the **aa-genprof** and **aa-logprof** tools to create or update their AppArmor profiles.

Because CGI programs are executed by the Apache Web server, the profile for Apache itself, `usr.sbin.httpd2-prefork` for Apache2 on SUSE Linux Enterprise Server, must be modified to add execute permissions to each of these programs. For example, adding the line `/srv/www/cgi-bin/my_hit_counter.pl rPx` grants Apache permission to execute the Perl script `my_hit_counter.pl` and requires that there be a dedicated profile for `my_hit_counter.pl`. If `my_hit_counter.pl` does not have a dedicated profile associated with it, the rule should say `/srv/www/cgi-bin/my_hit_counter.pl rix` to cause `my_hit_counter.pl` to inherit the `usr.sbin.httpd2-prefork` profile.

Some users might find it inconvenient to specify execute permission for every CGI script that Apache might invoke. Instead, the administrator can grant controlled access to collections of CGI scripts. For example, adding the line `/srv/www/cgi-bin/*.{pl,py,pyc} rix` allows Apache to execute all files in `/srv/www/cgi-bin/` ending in `.pl` (Perl scripts) and `.py` or `.pyc` (Python scripts). As above, the `ix` part of the rule causes Python scripts to inherit the Apache profile, which is appropriate if you do not want to write individual profiles for each CGI script.

 Note

> If you want the subprocess confinement module (`apache2-mod-apparmor`) functionality when Web applications handle Apache modules (`mod_perl` and `mod_php`), use the ChangeHat features when you add a profile in YaST or at the command line. To take advantage of the subprocess confinement, refer to *Section 25.2, "Managing ChangeHat-Aware Applications"*.

Profiling Web applications that use `mod_perl` and `mod_php` requires slightly different handling. In this case, the "program" is a script interpreted directly by the module within the Apache process, so no exec happens. Instead, the AppArmor version of Apache calls **change_hat()** using a subprofile (a "hat") corresponding to the name of the URI requested.

Note

> The name presented for the script to execute might not be the URI, depending on how Apache has been configured for where to look for module scripts. If you have configured your Apache to place scripts in a different place, the different names appear in the log file when AppArmor complains about access violations. See *Chapter 27, Managing Profiled Applications*.

For `mod_perl` and `mod_php` scripts, this is the name of the Perl script or the PHP page requested. For example, adding this subprofile allows the `localtime.php` page to execute and access to the local system time and locale files:

```
/usr/bin/httpd2-prefork {
  # ...
  ^/cgi-bin/localtime.php {
    /etc/localtime                  r,
    /srv/www/cgi-bin/localtime.php  r,
    /usr/lib/locale/**              r,
  }
}
```

If no subprofile has been defined, the AppArmor version of Apache applies the `DEFAULT_URI` hat. This subprofile is sufficient to display a Web page. The `DEFAULT_URI` hat that AppArmor provides by default is the following:

```
^DEFAULT_URI {
    /usr/sbin/suexec2             mixr,
    /var/log/apache2/**           rwl,
    @{HOME}/public_html           r,
    @{HOME}/public_html/**        r,
    /srv/www/htdocs               r,
    /srv/www/htdocs/**            r,
    /srv/www/icons/*.{gif,jpg,png}  r,
    /srv/www/vhosts               r,
    /srv/www/vhosts/**            r,
    /usr/share/apache2/**         r,
    /var/lib/php/sess_*           rwl
}
```

To use a single AppArmor profile for all Web pages and CGI scripts served by Apache, a good approach is to edit the `DEFAULT_URI` subprofile. For more information on confining Web applications with Apache, see *Chapter 25, Profiling Your Web Applications Using ChangeHat*.

20.4.2   Immunizing Network Agents

To find network server daemons and network clients (such as **fetchmail** or Firefox) that need to be profiled, you should inspect the open ports on your machine. Also consider the programs that are answering on those ports, and provide profiles for as many of those programs as possible. If you provide profiles for all programs with open network ports, an attacker cannot get to the file system on your machine without passing through an AppArmor profile policy.

Scan your server for open network ports manually from outside the machine using a scanner (such as nmap), or from inside the machine using the **netstat --inet -n -p** command as root. Then, inspect the machine to determine which programs are answering on the discovered open ports.

 Tip

Refer to the man page of the **netstat** command for a detailed reference of all possible options.

21 Profile Components and Syntax

Building AppArmor profiles to confine an application is very straightforward and intuitive. AppArmor ships with several tools that assist in profile creation. It does not require you to do any programming or script handling. The only task that is required of the administrator is to determine a policy of strictest access and execute permissions for each application that needs to be hardened.

Updates or modifications to the application profiles are only required if the software configuration or the desired range of activities changes. AppArmor offers intuitive tools to handle profile updates and modifications.

You are ready to build AppArmor profiles after you select the programs to profile. To do so, it is important to understand the components and syntax of profiles. AppArmor profiles contain several building blocks that help build simple and reusable profile code:

Include Files

Include statements are used to pull in parts of other AppArmor profiles to simplify the structure of new profiles.

Abstractions

Abstractions are include statements grouped by common application tasks.

Program Chunks

Program chunks are include statements that contain chunks of profiles that are specific to program suites.

Capability Entries

Capability entries are profile entries for any of the POSIX.1e http://en.wikipedia.org/wiki/POSIX#POSIX.1 ↗ Linux capabilities allowing a fine-grained control over what a confined process is allowed to do through system calls that require privileges.

Network Access Control Entries

Network Access Control Entries mediate network access based on the address type and family.

Local Variable Definitions

Local variables define shortcuts for paths.

File Access Control Entries

File Access Control Entries specify the set of files an application can access.

rlimit Entries

rlimit entries set and control an application's resource limits.

For help determining the programs to profile, refer to *Section 20.2, "Determining Programs to Immunize"*. To start building AppArmor profiles with YaST, proceed to *Chapter 23, Building and Managing Profiles with YaST*. To build profiles using the AppArmor command line interface, proceed to *Chapter 24, Building Profiles from the Command Line*.

21.1   Breaking an AppArmor Profile into Its Parts

The easiest way of explaining what a profile consists of and how to create one is to show the details of a sample profile, in this case for a hypothetical application called **/usr/bin/foo**:

```
#include <tunables/global> ❶

# a comment naming the application to confine
/usr/bin/foo ❷  { ❸
   #include <abstractions/base> ❹

   capability setgid ❺,
   network inet tcp ❻,

   link /etc/sysconfig/foo -> /etc/foo.conf, ❼
   /bin/mount            ux,
   /dev/{,u} ❽ random    r,
   /etc/ld.so.cache      r,
   /etc/foo/*            r,
   /lib/ld-*.so*         mr,
   /lib/lib*.so*         mr,
   /proc/[0-9]**         r,
   /usr/lib/**           mr,
   /tmp/                 r, ❾
   /tmp/foo.pid          wr,
   /tmp/foo.*            lrw,
   /@{HOME} ❿ /.foo_file   rw,
   /@{HOME}/.foo_lock    kw,
   owner ⓫ /shared/foo/** rw,
   /usr/bin/foobar       Cx, ⓬
   /bin/**               Px -> bin_generic, ⓭

   # a comment about foo's local (children) profile for /usr/bin/foobar.

   profile /usr/bin/foobar ⓮ {
```

```
      /bin/bash         rmix,
      /bin/cat          rmix,
      /bin/more         rmix,
      /var/log/foobar*  rwl,
      /etc/foobar       r,
   }

 # foo's hat, bar.
  ^bar⑮ {
   /lib/ld-*.so*        mr,
   /usr/bin/bar         px,
   /var/spool/*         rwl,
   }
}
```

① This loads a file containing variable definitions.

② The normalized path to the program that is confined.

③ The curly braces ({}) serve as a container for include statements, subprofiles, path entries, capability entries, and network entries.

④ This directive pulls in components of AppArmor profiles to simplify profiles.

⑤ Capability entry statements enable each of the 29 POSIX.1e draft capabilities.

⑥ A directive determining the kind of network access allowed to the application. For details, refer to *Section 21.5, "Network Access Control"*.

⑦ A link pair rule specifying the source and the target of a link. See *Section 21.7.6, "Link Pair"* for more information.

⑧ The curly braces ({}) here allow for each of the listed possibilities, one of which is the empty string.

⑨ A path entry specifying what areas of the file system the program can access. The first part of a path entry specifies the absolute path of a file (including regular expression globbing) and the second part indicates permissible access modes (for example r for read, w for write, and x for execute). A whitespace of any kind (spaces or tabs) can precede the path name, but must separate the path name and the mode specifier. Spaces between the access mode and the trailing comma are optional. Find a comprehensive overview of the available access modes in *Section 21.7, "File Permission Access Modes"*.

⑩ This variable expands to a value that can be changed without changing the entire profile.

⑪ An owner conditional rule, granting read and write permission on files owned by the user. Refer to *Section 21.7.8, "Owner Conditional Rules"* for more information.

⑫ This entry defines a transition to the local profile `/usr/bin/foobar`. Find a comprehensive overview of the available execute modes in *Section 21.8, "Execute Modes"*.

⑬ A named profile transition to the profile bin_generic located in the global scope. See *Section 21.8.7, "Named Profile Transitions"* for details.

⑭ The local profile `/usr/bin/foobar` is defined in this section.

⑮ This section references a "hat" subprofile of the application. For more details on AppArmor's ChangeHat feature, refer to *Chapter 25, Profiling Your Web Applications Using ChangeHat*.

When a profile is created for a program, the program can access only the files, modes, and POSIX capabilities specified in the profile. These restrictions are in addition to the native Linux access controls.

Example: To gain the capability `CAP_CHOWN`, the program must have both access to `CAP_CHOWN` under conventional Linux access controls (typically, be a `root`-owned process) and have the capability `chown` in its profile. Similarly, to be able to write to the file `/foo/bar` the program must have both the correct user ID and mode bits set in the files attributes and have `/foo/bar w` in its profile.

Attempts to violate AppArmor rules are recorded in `/var/log/audit/audit.log` if the `audit` package is installed, or in `/var/log/messages`, or only in `journalctl` if no traditional syslog is installed. Often AppArmor rules prevent an attack from working because necessary files are not accessible and, in all cases, AppArmor confinement restricts the damage that the attacker can do to the set of files permitted by AppArmor.

21.2 Profile Types

AppArmor knows four different types of profiles: standard profiles, unattached profiles, local profiles and hats. Standard and unattached profiles are stand-alone profiles, each stored in a file under `/etc/apparmor.d/`. Local profiles and hats are children profiles embedded inside of a parent profile used to provide tighter or alternate confinement for a subtask of an application.

21.2.1 Standard Profiles

The default AppArmor profile is attached to a program by its name, so a profile name must match the path to the application it is to confine.

```
/usr/bin/foo {
```

```
...
}
```

This profile will be automatically used whenever an unconfined process executes `/usr/bin/foo`.

21.2.2 Unattached Profiles

Unattached profiles do not reside in the file system namespace and therefore are not automatically attached to an application. The name of an unattached profile is preceded by the keyword `profile`. You can freely choose a profile name, except for the following limitations: the name must not begin with a `:` or `.` character. If it contains a whitespace, it must be quoted. If the name begins with a `/`, the profile is considered to be a standard profile, so the following two profiles are identical:

```
profile /usr/bin/foo {
...
}
/usr/bin/foo {
...
}
```

Unattached profiles are never used automatically, nor can they be transitioned to through a `Px` rule. They need to be attached to a program by either using a named profile transition (see *Section 21.8.7, "Named Profile Transitions"*) or with the `change_profile` rule (see *Section 21.2.5, "Change rules"*).

Unattached profiles are useful for specialized profiles for system utilities that generally should not be confined by a system-wide profile (for example, `/bin/bash`). They can also be used to set up roles or to confine a user.

21.2.3 Local Profiles

Local profiles provide a convenient way to provide specialized confinement for utility programs launched by a confined application. They are specified like standard profiles, except that they are embedded in a parent profile and begin with the `profile` keyword:

```
/parent/profile {
  ...
```

```
    profile /local/profile {
        ...
    }
}
```

To transition to a local profile, either use a `cx` rule (see *Section 21.8.2, "Discrete Local Profile Execute Mode (Cx)"*) or a named profile transition (see *Section 21.8.7, "Named Profile Transitions"*).

21.2.4   Hats

AppArmor "hats" are a local profiles with some additional restrictions and an implicit rule allowing for `change_hat` to be used to transition to them. Refer to *Chapter 25, Profiling Your Web Applications Using ChangeHat* for a detailed description.

21.2.5   Change rules

AppArmor provides `change_hat` and `change_profile` rules that control domain transitioning. `change_hat` are specified by defining hats in a profile, while `change_profile` rules refer to another profile and start with the keyword `change_profile`:

```
change_profile -> /usr/bin/foobar,
```

Both `change_hat` and `change_profile` provide for an application directed profile transition, without having to launch a separate application. `change_profile` provides a generic one way transition between any of the loaded profiles. `change_hat` provides for a returnable parent child transition where an application can switch from the parent profile to the hat profile and if it provides the correct secret key return to the parent profile at a later time.

`change_profile` is best used in situations where an application goes through a trusted setup phase and then can lower its privilege level. Any resources mapped or opened during the start-up phase may still be accessible after the profile change, but the new profile will restrict the opening of new resources, and will even limit some resources opened before the switch. Specifically, memory resources will still be available while capability and file resources (as long as they are not memory mapped) can be limited.

`change_hat` is best used in situations where an application runs a virtual machine or an interpreter that does not provide direct access to the applications resources (for example Apache's `mod_php`). Since `change_hat` stores the return secret key in the application's memory the phase of reduced privilege should not have direct access to memory. It is also important that file access is properly separated, since the hat can restrict accesses to a file handle but does not close it. If an application does buffering and provides access to the open files with buffering, the accesses to these files might not be seen by the kernel and hence not restricted by the new profile.

 Warning: Safety of Domain Transitions

> The `change_hat` and `change_profile` domain transitions are less secure than a domain transition done through an exec because they do not affect a process's memory mappings, nor do they close resources that have already been opened.

21.3   Include Statements

Include statements are directives that pull in components of other AppArmor profiles to simplify profiles. Include files retrieve access permissions for programs. By using an include, you can give the program access to directory paths or files that are also required by other programs. Using includes can reduce the size of a profile.

Include statements normally begin with a hash (`#`) sign. This is confusing because the same hash sign is used for comments inside profile files. Because of this, `#include` is treated as an include only if there is no preceding `#` (`##include` is a comment) and there is no whitespace between `#` and `include` (`# include` is a comment).

You can also use `include` without the leading `#`.

```
include "/etc/apparmor.d/abstractions/foo"
```

is the same as using

```
#include "/etc/apparmor.d/abstractions/foo"
```

 Note: No Trailing ','

> Note that because includes follow the C pre-processor syntax, they do not have a trailing ',' like most AppArmor rules.

By slight changes in syntax, you can modify the behavior of `include`. If you use `""` around the including path, you instruct the parser to do an absolute or relative path lookup.

```
include "/etc/apparmor.d/abstractions/foo"    # absolute path
```

```
include "abstractions/foo"   # relative path to the directory of current file
```

Note that when using relative path includes, when the file is included, it is considered the new current file for its includes. For example, suppose you are in the /etc/apparmor.d/bar file, then

```
include "abstractions/foo"
```

includes the file /etc/apparmor.d/abstractions/foo. If then there is

```
include "example"
```

inside the /etc/apparmor.d/abstractions/foo file, it includes /etc/apparmor.d/abstractions/example.

The use of <> specifies to try the include path (specified by -I, defaults to the /etc/apparmor.d directory) in an ordered way. So assuming the include path is

```
-I /etc/apparmor.d/ -I /usr/share/apparmor/
```

then the include statement

```
include <abstractions/foo>
```

will try /etc/apparmor.d/abstractions/foo, and if that file does not exist, the next try is /usr/share/apparmor/abstractions/foo.

 Tip

The default include path can be overridden manually by passing -I to the **apparmor_parser**, or by setting the include paths in /etc/apparmor/parser.conf:

```
Include /usr/share/apparmor/
Include /etc/apparmor.d/
```

Multiple entries are allowed, and they are taken in the same order as when they are when using -I or --Include from the **apparmor_parser** command line.

If an include ends with '/', this is considered a directory include, and all files within the directory are included.

To assist you in profiling your applications, AppArmor provides three classes of includes: abstractions, program chunks and tunables.

21.3.1 Abstractions

Abstractions are includes that are grouped by common application tasks. These tasks include access to authentication mechanisms, access to name service routines, common graphics requirements, and system accounting. Files listed in these abstractions are specific to the named task. Programs that require one of these files usually also require other files listed in the abstraction file (depending on the local configuration and the specific requirements of the program). Find abstractions in `/etc/apparmor.d/abstractions`.

21.3.2 Program Chunks

The program-chunks directory (`/etc/apparmor.d/program-chunks`) contains some chunks of profiles that are specific to program suites and not generally useful outside of the suite, thus are never suggested for use in profiles by the profile wizards (**aa-logprof** and **aa-genprof**). Currently, program chunks are only available for the postfix program suite.

21.3.3 Tunables

The tunables directory (`/etc/apparmor.d/tunables`) contains global variable definitions. When used in a profile, these variables expand to a value that can be changed without changing the entire profile. Add all the tunables definitions that should be available to every profile to `/etc/apparmor.d/tunables/global`.

21.4 Capability Entries (POSIX.1e)

Capability rules are simply the word `capability` followed by the name of the POSIX.1e capability as defined in the `capabilities(7)` man page. You can list multiple capabilities in a single rule, or grant all implemented capabilities with the bare keyword `capability`.

```
capability dac_override sys_admin,    # multiple capabilities
capability,                           # grant all capabilities
```

21.5 Network Access Control

AppArmor allows mediation of network access based on the address type and family. The following illustrates the network access rule syntax:

```
network [[<domain>❶][<type❷>][<protocol❸>]]
```

❶ Supported domains: `inet`, `ax25`, `ipx`, `appletalk`, `netrom`, `bridge`, `x25`, `inet6`, `rose`, `netbeui`, `security`, `key`, `packet`, `ash`, `econet`, `atmsvc`, `sna`, `irda`, `pppox`, `wanpipe`, `bluetooth`, `unix`, `atmpvc`, `netlink`, `llc`, `can`, `tipc`, `iucv`, `rxrpc`, `isdn`, `phonet`, `ieee802154`, `caif`, `alg`, `nfc`, `vsock`

❷ Supported types: `stream`, `dgram`, `seqpacket`, `rdm`, `raw`, `packet`

❸ Supported protocols: `tcp`, `udp`, `icmp`

The AppArmor tools support only family and type specification. The AppArmor module emits only `network DOMAIN TYPE` in "ACCESS DENIED" messages. And only these are output by the profile generation tools, both YaST and command line.

The following examples illustrate possible network-related rules to be used in AppArmor profiles. Note that the syntax of the last two are not currently supported by the AppArmor tools.

```
network❶,
network inet❷,
network inet6❸,
network inet stream❹,
network inet tcp❺,
network tcp❻,
```

❶ Allow all networking. No restrictions applied with regard to domain, type, or protocol.

❷ Allow general use of IPv4 networking.

❸ Allow general use of IPv6 networking.

❹ Allow the use of IPv4 TCP networking.

❺ Allow the use of IPv4 TCP networking, paraphrasing the rule above.

❻ Allow the use of both IPv4 and IPv6 TCP networking.

21.6 Profile Names, Flags, Paths, and Globbing

A profile is usually attached to a program by specifying a full path to the program's executable. For example in the case of a standard profile (see *Section 21.2.1, "Standard Profiles"*), the profile is defined by

```
/usr/bin/foo { ... }
```

The following sections describe several useful techniques that can be applied when naming a profile or putting a profile in the context of other existing ones, or specifying file paths.

AppArmor explicitly distinguishes directory path names from file path names. Use a trailing /for any directory path that needs to be explicitly distinguished:

/some/random/example/* r
> Allow read access to files in the /some/random/example directory.

/some/random/example/ r
> Allow read access to the directory only.

/some/**/ r
> Give read access to any directories below /some (but not /some/ itself).

/some/random/example/** r
> Give read access to files and directories under /some/random/example (but not /some/random/example/ itself).

/some/random/example/**[^/] r
> Give read access to files under /some/random/example. Explicitly exclude directories ([^/]).

Globbing (or regular expression matching) is when you modify the directory path using wild cards to include a group of files or subdirectories. File resources can be specified with a globbing syntax similar to that used by popular shells, such as csh, Bash, and zsh.

*	Substitutes for any number of any characters, except / . Example: An arbitrary number of file path elements.

**	Substitutes for any number of characters, including /. Example: An arbitrary number of path elements, including entire directories.
?	Substitutes for any single character, except /.
[abc]	Substitutes for the single character a, b, or c. Example: a rule that matches /home[01]/*/.plan allows a program to access .plan files for users in both /home0 and /home1.
[a-c]	Substitutes for the single character a, b, or c.
{ab,cd}	Expands to one rule to match ab and one rule to match cd. Example: a rule that matches /{usr,www}/pages/** grants access to Web pages in both /usr/pages and /www/pages.
[^a]	Substitutes for any character except a.

21.6.1 Profile Flags

Profile flags control the behavior of the related profile. You can add profile flags to the profile definition by editing it manually, see the following syntax:

```
/path/to/profiled/binary flags=(list_of_flags) {
  [...]
}
```

You can use multiple flags separated by a comma ',' or space ' '. There are three basic types of profile flags: mode, relative, and attach flags.

Mode flag is `complain` (illegal accesses are allowed and logged). If it is omitted, the profile is in `enforce` mode (enforces the policy).

 Tip

> A more flexible way of setting the whole profile into complain mode is to create a symbolic link from the profile file inside the `/etc/apparmor.d/force-complain/` directory.

```
ln -s /etc/apparmor.d/bin.ping /etc/apparmor.d/force-complain/bin.ping
```

Relative flags are `chroot_relative` (states that the profile is relative to the chroot instead of namespace) or `namespace_relative` (the default, with the path being relative to outside the chroot). They are mutually exclusive.

Attach flags consist of two pairs of mutually exclusive flags: `attach_disconnected` or `no_attach_disconnected` (determine if path names resolved to be outside of the namespace are attached to the root, which means they have the '/' character at the beginning), and `chroot_attach` or `chroot_no_attach` (control path name generation when in a chroot environment while a file is accessed that is external to the chroot but within the namespace).

21.6.2 Using Variables in Profiles

AppArmor allows to use variables holding paths in profiles. Use global variables to make your profiles portable and local variables to create shortcuts for paths.

A typical example of when global variables come in handy are network scenarios in which user home directories are mounted in different locations. Instead of rewriting paths to home directories in all affected profiles, you only need to change the value of a variable. Global variables are defined under `/etc/apparmor.d/tunables` and need to be made available via an include statement. Find the variable definitions for this use case (`@{HOME}` and `@{HOMEDIRS}`) in the `/etc/apparmor.d/tunables/home` file.

Local variables are defined at the head of a profile. This is useful to provide the base of for a chrooted path, for example:

```
@{CHROOT_BASE}=/tmp/foo
/sbin/rsyslogd {
...
# chrooted applications
```

```
@{CHROOT_BASE}/var/lib/*/dev/log w,
@{CHROOT_BASE}/var/log/** w,
...
}
```

In the following example, while @{HOMEDIRS} lists where all the user home directories are stored, @{HOME} is a space-separated list of home directories. Later on, @{HOMEDIRS} is expanded by two new specific places where user home directories are stored.

```
@{HOMEDIRS}=/home/
@{HOME}=@{HOMEDIRS}/*/ /root/
[...]
@{HOMEDIRS}+=/srv/nfs/home/ /mnt/home/
```

 Note

> With the current AppArmor tools, variables can only be used when manually editing and maintaining a profile.

21.6.3   Pattern Matching

Profile names can contain globbing expressions allowing the profile to match against multiple binaries.

The following example is valid for systems where the **foo** binary resides either in /usr/bin or /bin.

```
/{usr/,}bin/foo { ... }
```

In the following example, when matching against the executable /bin/foo, the /bin/foo profile is an exact match so it is chosen. For the executable /bin/fat, the profile /bin/foo does not match, and because the /bin/f* profile is more specific (less general) than /bin/**, the /bin/f* profile is chosen.

```
/bin/foo { ... }

/bin/f*  { ... }

/bin/**  { ... }
```

For more information on profile name globbing examples, see the man page of AppArmor, **man 5 apparmor.d,**, section Globbing.

21.6.4 Namespaces

Namespaces are used to provide different profiles sets. Say one for the system, another for a chroot environment or container. Namespaces are hierarchical—a namespace can see its children but a child cannot see its parent. Namespace names start with a colon `:` followed by an alphanumeric string, a trailing colon `:` and an optional double slash `//`, such as

```
:childNameSpace://
```

Profiles loaded to a child namespace will be prefixed with their namespace name (viewed from a parent's perspective):

```
:childNameSpace://apache
```

Namespaces can be entered via the `change_profile` API, or named profile transitions:

```
/path/to/executable px -> :childNameSpace://apache
```

21.6.5 Profile Naming and Attachment Specification

Profiles can have a name, and an attachment specification. This allows for profiles with a logical name that can be more meaningful to users/administrators than a profile name that contains pattern matching (see *Section 21.6.3, "Pattern Matching"*). For example, the default profile

```
/** { ... }
```

can be named

```
profile default /** { ... }
```

Also, a profile with pattern matching can be named. For example:

```
/usr/lib/firefox-3.*/firefox-*bin { ... }
```

can be named

```
profile firefox /usr/lib/firefox-3.*/firefox-*bin { ... }
```

21.6.6 Alias Rules

Alias rules provide an alternative way to manipulate profile path mappings to site specific layouts. They are an alternative form of path rewriting to using variables, and are done post variable resolution. The alias rule says to treat rules that have the same source prefix as if the rules are at target prefix.

```
alias /home/ -> /usr/home/
```

All the rules that have a prefix match to /home/ will provide access to /usr/home/. For example

```
/home/username/** r,
```

allows as well access to

```
/usr/home/username/** r,
```

Aliases provide a quick way of remapping rules without the need to rewrite them. They keep the source path still accessible—in our example, the alias rule keeps the paths under /home/ still accessible.

With the alias rule, you can point to multiple targets at the same time.

```
alias /home/ -> /usr/home/
alias /home/ -> /mnt/home/
```

 Note

> With the current AppArmor tools, alias rules can only be used when manually editing and maintaining a profile.

 Tip

> Insert global alias definitions in the file /etc/apparmor.d/tunables/alias.

21.7 File Permission Access Modes

File permission access modes consist of combinations of the following modes:

r	Read mode

w	Write mode (mutually exclusive to a)
a	Append mode (mutually exclusive to w)
k	File locking mode
l	Link mode
link FILE -> TARGET	Link pair rule (cannot be combined with other access modes)

21.7.1 Read Mode (r)

Allows the program to have read access to the resource. Read access is required for shell scripts and other interpreted content and determines if an executing process can core dump.

21.7.2 Write Mode (w)

Allows the program to have write access to the resource. Files must have this permission if they are to be unlinked (removed).

21.7.3 Append Mode (a)

Allows a program to write to the end of a file. In contrast to the w mode, the append mode does not include the ability to overwrite data, to rename, or to remove a file. The append permission is typically used with applications who need to be able to write to log files, but which should not be able to manipulate any existing data in the log files. As the append permission is a subset of the permissions associated with the write mode, the w and a permission flags cannot be used together and are mutually exclusive.

21.7.4 File Locking Mode (k)

The application can take file locks. Former versions of AppArmor allowed files to be locked if an application had access to them. By using a separate file locking mode, AppArmor makes sure locking is restricted only to those files which need file locking and tightens security as locking can be used in several denial of service attack scenarios.

21.7.5 Link Mode (l)

The link mode mediates access to hard links. When a link is created, the target file must have the same access permissions as the link created (but the destination does not need link access).

21.7.6 Link Pair

The link mode grants permission to link to arbitrary files, provided the link has a subset of the permissions granted by the target (subset permission test).

```
/srv/www/htdocs/index.html rl,
```

By specifying origin and destination, the link pair rule provides greater control over how hard links are created. Link pair rules by default do not enforce the link subset permission test that the standard rules link permission requires.

```
link /srv/www/htdocs/index.html -> /var/www/index.html
```

To force the rule to require the test, the subset keyword is used. The following rules are equivalent:

```
/var/www/index.html l,
link subset /var/www/index.html -> /**,
```

 Note

> Currently link pair rules are not supported by YaST and the command line tools. Manually edit your profiles to use them. Updating such profiles using the tools is safe, because the link pair entries will not be touched.

21.7.7 Optional allow and file Rules

The allow prefix is optional, and it is idiomatically implied if not specified and the deny (see *Section 21.7.9, "Deny Rules"*) keyword is not used.

```
allow file /example r,
allow /example r,
allow network,
```

You can also use the optional file keyword. If you omit it and there are no other rule types that start with a keyword, such as network or mount, it is automatically implied.

```
file /example/rule r,
```

is equivalent to

```
/example/rule r,
```

The following rule grants access to all files:

```
file,
```

which is equal to

```
/** rwmlk,
```

File rules can use leading or trailing permissions. The permissions should not be specified as a trailing permission, but rather used at the start of the rule. This is important in that it makes file rules behave like any other rule types.

```
/path rw,              # old style
rw /path,              # leading permission
file rw /path,         # with explicit 'file' keyword
allow file rw /path,   # optional 'allow' keyword added
```

21.7.8 Owner Conditional Rules

The file rules can be extended so that they can be conditional upon the user being the owner of the file (the fsuid needs to match the file's uid). For this purpose the owner keyword is put in front of the rule. Owner conditional rules accumulate like regular file rules do.

```
owner /home/*/** rw
```

When using file ownership conditions with link rules the ownership test is done against the target file so the user must own the file to be able to link to it.

 Note: Precedence of Regular File Rules

Owner conditional rules are considered a subset of regular file rules. If a regular file rule overlaps with an owner conditional file rule, the rules are merged. Consider the following example.

```
/foo r,
owner /foo rw,   # or w,
```

The rules are merged—it results in r for everybody, and w for the owner only.

Tip

To address everybody *but* the owner of the file, use the keyword `other`.

```
owner /foo rw,
other /foo r,
```

21.7.9   Deny Rules

Deny rules can be used to annotate or quiet known rejects. The profile generating tools will not ask about a known reject treated with a deny rule. Such a reject will also not show up in the audit logs when denied, keeping the log files lean. If this is not desired, put the keyword `audit` in front of the deny entry.

It is also possible to use deny rules in combination with allow rules. This allows you to specify a broad allow rule, and then subtract a few known files that should not be allowed. Deny rules can also be combined with owner rules, to deny files owned by the user. The following example allows read/write access to everything in a users directory except write access to the `.ssh/` files:

```
deny /home/*/.ssh/** w,
owner /home/*/** rw,
```

The extensive use of deny rules is generally not encouraged, because it makes it much harder to understand what a profile does. However a judicious use of deny rules can simplify profiles. Therefore the tools only generate profiles denying specific files and will not use globbing in deny rules. Manually edit your profiles to add deny rules using globbing. Updating such profiles using the tools is safe, because the deny entries will not be touched.

21.8   Execute Modes

Execute modes, also named profile transitions, consist of the following modes:

Px	Discrete profile execute mode
Cx	Discrete local profile execute mode
Ux	Unconfined execute mode

ix	Inherit execute mode
m	Allow `PROT_EXEC` with **`mmap(2)`** calls

21.8.1 Discrete Profile Execute Mode (Px)

This mode requires that a discrete security profile is defined for a resource executed at an AppArmor domain transition. If there is no profile defined, the access is denied.

Incompatible with `Ux`, `ux`, `px`, and `ix`.

21.8.2 Discrete Local Profile Execute Mode (Cx)

As `Px`, but instead of searching the global profile set, `Cx` only searches the local profiles of the current profile. This profile transition provides a way for an application to have alternate profiles for helper applications.

 Note: Limitations of the Discrete Local Profile Execute Mode (Cx)

Currently, Cx transitions are limited to top level profiles and cannot be used in hats and children profiles. This restriction will be removed in the future.

Incompatible with `Ux`, `ux`, `Px`, `px`, `cx`, and `ix`.

21.8.3 Unconfined Execute Mode (Ux)

Allows the program to execute the resource without any AppArmor profile applied to the executed resource. This mode is useful when a confined program needs to be able to perform a privileged operation, such as rebooting the machine. By placing the privileged section in another executable and granting unconfined execution rights, it is possible to bypass the mandatory constraints imposed on all confined processes. Allowing a root process to go unconfined means it can change AppArmor policy itself. For more information about what is constrained, see the `apparmor(7)` man page.

This mode is incompatible with `ux`, `px`, `Px`, and `ix`.

21.8.4 Unsafe Exec Modes

Use the lowercase versions of exec modes—px, cx, ux —only in very special cases. They do not scrub the environment of variables such as LD_PRELOAD. As a result, the calling domain may have an undue amount of influence over the called resource. Use these modes only if the child absolutely *must* be run unconfined and LD_PRELOAD must be used. Any profile using such modes provides negligible security. Use at your own risk.

21.8.5 Inherit Execute Mode (ix)

ix prevents the normal AppArmor domain transition on **execve(2)** when the profiled program executes the named program. Instead, the executed resource inherits the current profile.

This mode is useful when a confined program needs to call another confined program without gaining the permissions of the target's profile or losing the permissions of the current profile. There is no version to scrub the environment because ix executions do not change privileges.

Incompatible with cx, ux, and px. Implies m.

21.8.6 Allow Executable Mapping (m)

This mode allows a file to be mapped into memory using **mmap(2)** 's PROT_EXEC flag. This flag marks the pages executable. It is used on some architectures to provide non executable data pages, which can complicate exploit attempts. AppArmor uses this mode to limit which files a well-behaved program (or all programs on architectures that enforce non executable memory access controls) may use as libraries, to limit the effect of invalid -L flags given to **ld(1)** and LD_PRELOAD, LD_LIBRARY_PATH, given to **ld.so(8)**.

21.8.7 Named Profile Transitions

By default, the px and cx (and their clean exec variants, too) transition to a profile whose name matches the executable name. With named profile transitions, you can specify a profile to be transitioned to. This is useful if multiple binaries need to share a single profile, or if they need to use a different profile than their name would specify. Named profile transitions can be used with cx, Cx, px and Px. Currently there is a limit of twelve named profile transitions per profile.

Named profile transitions use `->` to indicate the name of the profile that needs to be transitioned to:

```
/usr/bin/foo
{
  /bin/** px -> shared_profile,
  ...
  /usr/*bash cx -> local_profile,
  ...
  profile local_profile
  {
    ...
  }
}
```

Note: Difference Between Normal and Named Transitions

When used with globbing, normal transitions provide a "one to many" relationship—`/bin/** px` will transition to `/bin/ping`, `/bin/cat`, etc, depending on the program being run.

Named transitions provide a "many to one" relationship—all programs that match the rule regardless of their name will transition to the specified profile.

Named profile transitions show up in the log as having the mode `Nx`. The name of the profile to be changed to is listed in the `name2` field.

21.8.8 Fallback Modes for Profile Transitions

The `px` and `cx` transitions specify a hard dependency—if the specified profile does not exist, the exec will fail. With the inheritance fallback, the execution will succeed but inherit the current profile. To specify inheritance fallback, `ix` is combined with `cx`, `Cx`, `px` and `Px` into the modes `cix`, `Cix`, `pix` and `Pix`.

```
/path Cix -> profile_name,
```

or

```
Cix /path -> profile_name,
```

where `-> profile_name` is optional.

The same applies if you add the unconfined `ux` mode, where the resulting modes are `cux`, `CUx`, `pux` and `PUx`. These modes allow falling back to "unconfined" when the specified profile is not found.

```
/path PUx -> profile_name,
```

or

```
PUx /path -> profile_name,
```

where `-> profile_name` is optional.

The fallback modes can be used with named profile transitions, too.

21.8.9 Variable Settings in Execution Modes

When choosing one of the Px, Cx or Ux execution modes, take into account that the following environment variables are removed from the environment before the child process inherits it. As a consequence, applications or processes relying on any of these variables do not work anymore if the profile applied to them carries Px, Cx or Ux flags:

- `GCONV_PATH`

- `GETCONF_DIR`

- `HOSTALIASES`

- `LD_AUDIT`

- `LD_DEBUG`

- `LD_DEBUG_OUTPUT`

- `LD_DYNAMIC_WEAK`

- `LD_LIBRARY_PATH`

- `LD_ORIGIN_PATH`

- `LD_PRELOAD`

- `LD_PROFILE`

- `LD_SHOW_AUXV`

- `LD_USE_LOAD_BIAS`

- `LOCALDOMAIN`

- `LOCPATH`

- `MALLOC_TRACE`

- `NLSPATH`

- `RESOLV_HOST_CONF`

- `RES_OPTIONS`

- `TMPDIR`

- `TZDIR`

21.8.10 safe and unsafe Keywords

You can use the `safe` and `unsafe` keywords for rules instead of using the case modifier of execution modes. For example

```
/example_rule Px,
```

is the same as any of the following

```
safe /example_rule px,
safe /example_rule Px,
safe px /example_rule,
safe Px /example_rule,
```

and the rule

```
/example_rule px,
```

is the same as any of

```
unsafe /example_rule px,
unsafe /example_rule Px,
unsafe px /example_rule,
unsafe Px /example_rule,
```

The `safe`/`unsafe` keywords are mutually exclusive and can be used in a file rule after the `owner` keyword, so the order of rule keywords is

```
[audit] [deny] [owner] [safe|unsafe] file_rule
```

21.9 Resource Limit Control

AppArmor can set and control an application's resource limits (rlimits, also known as ulimits). By default, AppArmor does not control application's rlimits, and it will only control those limits specified in the confining profile. For more information about resource limits, refer to the `setrlimit(2)`, `ulimit(1)`, or `ulimit(3)` man pages.

AppArmor leverages the system's rlimits and as such does not provide an additional auditing that would normally occur. It also cannot raise rlimits set by the system, AppArmor rlimits can only reduce an application's current resource limits.

The values will be inherited by the children of a process and will remain even if a new profile is transitioned to or the application becomes unconfined. So when an application transitions to a new profile, that profile can further reduce the application's rlimits.

AppArmor's rlimit rules will also provide mediation of setting an application's hard limits, should it try to raise them. The application cannot raise its hard limits any further than specified in the profile. The mediation of raising hard limits is not inherited as the set value is, so that when the application transitions to a new profile it is free to raise its limits as specified in the profile.

AppArmor's rlimit control does not affect an application's soft limits beyond ensuring that they are less than or equal to the application's hard limits.

AppArmor's hard limit rules have the general form of:

```
set rlimit RESOURCE <= value,
```

where *RESOURCE* and *VALUE* are to be replaced with the following values:

`cpu`

> CPU time limit in seconds.

`fsize`, `data`, `stack`, `core`, `rss`, `as`, `memlock`, `msgqueue`

> a number in bytes, or a number with a suffix where the suffix can be K/KB (kilobytes), M/MB (megabytes), G/GB (gigabytes), for example

```
rlimit data <= 100M,
```

`fsize`, `nofile`, `locks`, `sigpending`, `nproc`[*], `rtprio`

> a number greater or equal to 0

`nice`

> a value between -20 and 19

*The nproc rlimit is handled different than all the other rlimits. Instead of indicating the standard process rlimit it controls the maximum number of processes that can be running under the profile at any time. When the limit is exceeded the creation of new processes under the profile will fail until the number of currently running processes is reduced.

 Note

> Currently the tools cannot be used to add rlimit rules to profiles. The only way to add rlimit controls to a profile is to manually edit the profile with a text editor. The tools will still work with profiles containing rlimit rules and will not remove them, so it is safe to use the tools to update profiles containing them.

21.10   Auditing Rules

AppArmor provides the ability to audit given rules so that when they are matched an audit message will appear in the audit log. To enable audit messages for a given rule, the `audit` keyword is put in front of the rule:

```
audit /etc/foo/*          rw,
```

If it is desirable to audit only a given permission the rule can be split into two rules. The following example will result in audit messages when files are opened for writing, but not when they are opened for reading:

```
audit /etc/foo/*   w,
/etc/foo/*          r,
```

 Note

> Audit messages are not generated for every read or write of a file but only when a file is opened for reading or writing.

Audit control can be combined with `owner`/`other` conditional file rules to provide auditing when users access files they own/do not own:

```
audit owner /home/*/.ssh/**     rw,
audit other /home/*/.ssh/**     r,
```

22 AppArmor Profile Repositories

AppArmor ships with a set of profiles enabled by default. These are created by the AppArmor developers, and are stored in `/etc/apparmor.d`. In addition to these profiles, SUSE Linux Enterprise Server ships profiles for individual applications together with the relevant application. These profiles are not enabled by default, and reside under another directory than the standard AppArmor profiles, `/etc/apparmor/profiles/extras`.

The AppArmor tools (YaST, **aa-genprof** and **aa-logprof**) support the use of a local repository. Whenever you start to create a new profile from scratch, and there already is an inactive profile in your local repository, you are asked whether you want to use the existing inactive one from `/etc/apparmor/profiles/extras` and whether you want to base your efforts on it. If you decide to use this profile, it gets copied over to the directory of profiles enabled by default (`/etc/apparmor.d`) and loaded whenever AppArmor is started. Any further adjustments will be done to the active profile under `/etc/apparmor.d`.

23 Building and Managing Profiles with YaST

YaST provides a basic way to build profiles and manage AppArmor® profiles. It provides two interfaces: a graphical one and a text-based one. The text-based interface consumes less resources and bandwidth, making it a better choice for remote administration, or for times when a local graphical environment is inconvenient. Although the interfaces have differing appearances, they offer the same functionality in similar ways. Another alternative is to use AppArmor commands, which can control AppArmor from a terminal window or through remote connections. The command line tools are described in *Chapter 24, Building Profiles from the Command Line*.

Start YaST from the main menu and enter your `root` password when prompted for it. Alternatively, start YaST by opening a terminal window, logging in as `root`, and entering **yast2** for the graphical mode or **yast** for the text-based mode.

In the *Security and Users* section, there is an *AppArmor Configuration* icon. Click it to launch the AppArmor YaST module.

23.1 Manually Adding a Profile

AppArmor enables you to create an AppArmor profile by manually adding entries into the profile. Select the application for which to create a profile, then add entries.

1. Start YaST, select *AppArmor Configuration*, and click *Manually Add Profile* in the main window.

2. Browse your system to find the application for which to create a profile.

3. When you find the application, select it and click *Open*. A basic, empty profile appears in the *AppArmor Profile Dialog* window.

4. In *AppArmor Profile Dialog*, add, edit, or delete AppArmor profile entries by clicking the corresponding buttons and referring to *Section 23.2.1, "Adding an Entry"*, *Section 23.2.2, "Editing an Entry"*, or *Section 23.2.3, "Deleting an Entry"*.

5. When finished, click *Done*.

23.2 Editing Profiles

 Tip

> YaST offers basic manipulation for AppArmor profiles, such as creating or editing. However, the most straightforward way to edit an AppArmor profile is to use a text editor such as **vi**:

```
root # vi /etc/apparmor.d/usr.sbin.httpd2-prefork
```

 Tip

> The **vi** editor also includes syntax (error) highlighting and syntax error highlighting, which visually warns you when the syntax of the edited AppArmor profile is wrong.

AppArmor enables you to edit AppArmor profiles manually by adding, editing, or deleting entries. To edit a profile, proceed as follows:

1. Start YaST, select *AppArmor Configuration*, and click *Manage Existing Profiles* in the main window.

Edit Profile - Choose profile to edit

Profile Name

/sbin/klogd
/sbin/syslog-ng
/sbin/syslogd
/usr/lib/apache2/mpm-prefork/apache2
/usr/lib/dovecot/anvil
/usr/lib/dovecot/auth
/usr/lib/dovecot/config
/usr/lib/dovecot/deliver
/usr/lib/dovecot/dict
/usr/lib/dovecot/dovecot-auth
/usr/lib/dovecot/dovecot-lda
/usr/lib/dovecot/imap
/usr/lib/dovecot/imap-login
/usr/lib/dovecot/lmtp
/usr/lib/dovecot/log
/usr/lib/dovecot/managesieve

Edit   Delete

Help   Abort   Back   Next

2. From the list of profiled applications, select the profile to edit.

3. Click *Edit*. The *AppArmor Profile Dialog* window displays the profile.

4. In the *AppArmor Profile Dialog* window, add, edit, or delete AppArmor profile entries by clicking the corresponding buttons and referring to *Section 23.2.1, "Adding an Entry"*, *Section 23.2.2, "Editing an Entry"*, **or** *Section 23.2.3, "Deleting an Entry"*.

5. When you are finished, click *Done*.

6. In the pop-up that appears, click *Yes* to confirm your changes to the profile and reload the AppArmor profile set.

 Tip: Syntax Checking in AppArmor

> AppArmor contains a syntax check that notifies you of any syntax errors in profiles you are trying to process with the YaST AppArmor tools. If an error occurs, edit the profile manually as `root` and reload the profile set with `systemctl reload apparmor`.

23.2.1 Adding an Entry

The *Add Entry* button in the *AppArmor Profile Window* lists types of entries you can add to the AppArmor profile.

From the list, select one of the following:

File

> In the pop-up window, specify the absolute path of a file, including the type of access permitted. When finished, click *OK*.
>
> You can use globbing if necessary. For globbing information, refer to *Section 21.6, "Profile Names, Flags, Paths, and Globbing"*. For file access permission information, refer to *Section 21.7, "File Permission Access Modes"*.

Directory

> In the pop-up window, specify the absolute path of a directory, including the type of access permitted. You can use globbing if necessary. When finished, click *OK*.
>
> For globbing information, refer to *Section 21.6, "Profile Names, Flags, Paths, and Globbing"*. For file access permission information, refer to *Section 21.7, "File Permission Access Modes"*.

Network Rule

In the pop-up window, select the appropriate network family and the socket type. For more information, refer to *Section 21.5, "Network Access Control"*.

Capability

In the pop-up window, select the appropriate capabilities. These are statements that enable each of the 32 POSIX.1e capabilities. Refer to *Section 21.4, "Capability Entries (POSIX.1e)"* for more information about capabilities. When finished making your selections, click *OK*.

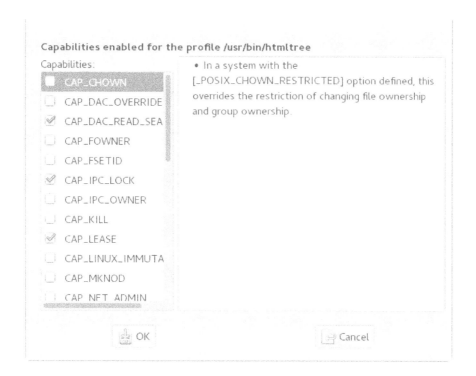

Include File

> In the pop-up window, browse to the files to use as includes. Includes are directives that pull in components of other AppArmor profiles to simplify profiles. For more information, refer to *Section 21.3, "Include Statements"*.

Hat

> In the pop-up window, specify the name of the subprofile (*hat*) to add to your current profile and click *Create Hat*. For more information, refer to *Chapter 25, Profiling Your Web Applications Using ChangeHat*.

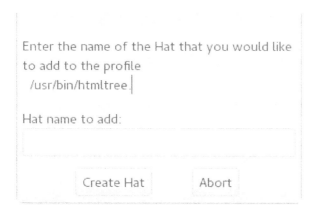

23.2.2   Editing an Entry

When you select *Edit Entry*, a pop-up window opens. From here, edit the selected entry.

In the pop-up window, edit the entry you need to modify. You can use globbing if necessary. When finished, click *OK*.

For globbing information, refer to *Section 21.6, "Profile Names, Flags, Paths, and Globbing"*. For access permission information, refer to *Section 21.7, "File Permission Access Modes"*.

23.2.3   Deleting an Entry

To delete an entry in a given profile, select *Delete Entry*. AppArmor removes the selected profile entry.

23.3   Deleting a Profile

AppArmor enables you to delete an AppArmor profile manually. Simply select the application for which to delete a profile then delete it as follows:

1. Start YaST, select *AppArmor Configuration*, and click *Manage Existing Profiles* in the main window.

2. Select the profile to delete.

3. Click *Delete*.

4. In the pop-up that opens, click *Yes* to delete the profile and reload the AppArmor profile set.

23.4   Managing AppArmor

You can change the status of AppArmor by enabling or disabling it. Enabling AppArmor protects your system from potential program exploitation. Disabling AppArmor, even if your profiles have been set up, removes protection from your system. To change the status of AppArmor, start YaST, select *AppArmor Configuration*, and click *Settings* in the main window.

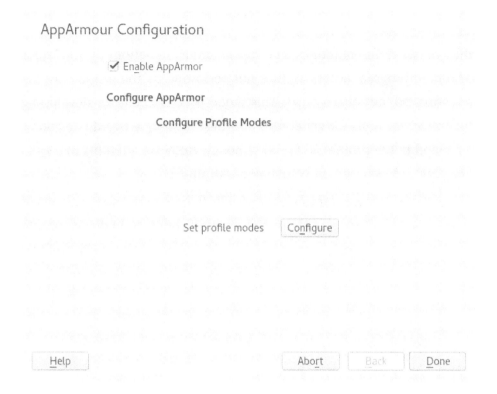

AppArmour Configuration

☑ Enable AppArmor

Configure AppArmor

Configure Profile Modes

Set profile modes   Configure

Help   Abort   Back   Done

To change the status of AppArmor, continue as described in *Section 23.4.1, "Changing AppArmor Status"*. To change the mode of individual profiles, continue as described in *Section 23.4.2, "Changing the Mode of Individual Profiles"*.

23.4.1   Changing AppArmor Status

When you change the status of AppArmor, set it to enabled or disabled. When AppArmor is enabled, it is installed, running, and enforcing the AppArmor security policies.

1. Start YaST, select *AppArmor Configuration*, and click *Settings* in the main window.

2. Enable AppArmor by checking *Enable AppArmor* or disable AppArmor by deselecting it.

3. Click *Done* in the *AppArmor Configuration* window.

 Tip

You always need to restart running programs to apply the profiles to them.

23.4.2 Changing the Mode of Individual Profiles

AppArmor can apply profiles in two different modes. In *complain* mode, violations of AppArmor profile rules, such as the profiled program accessing files not permitted by the profile, are detected. The violations are permitted, but also logged. This mode is convenient for developing profiles and is used by the AppArmor tools for generating profiles. Loading a profile in *enforce* mode enforces the policy defined in the profile, and reports policy violation attempts to `rsyslogd` (or `auditd` or `journalctl`, depending on system configuration).

The *Profile Mode Configuration* dialog allows you to view and edit the mode of currently loaded AppArmor profiles. This feature is useful for determining the status of your system during profile development. During systemic profiling (see *Section 24.6.2, "Systemic Profiling"*), you can use this tool to adjust and monitor the scope of the profiles for which you are learning behavior.

To edit an application's profile mode, proceed as follows:

1. Start YaST, select *AppArmor Configuration*, and click *Settings* in the main window.

2. In the *Configure Profile Modes* section, select *Configure*.

3. Select the profile for which to change the mode.

4. Select *Toggle Mode* to set this profile to *complain* mode or to *enforce* mode.

5. Apply your settings and leave YaST with *Done*.

To change the mode of all profiles, use *Set All to Enforce* or *Set All to Complain*.

 Tip: Listing the Profiles Available

By default, only active profiles are listed (any profile that has a matching application installed on your system). To set up a profile before installing the respective application, click *Show All Profiles* and select the profile to configure from the list that appears.

24 Building Profiles from the Command Line

AppArmor® provides the user the ability to use a command line interface rather than a graphical interface to manage and configure the system security. Track the status of AppArmor and create, delete, or modify AppArmor profiles using the AppArmor command line tools.

 Tip: Background Information

> Before starting to manage your profiles using the AppArmor command line tools, check out the general introduction to AppArmor given in *Chapter 20, Immunizing Programs* and *Chapter 21, Profile Components and Syntax*.

24.1 Checking the AppArmor Status

AppArmor can be in any one of three states:

Unloaded

> AppArmor is not activated in the kernel.

Running

> AppArmor is activated in the kernel and is enforcing AppArmor program policies.

Stopped

> AppArmor is activated in the kernel, but no policies are enforced.

Detect the state of AppArmor by inspecting `/sys/kernel/security/apparmor/profiles`. If `cat /sys/kernel/security/apparmor/profiles` reports a list of profiles, AppArmor is running. If it is empty and returns nothing, AppArmor is stopped. If the file does not exist, AppArmor is unloaded.

Manage AppArmor with `systemctl`. It lets you perform the following operations:

`sudo systemctl start apparmor`

> Behavior depends on the state of AppArmor. If it is not activated, `start` activates and starts it, putting it in the running state. If it is stopped, `start` causes the re-scan of AppArmor profiles usually found in `/etc/apparmor.d` and puts AppArmor in the running state. If AppArmor is already running, `start` reports a warning and takes no action.

Note: Already Running Processes

Already running processes need to be restarted to apply the AppArmor profiles on them.

`sudo systemctl stop apparmor`

Stops AppArmor if it is running by removing all profiles from kernel memory, effectively disabling all access controls, and putting AppArmor into the stopped state. If the AppArmor is already stopped, `stop` tries to unload the profiles again, but nothing happens.

`sudo systemctl reload apparmor`

Causes the AppArmor module to re-scan the profiles in `/etc/apparmor.d` without unconfining running processes. Freshly created profiles are enforced and recently deleted ones are removed from the `/etc/apparmor.d` directory.

24.2   Building AppArmor Profiles

The AppArmor module profile definitions are stored in the `/etc/apparmor.d` directory as plain text files. For a detailed description of the syntax of these files, refer to *Chapter 21, Profile Components and Syntax*.

All files in the `/etc/apparmor.d` directory are interpreted as profiles and are loaded as such. Renaming files in that directory is not an effective way of preventing profiles from being loaded. You must remove profiles from this directory to prevent them from being read and evaluated effectively, or call **aa-disable** on the profile, which will create a symbolic link in `/etc/apparmor.d/disabled/`.

You can use a text editor, such as **vi**, to access and make changes to these profiles. The following sections contain detailed steps for building profiles:

Adding or Creating AppArmor Profiles

Refer to *Section 24.3, "Adding or Creating an AppArmor Profile"*

Editing AppArmor Profiles

Refer to *Section 24.4, "Editing an AppArmor Profile"*

Deleting AppArmor Profiles

Refer to *Section 24.5, "Deleting an AppArmor Profile"*

24.3 Adding or Creating an AppArmor Profile

To add or create an AppArmor profile for an application, you can use a systemic or stand-alone profiling method, depending on your needs. Learn more about these two approaches in *Section 24.6, "Two Methods of Profiling"*.

24.4 Editing an AppArmor Profile

The following steps describe the procedure for editing an AppArmor profile:

1. If you are not currently logged in as `root`, enter **su** in a terminal window.

2. Enter the `root` password when prompted.

3. Go to the profile directory with **cd /etc/apparmor.d/**.

4. Enter **ls** to view all profiles currently installed.

5. Open the profile to edit in a text editor, such as vim.

6. Make the necessary changes, then save the profile.

7. Restart AppArmor by entering **systemctl reload apparmor** in a terminal window.

24.5 Deleting an AppArmor Profile

The following steps describe the procedure for deleting an AppArmor profile.

1. If you are not currently logged in as `root`, enter **su** in a terminal window.

2. Enter the `root` password when prompted.

3. Go to the AppArmor directory with **cd /etc/apparmor.d/**.

4. Enter **ls** to view all the AppArmor profiles that are currently installed.

5. Delete the profile with **rm** *PROFILENAME*.

6. Restart AppArmor by entering **systemctl reload apparmor** in a terminal window.

24.6 Two Methods of Profiling

Given the syntax for AppArmor profiles in *Chapter 21, Profile Components and Syntax*, you could create profiles without using the tools. However, the effort involved would be substantial. To avoid such a situation, use the AppArmor tools to automate the creation and refinement of profiles.

There are two ways to approach AppArmor profile creation. Tools are available for both methods.

Stand-Alone Profiling

A method suitable for profiling small applications that have a finite runtime, such as user client applications like mail clients. For more information, refer to *Section 24.6.1, "Stand-Alone Profiling"*.

Systemic Profiling

A method suitable for profiling many programs at once and for profiling applications that may run for days, weeks, or continuously across reboots, such as network server applications like Web servers and mail servers. For more information, refer to *Section 24.6.2, "Systemic Profiling"*.

Automated profile development becomes more manageable with the AppArmor tools:

1. Decide which profiling method suits your needs.

2. Perform a static analysis. Run either **aa-genprof** or **aa-autodep**, depending on the profiling method chosen.

3. Enable dynamic learning. Activate learning mode for all profiled programs.

24.6.1 Stand-Alone Profiling

Stand-alone profile generation and improvement is managed by a program called **aa-genprof**. This method is easy because **aa-genprof** takes care of everything, but is limited because it requires **aa-genprof** to run for the entire duration of the test run of your program (you cannot reboot the machine while you are still developing your profile).

To use **aa-genprof** for the stand-alone method of profiling, refer to *Section 24.6.3.8, "aa-genprof— Generating Profiles"*.

24.6.2 Systemic Profiling

This method is called *systemic profiling* because it updates all of the profiles on the system at once, rather than focusing on the one or few targeted by **aa-genprof** or stand-alone profiling. With systemic profiling, profile construction and improvement are somewhat less automated, but more flexible. This method is suitable for profiling long-running applications whose behavior continues after rebooting, or many programs at once.

Build an AppArmor profile for a group of applications as follows:

1. Create profiles for the individual programs that make up your application.

   Although this approach is systemic, AppArmor only monitors those programs with profiles and their children. To get AppArmor to consider a program, you must at least have **aa-autodep** create an approximate profile for it. To create this approximate profile, refer to *Section 24.6.3.1, "aa-autodep—Creating Approximate Profiles"*.

2. Put relevant profiles into learning or complain mode.

   Activate learning or complain mode for all profiled programs by entering

   ```
   aa-complain /etc/apparmor.d/*
   ```

   in a terminal window while logged in as `root`. This functionality is also available through the YaST Profile Mode module, described in *Section 23.4.2, "Changing the Mode of Individual Profiles"*.

   When in learning mode, access requests are not blocked, even if the profile dictates that they should be. This enables you to run through several tests (as shown in *Step 3*) and learn the access needs of the program so it runs properly. With this information, you can decide how secure to make the profile.

   Refer to *Section 24.6.3.2, "aa-complain—Entering Complain or Learning Mode"* for more detailed instructions for using learning or complain mode.

3. Exercise your application.

   Run your application and exercise its functionality. How much to exercise the program is up to you, but you need the program to access each file representing its access needs. Because the execution is not being supervised by **aa-genprof**, this step can go on for days or weeks and can span complete system reboots.

4. Analyze the log.

In systemic profiling, run **aa-logprof** directly instead of letting **aa-genprof** run it (as in stand-alone profiling). The general form of **aa-logprof** is:

```
aa-logprof [ -d /path/to/profiles ] [ -f /path/to/logfile ]
```

Refer to *Section 24.6.3.9, "aa-logprof—Scanning the System Log"* for more information about using **aa-logprof**.

5. Repeat *Step 3* and *Step 4*.

   This generates optimal profiles. An iterative approach captures smaller data sets that can be trained and reloaded into the policy engine. Subsequent iterations generate fewer messages and run faster.

6. Edit the profiles.

   You should review the profiles that have been generated. You can open and edit the profiles in `/etc/apparmor.d/` using a text editor.

7. Return to enforce mode.

   This is when the system goes back to enforcing the rules of the profiles, not only logging information. This can be done manually by removing the `flags=(complain)` text from the profiles or automatically by using the **aa-enforce** command, which works identically to the **aa-complain** command, except it sets the profiles to enforce mode. This functionality is also available through the YaST Profile Mode module, described in *Section 23.4.2, "Changing the Mode of Individual Profiles"*.

   To ensure that all profiles are taken out of complain mode and put into enforce mode, enter **aa-enforce /etc/apparmor.d/***.

8. Re-scan all profiles.

   To have AppArmor re-scan all of the profiles and change the enforcement mode in the kernel, enter **systemctl reload apparmor**.

24.6.3   Summary of Profiling Tools

All of the AppArmor profiling utilities are provided by the `apparmor-utils` RPM package and are stored in `/usr/sbin`. Each tool has a different purpose.

24.6.3.1   aa-autodep—Creating Approximate Profiles

This creates an approximate profile for the program or application selected. You can generate approximate profiles for binary executables and interpreted script programs. The resulting profile is called "approximate" because it does not necessarily contain all of the profile entries that the program needs to be properly confined by AppArmor. The minimum **aa-autodep** approximate profile has, at minimum, a base include directive, which contains basic profile entries needed by most programs. For certain types of programs, **aa-autodep** generates a more expanded profile. The profile is generated by recursively calling **ldd(1)** on the executables listed on the command line.

To generate an approximate profile, use the **aa-autodep** program. The program argument can be either the simple name of the program, which **aa-autodep** finds by searching your shell's path variable, or it can be a fully qualified path. The program itself can be of any type (ELF binary, shell script, Perl script, etc.). **aa-autodep** generates an approximate profile to improve through the dynamic profiling that follows.

The resulting approximate profile is written to the `/etc/apparmor.d` directory using the AppArmor profile naming convention of naming the profile after the absolute path of the program, replacing the forward slash (`/`) characters in the path with period (`.`) characters. The general syntax of **aa-autodep** is to enter the following in a terminal window when logged in as `root`:

```
aa-autodep [ -d /PATH/TO/PROFILES ] [PROGRAM1 PROGRAM2...]
```

If you do not enter the program name or names, you are prompted for them. `/path/to/profiles` overrides the default location of `/etc/apparmor.d`, should you keep profiles in a location other than the default.

To begin profiling, you must create profiles for each main executable service that is part of your application (anything that might start without being a child of another program that already has a profile). Finding all such programs depends on the application in question. Here are several strategies for finding such programs:

Directories

> If all the programs to profile are in one directory and there are no other programs in that directory, the simple command **aa-autodep** `/path/to/your/programs/*` creates basic profiles for all programs in that directory.

pstree -p

> You can run your application and use the standard Linux **pstree** command to find all processes running. Then manually hunt down the location of these programs and run the **aa-autodep** for each one. If the programs are in your path, **aa-autodep** finds them for you. If they are not in your path, the standard Linux command **find** might be helpful in finding your programs. Execute **find / -name '** *MY_APPLICATION*' -print to determine an application's path (*MY_APPLICATION* being an example application). You may use wild cards if appropriate.

24.6.3.2 aa-complain—Entering Complain or Learning Mode

The complain or learning mode tool (**aa-complain**) detects violations of AppArmor profile rules, such as the profiled program accessing files not permitted by the profile. The violations are permitted, but also logged. To improve the profile, turn complain mode on, run the program through a suite of tests to generate log events that characterize the program's access needs, then postprocess the log with the AppArmor tools to transform log events into improved profiles.

Manually activating complain mode (using the command line) adds a flag to the top of the profile so that /bin/foo becomes /bin/foo flags=(complain). To use complain mode, open a terminal window and enter one of the following lines as root:

- If the example program (*PROGRAM1*) is in your path, use:

```
aa-complain [PROGRAM1 PROGRAM2 ...]
```

- If the program is not in your path, specify the entire path as follows:

```
aa-complain /sbin/PROGRAM1
```

- If the profiles are not in /etc/apparmor.d, use the following to override the default location:

```
aa-complain /path/to/profiles/PROGRAM1
```

- Specify the profile for /sbin/program1 as follows:

```
aa-complain /etc/apparmor.d/sbin.PROGRAM1
```

Each of the above commands activates the complain mode for the profiles or programs listed. If the program name does not include its entire path, **aa-complain** searches $PATH for the program. For example, **aa-complain /usr/sbin/*** finds profiles associated with all of the programs in /usr/sbin and puts them into complain mode. **aa-complain /etc/apparmor.d/*** puts all of the profiles in /etc/apparmor.d into complain mode.

 Tip: Toggling Profile Mode with YaST

YaST offers a graphical front-end for toggling complain and enforce mode. See *Section 23.4.2, "Changing the Mode of Individual Profiles"* for information.

24.6.3.3 aa-decode—Decoding Hex-encoded Strings in AppArmor Log Files

aa-decode will decode hex-encoded strings in the AppArmor log output. It can also process the audit log on standard input, convert any hex-encoded AppArmor log entries, and display them on standard output.

24.6.3.4 aa-disable—Disabling an AppArmor Security Profile

Use **aa-disable** to disable the enforcement mode for one or more AppArmor profiles. This command will unload the profile from the kernel, and prevent the profile from being loaded on AppArmor start-up. Use **aa-enforce** or **aa-complain** utilities to change this behavior.

24.6.3.5 aa-easyprof—Easy Profile Generation

aa-easyprof provides an easy-to-use interface for AppArmor profile generation. **aa-easyprof** supports the use of templates and profile groups to quickly profile an application. While **aa-easyprof** can help with profile generation, its utility is dependent on the quality of the templates, profile groups and abstractions used. Also, this tool may create a profile that is less restricted than when creating a profile manually or with **aa-genprof** and **aa-logprof**.

For more information, see the man page of **aa-easyprof** (8).

24.6.3.6 aa-enforce—Entering Enforce Mode

The enforce mode detects violations of AppArmor profile rules, such as the profiled program accessing files not permitted by the profile. The violations are logged and not permitted. The default is for enforce mode to be enabled. To log the violations only, but still permit them, use complain mode.

Manually activating enforce mode (using the command line) removes the complain flag from the top of the profile so that `/bin/foo flags=(complain)` becomes `/bin/foo`. To use enforce mode, open a terminal window and enter one of the following lines as `root`.

- If the example program (`PROGRAM1`) is in your path, use:

```
aa-enforce [PROGRAM1 PROGRAM2 ...]
```

- If the program is not in your path, specify the entire path, as follows:

```
aa-enforce /sbin/PROGRAM1
```

- If the profiles are not in `/etc/apparmor.d`, use the following to override the default location:

```
aa-enforce -d /path/to/profiles/    program1
```

- Specify the profile for `/sbin/program1` as follows:

```
aa-enforce /etc/apparmor.d/sbin.PROGRAM1
```

Each of the above commands activates the enforce mode for the profiles and programs listed.

If you do not enter the program or profile names, you are prompted to enter one. `/path/to/profiles` overrides the default location of `/etc/apparmor.d`.

The argument can be either a list of programs or a list of profiles. If the program name does not include its entire path, **aa-enforce** searches `$PATH` for the program.

 Tip: Toggling Profile Mode with YaST

> YaST offers a graphical front-end for toggling complain and enforce mode. See *Section 23.4.2, "Changing the Mode of Individual Profiles"* for information.

24.6.3.7 aa-exec—Confining a Program with the Specified Profile

Use **aa-exec** to launch a program confined by a specified profile and/or profile namespace. If both a profile and namespace are specified, the program will be confined by the profile in the new namespace. If only a profile namespace is specified, the profile name of the current confinement will be used. If neither a profile nor namespace is specified, the command will be run using the standard profile attachment—as if you did not use the **aa-exec** command.

For more information on the command's options, see its manual page **man 8 aa-exec**.

24.6.3.8 aa-genprof—Generating Profiles

aa-genprof is AppArmor's profile generating utility. It runs **aa-autodep** on the specified program, creating an approximate profile (if a profile does not already exist for it), sets it to complain mode, reloads it into AppArmor, marks the log, and prompts the user to execute the program and exercise its functionality. Its syntax is as follows:

```
aa-genprof [ -d /path/to/profiles ]  PROGRAM
```

To create a profile for the Apache Web server program httpd2-prefork, do the following as `root`:

1. Enter **systemctl stop apache2**.

2. Next, enter **aa-genprof httpd2-prefork**.
   Now **aa-genprof** does the following:

   1. Resolves the full path of httpd2-prefork using your shell's path variables. You can also specify a full path. On SUSE Linux Enterprise Server, the default full path is `/usr/sbin/httpd2-prefork`.

   2. Checks to see if there is an existing profile for httpd2-prefork. If there is one, it updates it. If not, it creates one using the **aa-autodep** as described in *Section 24.6.3, "Summary of Profiling Tools"*.

   3. Puts the profile for this program into learning or complain mode so that profile violations are logged, but are permitted to proceed. A log event looks like this (see `/var/log/audit/audit.log`):

   ```
   type=APPARMOR_ALLOWED msg=audit(1189682639.184:20816): \
   apparmor="DENIED" operation="file_mmap" parent=2692 \
   ```

```
profile="/usr/sbin/httpd2-prefork//HANDLING_UNTRUSTED_INPUT" \
name="/var/log/apache2/access_log-20140116" pid=28730 comm="httpd2-prefork" \
requested_mask="::r" denied_mask="::r" fsuid=30 ouid=0
```

If you are not running the audit daemon, the AppArmor events are logged directly to `systemd` journal (see *Book "Administration Guide", Chapter 15 "***journalctl***: Query the* `systemd` *Journal"*):

```
Sep 13 13:20:30 K23 kernel: audit(1189682430.672:20810): \
apparmor="DENIED" operation="file_mmap" parent=2692 \
profile="/usr/sbin/httpd2-prefork//HANDLING_UNTRUSTED_INPUT" \
name="/var/log/apache2/access_log-20140116" pid=28730 comm="httpd2-prefork" \
requested_mask="::r" denied_mask="::r" fsuid=30 ouid=0
```

They also can be viewed using the **dmesg** command:

```
audit(1189682430.672:20810): apparmor="DENIED" \
operation="file_mmap" parent=2692 \
profile="/usr/sbin/httpd2-prefork//HANDLING_UNTRUSTED_INPUT" \
name="/var/log/apache2/access_log-20140116" pid=28730 comm="httpd2-prefork" \
requested_mask="::r" denied_mask="::r" fsuid=30 ouid=0
```

4. Marks the log with a beginning marker of log events to consider. For example:

```
Sep 13 17:48:52 figwit root: GenProf: e2ff78636296f16d0b5301209a04430d
```

3. When prompted by the tool, run the application to profile in another terminal window and perform as many of the application functions as possible. Thus, the learning mode can log the files and directories to which the program requires access to function properly. For example, in a new terminal window, enter **systemctl start apache2**.

4. Select from the following options that are available in the **aa-genprof** terminal window after you have executed the program function:

- S runs **aa-genprof** on the system log from where it was marked when **aa-genprof** was started and reloads the profile. If system events exist in the log, AppArmor parses the learning mode log files. This generates a series of questions that you must answer to guide **aa-genprof** in generating the security profile.

- F exits the tool.

Note

> If requests to add hats appear, proceed to *Chapter 25, Profiling Your Web Applications Using ChangeHat*.

5. Answer two types of questions:

   - A resource is requested by a profiled program that is not in the profile (see *Example 24.1, "Learning Mode Exception: Controlling Access to Specific Resources"*).

   - A program is executed by the profiled program and the security domain transition has not been defined (see *Example 24.2, "Learning Mode Exception: Defining Permissions for an Entry"*).

Each of these categories results in a series of questions that you must answer to add the resource or program to the profile. *Example 24.1, "Learning Mode Exception: Controlling Access to Specific Resources"* and *Example 24.2, "Learning Mode Exception: Defining Permissions for an Entry"* provide examples of each one. Subsequent steps describe your options in answering these questions.

   - Dealing with execute accesses is complex. You must decide how to proceed with this entry regarding which execute permission type to grant to this entry:

EXAMPLE 24.1: LEARNING MODE EXCEPTION: CONTROLLING ACCESS TO SPECIFIC RESOURCES

```
Reading log entries from /var/log/audit/audit.log.
Updating AppArmor profiles in /etc/apparmor.d.

Profile:  /usr/sbin/xinetd
Program:  xinetd
Execute:  /usr/lib/cups/daemon/cups-lpd
Severity: unknown

(I)nherit / (P)rofile / (C)hild / (N)ame / (U)nconfined / (X)ix / (D)eny /
 Abo(r)t / (F)inish
```

Inherit (ix)

   The child inherits the parent's profile, running with the same access controls as the parent. This mode is useful when a confined program needs to call another confined program without gaining the permissions of the target's profile or losing the permissions of the current profile. This mode is often used when the child program is a *helper application*, such as the `/usr/bin/mail` client using `less` as a pager.

Profile (px/Px)

The child runs using its own profile, which must be loaded into the kernel. If the profile is not present, attempts to execute the child fail with permission denied. This is most useful if the parent program is invoking a global service, such as DNS lookups or sending mail with your system's MTA.

Choose the *profile with clean exec* (Px) option to scrub the environment of environment variables that could modify execution behavior when passed to the child process.

Child (cx/Cx)

Sets up a transition to a subprofile. It is like px/Px transition, except to a child profile.

Choose the *profile with clean exec* (Cx) option to scrub the environment of environment variables that could modify execution behavior when passed to the child process.

Unconfined (ux/Ux)

The child runs completely unconfined without any AppArmor profile applied to the executed resource.

Choose the *unconfined with clean exec* (Ux) option to scrub the environment of environment variables that could modify execution behavior when passed to the child process. Note that running unconfined profiles introduces a security vulnerability that could be used to evade AppArmor. Only use it as a last resort.

mmap (m)

This permission denotes that the program running under the profile can access the resource using the mmap system call with the flag `PROT_EXEC`. This means that the data mapped in it can be executed. You are prompted to include this permission if it is requested during a profiling run.

Deny

Adds a `deny` rule to the profile, and permanently prevents the program from accessing the specified directory path entries. AppArmor then continues to the next event.

Abort

Aborts `aa-logprof`, losing all rule changes entered so far and leaving all profiles unmodified.

Finish

Closes `aa-logprof`, saving all rule changes entered so far and modifying all profiles.

- *Example 24.2, "Learning Mode Exception: Defining Permissions for an Entry"* shows AppArmor suggest allowing a globbing pattern `/var/run/nscd/*` for reading, then using an abstraction to cover common Apache-related access rules.

EXAMPLE 24.2: LEARNING MODE EXCEPTION: DEFINING PERMISSIONS FOR AN ENTRY

```
Profile:   /usr/sbin/httpd2-prefork
Path:      /var/run/nscd/dbSz9CTr
Mode:      r
Severity: 3

  1 - /var/run/nscd/dbSz9CTr
 [2 - /var/run/nscd/*]

(A)llow / [(D)eny] / (G)lob / Glob w/(E)xt / (N)ew / Abo(r)t / (F)inish /
 (O)pts
Adding /var/run/nscd/* r to profile.

Profile:   /usr/sbin/httpd2-prefork
Path:      /proc/11769/attr/current
Mode:      w
Severity: 9

 [1 - #include <abstractions/apache2-common>]
  2 - /proc/11769/attr/current
  3 - /proc/*/attr/current

(A)llow / [(D)eny] / (G)lob / Glob w/(E)xt / (N)ew / Abo(r)t / (F)inish /
 (O)pts
Adding #include <abstractions/apache2-common> to profile.
```

AppArmor provides one or more paths or includes. By entering the option number, select the desired options then proceed to the next step.

Note

Not all of these options are always presented in the AppArmor menu.

`#include`

This is the section of an AppArmor profile that refers to an include file, which procures access permissions for programs. By using an include, you can give the program access to directory paths or files that are also required by other programs. Using includes can reduce the size of a profile. It is good practice to select includes when suggested.

Globbed Version

This is accessed by selecting *Glob* as described in the next step. For information about globbing syntax, refer to *Section 21.6, "Profile Names, Flags, Paths, and Globbing"*.

Actual Path

This is the literal path to which the program needs access so that it can run properly.

After you select the path or include, process it as an entry into the AppArmor profile by selecting *Allow* or *Deny*. If you are not satisfied with the directory path entry as it is displayed, you can also *Glob* it.

The following options are available to process the learning mode entries and build the profile:

Select `Enter`

Allows access to the selected directory path.

Allow

Allows access to the specified directory path entries. AppArmor suggests file permission access. For more information, refer to *Section 21.7, "File Permission Access Modes"*.

Deny

Prevents the program from accessing the specified directory path entries. AppArmor then continues to the next event.

New

> Prompts you to enter your own rule for this event, allowing you to specify a regular expression. If the expression does not actually satisfy the event that prompted the question in the first place, AppArmor asks for confirmation and lets you reenter the expression.

Glob

> Select a specific path or create a general rule using wild cards that match a broader set of paths. To select any of the offered paths, enter the number that is printed in front of the path then decide how to proceed with the selected item. For more information about globbing syntax, refer to *Section 21.6, "Profile Names, Flags, Paths, and Globbing"*.

Glob w/Ext

> This modifies the original directory path while retaining the file name extension. For example, `/etc/apache2/file.ext` becomes `/etc/apache2/*.ext`, adding the wild card (asterisk) in place of the file name. This allows the program to access all files in the suggested directory that end with the `.ext` extension.

Abort

> Aborts `aa-logprof`, losing all rule changes entered so far and leaving all profiles unmodified.

Finish

> Closes `aa-logprof`, saving all rule changes entered so far and modifying all profiles.

6. To view and edit your profile using `vi`, enter `vi /etc/apparmor.d/` *PROFILENAME* in a terminal window. To enable syntax highlighting when editing an AppArmor profile in vim, use the commands `:syntax on` then `:set syntax=apparmor`. For more information about vim and syntax highlighting, refer to *Section 24.6.3.14, "apparmor.vim"*.

7. Restart AppArmor and reload the profile set including the newly created one using the `systemctl reload apparmor` command.

Like the graphical front-end for building AppArmor profiles, the YaST Add Profile Wizard, `aa-genprof` also supports the use of the local profile repository under `/etc/apparmor/profiles/extras` and the remote AppArmor profile repository.

To use a profile from the local repository, proceed as follows:

1. Start **aa-genprof** as described above.

   If **aa-genprof** finds an inactive local profile, the following lines appear on your terminal window:

   ```
   Profile: /usr/bin/opera

    [1 - Inactive local profile for /usr/bin/opera]

   [(V)iew Profile] / (U)se Profile / (C)reate New Profile / Abo(r)t / (F)inish
   ```

2. To use this profile, press U (*Use Profile*) and follow the profile generation procedure outlined above.

   To examine the profile before activating it, press V (*View Profile*).

   To ignore the existing profile, press C (*Create New Profile*) and follow the profile generation procedure outlined above to create the profile from scratch.

3. Leave **aa-genprof** by pressing F (*Finish*) when you are done and save your changes.

24.6.3.9   aa-logprof—Scanning the System Log

aa-logprof is an interactive tool used to review the complain and enforce mode events found in the log entries in `/var/log/audit/audit.log`, or directly in the `systemd` journal (see *Book "Administration Guide", Chapter 15 "***journalctl***: Query the* `systemd` *Journal"*), and generate new entries in AppArmor security profiles.

When you run **aa-logprof**, it begins to scan the log files produced in complain and enforce mode and, if there are new security events that are not covered by the existing profile set, it gives suggestions for modifying the profile. **aa-logprof** uses this information to observe program behavior.

If a confined program forks and executes another program, **aa-logprof** sees this and asks the user which execution mode should be used when launching the child process. The execution modes *ix, px, Px, ux, Ux, cx, Cx,* and named profiles, are options for starting the child process. If a separate profile exists for the child process, the default selection is *Px*. If one does not exist, the profile defaults to *ix*. Child processes with separate profiles have **aa-autodep** run on them and are loaded into AppArmor, if it is running.

When **aa-logprof** exits, profiles are updated with the changes. If AppArmor is active, the updated profiles are reloaded and, if any processes that generated security events are still running in the null-XXXX profiles (unique profiles temporarily created in complain mode), those processes are set to run under their proper profiles.

To run **aa-logprof**, enter **aa-logprof** into a terminal window while logged in as root. The following options can be used for **aa-logprof**:

aa-logprof -d */path/to/profile/directory/*

> Specifies the full path to the location of the profiles if the profiles are not located in the standard directory, /etc/apparmor.d/.

aa-logprof -f */path/to/logfile/*

> Specifies the full path to the location of the log file if the log file is not located in the default directory or /var/log/audit/audit.log.

aa-logprof -m "string marker in logfile"

> Marks the starting point for **aa-logprof** to look in the system log. **aa-logprof** ignores all events in the system log before the specified mark. If the mark contains spaces, it must be surrounded by quotes to work correctly. For example:

```
aa-logprof -m "17:04:21"
```

> or

```
aa-logprof -m e2ff78636296f16d0b5301209a04430d
```

aa-logprof scans the log, asking you how to handle each logged event. Each question presents a numbered list of AppArmor rules that can be added by pressing the number of the item on the list.

By default, **aa-logprof** looks for profiles in /etc/apparmor.d/. Often running **aa-logprof** as root is enough to update the profile. However, there might be times when you need to search archived log files, such as if the program exercise period exceeds the log rotation window (when the log file is archived and a new log file is started). If this is the case, you can enter **zcat -f** `**ls -1tr** */path/to/logfile*`` | aa-logprof -f -.

24.6.3.10 aa-logprof Example 1

The following is an example of how **aa-logprof** addresses httpd2-prefork accessing the file /etc/group. [] indicates the default option.

In this example, the access to **/etc/group** is part of httpd2-prefork accessing name services. The appropriate response is 1, which includes a predefined set of AppArmor rules. Selecting 1 to #include the name service package resolves all of the future questions pertaining to DNS lookups and makes the profile less brittle in that any changes to DNS configuration and the associated name service profile package can be made once, rather than needing to revise many profiles.

```
Profile:   /usr/sbin/httpd2-prefork
Path:      /etc/group
New Mode: r

[1 - #include <abstractions/nameservice>]
 2 - /etc/group
[(A)llow] / (D)eny / (N)ew / (G)lob / Glob w/(E)xt / Abo(r)t / (F)inish
```

Select one of the following responses:

Select `Enter`

> Triggers the default action, which is, in this example, allowing access to the specified directory path entry.

Allow

> Allows access to the specified directory path entries. AppArmor suggests file permission access. For more information about this, refer to *Section 21.7, "File Permission Access Modes"*.

Deny

> Permanently prevents the program from accessing the specified directory path entries. AppArmor then continues to the next event.

New

> Prompts you to enter your own rule for this event, allowing you to specify whatever form of regular expression you want. If the expression entered does not actually satisfy the event that prompted the question in the first place, AppArmor asks for confirmation and lets you reenter the expression.

Glob

> Select either a specific path or create a general rule using wild cards that matches on a broader set of paths. To select any of the offered paths, enter the number that is printed in front of the paths then decide how to proceed with the selected item.
>
> For more information about globbing syntax, refer to *Section 21.6, "Profile Names, Flags, Paths, and Globbing"*.

Glob w/Ext

This modifies the original directory path while retaining the file name extension. For example, `/etc/apache2/file.ext` becomes `/etc/apache2/*.ext`, adding the wild card (asterisk) in place of the file name. This allows the program to access all files in the suggested directory that end with the `.ext` extension.

Abort

Aborts **aa-logprof**, losing all rule changes entered so far and leaving all profiles unmodified.

Finish

Closes **aa-logprof**, saving all rule changes entered so far and modifying all profiles.

24.6.3.11   aa-logprof Example 2

For example, when profiling vsftpd, see this question:

```
Profile:   /usr/sbin/vsftpd
Path:      /y2k.jpg

New Mode: r

[1 - /y2k.jpg]

(A)llow / [(D)eny] / (N)ew / (G)lob / Glob w/(E)xt / Abo(r)t / (F)inish
```

Several items of interest appear in this question. First, note that vsftpd is asking for a path entry at the top of the tree, even though vsftpd on SUSE Linux Enterprise Server serves FTP files from `/srv/ftp` by default. This is because vsftpd uses chroot and, for the portion of the code inside the chroot jail, AppArmor sees file accesses in terms of the chroot environment rather than the global absolute path.

The second item of interest is that you should grant FTP read access to all JPEG files in the directory, so you could use *Glob w/Ext* and use the suggested path of `/*.jpg`. Doing so collapses all previous rules granting access to individual `.jpg` files and forestalls any future questions pertaining to access to `.jpg` files.

Finally, you should grant more general access to FTP files. If you select *Glob* in the last entry, **aa-logprof** replaces the suggested path of `/y2k.jpg` with `/*`. Alternatively, you should grant even more access to the entire directory tree, in which case you could use the *New* path option and enter `/**.jpg` (which would grant access to all `.jpg` files in the entire directory tree) or `/**` (which would grant access to all files in the directory tree).

These items deal with read accesses. Write accesses are similar, except that it is good policy to be more conservative in your use of regular expressions for write accesses. Dealing with execute accesses is more complex. Find an example in *Example 24.1, "Learning Mode Exception: Controlling Access to Specific Resources".*

In the following example, the `/usr/bin/mail` mail client is being profiled and **aa-logprof** has discovered that **/usr/bin/mail** executes **/usr/bin/less** as a helper application to "page" long mail messages. Consequently, it presents this prompt:

```
/usr/bin/nail -> /usr/bin/less
(I)nherit / (P)rofile / (C)hild / (N)ame / (U)nconfined / (X)ix / (D)eny
```

Note

The actual executable file for `/usr/bin/mail` turns out to be `/usr/bin/nail`, which is not a typographical error.

The program `/usr/bin/less` appears to be a simple one for scrolling through text that is more than one screen long and that is in fact what `/usr/bin/mail` is using it for. However, **less** is actually a large and powerful program that uses many other helper applications, such as **tar** and **rpm**.

Tip

Run **less** on a tar file or an RPM file and it shows you the inventory of these containers.

You do not want to run **rpm** automatically when reading mail messages (that leads directly to a Microsoft* Outlook–style virus attack, because RPM has the power to install and modify system programs), so, in this case, the best choice is to use *Inherit*. This results in the less program executed from this context running under the profile for `/usr/bin/mail`. This has two consequences:

- You need to add all of the basic file accesses for `/usr/bin/less` to the profile for `/usr/bin/mail`.

- You can avoid adding the helper applications, such as **tar** and **rpm**, to the `/usr/bin/mail` profile so that when `/usr/bin/mail` runs `/usr/bin/less` in this context, the less program is far less dangerous than it would be without AppArmor protection. Another option is to use the Cx execute modes. For more information on execute modes, see *Section 21.8, "Execute Modes"*.

In other circumstances, you might instead want to use the *Profile* option. This has the following effects on **aa-logprof**:

- The rule written into the profile uses px/Px, which forces the transition to the child's own profile.

- **aa-logprof** constructs a profile for the child and starts building it, in the same way that it built the parent profile, by assigning events for the child process to the child's profile and asking the **aa-logprof** user questions. The profile will also be applied if you run the child as a stand-alone program.

If a confined program forks and executes another program, **aa-logprof** sees this and asks the user which execution mode should be used when launching the child process. The execution modes of inherit, profile, unconfined, child, named profile, or an option to deny the execution are presented.

If a separate profile exists for the child process, the default selection is profile. If a profile does not exist, the default is inherit. The inherit option, or `ix`, is described in *Section 21.7, "File Permission Access Modes"*.

The profile option indicates that the child program should run in its own profile. A secondary question asks whether to sanitize the environment that the child program inherits from the parent. If you choose to sanitize the environment, this places the execution modifier `Px` in your AppArmor profile. If you select not to sanitize, `px` is placed in the profile and no environment sanitizing occurs. The default for the execution mode is `Px` if you select profile execution mode.

The unconfined execution mode is not recommended and should only be used in cases where there is no other option to generate a profile for a program reliably. Selecting unconfined opens a warning dialog asking for confirmation of the choice. If you are sure and choose *Yes*, a second dialog ask whether to sanitize the environment. To use the execution mode Ux in your profile, select *Yes*. To use the execution mode ux in your profile instead, select *No*. The default value selected is Ux for unconfined execution mode.

Important: Running Unconfined

Selecting ux or Ux is very dangerous and provides no enforcement of policy (from a security perspective) of the resulting execution behavior of the child program.

24.6.3.12 aa-unconfined—Identifying Unprotected Processes

The **aa-unconfined** command examines open network ports on your system, compares that to the set of profiles loaded on your system, and reports network services that do not have AppArmor profiles. It requires root privileges and that it not be confined by an AppArmor profile.

aa-unconfined must be run as root to retrieve the process executable link from the /proc file system. This program is susceptible to the following race conditions:

- An unlinked executable is mishandled

- A process that dies between **netstat(8)** and further checks is mishandled

Note

This program lists processes using TCP and UDP only. In short, this program is unsuitable for forensics use and is provided only as an aid to profiling all network-accessible processes in the lab.

24.6.3.13 aa-notify

aa-notify is a handy utility that displays AppArmor notifications in your desktop environment. This is very convenient if you do not want to inspect the AppArmor log file, but rather let the desktop inform you about events that violate the policy. To enable AppArmor desktop notifications, run **aa-notify**:

```
sudo aa-notify -p -u USERNAME --display DISPLAY_NUMBER
```

where *USERNAME* is your user name under which you are logged in, and *DISPLAY_NUMBER* is the X Window display number you are currently using, such as `:0`. The process is run in the background, and shows a notification each time a deny event happens.

 Tip

> The active X Window display number is saved in the `$DISPLAY` variable, so you can use `--display $DISPLAY` to avoid finding out the current display number.

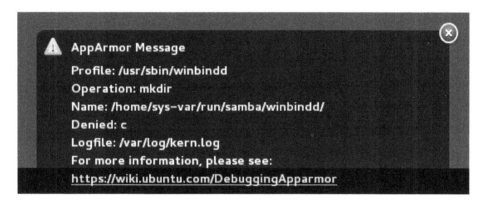

FIGURE 24.1: aa-notify Message in GNOME

With the `-s` *DAYS* option, you can also configure **aa-notify** to display a summary of notifications for the specified number of past days. For more information on **aa-notify**, see its man page `man 8 aa-notify`.

24.6.3.14 apparmor.vim

A syntax highlighting file for the vim text editor highlights various features of an AppArmor profile with colors. Using vim and the AppArmor syntax mode for vim, you can see the semantic implications of your profiles with color highlighting. Use vim to view and edit your profile by typing vim at a terminal window.

To enable the syntax coloring when you edit an AppArmor profile in vim, use the commands `:syntax on` then `:set syntax=apparmor`. To make sure vim recognizes the edited file type correctly as an AppArmor profile, add

```
# vim:ft=apparmor
```

at the end of the profile.

 Tip

vim comes with AppArmor highlighting automatically enabled for files in /etc/appar-mor.d/.

When you enable this feature, vim colors the lines of the profile for you:

Blue

Comments

White

Ordinary read access lines

Brown

Capability statements and complain flags

Yellow

Lines that grant write access

Green

Lines that grant execute permission (either ix or px)

Red

Lines that grant unconfined access (ux)

Red background

Syntax errors that will not load properly into the AppArmor modules

Use the `apparmor.vim` and `vim` man pages and the `:help syntax` from within the vim editor for further vim help about syntax highlighting. The AppArmor syntax is stored in `/usr/share/vim/current/syntax/apparmor.vim`.

24.7 Important File Names and Directories

The following list contains the most important files and directories used by the AppArmor framework. If you intend to manage and troubleshoot your profiles manually, make sure that you know about these files and directories:

`/sys/kernel/security/apparmor/profiles`
> Virtualized file representing the currently loaded set of profiles.

`/etc/apparmor/`
> Location of AppArmor configuration files.

`/etc/apparmor/profiles/extras/`
> A local repository of profiles shipped with AppArmor, but not enabled by default.

`/etc/apparmor.d/`
> Location of profiles, named with the convention of replacing the `/` in paths with `.` (not for the root `/`) so profiles are easier to manage. For example, the profile for the program `/usr/sbin/ntpd` is named `usr.sbin.ntpd`.

`/etc/apparmor.d/abstractions/`
> Location of abstractions.

`/etc/apparmor.d/program-chunks/`
> Location of program chunks.

`/proc/*/attr/current`
> Check this file to review the confinement status of a process and the profile that is used to confine the process. The **ps** `auxZ` command retrieves this information automatically.

25 Profiling Your Web Applications Using ChangeHat

An AppArmor® profile represents the security policy for an individual program instance or process. It applies to an executable program, but if a portion of the program needs different access permissions than other portions, the program can "change hats" to use a different security context, distinctive from the access of the main program. This is known as a *hat* or *subprofile*.

ChangeHat enables programs to change to or from a *hat* within an AppArmor profile. It enables you to define security at a finer level than the process. This feature requires that each application be made "ChangeHat-aware", meaning that it is modified to make a request to the AppArmor module to switch security domains at specific times during the application execution. One example of a ChangeHat-aware application is the Apache Web server.

A profile can have an arbitrary number of subprofiles, but there are only two levels: a subprofile cannot have further child profiles. A subprofile is written as a separate profile. Its name consists of the name of the containing profile followed by the subprofile name, separated by a ^.

Subprofiles are either stored in the same file as the parent profile, or in a separate file. The latter case is recommended on sites with many hats—it allows the policy caching to handle changes at the per hat level. If all the hats are in the same file as the parent profile, then the parent profile and all hats must be recompiled.

An external subprofile that is going to be used as a hat, must begin with the word hat or the ^ character.

The following two subprofiles *cannot* be used as a hat:

```
/foo//bar { }
```

or

```
profile /foo//bar { }
```

While the following two are treated as hats:

```
^/foo//bar { }
```

or

```
hat /foo//bar { } # this syntax is not highlighted in vim
```

Note that the security of hats is considerably weaker than that of full profiles. Using certain types of bugs in a program, an attacker may be able to escape from a hat into the containing profile. This is because the security of hats is determined by a secret key handled by the containing process, and the code running in the hat must not have access to the key. Thus, change_hat is most useful with application servers, where a language interpreter (such as PERL, PHP, or Java) is isolating pieces of code such that they do not have direct access to the memory of the containing process.

The rest of this chapter describes using change_hat with Apache, to contain Web server components run using mod_perl and mod_php. Similar approaches can be used with any application server by providing an application module similar to the mod_apparmor described next in *Section 25.1.2, "Location and Directory Directives"*.

 Tip: For More Information

For more information, see the **change_hat** man page.

25.1 Configuring Apache for mod_apparmor

AppArmor provides a `mod_apparmor` module (package `apache2-mod-apparmor`) for the Apache program. This module makes the Apache Web server ChangeHat aware. Install it along with Apache.

When Apache is ChangeHat-aware, it checks for the following customized AppArmor security profiles in the order given for every URI request that it receives.

- URI-specific hat. For example, `^www_app_name/templates/classic/images/bar_left.gif`

- `DEFAULT_URI`

- `HANDLING_UNTRUSTED_INPUT`

 Note: Apache Configuration

If you install `apache2-mod-apparmor`, make sure the module is enabled, and then restart Apache by executing the following command:

```
a2enmod apparmor && sudo systemctl reload apache2
```

Apache is configured by placing directives in plain text configuration files. The main configuration file is usually `/etc/apache2/httpd.conf`. When you compile Apache, you can indicate the location of this file. Directives can be placed in any of these configuration files to alter the way Apache behaves. When you make changes to the main configuration files, you need to reload Apache with **`sudo systemctl reload apache2`**, so the changes are recognized.

25.1.1 Virtual Host Directives

`<VirtualHost>` and `</VirtualHost>` directives are used to enclose a group of directives that will apply only to a particular virtual host. For more information on Apache virtual host directives, refer to http://httpd.apache.org/docs/2.4/en/mod/core.html#virtualhost ↗.

The ChangeHat-specific configuration keyword is `AADefaultHatName`. It is used similarly to `AAHatName`, for example, `AADefaultHatName My_Funky_Default_Hat`.

It allows you to specify a default hat to be used for virtual hosts and other Apache server directives, so that you can have different defaults for different virtual hosts. This can be overridden by the `AAHatName` directive and is checked for only if there is not a matching `AAHatName` or hat named by the URI. If the `AADefaultHatName` hat does not exist, it falls back to the `DEFAULT_URI` hat if it exists/

If none of those are matched, it goes back to the "parent" Apache hat.

25.1.2 Location and Directory Directives

Location and directory directives specify hat names in the program configuration file so the Apache calls the hat regarding its security. For Apache, you can find documentation about the location and directory directives at http://httpd.apache.org/docs/2.4/en/sections.html ↗.

The location directive example below specifies that, for a given location, `mod_apparmor` should use a specific hat:

```
<Location /foo/>
  AAHatName MY_HAT_NAME
</Location>
```

This tries to use `MY_HAT_NAME` for any URI beginning with `/foo/` (`/foo/`, `/foo/bar`, `/foo/cgi/path/blah_blah/blah`, etc.).

The directory directive works similarly to the location directive, except it refers to a path in the file system as in the following example:

```
<Directory "/srv/www/www.example.org/docs">
  # Note lack of trailing slash
  AAHatName example.org
</Directory>
```

25.2 Managing ChangeHat-Aware Applications

In the previous section you learned about `mod_apparmor` and the way it helps you to secure a specific Web application. This section walks you through a real-life example of creating a hat for a Web application, and using AppArmor's change_hat feature to secure it. Note that this chapter focuses on AppArmor's command line tools, as YaST's AppArmor module has limited functionality.

25.2.1 With AppArmor's Command Line Tools

For illustration purposes, let us choose the Web application called *Adminer* (http://www.adminer.org/en/ ↗). It is a full-featured SQL database management tool written in PHP, yet consisting of a single PHP file. For Adminer to work, you need to set up an Apache Web server, PHP and its Apache module, and one of the database drivers available for PHP—MariaDB in this example. You can install the required packages with

```
zypper in apache2 apache2-mod_apparmor apache2-mod_php5 php5 php5-mysql
```

To set up the Web environment for running Adminer, follow these steps:

PROCEDURE 25.1: SETTING UP A WEB SERVER ENVIRONMENT

1. Make sure `apparmor` and `php5` modules are enabled for Apache. To enable the modules in any case, use:

   ```
   a2enmod apparmor php5
   ```

   and then restart Apache with

   ```
   sudo systemctl restart apache2
   ```

2. Make sure MariaDB is running. If unsure, restart it with

```
sudo systemctl restart mysql
```

3. Download Adminer from http://www.adminer.org ↗, copy it to `/srv/www/htdocs/adminer/`, and rename it to `adminer.php`, so that its full path is `/srv/www/htdocs/adminer/adminer.php`.

4. Test Adminer in your Web browser by entering `http://localhost/adminer/adminer.php` in its URI address field. If you installed Adminer to a remote server, replace `localhost` with the real host name of the server.

FIGURE 25.1: ADMINER LOGIN PAGE

 Tip

If you encounter problems viewing the Adminer login page, try to look for help in the Apache error log `/var/log/apache2/error.log`. Another reason you cannot access the Web page may be that your Apache is already under AppArmor control and its AppArmor profile is too tight to permit viewing Adminer. Check it with **aa-status**, and if needed, set Apache temporarily in complain mode with

```
aa-complain usr.sbin.httpd2-prefork
```

After the Web environment for Adminer is ready, you need to configure Apache's mod_apparmor, so that AppArmor can detect accesses to Adminer and change to the specific "hat".

1. Apache has several configuration files under `/etc/apache2/` and `/etc/apache2/con-f.d/`. Choose your preferred one and open it in a text editor. In this example, the **vim** editor is used to create a new configuration file `/etc/apache2/conf.d/apparmor.conf`.

```
vim /etc/apache2/conf.d/apparmor.conf
```

2. Copy the following snippet into the edited file.

```
<Directory /srv/www/htdocs/adminer>
  AAHatName adminer
</Directory>
```

It tells Apache to let AppArmor know about a change_hat event when the Web user accesses the directory `/adminer` (and any file/directory inside) in Apache's document root. Remember, we placed the `adminer.php` application there.

3. Save the file, close the editor, and restart Apache with

```
sudo systemctl restart apache2
```

Apache now knows about our Adminer and changing a "hat" for it. It is time to create the related hat for Adminer in the AppArmor configuration. If you do not have an AppArmor profile yet, create one before proceeding. Remember that if your Apache's main binary is `/usr/sbin/httpd2-prefork`, then the related profile is named `/etc/apparmor.d/usr.sbin.httpd2-prefork`.

1. Open (or create one if it does not exist) the file `/etc/apparmor.d/usr.s-bin.httpd2-prefork` in a text editor. Its contents should be similar to the following:

```
#include <tunables/global>

/usr/sbin/httpd2-prefork {
  #include <abstractions/apache2-common>
  #include <abstractions/base>
  #include <abstractions/php5>

  capability kill,
  capability setgid,
  capability setuid,

  /etc/apache2/** r,
```

```
  /run/httpd.pid rw,
  /usr/lib{,32,64}/apache2*/** mr,
  /var/log/apache2/** rw,

  ^DEFAULT_URI {
    #include <abstractions/apache2-common>
    /var/log/apache2/** rw,
  }

  ^HANDLING_UNTRUSTED_INPUT {
    #include <abstractions/apache2-common>
    /var/log/apache2/** w,
  }
}
```

2. Before the last closing curly bracket (}), insert the following section:

```
^adminer flags=(complain) {
}
```

Note the (complain) addition after the hat name—it tells AppArmor to leave the adminer hat in complain mode. That is because we need to learn the hat profile by accessing Adminer later on.

3. Save the file, and then restart AppArmor, then Apache.

```
systemctl reload apparmor apache2
```

4. Check if the adminer hat really is in complain mode.

```
# aa-status
apparmor module is loaded.
39 profiles are loaded.
37 profiles are in enforce mode.
[...]
   /usr/sbin/httpd2-prefork
   /usr/sbin/httpd2-prefork//DEFAULT_URI
   /usr/sbin/httpd2-prefork//HANDLING_UNTRUSTED_INPUT
[...]
2 profiles are in complain mode.
   /usr/bin/getopt
   /usr/sbin/httpd2-prefork//adminer
[...]
```

As we can see, the httpd2-prefork//adminer is loaded in complain mode.

Our last task is to find out the right set of rules for the `adminer` hat. That is why we set the `adminer` hat into complain mode—the logging facility collects useful information about the access requirements of `adminer.php` as we use it via the Web browser. **aa-logprof** then helps us with creating the hat's profile.

PROCEDURE 25.4: GENERATING RULES FOR THE `adminer` HAT

1. Open Adminer in the Web browser. If you installed it locally, then the URI is `http://localhost/adminer/adminer.php`.

2. Choose the database engine you want to use (MariaDB in our case), and log in to Adminer using the existing database user name and password. You do not need to specify the database name as you can do so after logging in. Perform any operations with Adminer you like—create a new database, create a new table for it, set user privileges, and so on.

3. After the short testing of Adminer's user interface, switch back to console and examine the log for collected data.

```
# aa-logprof
Reading log entries from /var/log/messages.
Updating AppArmor profiles in /etc/apparmor.d.
Complain-mode changes:

Profile:  /usr/sbin/httpd2-prefork^adminer
Path:     /dev/urandom
Mode:     r
Severity: 3

  1 - #include <abstractions/apache2-common>
[...]
 [8 - /dev/urandom]

[(A)llow] / (D)eny / (G)lob / Glob w/(E)xt / (N)ew / Abo(r)t / (F)inish / (O)pts
```

From the **aa-logprof** message, it is clear that our new `adminer` hat was correctly detected:

```
Profile:  /usr/sbin/httpd2-prefork^adminer
```

The **aa-logprof** command will ask you to pick the right rule for each discovered AppArmor event. Specify the one you want to use, and confirm with *Allow*. For more information on working with the **aa-genprof** and **aa-logprof** interface, see *Section 24.6.3.8, "aa-genprof—Generating Profiles"*.

Tip

> **aa-logprof** usually offers several valid rules for the examined event. Some are *abstractions*—predefined sets of rules affecting a specific common group of targets. Sometimes it is useful to include such an abstraction instead of a direct URI rule:
>
> ```
> 1 - #include <abstractions/php5>
> [2 - /var/lib/php5/sess_3jdmii9cacj1e3jnahbtopajl7p064ai242]
> ```
>
> In the example above, it is recommended hitting *1* and confirming with *A* to allow the abstraction.

4. After the last change, you will be asked to save the changed profile.

```
The following local profiles were changed. Would you like to save them?
 [1 - /usr/sbin/httpd2-prefork]

 (S)ave Changes / [(V)iew Changes] / Abo(r)t
```

Hit *S* to save the changes.

5. Set the profile to enforce mode with **aa-enforce**

```
aa-enforce usr.sbin.httpd2-prefork
```

and check its status with **aa-status**

```
# aa-status
apparmor module is loaded.
39 profiles are loaded.
38 profiles are in enforce mode.
[...]
   /usr/sbin/httpd2-prefork
   /usr/sbin/httpd2-prefork//DEFAULT_URI
   /usr/sbin/httpd2-prefork//HANDLING_UNTRUSTED_INPUT
   /usr/sbin/httpd2-prefork//adminer
[...]
```

As you can see, the //adminer hat jumped from *complain* to *enforce* mode.

6. Try to run Adminer in the Web browser, and if you encounter problems running it, switch it to the complain mode, repeat the steps that previously did not work well, and update the profile with **aa-logprof** until you are satisfied with the application's functionality.

Note: Hat and Parent Profile Relationship

The profile `^adminer` is only available in the context of a process running under the parent profile `usr.sbin.httpd2-prefork`.

25.2.2   Adding Hats and Entries to Hats in YaST

When you use the *Edit Profile* dialog (for instructions, refer to *Section 23.2, "Editing Profiles"*) or when you add a new profile using *Manually Add Profile* (for instructions, refer to *Section 23.1, "Manually Adding a Profile"*), you are given the option of adding hats (subprofiles) to your AppArmor profiles. Add a ChangeHat subprofile from the *AppArmor Profile Dialog* window as in the following.

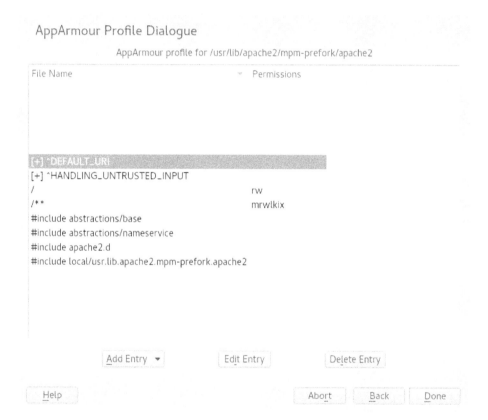

1. From the *AppArmor Profile Dialog* window, click *Add Entry* then select *Hat*. The *EnterHat Name* dialog opens:

Please enter the name of the Hat that you would like to add to the profile /usr/sbin/httpd2-prefork.

Hat name to add:

adminer

Create Hat   Abort

2. Enter the name of the hat to add to the AppArmor profile. The name is the URI that, when accessed, receives the permissions set in the hat.

3. Click *Create Hat*. You are returned to the *AppArmor Profile Dialog* screen.

4. After adding the new hat, click *Done*.

26 Confining Users with pam_apparmor

An AppArmor profile applies to an executable program; if a portion of the program needs different access permissions than other portions need, the program can change hats via change_hat to a different role, also known as a subprofile. The `pam_apparmor` PAM module allows applications to confine authenticated users into subprofiles based on group names, user names, or a default profile. To accomplish this, `pam_apparmor` needs to be registered as a PAM session module.

The package `pam_apparmor` is not installed by default, you can install it using YaST or **zypper**. Details about how to set up and configure `pam_apparmor` can be found in `/usr/share/doc/packages/pam_apparmor/README` after the package has been installed. For details on PAM, refer to *Chapter 2, Authentication with PAM*.

27 Managing Profiled Applications

After creating profiles and immunizing your applications, SUSE® Linux Enterprise Server becomes more efficient and better protected as long as you perform AppArmor® profile maintenance (which involves analyzing log files, refining your profiles, backing up your set of profiles and keeping it up-to-date). You can deal with these issues before they become a problem by setting up event notification by e-mail, updating profiles from system log entries by running the aa-logprof tool, and dealing with maintenance issues.

27.1 Reacting to Security Event Rejections

When you receive a security event rejection, examine the access violation and determine if that event indicated a threat or was part of normal application behavior. Application-specific knowledge is required to make the determination. If the rejected action is part of normal application behavior, run **aa-logprof** at the command line.

If the rejected action is not part of normal application behavior, this access should be considered a possible intrusion attempt (that was prevented) and this notification should be passed to the person responsible for security within your organization.

27.2 Maintaining Your Security Profiles

In a production environment, you should plan on maintaining profiles for all of the deployed applications. The security policies are an integral part of your deployment. You should plan on taking steps to back up and restore security policy files, plan for software changes, and allow any needed modification of security policies that your environment dictates.

27.2.1 Backing Up Your Security Profiles

Backing up profiles might save you from having to re-profile all your programs after a disk crash. Also, if profiles are changed, you can easily restore previous settings by using the backed up files.

Back up profiles by copying the profile files to a specified directory.

1. You should first archive the files into one file. To do this, open a terminal window and enter the following as `root`:

   ```
   tar zclpf profiles.tgz /etc/apparmor.d
   ```

   The simplest method to ensure that your security policy files are regularly backed up is to include the directory `/etc/apparmor.d` in the list of directories that your backup system archives.

2. You can also use **scp** or a file manager like Nautilus to store the files on some kind of storage media, the network, or another computer.

27.2.2   Changing Your Security Profiles

Maintenance of security profiles includes changing them if you decide that your system requires more or less security for its applications. To change your profiles in AppArmor, refer to *Section 23.2, "Editing Profiles"*.

27.2.3   Introducing New Software into Your Environment

When you add a new application version or patch to your system, you should always update the profile to fit your needs. You have several options, depending on your company's software deployment strategy. You can deploy your patches and upgrades into a test or production environment. The following explains how to do this with each method.

If you intend to deploy a patch or upgrade in a test environment, the best method for updating your profiles is to run **aa-logprof** in a terminal as `root`. For detailed instructions, refer to *Section 24.6.3.9, "aa-logprof—Scanning the System Log"*.

If you intend to deploy a patch or upgrade directly into a production environment, the best method for updating your profiles is to monitor the system frequently to determine if any new rejections should be added to the profile and update as needed using **aa-logprof**. For detailed instructions, refer to *Section 24.6.3.9, "aa-logprof—Scanning the System Log"*.

28 Support

This chapter outlines maintenance-related tasks. Learn how to update AppArmor® and get a list of available man pages providing basic help for using the command line tools provided by AppArmor. Use the troubleshooting section to learn about some common problems encountered with AppArmor and their solutions. Report defects or enhancement requests for AppArmor following the instructions in this chapter.

28.1 Updating AppArmor Online

Updates for AppArmor packages are provided in the same way as any other update for SUSE Linux Enterprise Server. Retrieve and apply them exactly like for any other package that ships as part of SUSE Linux Enterprise Server.

28.2 Using the Man Pages

There are man pages available for your use. In a terminal, enter `man apparmor` to open the AppArmor man page. Man pages are distributed in sections numbered 1 through 8. Each section is specific to a category of documentation:

TABLE 28.1: MAN PAGES: SECTIONS AND CATEGORIES

Section	Category
1	User commands
2	System calls
3	Library functions
4	Device driver information
5	Configuration file formats
6	Games
7	High level concepts

Section	Category
8	Administrator commands

The section numbers are used to distinguish man pages from each other. For example, `exit(2)` describes the exit system call, while `exit(3)` describes the exit C library function.

The AppArmor man pages are:

- `aa-audit(8)`

- `aa-autodep(8)`

- `aa-complain(8)`

- `aa-decode(8)`

- `aa-disable(8)`

- `aa-easyprof(8)`

- `aa-enforce(8)`

- `aa-enxec(8)`

- `aa-genprof(8)`

- `aa-logprof(8)`

- `aa-notify(8)`

- `aa-status(8)`

- `aa-unconfined(8)`

- `aa_change_hat(8)`

- `logprof.conf(5)`

- `apparmor.d(5)`

- `apparmor.vim(5)`

- `apparmor(7)`

- `apparmor_parser(8)`

- `apparmor_status(8)`

28.3 For More Information

Find more information about the AppArmor product at: http://wiki.apparmor.net ↗. Find the product documentation for AppArmor in the installed system at `/usr/share/doc/manual`.

There is a mailing list for AppArmor that users can post to or join to communicate with developers. See https://lists.ubuntu.com/mailman/listinfo/apparmor ↗ for details.

28.4 Troubleshooting

This section lists the most common problems and error messages that may occur using AppArmor.

28.4.1 How to React to odd Application Behavior?

If you notice odd application behavior or any other type of application problem, you should first check the reject messages in the log files to see if AppArmor is too closely constricting your application. If you detect reject messages that indicate that your application or service is too closely restricted by AppArmor, update your profile to properly handle your use case of the application. Do this with **aa-logprof** (*Section 24.6.3.9, "aa-logprof—Scanning the System Log"*).

If you decide to run your application or service without AppArmor protection, remove the application's profile from `/etc/apparmor.d` or move it to another location.

28.4.2 My Profiles Do not Seem to Work Anymore ...

If you have been using previous versions of AppArmor and have updated your system (but kept your old set of profiles) you might notice some applications which seemed to work perfectly before you updated behaving strangely, or not working.

This version of AppArmor introduces a set of new features to the profile syntax and the AppArmor tools that might cause trouble with older versions of the AppArmor profiles. Those features are:

- File Locking

- Network Access Control

- The `SYS_PTRACE` Capability

- Directory Path Access

The current version of AppArmor mediates file locking and introduces a new permission mode (`k`) for this. Applications requesting file locking permission might misbehave or fail altogether if confined by older profiles which do not explicitly contain permissions to lock files. If you suspect this being the case, check the log file under `/var/log/audit/audit.log` for entries like the following:

```
type=AVC msg=audit(1389862802.727:13939): apparmor="DENIED" \
operation="file_lock" parent=2692 profile="/usr/bin/opera" \
name="/home/tux/.qt/.qtrc.lock" pid=28730 comm="httpd2-prefork" \
requested_mask="::k" denied_mask="::k" fsuid=30 ouid=0
```

Update the profile using the **aa-logprof** command as outlined below.

The new network access control syntax based on the network family and type specification, described in *Section 21.5, "Network Access Control"*, might cause application misbehavior or even stop applications from working. If you notice a network-related application behaving strangely, check the log file under `/var/log/audit/audit.log` for entries like the following:

```
type=AVC msg=audit(1389864332.233:13947): apparmor="DENIED" \
operation="socket_create" family="inet" parent=29985 profile="/bin/ping" \
sock_type="raw" pid=30251 comm="ping"
```

This log entry means that our example application, **/bin/ping** in this case, failed to get AppArmor's permission to open a network connection. This permission needs to be explicitly stated to make sure that an application has network access. To update the profile to the new syntax, use the **aa-logprof** command as outlined below.

The current kernel requires the `SYS_PTRACE` capability, if a process tries to access files in `/proc/PID/fd/*`. New profiles need an entry for the file and the capability, where old profiles only needed the file entry. For example:

```
/proc/*/fd/**  rw,
```

in the old syntax would translate to the following rules in the new syntax:

```
capability SYS_PTRACE,
/proc/*/fd/**  rw,
```

To update the profile to the new syntax, use the YaST Update Profile Wizard or the **aa-logprof** command as outlined below.

With this version of AppArmor, a few changes have been made to the profile rule syntax to better distinguish directory from file access. Therefore, some rules matching both file and directory paths in the previous version might now match a file path only. This could lead to AppArmor not being able to access a crucial directory, and thus trigger misbehavior of your application and various log messages. The following examples highlight the most important changes to the path syntax.

Using the old syntax, the following rule would allow access to files and directories in `/proc/net`. It would allow directory access only to read the entries in the directory, but not give access to files or directories under the directory, for example `/proc/net/dir/foo` would be matched by the asterisk (*), but as `foo` is a file or directory under `dir`, it cannot be accessed.

```
/proc/net/*  r,
```

To get the same behavior using the new syntax, you need two rules instead of one. The first allows access to the file under `/proc/net` and the second allows access to directories under `/proc/net`. Directory access can only be used for listing the contents, not actually accessing files or directories underneath the directory.

```
/proc/net/*  r,
/proc/net/*/  r,
```

The following rule works similarly both under the old and the new syntax, and allows access to both files and directories under `/proc/net` (but does not allow a directory listing of `/proc/net/` itself):

```
/proc/net/**  r,
```

To distinguish file access from directory access using the above expression in the new syntax, use the following two rules. The first one only allows to recursively access directories under `/proc/net` while the second one explicitly allows for recursive file access only.

```
/proc/net/**/  r,
/proc/net/**[^/]  r,
```

The following rule works similarly both under the old and the new syntax and allows access to both files and directories beginning with `foo` under `/proc/net`:

```
/proc/net/foo**   r,
```

To distinguish file access from directory access in the new syntax and use the `**` globbing pattern, use the following two rules. The first one would have matched both files and directories in the old syntax, but only matches files in the new syntax because of the missing trailing slash. The second rule matched neither file nor directory in the old syntax, but matches directories only in the new syntax:

```
/proc/net/**foo   r,
/proc/net/**foo/   r,
```

The following rules illustrate how the use of the `?` globbing pattern has changed. In the old syntax, the first rule would have matched both files and directories (four characters, last character could be any but a slash). In the new syntax, it matches only files (trailing slash is missing). The second rule would match nothing in the old profile syntax, but matches directories only in the new syntax. The last rule matches explicitly matches a file called `bar` under `/proc/net/foo?`. Using the old syntax, this rule would have applied to both files and directories:

```
/proc/net/foo?   r,
/proc/net/foo?/   r,
/proc/net/foo?/bar   r,
```

To find and resolve issues related to syntax changes, take some time after the update to check the profiles you want to keep and proceed as follows for each application you kept the profile for:

1. Put the application's profile into complain mode:

   ```
   aa-complain /path/to/application
   ```

   Log entries are made for any actions violating the current profile, but the profile is not enforced and the application's behavior not restricted.

2. Run the application covering all the tasks you need this application to be able to perform.

3. Update the profile according to the log entries made while running the application:

   ```
   aa-logprof /path/to/application
   ```

4. Put the resulting profile back into enforce mode:

```
aa-enforce /path/to/application
```

28.4.3 Resolving Issues with Apache

After installing additional Apache modules (like `apache2-mod_apparmor`) or making configuration changes to Apache, profile Apache again to find out if additional rules need to be added to the profile. If you do not profile Apache again, it could be unable to start properly or be unable to serve Web pages.

28.4.4 How to Exclude Certain Profiles from the List of Profiles Used?

Run **aa-disable** *PROGRAMNAME* to disable the profile for *PROGRAMNAME*. This command creates a symbolic link to the profile in `/etc/apparmor.d/disable/`. To reactivate the profile, delete the link, and run **systemctl reload apparmor**.

28.4.5 Can I Manage Profiles for Applications not Installed on my System?

Managing profiles with AppArmor requires you to have access to the log of the system on which the application is running. So you do not need to run the application on your profile build host as long as you have access to the machine that runs the application. You can run the application on one system, transfer the logs (`/var/log/audit.log` or, if `audit` is not installed, **journalctl | grep -i apparmor > path_to_logfile**) to your profile build host and run **aa-logprof -f** *PATH_TO_LOGFILE*.

28.4.6 How to Spot and fix AppArmor Syntax Errors?

Manually editing AppArmor profiles can introduce syntax errors. If you attempt to start or restart AppArmor with syntax errors in your profiles, error results are shown. This example shows the syntax of the entire parser error.

```
localhost:~ # rcapparmor start
```

```
Loading AppArmor profiles AppArmor parser error in /etc/apparmor.d/usr.sbin.squid at line
 410: syntax error, unexpected TOK_ID, expecting TOK_MODE
 Profile /etc/apparmor.d/usr.sbin.squid failed to load
```

Using the AppArmor YaST tools, a graphical error message indicates which profile contained the error and requests you to fix it.

Errors found in AppArmor profiles

These problems must be corrected before AppArmor can be started or the profile management tools can be used.

- /etc/apparmor.d/usr.sbin.traceroute contains syntax errors. Line [foo]

You can find a description of AppArmor profile syntax by running man apparmor.d

Comprehensive documentation about AppArmor is available in the Administration guide. This is available in the directory:

/usr/share/doc/manual/suselinux-manual_LANGUAGE.
Please refer to this for more detailed information about AppArmor

  OK

To fix a syntax error, log in to a terminal window as `root`, open the profile, and correct the syntax. Reload the profile set with **`systemctl reload apparmor`**.

 Tip: AppArmor Syntax Highlighting in vi

> The editor `vi` on SUSE Linux Enterprise Server supports syntax highlighting for AppArmor profiles. Lines containing syntax errors will be displayed with a red background.

28.5 Reporting Bugs for AppArmor

The developers of AppArmor are eager to deliver products of the highest quality. Your feedback and your bug reports help us keep the quality high. Whenever you encounter a bug in AppArmor, file a bug report against this product:

1. Use your Web browser to go to http://bugzilla.suse.com/ ↗ and click *Log In*.

2. Enter the account data of your SUSE account and click *Login*. If you do not have a SUSE account, click *Create Account* and provide the required data.

3. If your problem has already been reported, check this bug report and add extra information to it, if necessary.

4. If your problem has not been reported yet, select *New* from the top navigation bar and proceed to the *Enter Bug* page.

5. Select the product against which to file the bug. In your case, this would be your product's release. Click *Submit*.

6. Select the product version, component (AppArmor in this case), hardware platform, and severity.

7. Enter a brief headline describing your problem and add a more elaborate description including log files. You may create attachments to your bug report for screenshots, log files, or test cases.

8. Click *Submit* after you have entered all the details to send your report to the developers.

29   AppArmor Glossary

Abstraction

See *profile foundation classes* below.

Apache

Apache is a freely-available Unix-based Web server. It is currently the most commonly used Web server on the Internet. Find more information about Apache at the Apache Web site at http://www.apache.org ↗.

application fire-walling

AppArmor confines applications and limits the actions they are permitted to take. It uses privilege confinement to prevent attackers from using malicious programs on the protected server and even using trusted applications in unintended ways.

attack signature

Pattern in system or network activity that alerts of a possible virus or hacker attack. Intrusion detection systems might use attack signatures to distinguish between legitimate and potentially malicious activity.

By not relying on attack signatures, AppArmor provides "proactive" instead of "reactive" defense from attacks. This is better because there is no window of vulnerability where the attack signature must be defined for AppArmor as it does for products using attack signatures.

GUI

Graphical user interface. Refers to a software front-end meant to provide an attractive and easy-to-use interface between a computer user and application. Its elements include windows, icons, buttons, cursors, and scrollbars.

globbing

File name substitution. Instead of specifying explicit file name paths, you can use helper characters * (substitutes any number of characters except special ones such as / or ?) and ? (substitutes exactly one character) to address multiple files/directories at once. ** is a special substitution that matches any file or directory below the current directory.

HIP

Host intrusion prevention. Works with the operating system kernel to block abnormal application behavior in the expectation that the abnormal behavior represents an unknown attack. Blocks malicious packets on the host at the network level before they can "hurt" the application they target.

mandatory access control

A means of restricting access to objects that is based on fixed security attributes assigned to users, files, and other objects. The controls are mandatory in the sense that they cannot be modified by users or their programs.

profile

AppArmor profile completely defines what system resources an individual application can access, and with what privileges.

profile foundation classes

Profile building blocks needed for common application activities, such as DNS lookup and user authentication.

RPM

The RPM Package Manager. An open packaging system available for anyone to use. It works on Red Hat Linux, SUSE Linux Enterprise Server, and other Linux and Unix systems. It is capable of installing, uninstalling, verifying, querying, and updating computer software packages. See http://www.rpm.org/ ↗ for more information.

SSH

Secure Shell. A service that allows you to access your server from a remote computer and issue text commands through a secure connection.

streamlined access control

AppArmor provides streamlined access control for network services by specifying which files each program is allowed to read, write, and execute. This ensures that each program does what it is supposed to do and nothing else.

URI

Universal resource identifier. The generic term for all types of names and addresses that refer to objects on the World Wide Web. A URL is one kind of URI.

URL

Uniform Resource Locator. The global address of documents and other resources on the Web.

The first part of the address indicates what protocol to use and the second part specifies the IP address or the domain name where the resource is located.

For example, when you visit `http://www.suse.com`, you are using the HTTP protocol, as the beginning of the URL indicates.

vulnerabilities

An aspect of a system or network that leaves it open to attack. Characteristics of computer systems that allow an individual to keep it from correctly operating or that allows unauthorized users to take control of the system. Design, administrative, or implementation weaknesses or flaws in hardware, firmware, or software. If exploited, a vulnerability could lead to an unacceptable impact in the form of unauthorized access to information or the disruption of critical processing.

310

V SELinux

V SELinux

30 Configuring SELinux

In this chapter, you will learn how to set up and manage SELinux on SUSE Linux Enterprise Server. The following topics are covered:

- Why Use SELinux?

- Understanding SELinux

- Setting Up SELinux

- Managing SELinux

30.1 Why Use SELinux?

SELinux was developed as an additional Linux security solution that uses the security framework in the Linux kernel. The purpose was to allow for a more granular security policy that goes beyond what is offered by the default existing permissions of Read, Write, and Execute, and beyond assigning permissions to the different capabilities that are available on Linux. SELinux does this by trapping all system calls that reach the kernel, and denying them by default. This means that on a system that has SELinux enabled and nothing else configured, nothing will work. To allow your system to do anything, as an administrator you will need to write rules and put them in a policy.

An example explains why a solution such as SELinux (or its counterpart AppArmor) is needed:

"One morning, I found out that my server was hacked. The server was running a fully patched SLES installation. A firewall was configured on it and no unnecessary services were offered by this server. Further analysis revealed that the hacker had come in through a vulnerable PHP script that was a part of one of the Apache virtual hosts that were running on this server. The intruder had managed to get access to a shell, using the wwwrun account that was used by the Apache Web server. As this wwwrun user, the intruder had created several scripts in the /var/tmp and the /tmp directories, which were a part of a botnet that was launching a Distributed Denial of Service attack against several servers."

The interesting thing about this hack is that it occurred on a server where nothing was really wrong. All permissions where set OK, but the intruder had managed to get into the system. What becomes clearly evident from this example is that in some cases additional security is needed—a security that goes beyond what is offered by using SELinux. As a less complete and less complex alternative, AppArmor can be used.

AppArmor confines specific processes in their abilities to read/write and execute files (and other things). Its view is mostly that things that happen inside a process cannot escape.

SELinux instead uses labels attached to objects (for example, files, binaries, network sockets) and uses them to determine privilege boundaries, thereby building up a level of confinement that can span more than a process or even the whole system.

SELinux was developed by the US National Security Agency (NSA), and since the beginning Red Hat has been heavily involved in its development. The first version of SELinux was offered in the era of Red Hat Enterprise Linux 4™, around the year 2006. In the beginning it offered support for essential services only, but over the years it has developed into a system that offers many rules that are collected in policies to offer protection to a broad range of services.

SELinux was developed in accordance with some certification standards like Common Criteria and FIPS 140. Because some customers specifically requested solutions that met these standards, SELinux rapidly became relatively popular.

As an alternative to SELinux, Immunix, a company that was purchased by Novell in 2005, had developed AppArmor. AppArmor was built on top of the same security principles as SELinux, but took a completely different approach, where it was possible to restrict services to exactly what they needed to do by using an easy to use wizard-driven procedure. Nevertheless, AppArmor has never reached the same status as SELinux, even if there are some good arguments to secure a server with AppArmor rather than with SELinux.

Because many organizations are requesting SELinux to be in the Linux distributions they are using, SUSE is offering support for the SELinux framework in SUSE Linux Enterprise Server. This does not mean that the default installation of SUSE Linux Enterprise Server will switch from AppArmor to SELinux in the near future.

30.1.1 Support Status

The SELinux framework is supported on SUSE Linux Enterprise Server. This means that SLES offers all binaries and libraries you need to be able to use SELinux on your server. You may however miss some software that you may be familiar with from other Linux distributions.

SELinux support is at a fairly early stage in SUSE Linux Enterprise Server, which means that unexpected behavior may occur. To limit this risk as much as possible, it is best to use only the binaries that have been provided by default on SUSE Linux Enterprise Server.

30.1.2   Understanding SELinux Components

Before starting the configuration of SELinux, you should know a bit about how SELinux is organized. Three components play a role:

- The security framework in the Linux kernel

- The SELinux libraries and binaries

- The SELinux policy

The default kernel of SUSE Linux Enterprise Server supports SELinux and the tools that are needed to manage it. The most important part of the work of the administrator with regard to SELinux is managing the policy.

In the SELinux policy, security labels are applied to different objects on a Linux server. These objects typically are users, ports, processes and files. Using these security labels, rules are created that define what is and what is not allowed on a server. Remember, by default SELinux denies everything, and by creating the appropriate rules you can allow the access that is strictly necessary. Rules should therefore exist for all programs that you want to use on a system. Alternatively, you should configure parts of a system to run in unconfined mode, which means that specific ports, programs, users, files and directories are not protected by SELinux. This mode is useful if you only want to use SELinux to protect some essential services, while you are not specifically worried about other services. To get a really secure system, you should avoid this.

To ensure the appropriate protection of your system, you need an SELinux policy. This must be a tailor-made policy in which all files are provided with a label, and all services and users have a security label as well to express which files and directories can be accessed by which user and processed on the server. Developing such a policy is a tremendous amount of work.

The complexity of SELinux is also one of the main arguments against using it. Because a typical Linux system is so very complex, it is easy to overlook something and leave an opening that intruders can abuse to get into your system. And even if it is set up completely the way it should be, it still is very hard for an administrator to overlook all aspects with SELinux. With regard to the complexity, AppArmor takes a completely different approach and works with automated procedures that allow the administrator to set up AppArmor protection and understand exactly what is happening.

Note that a freely available SELinux policy might work on your server, but is unlikely to offer the same protection as a custom policy. SUSE also does not support third-party policies.

30.2 Policy

As mentioned, the policy is the key component in SELinux. It defines rules that specify which objects can access which files, directories, ports and processes on a system. To do this, a security context is defined for all of these. On an SELinux system where the policy has been applied to label the file system, you can use the **ls -Z** command on any directory to find the security context for the files in that directory. *Example 30.1: "Security Context Settings Using* ls -Z*"* shows the security context settings for the directories in the / directory of a SUSE Linux Enterprise Server system with an SELinux-labeled file system.

EXAMPLE 30.1: SECURITY CONTEXT SETTINGS USING ls -Z

```
ls -Z
system_u:object_r:bin_t bin
system_u:object_r:boot_t boot
system_u:object_r:device_t dev
system_u:object_r:etc_t etc
system_u:object_r:home_root_t home
system_u:object_r:lib_t lib
system_u:object_r:lib_t lib64
system_u:object_r:lost_found_t lost+found
system_u:object_r:mnt_t media
system_u:object_r:mnt_t mnt
system_u:object_r:usr_t opt
system_u:object_r:proc_t proc
system_u:object_r:default_t root
system_u:object_r:bin_t sbin
system_u:object_r:security_t selinux
system_u:object_r:var_t srv
system_u:object_r:sysfs_t sys
system_u:object_r:tmp_t tmp
system_u:object_r:usr_t usr
system_u:object_r:var_t var
```

The most important line in the security context is the context type. This is the part of the security context that ends in _t. It tells SELinux which kind of access the object is allowed. In the policy, rules are specified to define which type of user or which type of role has access to which type of context. For example, this can happen by using a rule like the following:

```
allow user_t bin_t:file {read execute gettattr};
```

This example rule states that the user who has the context type user_t (this user is called the source object) is allowed to access objects of class "file" with the context type bin_t (the target), using the permissions read, execute and getattr.

The standard policy that you are going to use contains a huge amount of rules. To make it more manageable, policies are often split into modules. This allows administrator to switch protection on or off for different parts of the system.

When compiling the policy for your system, you will have a choice to either work with a modular policy, or a monolithic policy, where one huge policy is used to protect everything on your system. It is strongly recommended to use a modular policy and not a monolithic policy. Modular policies are much easier to manage.

30.3 Installing SELinux Packages and Modifying GRUB 2

The easiest way to make sure that all SELinux components are installed is by using YaST. The procedure described below shows what to do on an installed SUSE Linux Enterprise Server:

1. Log in to your server as `root` and start YaST.

2. Select *Software* › *Software Management*

3. *Select View* › *Patterns* and select the entire *C/C++ Development* category for installation.

4. *Select View* › *Search* and make sure that *Search in Name*, *Keywords* and *Summary* are selected. Now enter the keyword `selinux` and click *Search*. You now see a list of packages.

5. Make sure that all the packages you have found are selected and click *Accept* to install them.

FIGURE 30.1: SELECTING ALL SELINUX PACKAGES IN YAST

After installing the SELinux packages, you need to modify the GRUB 2 boot loader. Do this from YaST, select *System* > *Boot Loader* > *Kernel Parameters*. Now add the following parameters to the *Optional Kernel Command Line Parameters*:

```
security=selinux selinux=1 enforcing=0
```

These options are used for the following purposes:

`security=selinux`

    This option tells the kernel to use SELinux and not AppArmor

`selinux=1`

    This option switches on SELinux

`enforcing=0`

    This option puts SELinux in permissive mode. In this mode, SELinux is fully functional, but does not enforce any of the security settings in the policy. Use this mode for configuring your system. To switch on SELinux protection, when the system is fully operational, change the option to `enforcing=1` and add `SELINUX=enforcing` in `/etc/selinux/config`.

After installing the SELinux packages and enabling the SELinux GRUB 2 boot options, reboot your server to activate the configuration.

30.4   SELinux Policy

The policy is an essential component of SELinux. SUSE Linux Enterprise Server 12 SP3 includes the *minimum* SELinux reference policy in the package `selinux-policy-minimum`. The examples in this chapter refer to this policy if not stated otherwise.

 Tip

    To install a different policy, you need to download it from https://build.opensuse.org/package/binaries/security:SELinux/selinux-policy?repository=SLE_12 and install:

```
sudo zypper in selinux-policy-targeted-VERSION_NUMBER.noarch.rpm
```

After installing the policy, you are ready to start file system labeling. Run

```
restorecon -Rp /
```

to start the **/sbin/setfiles** command to label all files on your system. The /etc/selin-ux/minimum/contexts/files/file_contexts input file is used. The file_contexts file needs to match your actual file system as much as possible. Otherwise, it can lead to a completely unbootable system. If that happens, modify the records in file_contexts with the **semanage fcontext** command to match the real structure of the file system your server is using. For example

```
semanage fcontext -a -t samba_share_t /etc/example_file
```

changes the file type from the default etc_t to samba_share_t and adds the following record to the related file_contexts.local file:

```
/etc/example_file     unconfined_u:object_r:samba_share_t:s0
```

Then run

```
restorecon -v /etc/example_file
```

for the type change to take effect.

Before doing this, make sure to read the rest of this chapter, so you fully understand how context type is applied to files and directories. Do not forget to make a backup of the file_contexts file before starting.

 Note: The User nobody

While using **semanage**, you may get a message that complains about the home directory of nobody. In this case, change the login shell of user nobody to /sbin/nologin. Then the settings of nobody match the current policy settings.

After another reboot SELinux should be operational. To verify this, use the command **sestatus -v**. It should give you an output similar to *Example 30.2: "Verifying that SELinux is functional"*.

EXAMPLE 30.2: VERIFYING THAT SELINUX IS FUNCTIONAL

```
sestatus -v
SELinux status:            enabled
SELinuxfs mount:           /selinux
Current mode:              permissive
```

```
Mode from config file:        permissive
Policy version:               26
Policy from config file:      minimum

Process contexts:
Current context:              root:staff_r:staff_t
Init context:                 system_u:system_r:init_t
/sbin/mingetty                system_u:system_r:sysadm_t
/usr/sbin/sshd                system_u:system_r:sshd_t

File contexts:
Controlling term:             root:object_r:user_devpts_t
/etc/passwd                   system_u:object_r:etc_t
/etc/shadow                   system_u:object_r:shadow_t
/bin/bash                     system_u:object_r:shell_exec_t
/bin/login                    system_u:object_r:login_exec_t
/bin/sh                       system_u:object_r:bin_t -> system_u:object_r:shell_exec_t
/sbin/agetty                  system_u:object_r:getty_exec_t
/sbin/init                    system_u:object_r:init_exec_t
/sbin/mingetty                system_u:object_r:getty_exec_t
/usr/sbin/sshd                system_u:object_r:sshd_exec_t
/lib/libc.so.6                system_u:object_r:lib_t -> system_u:object_r:lib_t
/lib/ld-linux.so.2            system_u:object_r:lib_t -> system_u:object_r:ld_so_t
```

30.5 Configuring SELinux

At this point you have a completely functional SELinux system and it is time to further configure it. In the current status, SELinux is operational but not in enforcing mode. This means that it does not limit you in doing anything, it logs everything that it should be doing if it were in enforcing mode. This is good, because based on the log files you can find what it is that it would prevent you from doing. As a first test, put SELinux in enforcing mode and find out if you can still use your server after doing so: check that the option `enforcing=1` is set in the GRUB 2 configuration file, while `SELINUX=enforcing` is set in `/etc/selinux/config`. Reboot your server and see if it still comes up the way you expect it to. If it does, leave it like that and start modifying the server in a way that everything works as expected. However, you may not even be able to boot the server properly. In that case, switch back to the mode where SELinux is not enforcing and start tuning your server.

Before you start tuning your server, verify the SELinux installation. You have already used the command **sestatus -v** to view the current mode, process, and file contexts. Next, run

```
semanage boolean -l
```

which lists all Boolean switches that are available, and at the same time verifies that you can access the policy. *Example 30.3, "Getting a List of Booleans and Verifying Policy Access"* shows part of the output of this command.

EXAMPLE 30.3: GETTING A LIST OF BOOLEANS AND VERIFYING POLICY ACCESS

```
semanage boolean -l
SELinux boolean                                Description
ftp_home_dir                      -> off    ftp_home_dir
mozilla_read_content              -> off    mozilla_read_content
spamassassin_can_network          -> off    spamassassin_can_network
httpd_can_network_relay           -> off    httpd_can_network_relay
openvpn_enable_homedirs           -> off    openvpn_enable_homedirs
gpg_agent_env_file                -> off    gpg_agent_env_file
allow_httpd_awstats_script_anon_write -> off    allow_httpd_awstats_script_anon_write
httpd_can_network_connect_db      -> off    httpd_can_network_connect_db
allow_ftpd_full_access            -> off    allow_ftpd_full_access
samba_domain_controller           -> off    samba_domain_controller
httpd_enable_cgi                  -> off    httpd_enable_cgi
virt_use_nfs                      -> off    virt_use_nfs
```

Another command that outputs useful information at this stage is

```
semanage fcontext -l
```

It shows the default file context settings as provided by the policy (see *Example 30.4: "Getting File Context Information"* for partial output of this command).

EXAMPLE 30.4: GETTING FILE CONTEXT INFORMATION

```
semanage fcontext -l
/var/run/usb(/.*)?                              all files
  system_u:object_r:hotplug_var_run_t
/var/run/utmp                                   regular file
  system_u:object_r:initrc_var_run_t
/var/run/vbe.*                                  regular file
  system_u:object_r:hald_var_run_t
/var/run/vmnat.*                                socket
  system_u:object_r:vmware_var_run_t
/var/run/vmware.*                               all files
  system_u:object_r:vmware_var_run_t
/var/run/vpnc(/.*)?                             all files
  system_u:object_r:vpnc_var_run_t
/var/run/watchdog\.pid                          regular file
  system_u:object_r:watchdog_var_run_t
/var/run/winbindd(/.*)?                         all files
  system_u:object_r:winbind_var_run_t
```

```
/var/run/wnn-unix(/.*)                          all files
  system_u:object_r:canna_var_run_t
/var/run/wpa_supplicant(/.*)?                    all files
  system_u:object_r:NetworkManager_var_run_t
/var/run/wpa_supplicant-global                   socket
  system_u:object_r:NetworkManager_var_run_t
/var/run/xdmctl(/.*)?                            all files
  system_u:object_r:xdm_var_run_t
/var/run/yiff-[0-9]+\.pid                        regular file
  system_u:object_r:soundd_var_run_t
```

30.6 Managing SELinux

The base SELinux configuration is now operational and it can now be configured to secure your server. In SELinux, an additional set of rules is used to define exactly which process or user can access which files, directories, or ports. To do this, SELinux applies a context to every file, directory, process, and port. This context is a security label that defines how this file, directory, process, or port should be treated. These context labels are used by the SELinux policy, which defines exactly what should be done with the context labels. By default, the policy blocks all non-default access, which means that, as an administrator, you need to enable all features that are non-default on your server.

30.6.1 Viewing the Security Context

As already mentioned, files, directories, and ports can be labeled. Within each label, different contexts are used. To be able to perform your daily administration work, the type context is what you are most interested in. As an administrator, you will mostly work with the type context. Many commands allow you to use the -Z option to list current context settings. In *Example 30.5: "The default context for directories in the root directory"* you can see what the context settings are for the directories in the root directory.

EXAMPLE 30.5: THE DEFAULT CONTEXT FOR DIRECTORIES IN THE ROOT DIRECTORY

```
ls -Z
dr-xr-xr-x. root root system_u:object_r:bin_t:s0        bin
dr-xr-xr-x. root root system_u:object_r:boot_t:s0       boot
drwxr-xr-x. root root system_u:object_r:cgroup_t:s0     cgroup
drwxr-xr-x+ root root unconfined_u:object_r:default_t:s0 data
drwxr-xr-x. root root system_u:object_r:device_t:s0     dev
```

```
drwxr-xr-x. root root system_u:object_r:etc_t:s0         etc
drwxr-xr-x. root root system_u:object_r:home_root_t:s0 home
dr-xr-xr-x. root root system_u:object_r:lib_t:s0         lib
dr-xr-xr-x. root root system_u:object_r:lib_t:s0         lib64
drwx------. root root system_u:object_r:lost_found_t:s0 lost+found
drwxr-xr-x. root root system_u:object_r:mnt_t:s0         media
drwxr-xr-x. root root system_u:object_r:autofs_t:s0      misc
drwxr-xr-x. root root system_u:object_r:mnt_t:s0         mnt
drwxr-xr-x. root root unconfined_u:object_r:default_t:s0 mnt2
drwxr-xr-x. root root unconfined_u:object_r:default_t:s0 mounts
drwxr-xr-x. root root system_u:object_r:autofs_t:s0      net
drwxr-xr-x. root root system_u:object_r:usr_t:s0         opt
dr-xr-xr-x. root root system_u:object_r:proc_t:s0        proc
drwxr-xr-x. root root unconfined_u:object_r:default_t:s0 repo
dr-xr-x---. root root system_u:object_r:admin_home_t:s0  root
dr-xr-xr-x. root root system_u:object_r:bin_t:s0         sbin
drwxr-xr-x. root root system_u:object_r:security_t:s0    selinux
drwxr-xr-x. root root system_u:object_r:var_t:s0         srv
-rw-r--r--. root root unconfined_u:object_r:swapfile_t:s0 swapfile
drwxr-xr-x. root root system_u:object_r:sysfs_t:s0       sys
drwxrwxrwt. root root system_u:object_r:tmp_t:s0         tmp
-rw-r--r--. root root unconfined_u:object_r:etc_runtime_t:s0 tmp2.tar
-rw-r--r--. root root unconfined_u:object_r:etc_runtime_t:s0 tmp.tar
drwxr-xr-x. root root system_u:object_r:usr_t:s0         usr
drwxr-xr-x. root root system_u:object_r:var_t:s0         var
```

In the listing above, you can see the complete context for all directories. It consists of a user, a role, and a type. The s0 setting indicates the security level in Multi Level Security environments. These environments are not discussed here. In such an environment, make sure that s0 is set. The Context Type defines what kind of activity is permitted in the directory. Compare, for example, the /root directory, which has the admin_home_t context type, and the /home directory, which has the home_root_t context type. In the SELinux policy, different kinds of access are defined for these context types.

Security labels are not only associated with files, but also with other items, such as ports and processes. In *Example 30.6: "Showing SELinux settings for processes with* ps Zaux*"* for example you can see the context settings for processes on your server.

EXAMPLE 30.6: SHOWING SELINUX SETTINGS FOR PROCESSES WITH ps Zaux

```
ps Zaux
LABEL                           USER     PID %CPU %MEM   VSZ  RSS TTY     STAT START
   TIME COMMAND
system_u:system_r:init_t        root       1  0.0  0.0 10640  808 ?       Ss   05:31
   0:00 init [5]
```

```
system_u:system_r:kernel_t        root       2  0.0  0.0      0     0 ?     S    05:31
   0:00 [kthreadd]
system_u:system_r:kernel_t        root       3  0.0  0.0      0     0 ?     S    05:31
   0:00 [ksoftirqd/0]
system_u:system_r:kernel_t        root       6  0.0  0.0      0     0 ?     S    05:31
   0:00 [migration/0]
system_u:system_r:kernel_t        root       7  0.0  0.0      0     0 ?     S    05:31
   0:00 [watchdog/0]
system_u:system_r:sysadm_t        root    2344  0.0  0.0  27640   852 ?     Ss   05:32
   0:00 /usr/sbin/mcelog --daemon --config-file /etc/mcelog/mcelog.conf
system_u:system_r:sshd_t          root    3245  0.0  0.0  69300  1492 ?     Ss   05:32
   0:00 /usr/sbin/sshd -o PidFile=/var/run/sshd.init.pid
system_u:system_r:cupsd_t         root    3265  0.0  0.0  68176  2852 ?     Ss   05:32
   0:00 /usr/sbin/cupsd
system_u:system_r:nscd_t          root    3267  0.0  0.0 772876  1380 ?     Ssl  05:32
   0:00 /usr/sbin/nscd
system_u:system_r:postfix_master_t root  3334  0.0  0.0  38320  2424 ?     Ss   05:32
   0:00 /usr/lib/postfix/master
system_u:system_r:postfix_qmgr_t postfix 3358  0.0  0.0  40216  2252 ?     S    05:32
   0:00 qmgr -l -t fifo -u
system_u:system_r:crond_t         root    3415  0.0  0.0  14900   800 ?     Ss   05:32
   0:00 /usr/sbin/cron
system_u:system_r:fsdaemon_t      root    3437  0.0  0.0  16468  1040 ?     S    05:32
   0:00 /usr/sbin/smartd
system_u:system_r:sysadm_t        root    3441  0.0  0.0  66916  2152 ?     Ss   05:32
   0:00 login -- root
system_u:system_r:sysadm_t        root    3442  0.0  0.0   4596   800 tty2  Ss+  05:32
   0:00 /sbin/mingetty tty2
```

30.6.2 Selecting the SELinux Mode

In SELinux, three different modes can be used:

Enforcing:

This is the default mode. SELinux protects your server according to the rules in the policy, and SELinux logs all of its activity to the audit log.

Permissive:

This mode is useful for troubleshooting. If set to Permissive, SELinux does not protect your server, but it still logs everything that happens to the log files.

Disabled:

In this mode, SELinux is switched off completely and no logging occurs. The file system labels however are not removed from the file system.

You have already read how you can set the current SELinux mode from GRUB 2 while booting using the enforcing boot parameter.

30.6.3 Modifying SELinux Context Types

An important part of the work of an administrator is setting context types on files to ensure appropriate working of SELinux.

If a file is created within a specific directory, it inherits the context type of the parent directory by default. If, however, a file is moved from one location to another location, it retains the context type that it had in the old location.

To set the context type for files, you can use the **semanage fcontext** command. With this command, you write the new context type to the policy, but it does not change the actual context type immediately! To apply the context types that are in the policy, you need to run the **restorecon** command afterward.

The challenge when working with **semanage fcontext** is to find out which context you actually need. You can use

```
semanage fcontext -l
```

to list all contexts in the policy, but it may be a bit hard to find out the actual context you need from that list as it is rather long (see *Example 30.7: "Viewing Default File Contexts"*).

EXAMPLE 30.7: VIEWING DEFAULT FILE CONTEXTS

```
semanage fcontext -l | less
SELinux fcontext                                type            Context

/                                               directory
 system_u:object_r:root_t:s0
/.*                                             all files
 system_u:object_r:default_t:s0
/[^/]+                                          regular file
 system_u:object_r:etc_runtime_t:s0
/\.autofsck                                     regular file
 system_u:object_r:etc_runtime_t:s0
/\.autorelabel                                  regular file
 system_u:object_r:etc_runtime_t:s0
/\.journal                                      all files       X:>>None>>
/\.suspended                                    regular file
 system_u:object_r:etc_runtime_t:s0
/a?quota\.(user|group)                          regular file
 system_u:object_r:quota_db_t:s0
```

```
/afs                                          directory
 system_u:object_r:mnt_t:s0
/bin                                          directory
 system_u:object_r:bin_t:s0
/bin/.*                                       all files
 system_u:object_r:bin_t:s0
```

There are three ways to find out which context settings are available for your services:

- Install the service and look at the default context settings that are used. This is the easiest and recommended option.

- Consult the man page for the specific service. Some services have a man page that ends in `_selinux`, which contains all the information you need to find the correct context settings. When you have found the right context setting, apply it using **semanage fcontext**. This command takes `-t` context type as its first argument, followed by the name of the directory or file to which you want to apply the context settings. To apply the context to everything that already exists in the directory where you want to apply the context, you add the regular expression `(/.*)?` to the name of the directory. This means: optionally, match a slash followed by any character. The examples section of the **semanage** man page has some useful usage examples for **semanage**. For more information on regular expressions, see for example the tutorial at http://www.regular-expressions.info/ ↗.

- Display a list of all context types that are available on your system:

  ```
  seinfo -t
  ```

  Since the command by itself outputs an overwhelming amount of information, it should be used in combination with **grep** or a similar command for filtering.

30.6.4   Applying File Contexts

To help you apply the SELinux context properly, the following procedure shows how to set a context using **semanage fcontext** and **restorecon**. You will notice that at first attempt, the Web server with a non-default document root does not work. After changing the SELinux context, it will:

1. Create the `/web` directory and then change to it:

   ```
   sudo mkdir /web  && cd /web
   ```

2. Use a text editor to create the file `/web/index.html` that contains the text welcome to my Web site.

3. Open the file `/etc/apache2/default-server.conf` with an editor, and change the DocumentRoot line to `DocumentRoot /web`

4. Start the Apache Web server:

```
sudo systemctl start apache2
```

5. Open a session to your local Web server:

```
w3m localhost
```

You will receive a *Connection refused* message. Press Enter , and then **q** to quit w3m.

6. Find the current context type for the default Apache `DocumentRoot`, which is `/srv/www/htdocs`. It should be set to `httpd_sys_content_t`:

```
ls -Z /srv/www
```

7. Set the new context in the policy and press Enter :

```
semanage fcontext -a -f "" -t httpd_sys_content_t '/web(/.*) ?'
```

8. Apply the new context type:

```
restorecon /web
```

9. Show the context of the files in the directory `/web`. You will see that the new context type has been set properly to the `/web` directory, but not to its contents.

```
ls -Z /web
```

10. Apply the new context recursively to the `/web` directory. The type context has now been set correctly.

```
restorecon -R /web
```

11. Restart the Web server:

```
sudo systemctl restart apache2
```

You should now be able to access the contents of the `/web` directory.

30.6.5 Configuring SELinux Policies

The easiest way to change the behavior of the policy is by working with Booleans. These are on-off switches that you can use to change the settings in the policy. To find out which Booleans are available, run

```
semanage boolean -l
```

It will show a long list of Booleans, with a short description of what each of these Booleans will do for you. When you have found the Boolean you want to set, you can use **setsebool -P**, followed by the name of the Boolean that you want to change. It is important to use the -P option at all times when using **setsebool**. This option writes the setting to the policy file on disk, and this is the only way to make sure that the Boolean is applied automatically after a reboot.

The procedure below gives an example of changing Boolean settings

1. List Booleans that are related to FTP servers.

   ```
   semanage boolean -l | grep ftp
   ```

2. Turn the Boolean off:

   ```
   setsebool allow_ftpd_anon_write off
   ```

   Note that it does not take much time to write the change. Then verify that the Boolean is indeed turned off:

   ```
   semanage boolean -l|grep ftpd_anon
   ```

3. Reboot your server.

4. Check again to see if the `allow_ftpd_anon_write` Boolean is still turned on. As it has not yet been written to the policy, you will notice that it is off.

5. Switch the Boolean and write the setting to the policy:

   ```
   setsebool -P allow_ftpd_anon_write
   ```

30.6.6 Working with SELinux Modules

By default, SELinux uses a modular policy. This means that the policy that implements SELinux features is not just one huge policy, but it consists of many smaller modules. Each module covers a specific part of the SELinux configuration. The concept of the SELinux module was introduced to make it easier for third party vendors to make their services compatible with SELinux. To get an overview of the SELinux modules, you can use the **semodule -l** command. This command lists all current modules in use by SELinux and their version numbers.

As an administrator, you can switch modules on or off. This can be useful if you want to disable only a part of SELinux and not everything to run a specific service without SELinux protection. Especially in the case of SUSE Linux Enterprise Server, where there is not a completely supported SELinux policy yet, it can make sense to switch off all modules that you do not need so that you can focus on the services that really do need SELinux protection. To switch off an SELinux module, use

```
semodule -d MODULENAME
```

To switch it on again, you can use

```
semodule -e modulename
```

As an administrator, you do not typically change the contents of the policy files that come from the SELinux Policy RPM. You would rather use **semanage fcontext** to change file contexts. If you are using **audit2allow** to generate policies for your server, you should change the policy files after all.

To change the contents of any of the policy module files, compile the changes into a new policy module file. To do this, first install the `selinux-policy-devel` package. Then, in the directory where the files created by **audit2allow** are located, run:

```
make -f /usr/share/selinux/devel/Makefile
```

When **make** has completed, you can manually load the modules into the system, using **semodule -i**.

30.7 Troubleshooting

By default, if SELinux is the reason something is not working, a log message to this effect is sent to the `/var/log/audit/audit.log` file. That is, if the auditd service is running. If you see an empty `/var/log/audit`, start the auditd service using

```
sudo systemctl start auditd
```

and enable it in the targets of your system, using

```
sudo systemctl enable auditd
```

In *Example 30.8: "Example Lines from /etc/audit/audit.log"* you can see a partial example of the contents of /var/log/audit/audit.log

EXAMPLE 30.8: EXAMPLE LINES FROM /etc/audit/audit.log

```
type=DAEMON_START msg=audit(1348173810.874:6248): auditd start, ver=1.7.7 format=raw
 kernel=3.0.13-0.27-default auid=0 pid=4235 subj=system_u:system_r:auditd_t res=success
type=AVC msg=audit(1348173901.081:292): avc:  denied  { write } for
  pid=3426 comm="smartd" name="smartmontools" dev=sda6 ino=581743
 scontext=system_u:system_r:fsdaemon_t tcontext=system_u:object_r:var_lib_t tclass=dir
type=AVC msg=audit(1348173901.081:293): avc:  denied  { remove_name } for  pid=3426
 comm="smartd" name="smartd.WDC_WD2500BEKT_75PVMT0-WD_WXC1A21E0454.ata.state~" dev=sda6
 ino=582390 scontext=system_u:system_r:fsdaemon_t tcontext=system_u:object_r:var_lib_t
 tclass=dir
type=AVC msg=audit(1348173901.081:294): avc:  denied  { unlink } for  pid=3426
 comm="smartd" name="smartd.WDC_WD2500BEKT_75PVMT0-WD_WXC1A21E0454.ata.state~" dev=sda6
 ino=582390 scontext=system_u:system_r:fsdaemon_t tcontext=system_u:object_r:var_lib_t
 tclass=file
type=AVC msg=audit(1348173901.081:295): avc:  denied  { rename } for  pid=3426
 comm="smartd" name="smartd.WDC_WD2500BEKT_75PVMT0-WD_WXC1A21E0454.ata.state" dev=sda6
 ino=582373 scontext=system_u:system_r:fsdaemon_t tcontext=system_u:object_r:var_lib_t
 tclass=file
type=AVC msg=audit(1348173901.081:296): avc:  denied  { add_name } for  pid=3426
 comm="smartd" name="smartd.WDC_WD2500BEKT_75PVMT0-WD_WXC1A21E0454.ata.state~"
 scontext=system_u:system_r:fsdaemon_t tcontext=system_u:object_r:var_lib_t tclass=dir
type=AVC msg=audit(1348173901.081:297): avc:  denied  { create } for  pid=3426
 comm="smartd" name="smartd.WDC_WD2500BEKT_75PVMT0-WD_WXC1A21E0454.ata.state"
 scontext=system_u:system_r:fsdaemon_t tcontext=system_u:object_r:var_lib_t tclass=file
type=AVC msg=audit(1348173901.081:298): avc:  denied  { write open } for  pid=3426
 comm="smartd" name="smartd.WDC_WD2500BEKT_75PVMT0-WD_WXC1A21E0454.ata.state" dev=sda6
 ino=582390 scontext=system_u:system_r:fsdaemon_t tcontext=system_u:object_r:var_lib_t
 tclass=file
type=AVC msg=audit(1348173901.081:299): avc:  denied  { getattr } for  pid=3426
 comm="smartd" path="/var/lib/smartmontools/smartd.WDC_WD2500BEKT_75PVMT0-
WD_WXC1A21E0454.ata.state" dev=sda6 ino=582390 scontext=system_u:system_r:fsdaemon_t
 tcontext=system_u:object_r:var_lib_t tclass=file
type=AVC msg=audit(1348173901.309:300): avc:  denied  { append } for  pid=1316
```

At first look, the lines in `audit.log` are a bit hard to read. However, on closer examination they are not that hard to understand. Every line can be broken down into sections. For example, the sections in the last line are:

`type=AVC`:

> every SELinux-related audit log line starts with the type identification `type=AVC`

`msg=audit(1348173901.309:300)`:

> This is the time stamp, which unfortunately is written in epoch time, the number of seconds that have passed since Jan 1, 1970. You can use **date -d** on the part up to the dot in the epoch time notation to find out when the event has happened:

```
date -d @1348173901
Thu Sep 20 16:45:01 EDT 2012
```

`avc: denied { append }`:

> the specific action that was denied. In this case the system has denied the appending of data to a file. While browsing through the audit log file, you can see other system actions, such as write open, getattr and more.

`for pid=1316`:

> the process ID of the command or process that initiated the action

`comm="rsyslogd"`:

> the specific command that was associated with that PID

`name="smartmontools"`:

> the name of the subject of the action

`dev=sda6 ino=582296`:

> the block device and inode number of the file that was involved

`scontext=system_u:system_r:syslogd_t`:

> the source context, which is the context of the initiator of the action

`tclass=file`:

> a class identification of the subject

Instead of interpreting the events in audit.log yourself, there is another approach. You can use the **audit2allow** command, which helps analyze the cryptic log messages in `/var/log/audit/audit.log`. An audit2allow troubleshooting session always consists of three different commands. First, you would use **audit2allow -w -a** to present the audit information in a more readable way. The **audit2allow -w -a** by default works on the audit.log file. If you want to analyze a specific message in the audit.log file, copy it to a temporary file and analyze the file with:

```
audit2allow -w -i FILENAME
```

EXAMPLE 30.9: ANALYZING AUDIT MESSAGES

```
audit2allow -w -i testfile
type=AVC msg=audit(1348173901.309:300): avc:  denied  { append } for  pid=1316
comm="rsyslogd" name="acpid" dev=sda6 ino=582296
scontext=system_u:system_r:syslogd_t tcontext=system_u:object_r:apmd_log_t tclass=file
```

This was caused by:

Missing type enforcement (TE) allow rule.

To generate a loadable module to allow this access, run

```
audit2allow
```

To find out which specific rule has denied access, you can use **audit2allow -a** to show the enforcing rules from all events that were logged to the audit.log file, or **audit2allow -i** *FILENAME* to show it for messages that you have stored in a specific file:

EXAMPLE 30.10: VIEWING WHICH LINES DENY ACCESS

```
audit2allow -i testfile
#============= syslogd_t ==============
allow syslogd_t apmd_log_t:file append;
```

To create an SELinux module with the name mymodule that you can load to allow the access that was previously denied, run

```
audit2allow -a -R -M mymodule
```

If you want to do this for all events that have been logged to the audit.log, use the -a -M command arguments. To do it only for specific messages that are in a specific file, use -i -M as in the example below:

EXAMPLE 30.11: CREATING A POLICY MODULE ALLOWING AN ACTION PREVIOUSLY DENIED

```
audit2allow -i testfile -M example
******************** IMPORTANT ***********************
```

```
To make this policy package active, execute:

semodule -i example.pp
```

As indicated by the **audit2allow** command, you can now run this module by using the **semodule -i** command, followed by the name of the module that **audit2allow** has created for you (example.pp in the above example).

VI *The Linux Audit Framework*

31 Understanding Linux Audit

The Linux audit framework as shipped with this version of SUSE Linux Enterprise Server provides a CAPP-compliant (Controlled Access Protection Profiles) auditing system that reliably collects information about any security-relevant event. The audit records can be examined to determine whether any violation of the security policies has been committed, and by whom.

Providing an audit framework is an important requirement for a CC-CAPP/EAL (Common Criteria-Controlled Access Protection Profiles/Evaluation Assurance Level) certification. Common Criteria (CC) for Information Technology Security Information is an international standard for independent security evaluations. Common Criteria helps customers judge the security level of any IT product they intend to deploy in mission-critical setups.

Common Criteria security evaluations have two sets of evaluation requirements, functional and assurance requirements. Functional requirements describe the security attributes of the product under evaluation and are summarized under the Controlled Access Protection Profiles (CAPP). Assurance requirements are summarized under the Evaluation Assurance Level (EAL). EAL describes any activities that must take place for the evaluators to be confident that security attributes are present, effective, and implemented. Examples for activities of this kind include documenting the developers' search for security vulnerabilities, the patch process, and testing.

This guide provides a basic understanding of how audit works and how it can be set up. For more information about Common Criteria itself, refer to the Common Criteria Web site (http://www.commoncriteriaportal.org/) ↗.

Linux audit helps make your system more secure by providing you with a means to analyze what is happening on your system in great detail. It does not, however, provide additional security itself—it does not protect your system from code malfunctions or any kind of exploits. Instead, audit is useful for tracking these issues and helps you take additional security measures, like AppArmor, to prevent them.

Audit consists of several components, each contributing crucial functionality to the overall framework. The audit kernel module intercepts the system calls and records the relevant events. The `auditd` daemon writes the audit reports to disk. Various command line utilities take care of displaying, querying, and archiving the audit trail.

Audit enables you to do the following:

Associate Users with Processes

Audit maps processes to the user ID that started them. This makes it possible for the administrator or security officer to exactly trace which user owns which process and is potentially doing malicious operations on the system.

 Important: Renaming User IDs

Audit does not handle the renaming of UIDs. Therefore avoid renaming UIDs (for example, changing `tux` from `uid=1001` to `uid=2000`) and obsolete UIDs rather than renaming them. Otherwise you would need to change **auditctl** data (audit rules) and would have problems retrieving old data correctly.

Review the Audit Trail

Linux audit provides tools that write the audit reports to disk and translate them into human readable format.

Review Particular Audit Events

Audit provides a utility that allows you to filter the audit reports for certain events of interest. You can filter for:

- User

- Group

- Audit ID

- Remote Host Name

- Remote Host Address

- System Call

- System Call Arguments

- File

- File Operations

- Success or Failure

Apply a Selective Audit

Audit provides the means to filter the audit reports for events of interest and to tune audit to record only selected events. You can create your own set of rules and have the audit daemon record only those of interest to you.

Guarantee the Availability of the Report Data

Audit reports are owned by `root` and therefore only removable by `root`. Unauthorized users cannot remove the audit logs.

Prevent Audit Data Loss

If the kernel runs out of memory, the audit daemon's backlog is exceeded, or its rate limit is exceeded, audit can trigger a shutdown of the system to keep events from escaping audit's control. This shutdown would be an immediate halt of the system triggered by the audit kernel component without synchronizing the latest logs to disk. The default configuration is to log a warning to syslog rather than to halt the system.

If the system runs out of disk space when logging, the audit system can be configured to perform clean shutdown. The default configuration tells the audit daemon to stop logging when it runs out of disk space.

31.1 Introducing the Components of Linux Audit

The following figure illustrates how the various components of audit interact with each other:

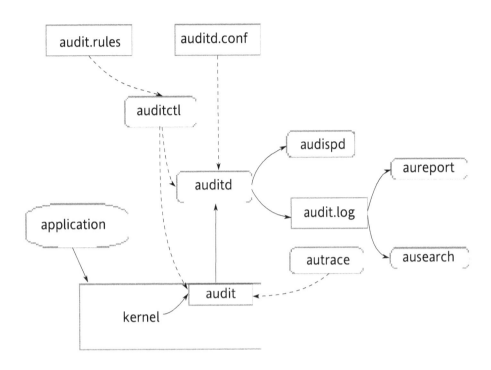

FIGURE 31.1: INTRODUCING THE COMPONENTS OF LINUX AUDIT

Straight arrows represent the data flow between components while dashed arrows represent lines of control between components.

auditd

The audit daemon is responsible for writing the audit messages that were generated through the audit kernel interface and triggered by application and system activity to disk. The way the audit daemon is started is controlled by `systemd`. The audit system functions (when started) are controlled by `/etc/audit/auditd.conf`. For more information about `auditd` and its configuration, refer to *Section 31.2, "Configuring the Audit Daemon"*.

`auditctl`

The **`auditctl`** utility controls the audit system. It controls the log generation parameters and kernel settings of the audit interface and the rule sets that determine which events are tracked. For more information about **`auditctl`**, refer to *Section 31.3, "Controlling the Audit System Using `auditctl`"*.

audit rules

The file `/etc/audit/audit.rules` contains a sequence of **auditctl** commands that are loaded at system boot time immediately after the audit daemon is started. For more information about audit rules, refer to *Section 31.4, "Passing Parameters to the Audit System"*.

aureport

The **aureport** utility allows you to create custom reports from the audit event log. This report generation can easily be scripted, and the output can be used by various other applications, for example, to plot these results. For more information about **aureport**, refer to *Section 31.5, "Understanding the Audit Logs and Generating Reports"*.

ausearch

The **ausearch** utility can search the audit log file for certain events using various keys or other characteristics of the logged format. For more information about **ausearch**, refer to *Section 31.6, "Querying the Audit Daemon Logs with `ausearch`"*.

audispd

The audit dispatcher daemon (`audispd`) can be used to relay event notifications to other applications instead of (or in addition to) writing them to disk in the audit log. For more information about `audispd`, refer to *Section 31.9, "Relaying Audit Event Notifications"*.

autrace

The **autrace** utility traces individual processes in a fashion similar to **strace**. The output of **autrace** is logged to the audit log. For more information about **autrace**, refer to *Section 31.7, "Analyzing Processes with `autrace`"*.

aulast

Prints a list of the last logged-in users, similarly to **last**. **aulast** searches back through the audit logs (or the given audit log file) and displays a list of all users logged in and out based on the range of time in the audit logs.

aulastlog

Prints the last login for all users of a machine similar to the way **lastlog** does. The login name, port, and last login time will be printed.

31.2 Configuring the Audit Daemon

Before you can actually start generating audit logs and processing them, configure the audit daemon itself. The `/etc/audit/auditd.conf` configuration file determines how the audit system functions when the daemon has been started. For most use cases, the default settings shipped with SUSE Linux Enterprise Server should suffice. For CAPP environments, most of these parameters need tweaking. The following list briefly introduces the parameters available:

```
log_file = /var/log/audit/audit.log
log_format = RAW
log_group = root
priority_boost = 4
flush = INCREMENTAL
freq = 20
num_logs = 5
disp_qos = lossy
dispatcher = /sbin/audispd
name_format = NONE
##name = mydomain
max_log_file = 6
max_log_file_action = ROTATE
space_left = 75
space_left_action = SYSLOG
action_mail_acct = root
admin_space_left = 50
admin_space_left_action = SUSPEND
disk_full_action = SUSPEND
disk_error_action = SUSPEND
##tcp_listen_port =
tcp_listen_queue = 5
tcp_max_per_addr = 1
##tcp_client_ports = 1024-65535
tcp_client_max_idle = 0
cp_client_max_idle = 0
```

Depending on whether you want your environment to satisfy the requirements of CAPP, you need to be extra restrictive when configuring the audit daemon. Where you need to use particular settings to meet the CAPP requirements, a "CAPP Environment" note tells you how to adjust the configuration.

`log_file, log_format` **and** `log_group`

> `log_file` specifies the location where the audit logs should be stored. `log_format` determines how the audit information is written to disk and `log_group` defines the group that owns the log files. Possible values for `log_format` are `raw` (messages are stored

exactly as the kernel sends them) or `nolog` (messages are discarded and not written to disk). The data sent to the audit dispatcher is not affected if you use the `nolog` mode. The default setting is `raw` and you should keep it if you want to be able to create reports and queries against the audit logs using the **aureport** and **ausearch** tools. The value for `log_group` can either be specified literally or using the group's ID.

 Note: CAPP Environment

In a CAPP environment, have the audit log reside on its own partition. By doing so, you can be sure that the space detection of the audit daemon is accurate and that you do not have other processes consuming this space.

`priority_boost`

Determine how much of a priority boost the audit daemon should get. Possible values are 0 to 20. The resulting nice value calculates like this: 0 - priority_boost

`flush` **and** `freq`

Specifies whether, how, and how often the audit logs should be written to disk. Valid values for `flush` are `none`, `incremental`, `data`, and `sync`. `none` tells the audit daemon not to make any special effort to write the audit data to disk. `incremental` tells the audit daemon to explicitly flush the data to disk. A frequency must be specified if `incremental` is used. A `freq` value of `20` tells the audit daemon to request that the kernel flush the data to disk after every 20 records. The `data` option keeps the data portion of the disk file synchronized at all times while the `sync` option takes care of both metadata and data.

 Note: CAPP Environment

In a CAPP environment, make sure that the audit trail is always fully up to date and complete. Therefore, use `sync` or `data` with the `flush` parameter.

`num_logs`

Specify the number of log files to keep if you have given `rotate` as the `max_log_file_ac-tion`. Possible values range from `0` to `99`. A value less than `2` means that the log files are not rotated. As you increase the number of files to rotate, you increase the amount of work required of the audit daemon. While doing this rotation, `auditd` cannot always service new data arriving from the kernel as quickly, which can result in a backlog condition (triggering `auditd` to react according to the failure flag, described in *Section 31.3,*

"Controlling the Audit System Using `auditctl`*")*. In this situation, increasing the backlog limit is recommended. Do so by changing the value of the `-b` parameter in the `/etc/audit/audit.rules` file.

`disp_qos` **and** `dispatcher`

The dispatcher is started by the audit daemon during its start. The audit daemon relays the audit messages to the application specified in `dispatcher`. This application must be a highly trusted one, because it needs to run as `root`. `disp_qos` determines whether you allow for `lossy` or `lossless` communication between the audit daemon and the dispatcher.

If you select `lossy`, the audit daemon might discard some audit messages when the message queue is full. These events still get written to disk if `log_format` is set to `raw`, but they might not get through to the dispatcher. If you select `lossless` the audit logging to disk is blocked until there is an empty spot in the message queue. The default value is `lossy`.

`name_format` **and** `name`

`name_format` controls how computer names are resolved. Possible values are `none` (no name will be used), `hostname` (value returned by gethostname), `fqd` (fully qualified host name as received through a DNS lookup), `numeric` (IP address) and `user`. `user` is a custom string that needs to be defined with the `name` parameter.

`max_log_file` **and** `max_log_file_action`

`max_log_file` takes a numerical value that specifies the maximum file size in megabytes that the log file can reach before a configurable action is triggered. The action to be taken is specified in `max_log_file_action`. Possible values for `max_log_file_action` are `ignore`, `syslog`, `suspend`, `rotate`, and `keep_logs`. `ignore` tells the audit daemon to do nothing when the size limit is reached, `syslog` tells it to issue a warning and send it to syslog, and `suspend` causes the audit daemon to stop writing logs to disk, leaving the daemon itself still alive. `rotate` triggers log rotation using the `num_logs` setting. `keep_logs` also triggers log rotation, but does not use the `num_log` setting, so always keeps all logs.

 Note: CAPP Environment

To keep a complete audit trail in CAPP environments, the `keep_logs` option should be used. If using a separate partition to hold your audit logs, adjust `max_log_file` and `num_logs` to use the entire space available on that partition. Note that the more files that need to be rotated, the longer it takes to get back to receiving audit events.

space_left and `space_left_action`

> `space_left` takes a numerical value in megabytes of remaining disk space that triggers a configurable action by the audit daemon. The action is specified in `space_left_action`. Possible values for this parameter are `ignore`, `syslog`, `email`, `exec`, `suspend`, `single`, and `halt`. `ignore` tells the audit daemon to ignore the warning and do nothing, `syslog` has it issue a warning to syslog, and `email` sends an e-mail to the account specified under `action_mail_acct`. `exec` plus a path to a script executes the given script. Note that it is not possible to pass parameters to the script. `suspend` tells the audit daemon to stop writing to disk but remain alive while `single` triggers the system to be brought down to single user mode. `halt` triggers a full shutdown of the system.

 Note: CAPP Environment

> Make sure that `space_left` is set to a value that gives the administrator enough time to react to the alert and allows it to free enough disk space for the audit daemon to continue to work. Freeing disk space would involve calling **aureport -t** and archiving the oldest logs on a separate archiving partition or resource. The actual value for `space_left` depends on the size of your deployment. Set `space_left_action` to `email`.

`action_mail_acct`

> Specify an e-mail address or alias to which any alert messages should be sent. The default setting is `root`, but you can enter any local or remote account as long as e-mail and the network are properly configured on your system and `/usr/lib/sendmail` exists.

admin_space_left and `admin_space_left_action`

> `admin_space_left` takes a numerical value in megabytes of remaining disk space. The system is already running low on disk space when this limit is reached and the administrator has one last chance to react to this alert and free disk space for the audit logs. The value of `admin_space_left` should be lower than the value for `space_left`. The possible values for `admin_space_left_action` are the same as for `space_left_action`.

 Note: CAPP Environment

> Set `admin_space_left` to a value that would allow the administrator's actions to be recorded. The action should be set to `single`.

`disk_full_action`

Specify which action to take when the system runs out of disk space for the audit logs. Valid values are `ignore`, `syslog`, `rotate`, `exec`, `suspend`, `single`, and `halt`. For an explanation of these values refer to `space_left` *and* `space_left_action` .

 Note: CAPP Environment

As the `disk_full_action` is triggered when there is absolutely no more room for any audit logs, you should bring the system down to single-user mode (`single`) or shut it down completely (`halt`).

`disk_error_action`

Specify which action to take when the audit daemon encounters any kind of disk error while writing the logs to disk or rotating the logs. The possible value are the same as for `space_left_action`.

 Note: CAPP Environment

Use `syslog`, `single`, or `halt` depending on your site's policies regarding the handling of any kind of hardware failure.

`tcp_listen_port`, `tcp_listen_queue`, `tcp_client_ports`, `tcp_client_max_idle`, **and** `tcp_max_per_addr`

The audit daemon can receive audit events from other audit daemons. The tcp parameters let you control incoming connections. Specify a port between 1 and 65535 with `tcp_listen_port` on which the `auditd` will listen. `tcp_listen_queue` lets you configure a maximum value for pending connections. Make sure not to set a value too small, since the number of pending connections may be high under certain circumstances, such as after a power outage. `tcp_client_ports` defines which client ports are allowed. Either specify a single port or a port range with numbers separated by a dash (for example 1-1023 for all privileged ports).

Specifying a single allowed client port may make it difficult for the client to restart their audit subsystem, as it will be unable to re-create a connection with the same host addresses and ports until the connection closure TIME_WAIT state times out. If a client does not respond anymore, `auditd` complains. Specify the number of seconds after which this will happen with `tcp_client_max_idle`. Keep in mind that this setting is valid for all clients and therefore should be higher than any individual client heartbeat setting, preferably by a factor of two. `tcp_max_per_addr` is a numeric value representing how many concurrent connections from one IP address are allowed.

 Tip

> We recommend using privileged ports for client and server to prevent non-root (CAP_NET_BIND_SERVICE) programs from binding to those ports.

When the daemon configuration in `/etc/audit/auditd.conf` is complete, the next step is to focus on controlling the amount of auditing the daemon does, and to assign sufficient resources and limits to the daemon so it can operate smoothly.

31.3   Controlling the Audit System Using `auditctl`

`auditctl` is responsible for controlling the status and some basic system parameters of the audit daemon. It controls the amount of auditing performed on the system. Using audit rules, **auditctl** controls which components of your system are subjected to the audit and to what extent they are audited. Audit rules can be passed to the audit daemon on the **auditctl** command line or by composing a rule set and instructing the audit daemon to process this file. By default, the `auditd` daemon is configured to check for audit rules under `/etc/audit/audit.rules`. For more details on audit rules, refer to *Section 31.4, "Passing Parameters to the Audit System"*.

The main **auditctl** commands to control basic audit system parameters are:

- **auditctl** `-e` to enable or disable audit
- **auditctl** `-f` to control the failure flag
- **auditctl** `-r` to control the rate limit for audit messages
- **auditctl** `-b` to control the backlog limit
- **auditctl** `-s` to query the current status of the audit daemon

 Tip

> Before running **auditctl -S** on your system, add `-F arch=b64` to prevent the architecture mismatch warning.

The `-e`, `-f`, `-r`, and `-b` options can also be specified in the `audit.rules` file to avoid having to enter them each time the audit daemon is started.

Any time you query the status of the audit daemon with **auditctl** `-s` or change the status flag with **auditctl** `-eFLAG`, a status message (including information on each of the above-mentioned parameters) is printed. The following example highlights the typical audit status message.

EXAMPLE 31.1: EXAMPLE OUTPUT OF `auditctl -s`

```
AUDIT_STATUS: enabled=1 flag=2 pid=3105 rate_limit=0 backlog_limit=8192 lost=0 backlog=0
```

TABLE 31.1: AUDIT STATUS FLAGS

Flag	Meaning [Possible Values]	Command
enabled	Set the enable flag. [0..2] 0 = disable, 1 = enable, 2 = enable and lock down the configuration	**auditctl** -e [0|1|2]
flag	Set the failure flag. [0..2] 0 = silent, 1 = printk, 2 = panic (immediate halt without synchronizing pending data to disk)	**auditctl** -f [0|1|2]
pid	Process ID under which auditd is running.	—
rate_limit	Set a limit in messages per second. If the rate is not zero and is exceeded, the action specified in the failure flag is triggered.	**auditctl** -r RATE
backlog_limit	Specify the maximum number of outstanding audit buffers allowed. If all buffers	**auditctl** -b BACKLOG

Flag	Meaning [Possible Values]	Command
	are full, the action specified in the failure flag is triggered.	
lost	Count the current number of lost audit messages.	—
backlog	Count the current number of outstanding audit buffers.	—

31.4 Passing Parameters to the Audit System

Commands to control the audit system can be invoked individually from the shell using **auditctl** or batch read from a file using **auditctl - R**. This latter method is used by the init scripts to load rules from the file `/etc/audit/audit.rules` after the audit daemon has been started. The rules are executed in order from top to bottom. Each of these rules would expand to a separate **auditctl** command. The syntax used in the rules file is the same as that used for the **auditctl** command.

Changes made to the running audit system by executing **auditctl** on the command line are not persistent across system restarts. For changes to persist, add them to the `/etc/audit/audit.rules` file and, if they are not currently loaded into audit, restart the audit system to load the modified rule set by using the **systemctl restart auditd** command.

EXAMPLE 31.2: EXAMPLE AUDIT RULES—AUDIT SYSTEM PARAMETERS

```
-b 1000 ❶
-f 1 ❷
-r 10 ❸
-e 1 ❹
```

❶ Specify the maximum number of outstanding audit buffers. Depending on the level of logging activity, you might need to adjust the number of buffers to avoid causing too heavy an audit load on your system.

❷ Specify the failure flag to use. See Table 31.1, "Audit Status Flags" for possible values.

❸ Specify the maximum number of messages per second that may be issued by the kernel. See Table 31.1, "Audit Status Flags" for details.

④　Enable or disable the audit subsystem.

Using audit, you can track any kind of file system access to important files, configurations or resources. You can add watches on these and assign keys to each kind of watch for better identification in the logs.

EXAMPLE 31.3: EXAMPLE AUDIT RULES—FILE SYSTEM AUDITING

```
-w /etc/shadow①
-w /etc -p rx②
-w /etc/passwd -k fk_passwd -p rwxa③
```

①　The `-w` option tells audit to add a watch to the file specified, in this case `/etc/shadow`. All system calls requesting access permissions to this file are analyzed.

②　This rule adds a watch to the `/etc` directory and applies permission filtering for read and execute access to this directory (`-p rx`). Any system call requesting any of these two permissions is analyzed. Only the creation of new files and the deletion of existing ones are logged as directory-related events. To get more specific events for files located under this particular directory, you should add a separate rule for each file. A file must exist before you add a rule containing a watch on it. Auditing files as they are created is not supported.

③　This rule adds a file watch to `/etc/passwd`. Permission filtering is applied for read, write, execute, and attribute change permissions. The `-k` option allows you to specify a key to use to filter the audit logs for this particular event later (for example with **ausearch**). You may use the same key on different rules to be able to group rules when searching for them. It is also possible to apply multiple keys to a rule.

System call auditing lets you track your system's behavior on a level even below the application level. When designing these rules, consider that auditing a great many system calls may increase your system load and cause you to run out of disk space. Consider carefully which events need tracking and how they can be filtered to be even more specific.

EXAMPLE 31.4: EXAMPLE AUDIT RULES—SYSTEM CALL AUDITING

```
-a exit,always -S mkdir①
-a exit,always -S access -F a1=4②
-a exit,always -S ipc -F a0=2③
-a exit,always -S open -F success!=0④
-a task,always -F auid=0⑤
-a task,always -F uid=0 -F auid=501 -F gid=wheel⑥
```

① This rule activates auditing for the `mkdir` system call. The `-a` option adds system call rules. This rule triggers an event whenever the `mkdir` system call is entered (`exit`, `always`). The `-S` option specifies the system call to which this rule should be applied.

② This rule adds auditing to the access system call, but only if the second argument of the system call (`mode`) is `4` (`R_OK`). `exit,always` tells audit to add an audit context to this system call when entering it, and to write out a report when it gets audited.

③ This rule adds an audit context to the IPC multiplexed system call. The specific `ipc` system call is passed as the first syscall argument and can be selected using `-F a0=IPC_CALL_NUMBER`.

④ This rule audits failed attempts to call open.

⑤ This rule is an example of a task rule (keyword: `task`). It is different from the other rules above in that it applies to processes that are forked or cloned. To filter these kind of events, you can only use fields that are known at fork time, such as UID, GID, and AUID. This example rule filters for all tasks carrying an audit ID of `0`.

⑥ This last rule makes heavy use of filters. All filter options are combined with a logical AND operator, meaning that this rule applies to all tasks that carry the audit ID of `501`, run as `root`, and have `wheel` as the group. A process is given an audit ID on user login. This ID is then handed down to any child process started by the initial process of the user. Even if the user changes his identity, the audit ID stays the same and allows tracing actions to the original user.

 Tip: Filtering System Call Arguments

> For more details on filtering system call arguments, refer to *Section 33.6, "Filtering System Call Arguments"*.

You cannot only add rules to the audit system, but also remove them. There are different methods for deleting the entire rule set at once or for deleting system call rules or file and directory watches:

EXAMPLE 31.5: DELETING AUDIT RULES AND EVENTS

```
-D ①
-d exit,always -S mkdir ②
-W /etc ③
```

① Clear the queue of audit rules and delete any preexisting rules. This rule is used as the first rule in `/etc/audit/audit.rules` files to make sure that the rules that are about to be added do not clash with any preexisting ones. The **auditctl** -D command is also used before doing an **autrace** to avoid having the trace rules clash with any rules present in the `audit.rules` file.

② This rule deletes a system call rule. The -d option must precede any system call rule that needs to be deleted from the rule queue, and must match exactly.

③ This rule tells audit to discard the rule with the directory watch on `/etc` from the rules queue. This rule deletes any rule containing a directory watch on `/etc`, regardless of any permission filtering or key options.

To get an overview of which rules are currently in use in your audit setup, run **auditctl** -l. This command displays all rules with one rule per line.

EXAMPLE 31.6: LISTING RULES WITH auditctl -l

```
exit,always watch=/etc perm=rx
exit,always watch=/etc/passwd perm=rwxa key=fk_passwd
exit,always watch=/etc/shadow perm=rwxa
exit,always syscall=mkdir
exit,always a1=4 (0x4) syscall=access
exit,always a0=2 (0x2) syscall=ipc
exit,always success!=0 syscall=open
```

 Note: Creating Filter Rules

You can build very sophisticated audit rules by using the various filter options. Refer to the **auditctl(8)** man page for more information about the options available for building audit filter rules, and audit rules in general.

31.5 Understanding the Audit Logs and Generating Reports

To understand what the **aureport** utility does, it is vital to know how the logs generated by the audit daemon are structured, and what exactly is recorded for an event. Only then can you decide which report types are most appropriate for your needs.

31.5.1 Understanding the Audit Logs

The following examples highlight two typical events that are logged by audit and how their trails in the audit log are read. The audit log or logs (if log rotation is enabled) are stored in the `/var/log/audit` directory. The first example is a simple **less** command. The second example covers a great deal of PAM activity in the logs when a user tries to remotely log in to a machine running audit.

EXAMPLE 31.7: A SIMPLE AUDIT EVENT—VIEWING THE AUDIT LOG

```
type=SYSCALL msg=audit(1234874638.599:5207): arch=c000003e syscall=2 success=yes exit=4
 a0=62fb60 a1=0 a2=31 a3=0 items=1 ppid=25400 pid
=25616 auid=0 uid=0 gid=0 euid=0 suid=0 fsuid=0 egid=0 sgid=0 fsgid=0 tty=pts1 ses=1164
 comm="less" exe="/usr/bin/less" key="doc_log"
type=CWD msg=audit(1234874638.599:5207):  cwd="/root"
type=PATH msg=audit(1234874638.599:5207): item=0 name="/var/log/audit/audit.log"
 inode=1219041 dev=08:06 mode=0100644 ouid=0 ogid=0 rdev=00:00
```

The above event, a simple **less /var/log/audit/audit.log**, wrote three messages to the log. All of them are closely linked together and you would not be able to make sense of one of them without the others. The first message reveals the following information:

type

> The type of event recorded. In this case, it assigns the SYSCALL type to an event triggered by a system call. The CWD event was recorded to record the current working directory at the time of the syscall. A PATH event is generated for each path passed to the system call. The open system call takes only one path argument, so only generates one PATH event. It is important to understand that the PATH event reports the path name string argument without any further interpretation, so a relative path requires manual combination with the path reported by the CWD event to determine the object accessed.

msg

> A message ID enclosed in brackets. The ID splits into two parts. All characters before the `:` represent a Unix epoch time stamp. The number after the colon represents the actual event ID. All events that are logged from one application's system call have the same event ID. If the application makes a second system call, it gets another event ID.

arch

> References the CPU architecture of the system call. Decode this information using the `-i` option on any of your **ausearch** commands when searching the logs.

`syscall`

> The type of system call as it would have been printed by an strace on this particular system call. This data is taken from the list of system calls under `/usr/include/asm/unistd.h` and may vary depending on the architecture. In this case, `syscall=2` refers to the open system call (see **man open(2)**) invoked by the less application.

`success`

> Whether the system call succeeded or failed.

`exit`

> The exit value returned by the system call. For the **open** system call used in this example, this is the file descriptor number. This varies by system call.

`a0` **to** `a3`

> The first four arguments to the system call in numeric form. The values of these are system call dependent. In this example (an **open** system call), the following are used:

```
a0=62fb60 a1=8000 a2=31 a3=0
```

> `a0` is the start address of the passed path name. `a1` is the flags. `8000` in hex notation translates to `100000` in octal notation, which in turn translates to `O_LARGEFILE`. `a2` is the mode, which, because `O_CREAT` was not specified, is unused. `a3` is not passed by the **open** system call. Check the manual page of the relevant system call to find out which arguments are used with it.

`items`

> The number of strings passed to the application.

`ppid`

> The process ID of the parent of the process analyzed.

`pid`

> The process ID of the process analyzed.

`auid`

> The audit ID. A process is given an audit ID on user login. This ID is then handed down to any child process started by the initial process of the user. Even if the user changes his identity (for example, becomes `root`), the audit ID stays the same. Thus you can always trace actions to the original user who logged in.

`uid`

> The user ID of the user who started the process. In this case, `0` for `root`.

gid

> The group ID of the user who started the process. In this case, `0` for `root`.

euid, suid, fsuid

> Effective user ID, set user ID, and file system user ID of the user that started the process.

egid, sgid, fsgid

> Effective group ID, set group ID, and file system group ID of the user that started the process.

tty

> The terminal from which the application was started. In this case, a pseudo-terminal used in an SSH session.

ses

> The login session ID. This process attribute is set when a user logs in and can tie any process to a particular user login.

comm

> The application name under which it appears in the task list.

exe

> The resolved path name to the binary program.

subj

> `auditd` records whether the process is subject to any security context, such as AppArmor. `unconstrained`, as in this case, means that the process is not confined with AppArmor. If the process had been confined, the binary path name plus the AppArmor profile mode would have been logged.

key

> If you are auditing many directories or files, assign key strings to each of these watches. You can use these keys with **ausearch** to search the logs for events of this type only.

The second message triggered by the example **less** call does not reveal anything apart from the current working directory when the **less** command was executed.

The third message reveals the following (the `type` and `message` flags have already been introduced):

`item`

> In this example, `item` references the `a0` argument—a path—that is associated with the original `SYSCALL` message. Had the original call had more than one path argument (such as a **cp** or **mv** command), an additional `PATH` event would have been logged for the second path argument.

`name`

> Refers to the path name passed as an argument to the open system call.

`inode`

> Refers to the inode number corresponding to `name`.

`dev`

> Specifies the device on which the file is stored. In this case, `08:06`, which stands for `/dev/sda1` or "first partition on the first IDE device."

`mode`

> Numerical representation of the file's access permissions. In this case, `root` has read and write permissions and his group (`root`) has read access while the entire rest of the world cannot access the file.

`ouid` **and** `ogid`

> Refer to the UID and GID of the inode itself.

`rdev`

> Not applicable for this example. The `rdev` entry only applies to block or character devices, not to files.

Example 31.8, "An Advanced Audit Event—Login via SSH" highlights the audit events triggered by an incoming SSH connection. Most of the messages are related to the PAM stack and reflect the different stages of the SSH PAM process. Several of the audit messages carry nested PAM messages in them that signify that a particular stage of the PAM process has been reached. Although the PAM messages are logged by audit, audit assigns its own message type to each event:

EXAMPLE 31.8: AN ADVANCED AUDIT EVENT—LOGIN VIA SSH

```
type=USER_AUTH msg=audit(1234877011.791:7731): user pid=26127 uid=0 ❶
```

```
auid=4294967295 ses=4294967295 msg='op=PAM:authentication acct="root" exe="/usr/sbin/
sshd"
(hostname=jupiter.example.com, addr=192.168.2.100, terminal=ssh res=success)'
type=USER_ACCT msg=audit(1234877011.795:7732): user pid=26127 uid=0 ②
auid=4294967295 ses=4294967295 msg='op=PAM:accounting acct="root" exe="/usr/sbin/sshd"
(hostname=jupiter.example.com, addr=192.168.2.100, terminal=ssh res=success)'
type=CRED_ACQ msg=audit(1234877011.799:7733): user pid=26125 uid=0 ③
auid=4294967295 ses=4294967295 msg='op=PAM:setcred acct="root" exe="/usr/sbin/sshd"
(hostname=jupiter.example.com, addr=192.168.2.100, terminal=/dev/pts/0 res=success)'
type=LOGIN msg=audit(1234877011.799:7734): login pid=26125 uid=0
old auid=4294967295 new auid=0 old ses=4294967295 new ses=1172
type=USER_START msg=audit(1234877011.799:7735): user pid=26125 uid=0 ④
auid=0 ses=1172 msg='op=PAM:session_open acct="root" exe="/usr/sbin/sshd"
(hostname=jupiter.example.com, addr=192.168.2.100, terminal=/dev/pts/0 res=success)'
type=USER_LOGIN msg=audit(1234877011.823:7736): user pid=26128 uid=0 ⑤
auid=0 ses=1172 msg='uid=0: exe="/usr/sbin/sshd"
(hostname=jupiter.example.com, addr=192.168.2.100, terminal=/dev/pts/0 res=success)'
type=CRED_REFR msg=audit(1234877011.828:7737): user pid=26128 uid=0 ⑥
auid=0 ses=1172 msg='op=PAM:setcred acct="root" exe="/usr/sbin/sshd"
(hostname=jupiter.example.com, addr=192.168.2.100, terminal=/dev/pts/0 res=success)'
```

① PAM reports that is has successfully requested user authentication for `root` from a remote host (jupiter.example.com, 192.168.2.100). The terminal where this is happening is `ssh`.

② PAM reports that it has successfully determined whether the user is authorized to log in.

③ PAM reports that the appropriate credentials to log in have been acquired and that the terminal changed to a normal terminal (`/dev/pts0`).

④ PAM reports that it has successfully opened a session for `root`.

⑤ The user has successfully logged in. This event is the one used by **aureport** `-l` to report about user logins.

⑥ PAM reports that the credentials have been successfully reacquired.

31.5.2   Generating Custom Audit Reports

The raw audit reports stored in the `/var/log/audit` directory tend to become very bulky and hard to understand. To more easily find relevant messages, use the **aureport** utility and create custom reports.

The following use cases highlight a few of the possible report types that you can generate with `aureport`:

Read Audit Logs from Another File

When the audit logs have moved to another machine or when you want to analyze the logs of several machines on your local machine without wanting to connect to each of these individually, move the logs to a local file and have `aureport` analyze them locally:

```
aureport -if myfile

Summary Report
======================
Range of time in logs: 03/02/09 14:13:38.225 - 17/02/09 14:52:27.971
Selected time for report: 03/02/09 14:13:38 - 17/02/09 14:52:27.971
Number of changes in configuration: 13
Number of changes to accounts, groups, or roles: 0
Number of logins: 6
Number of failed logins: 13
Number of authentications: 7
Number of failed authentications: 573
Number of users: 1
Number of terminals: 9
Number of host names: 4
Number of executables: 17
Number of files: 279
Number of AVC's: 0
Number of MAC events: 0
Number of failed syscalls: 994
Number of anomaly events: 0
Number of responses to anomaly events: 0
Number of crypto events: 0
Number of keys: 2
Number of process IDs: 1211
Number of events: 5320
```

The above command, `aureport` without any arguments, provides only the standard general summary report generated from the logs contained in `myfile`. To create more detailed reports, combine the `-if` option with any of the options below. For example, generate a login report that is limited to a certain time frame:

```
aureport -l -ts 14:00 -te 15:00 -if myfile

Login Report
============================================
```

```
# date time auid host term exe success event
=============================================
1. 17/02/09 14:21:09 root: 192.168.2.100 sshd /usr/sbin/sshd no 7718
2. 17/02/09 14:21:15 0 jupiter /dev/pts/3 /usr/sbin/sshd yes 7724
```

Convert Numeric Entities to Text

Some information, such as user IDs, are printed in numeric form. To convert these into a human-readable text format, add the `-i` option to your **aureport** command.

Create a Rough Summary Report

If you are interested in the current audit statistics (events, logins, processes, etc.), run **aureport** without any other option.

Create a Summary Report of Failed Events

If you want to break down the overall statistics of plain **aureport** to the statistics of failed events, use **aureport** `--failed`:

```
aureport --failed

Failed Summary Report
======================
Range of time in logs: 03/02/09 14:13:38.225 - 17/02/09 14:57:35.183
Selected time for report: 03/02/09 14:13:38 - 17/02/09 14:57:35.183
Number of changes in configuration: 0
Number of changes to accounts, groups, or roles: 0
Number of logins: 0
Number of failed logins: 13
Number of authentications: 0
Number of failed authentications: 574
Number of users: 1
Number of terminals: 5
Number of host names: 4
Number of executables: 11
Number of files: 77
Number of AVC's: 0
Number of MAC events: 0
Number of failed syscalls: 994
Number of anomaly events: 0
Number of responses to anomaly events: 0
Number of crypto events: 0
Number of keys: 2
Number of process IDs: 708
Number of events: 1583
```

Create a Summary Report of Successful Events

If you want to break down the overall statistics of a plain **aureport** to the statistics of successful events, use **aureport** --success:

```
aureport --success

Success Summary Report
=======================
Range of time in logs: 03/02/09 14:13:38.225 - 17/02/09 15:00:01.535
Selected time for report: 03/02/09 14:13:38 - 17/02/09 15:00:01.535
Number of changes in configuration: 13
Number of changes to accounts, groups, or roles: 0
Number of logins: 6
Number of failed logins: 0
Number of authentications: 7
Number of failed authentications: 0
Number of users: 1
Number of terminals: 7
Number of host names: 3
Number of executables: 16
Number of files: 215
Number of AVC's: 0
Number of MAC events: 0
Number of failed syscalls: 0
Number of anomaly events: 0
Number of responses to anomaly events: 0
Number of crypto events: 0
Number of keys: 2
Number of process IDs: 558
Number of events: 3739
```

Create Summary Reports

In addition to the dedicated summary reports (main summary and failed and success summary), use the --summary option with most of the other options to create summary reports for a particular area of interest only. Not all reports support this option, however. This example creates a summary report for user login events:

```
aureport -u -i --summary

User Summary Report
===========================
total  auid
===========================
5640  root
13  tux
```

3 wilber

Create a Report of Events

To get an overview of the events logged by audit, use the **aureport** -e command. This command generates a numbered list of all events including date, time, event number, event type, and audit ID.

```
aureport -e -ts 14:00 -te 14:21

Event Report
===================================
# date time event type auid success
===================================
1.  17/02/09 14:20:27 7462 DAEMON_START 0 yes
2.  17/02/09 14:20:27 7715 CONFIG_CHANGE 0 yes
3.  17/02/09 14:20:57 7716 USER_END 0 yes
4.  17/02/09 14:20:57 7717 CRED_DISP 0 yes
5.  17/02/09 14:21:09 7718 USER_LOGIN -1 no
6.  17/02/09 14:21:15 7719 USER_AUTH -1 yes
7.  17/02/09 14:21:15 7720 USER_ACCT -1 yes
8.  17/02/09 14:21:15 7721 CRED_ACQ -1 yes
9.  17/02/09 14:21:15 7722 LOGIN 0 yes
10. 17/02/09 14:21:15 7723 USER_START 0 yes
11. 17/02/09 14:21:15 7724 USER_LOGIN 0 yes
12. 17/02/09 14:21:15 7725 CRED_REFR 0 yes
```

Create a Report from All Process Events

To analyze the log from a process's point of view, use the **aureport** -p command. This command generates a numbered list of all process events including date, time, process ID, name of the executable, system call, audit ID, and event number.

```
aureport -p

Process ID Report
===================================
# date time pid exe syscall auid event
===================================
1. 13/02/09 15:30:01 32742 /usr/sbin/cron 0 0 35
2. 13/02/09 15:30:01 32742 /usr/sbin/cron 0 0 36
3. 13/02/09 15:38:34 32734 /usr/lib/gdm/gdm-session-worker 0 -1 37
```

Create a Report from All System Call Events

To analyze the audit log from a system call's point of view, use the **aureport** -s command. This command generates a numbered list of all system call events including date, time, number of the system call, process ID, name of the command that used this call, audit ID, and event number.

```
aureport -s

Syscall Report
======================================
# date time syscall pid comm auid event
======================================
1. 16/02/09 17:45:01 2 20343 cron -1 2279
2. 16/02/09 17:45:02 83 20350 mktemp 0 2284
3. 16/02/09 17:45:02 83 20351 mkdir 0 2285
```

Create a Report from All Executable Events

To analyze the audit log from an executable's point of view, use the **aureport** -x command. This command generates a numbered list of all executable events including date, time, name of the executable, the terminal it is run in, the host executing it, the audit ID, and event number.

```
aureport -x

Executable Report
====================================
# date time exe term host auid event
====================================
1. 13/02/09 15:08:26 /usr/sbin/sshd sshd 192.168.2.100 -1 12
2. 13/02/09 15:08:28 /usr/lib/gdm/gdm-session-worker :0 ? -1 13
3. 13/02/09 15:08:28 /usr/sbin/sshd ssh 192.168.2.100 -1 14
```

Create a Report about Files

To generate a report from the audit log that focuses on file access, use the **aureport** -f command. This command generates a numbered list of all file-related events including date, time, name of the accessed file, number of the system call accessing it, success or failure of the command, the executable accessing the file, audit ID, and event number.

```
aureport -f

File Report
=================================================
# date time file syscall success exe auid event
```

```
==================================================
1. 16/02/09 17:45:01 /etc/shadow 2 yes /usr/sbin/cron -1 2279
2. 16/02/09 17:45:02 /tmp/ 83 yes /bin/mktemp 0 2284
3. 16/02/09 17:45:02 /var 83 no /bin/mkdir 0 2285
```

Create a Report about Users

To generate a report from the audit log that illustrates which users are running what executables on your system, use the **aureport** -u command. This command generates a numbered list of all user-related events including date, time, audit ID, terminal used, host, name of the executable, and an event ID.

```
aureport -u

User ID Report
==================================
# date time auid term host exe event
==================================
1. 13/02/09 15:08:26 -1 sshd 192.168.2.100 /usr/sbin/sshd 12
2. 13/02/09 15:08:28 -1 :0 ? /usr/lib/gdm/gdm-session-worker 13
3. 14/02/09 08:25:39 -1 ssh 192.168.2.101 /usr/sbin/sshd 14
```

Create a Report about Logins

To create a report that focuses on login attempts to your machine, run the **aureport** -l command. This command generates a numbered list of all login-related events including date, time, audit ID, host and terminal used, name of the executable, success or failure of the attempt, and an event ID.

```
aureport -l -i

Login Report
============================================
# date time auid host term exe success event
============================================
1. 13/02/09 15:08:31 tux: 192.168.2.100 sshd /usr/sbin/sshd no 19
2. 16/02/09 12:39:05 root: 192.168.2.101 sshd /usr/sbin/sshd no 2108
3. 17/02/09 15:29:07 geeko: ? tty3 /bin/login yes 7809
```

Limit a Report to a Certain Time Frame

To analyze the logs for a particular time frame, such as only the working hours of Feb 16, 2009, first find out whether this data is contained in the current audit.log or whether the logs have been rotated in by running **aureport** -t:

```
aureport -t
```

```
Log Time Range Report
=====================
/var/log/audit/audit.log: 03/02/09 14:13:38.225 - 17/02/09 15:30:01.636
```

The current `audit.log` contains all the desired data. Otherwise, use the `-if` option to point the **aureport** commands to the log file that contains the needed data.

Then, specify the start date and time and the end date and time of the desired time frame and combine it with the report option needed. This example focuses on login attempts:

```
aureport -ts 02/16/09 8:00 -te 02/16/09 18:00 -l


Login Report
===========================================
# date time auid host term exe success event
===========================================
1. 16/02/09 12:39:05 root: 192.168.2.100 sshd /usr/sbin/sshd no 2108
2. 16/02/09 12:39:12 0 192.168.2.100 /dev/pts/1 /usr/sbin/sshd yes 2114
3. 16/02/09 13:09:28 root: 192.168.2.100 sshd /usr/sbin/sshd no 2131
4. 16/02/09 13:09:32 root: 192.168.2.100 sshd /usr/sbin/sshd no 2133
5. 16/02/09 13:09:37 0 192.168.2.100 /dev/pts/2 /usr/sbin/sshd yes 2139
```

The start date and time are specified with the `-ts` option. Any event that has a time stamp equal to or after your given start time appears in the report. If you omit the date, **aureport** assumes that you meant *today*. If you omit the time, it assumes that the start time should be midnight of the date specified.

Specify the end date and time with the `-te` option. Any event that has a time stamp equal to or before your given event time appears in the report. If you omit the date, **aureport** assumes that you meant today. If you omit the time, it assumes that the end time should be now. Use the same format for the date and time as for `-ts`.

All reports except the summary ones are printed in column format and sent to STDOUT, which means that this data can be written to other commands very easily. The visualization scripts introduced in *Section 31.8, "Visualizing Audit Data"* are examples of how to further process the data generated by audit.

31.6 Querying the Audit Daemon Logs with ausearch

The **aureport** tool helps you to create overall summaries of what is happening on the system, but if you are interested in the details of a particular event, **ausearch** is the tool to use.

ausearch allows you to search the audit logs using special keys and search phrases that relate to most of the flags that appear in event messages in `/var/log/audit/audit.log`. Not all record types contain the same search phrases. There are no `hostname` or `uid` entries in a `PATH` record, for example.

When searching, make sure that you choose appropriate search criteria to catch all records you need. On the other hand, you could be searching for a specific type of record and still get various other related records along with it. This is caused by different parts of the kernel contributing additional records for events that are related to the one to find. For example, you would always get a `PATH` record along with the `SYSCALL` record for an **open** system call.

 Tip: Using Multiple Search Options

> Any of the command line options can be combined with logical AND operators to narrow down your search.

Read Audit Logs from Another File

When the audit logs have moved to another machine or when you want to analyze the logs of several machines on your local machine without wanting to connect to each of these individually, move the logs to a local file and have **ausearch** search them locally:

```
ausearch - option -if myfile
```

Convert Numeric Results into Text

Some information, such as user IDs are printed in numeric form. To convert these into human readable text format, add the `-i` option to your **ausearch** command.

Search by Audit Event ID

If you have previously run an audit report or done an **autrace**, you should analyze the trail of a particular event in the log. Most of the report types described in *Section 31.5, "Understanding the Audit Logs and Generating Reports"* include audit event IDs in their output. An audit event ID is the second part of an audit message ID, which consists of a Unix epoch time stamp and the audit event ID separated by a colon. All events that are logged from one application's system call have the same event ID. Use this event ID with **ausearch** to retrieve this event's trail from the log.

Use a command similar to the following:

```
ausearch -a 5207
```

```
----
time->Tue Feb 17 13:43:58 2009
type=PATH msg=audit(1234874638.599:5207): item=0 name="/var/log/audit/audit.log"
 inode=1219041 dev=08:06 mode=0100644 ouid=0 ogid=0 rdev=00:00
type=CWD msg=audit(1234874638.599:5207):  cwd="/root"
type=SYSCALL msg=audit(1234874638.599:5207): arch=c000003e syscall=2 success=yes
 exit=4 a0=62fb60 a1=0 a2=31 a3=0 items=1 ppid=25400 pid=25616 auid=0 uid=0 gid=0
 euid=0 suid=0 fsuid=0 egid=0 sgid=0 fsgid=0 tty=pts1 ses=1164 comm="less" exe="/
usr/bin/less" key="doc_log"
```

The **ausearch** -a command grabs all records in the logs that are related to the audit event ID provided and displays them. This option can be combined with any other option.

Search by Message Type

To search for audit records of a particular message type, use the **ausearch** -m *MESSAGE_TYPE* command. Examples of valid message types include PATH, SYSCALL, and USER_LOGIN. Running **ausearch** -m without a message type displays a list of all message types.

Search by Login ID

To view records associated with a particular login user ID, use the **ausearch** -ul command. It displays any records related to the user login ID specified provided that user had been able to log in successfully.

Search by User ID

View records related to any of the user IDs (both user ID and effective user ID) with **ausearch** -ua. View reports related to a particular user ID with **ausearch** -ui *UID*. Search for records related to a particular effective user ID, use the **ausearch** -ue *EUID*. Searching for a user ID means the user ID of the user creating a process. Searching for an effective user ID means the user ID and privileges that are required to run this process.

Search by Group ID

View records related to any of the group IDs (both group ID and effective group ID) with the **ausearch** -ga command. View reports related to a particular user ID with **ausearch** -gi *GID*. Search for records related to a particular effective group ID, use **ausearch** -ge *EGID*.

Search by Command Line Name

View records related to a certain command, using the **ausearch** -c *COMM_NAME* command, for example, **ausearch** -c less for all records related to the **less** command.

Search by Executable Name

View records related to a certain executable with the **ausearch** `-x` *EXE* command, for example **ausearch** `-x /usr/bin/less` for all records related to the **/usr/bin/less** executable.

Search by System Call Name

View records related to a certain system call with the **ausearch** `-sc` *SYSCALL* command, for example, **ausearch** `-sc open` for all records related to the **open** system call.

Search by Process ID

View records related to a certain process ID with the **ausearch** `-p` *PID* command, for example **ausearch** `-p 13368` for all records related to this process ID.

Search by Event or System Call Success Value

View records containing a certain system call success value with **ausearch** `-sv` *SUC-CESS_VALUE*, for example, **ausearch** `-sv yes` for all successful system calls.

Search by File Name

View records containing a certain file name with **ausearch** `-f` *FILE_NAME*, for example, **ausearch** `-f /foo/bar` for all records related to the `/foo/bar` file. Using the file name alone would work as well, but using relative paths does not work.

Search by Terminal

View records of events related to a certain terminal only with **ausearch** `-tm` *TERM*, for example, **ausearch** `-tm ssh` to view all records related to events on the SSH terminal and **ausearch** `-tm tty` to view all events related to the console.

Search by Host Name

View records related to a certain remote host name with **ausearch** `-hn` *HOSTNAME*, for example, **ausearch** `-hn jupiter.example.com`. You can use a host name, fully qualified domain name, or numeric network address.

Search by Key Field

View records that contain a certain key assigned in the audit rule set to identify events of a particular type. Use the **ausearch** `-k` *KEY_FIELD*, for example, **ausearch** `-k CFG_etc` to display any records containing the `CFG_etc` key.

Search by Word

View records that contain a certain string assigned in the audit rule set to identify events of a particular type. The whole string will be matched on file name, host name, and terminal. Use the **ausearch** `-w` *WORD*.

Limit a Search to a Certain Time Frame

Use `-ts` and `-te` to limit the scope of your searches to a certain time frame. The `-ts` option is used to specify the start date and time and the `-te` option is used to specify the end date and time. These options can be combined with any of the above. The use of these options is similar to use with **aureport**.

31.7 Analyzing Processes with `autrace`

In addition to monitoring your system using the rules you set up, you can also perform dedicated audits of individual processes using the **autrace** command. **autrace** works similarly to the **strace** command, but gathers slightly different information. The output of **autrace** is written to `/var/log/audit/audit.log` and does not look any different from the standard audit log entries.

When performing an **autrace** on a process, make sure that any audit rules are purged from the queue to avoid these rules clashing with the ones **autrace** adds itself. Delete the audit rules with the **auditctl** `-D` command. This stops all normal auditing.

```
auditctl -D

No rules

autrace /usr/bin/less


Waiting to execute: /usr/bin/less
Cleaning up...
No rules
Trace complete. You can locate the records with 'ausearch -i -p 7642'
```

Always use the full path to the executable to track with **autrace**. After the trace is complete, **autrace** provides the event ID of the trace, so you can analyze the entire data trail with **ausearch**. To restore the audit system to use the audit rule set again, restart the audit daemon with **systemctl restart auditd**.

31.8 Visualizing Audit Data

Neither the data trail in `/var/log/audit/audit.log` nor the different report types generated by **aureport**, described in *Section 31.5.2, "Generating Custom Audit Reports"*, provide an intuitive reading experience to the user. The **aureport** output is formatted in columns and thus easily available to any sed, Perl, or awk scripts that users might connect to the audit framework to visualize the audit data.

The visualization scripts (see *Section 32.6, "Configuring Log Visualization"*) are one example of how to use standard Linux tools available with SUSE Linux Enterprise Server or any other Linux distribution to create easy-to-read audit output. The following examples help you understand how the plain audit reports can be transformed into human readable graphics.

The first example illustrates the relationship of programs and system calls. To get to this kind of data, you need to determine the appropriate **aureport** command that delivers the source data from which to generate the final graphic:

```
aureport -s -i

Syscall Report
=======================================
# date time syscall pid comm auid event
=======================================
1. 16/02/09 17:45:01 open 20343 cron unset 2279
2. 16/02/09 17:45:02 mkdir 20350 mktemp root 2284
3. 16/02/09 17:45:02 mkdir 20351 mkdir root 2285
...
```

The first thing that the visualization script needs to do on this report is to extract only those columns that are of interest, in this example, the `syscall` and the `comm` columns. The output is sorted and duplicates removed then the final output is written into the visualization program itself:

```
LC_ALL=C aureport -s -i | awk '/^[0-9]/ { print $6" "$4 }' | sort | uniq | mkgraph
```

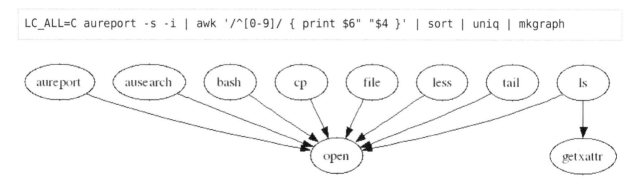

FIGURE 31.2: FLOW GRAPH—PROGRAM VERSUS SYSTEM CALL RELATIONSHIP

The second example illustrates the different types of events and how many of each type have been logged. The appropriate **aureport** command to extract this kind of information is **aureport -e**:

```
aureport -e -i --summary

Event Summary Report
======================
total   type
======================
2434  SYSCALL
816   USER_START
816   USER_ACCT
814   CRED_ACQ
810   LOGIN
806   CRED_DISP
779   USER_END
99    CONFIG_CHANGE
52    USER_LOGIN
```

Because this type of report already contains a two column output, it is only fed into the visualization script and transformed into a bar chart.

```
aureport -e -i --summary  | mkbar events
```

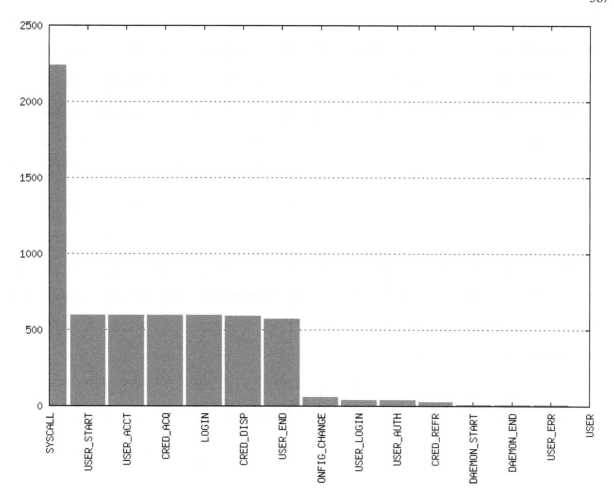

FIGURE 31.3: BAR CHART—COMMON EVENT TYPES

For background information about the visualization of audit data, refer to the Web site of the audit project at http://people.redhat.com/sgrubb/audit/visualize/index.html ↗.

31.9 Relaying Audit Event Notifications

The auditing system also allows external applications to access and use the `auditd` daemon in real time. This feature is provided by so called *audit dispatcher* which allows, for example, intrusion detection systems to use `auditd` to receive enhanced detection information.

`audispd` is a daemon which controls the audit dispatcher. It is normally started by `auditd`. `audispd` takes audit events and distributes them to the programs which want to analyze them in real time. Configuration of `auditd` is stored in `/etc/audisp/audispd.conf`. The file has the following options:

`q_depth`

> Specifies the size of the event dispatcher internal queue. If syslog complains about audit events getting dropped, increase this value. Default is 80.

`overflow_action`

> Specifies the way the audit daemon will react to the internal queue overflow. Possible values are `ignore` (nothing happens), `syslog` (issues a warning to syslog), `suspend` (audispd will stop processing events), `single` (the computer system will be put in single user mode), or `halt` (shuts the system down).

`priority_boost`

> Specifies the priority for the audit event dispatcher (in addition to the audit daemon priority itself). Default is 4 which means no change in priority.

`name_format`

> Specifies the way the computer node name is inserted into the audit event. Possible values are `none` (no computer name is inserted), `hostname` (name returned by the `gethostname` system call), `fqd` (fully qualified domain name of the machine), `numeric` (IP address of the machine), or `user` (user defined string from the `name` option). Default is `none`.

`name`

> Specifies a user defined string which identifies the machine. The `name_format` option must be set to `user`, otherwise this option is ignored.

`max_restarts`

> A non-negative number that tells the audit event dispatcher how many times it can try to restart a crashed plug-in. The default is 10.

EXAMPLE 31.9: EXAMPLE /ETC/AUDISP/AUDISPD.CONF

```
q_depth = 80
overflow_action = SYSLOG
priority_boost = 4
name_format = HOSTNAME
#name = mydomain
```

The plug-in programs install their configuration files in a special directory dedicated to `audispd` plug-ins. It is `/etc/audisp/plugins.d` by default. The plug-in configuration files have the following options:

`active`

> Specifies if the program will use `audispd`. Possible values are `yes` or `no`.

`direction`

> Specifies the way the plug-in was designed to communicate with audit. It informs the event dispatcher in which directions the events flow. Possible values are `in` or `out`.

`path`

> Specifies the absolute path to the plug-in executable. In case of internal plug-ins, this option specifies the plug-in name.

`type`

> Specifies the way the plug-in is to be run. Possible values are `builtin` or `always`. Use `builtin` for internal plug-ins (`af_unix` and `syslog`) and `always` for most (if not all) other plug-ins. Default is `always`.

`args`

> Specifies the argument that is passed to the plug-in program. Normally, plug-in programs read their arguments from their configuration file and do not need to receive any arguments. There is a limit of 2 arguments.

`format`

> Specifies the format of data that the audit dispatcher passes to the plug-in program. Valid options are `binary` or `string`. `binary` passes the data exactly as the event dispatcher receives them from the audit daemon. `string` instructs the dispatcher to change the event into a string that is parsable by the audit parsing library. Default is `string`.

EXAMPLE 31.10: EXAMPLE /ETC/AUDISP/PLUGINS.D/SYSLOG.CONF

```
active = no
direction = out
path = builtin_syslog
type = builtin
args = LOG_INFO
format = string
```

32 Setting Up the Linux Audit Framework

This chapter shows how to set up a simple audit scenario. Every step involved in configuring and enabling audit is explained in detail. After you have learned to set up audit, consider a real-world example scenario in *Chapter 33, Introducing an Audit Rule Set*.

To set up audit on SUSE Linux Enterprise Server, you need to complete the following steps:

PROCEDURE 32.1: SETTING UP THE LINUX AUDIT FRAMEWORK

1. Make sure that all required packages are installed: `audit`, `audit-libs`, and optionally `audit-libs-python`. To use the log visualization as described in *Section 32.6, "Configuring Log Visualization"*, install `gnuplot` and `graphviz` from the SUSE Linux Enterprise Server media.

2. Determine the components to audit. Refer to *Section 32.1, "Determining the Components to Audit"* for details.

3. Check or modify the basic audit daemon configuration. Refer to *Section 32.2, "Configuring the Audit Daemon"* for details.

4. Enable auditing for system calls. Refer to *Section 32.3, "Enabling Audit for System Calls"* for details.

5. Compose audit rules to suit your scenario. Refer to *Section 32.4, "Setting Up Audit Rules"* for details.

6. Generate logs and configure tailor-made reports. Refer to *Section 32.5, "Configuring Audit Reports"* for details.

7. Configure optional log visualization. Refer to *Section 32.6, "Configuring Log Visualization"* for details.

> **! Important: Controlling the Audit Daemon**
>
> Before configuring any of the components of the audit system, make sure that the audit daemon is not running by entering `systemctl status auditd` as `root`. On a default SUSE Linux Enterprise Server system, audit is started on boot, so you need to turn it off by entering `systemctl stop auditd`. Start the daemon after configuring it with `systemctl start auditd`.

32.1 Determining the Components to Audit

Before starting to create your own audit configuration, determine to which degree you want to use it. Check the following general rules to determine which use case best applies to you and your requirements:

- If you require a full security audit for CAPP/EAL certification, enable full audit for system calls and configure watches on various configuration files and directories, similar to the rule set featured in *Chapter 33, Introducing an Audit Rule Set*.

- If you need to trace a process based on the audit rules, use `autrace`.

- If you require file and directory watches to track access to important or security-sensitive data, create a rule set matching these requirements. Enable audit as described in *Section 32.3, "Enabling Audit for System Calls"* and proceed to *Section 32.4, "Setting Up Audit Rules"*.

32.2 Configuring the Audit Daemon

The basic setup of the audit daemon is done by editing `/etc/audit/auditd.conf`. You may also use YaST to configure the basic settings by calling *YaST › Security and Users › Linux Audit Framework (LAF)*. Use the tabs *Log File* and *Disk Space* for configuration.

```
log_file = /var/log/audit/audit.log
log_format = RAW
log_group = root
priority_boost = 4
flush = INCREMENTAL
freq = 20
num_logs = 5
disp_qos = lossy
dispatcher = /sbin/audispd
name_format = NONE
##name = mydomain
max_log_file = 6
max_log_file_action = ROTATE
space_left = 75
space_left_action = SYSLOG
action_mail_acct = root
admin_space_left = 50
admin_space_left_action = SUSPEND
disk_full_action = SUSPEND
```

```
disk_error_action = SUSPEND
##tcp_listen_port =
tcp_listen_queue = 5
tcp_max_per_addr = 1
##tcp_client_ports = 1024-65535
tcp_client_max_idle = 0
cp_client_max_idle = 0
```

The default settings work reasonably well for many setups. Some values, such as `num_logs`, `max_log_file`, `space_left`, and `admin_space_left` depend on the size of your deployment. If disk space is limited, you should reduce the number of log files to keep if they are rotated and you should get an earlier warning if disk space is running out. For a CAPP-compliant setup, adjust the values for `log_file`, `flush`, `max_log_file`, `max_log_file_action`, `space_left`, `space_left_action`, `admin_space_left`, `admin_space_left_action`, `disk_full_action`, and `disk_error_action`, as described in *Section 31.2, "Configuring the Audit Daemon"*. An example CAPP-compliant configuration looks like this:

```
log_file = PATH_TO_SEPARATE_PARTITION/audit.log
log_format = RAW
priority_boost = 4
flush = SYNC                       ### or DATA
freq = 20
num_logs = 4
dispatcher = /sbin/audispd
disp_qos = lossy
max_log_file = 5
max_log_file_action = KEEP_LOGS
space_left = 75
space_left_action = EMAIL
action_mail_acct = root
admin_space_left = 50
admin_space_left_action = SINGLE   ### or HALT
disk_full_action = SUSPEND         ### or HALT
disk_error_action = SUSPEND        ### or HALT
```

The `###` precedes comments where you can choose from several options. Do not add the comments to your actual configuration files.

 Tip: For More Information

Refer to *Section 31.2, "Configuring the Audit Daemon"* for detailed background information about the `auditd.conf` configuration parameters.

32.3 Enabling Audit for System Calls

If the audit framework is not installed, install the `audit` package. A standard SUSE Linux Enterprise Server system does not have auditd running by default. Enable it with:

```
systemctl enable auditd
```

There are different levels of auditing activity available:

Basic Logging

Out of the box (without any further configuration) auditd logs only events concerning its own configuration changes to `/var/log/audit/audit.log`. No events (file access, system call, etc.) are generated by the kernel audit component until requested by **auditctl**. However, other kernel components and modules may log audit events outside of the control of **auditctl** and these appear in the audit log. By default, the only module that generates audit events is AppArmor.

Advanced Logging with System Call Auditing

To audit system calls and get meaningful file watches, you need to enable audit contexts for system calls.

As you need system call auditing capabilities even when you are configuring plain file or directory watches, you need to enable audit contexts for system calls. To enable audit contexts for the duration of the current session only, execute **auditctl -e 1** as `root`. To disable this feature, execute **auditctl -e 0** as `root`.

The audit contexts are enabled by default. To turn this feature off temporarily, use **auditctl -e 0**.

32.4 Setting Up Audit Rules

Using audit rules, determine which aspects of the system should be analyzed by audit. Normally this includes important databases and security-relevant configuration files. You may also analyze various system calls in detail if a broad analysis of your system is required. A very detailed example configuration that includes most of the rules that are needed in a CAPP compliant environment is available in *Chapter 33, Introducing an Audit Rule Set*.

Audit rules can be passed to the audit daemon on the **auditctl** command line and by composing a rule set in /etc/audit/audit.rules which is processed whenever the audit daemon is
started. To customize /etc/audit/audit.rules either edit it directly, or use YaST: *Security
and Users › Linux Audit Framework (LAF) › Rules for 'auditctl'*. Rules passed on the command line
are not persistent and need to be re-entered when the audit daemon is restarted.

A simple rule set for very basic auditing on a few important files and directories could look
like this:

```
# basic audit system parameters
-D
-b 8192
-f 1
-e 1


# some file and directory watches with keys
-w /var/log/audit/ -k LOG_audit
-w /etc/audit/auditd.conf -k CFG_audit_conf -p rxwa
-w /etc/audit/audit.rules -k CFG_audit_rules -p rxwa

-w /etc/passwd -k CFG_passwd -p rwxa
-w /etc/sysconfig/ -k CFG_sysconfig

# an example system call rule
-a entry,always -S umask

### add your own rules
```

When configuring the basic audit system parameters (such as the backlog parameter -b) test
these settings with your intended audit rule set to determine whether the backlog size is appropriate for the level of logging activity caused by your audit rule set. If your chosen backlog size
is too small, your system might not be able to handle the audit load and consult the failure flag
(-f) when the backlog limit is exceeded.

 Important: Choosing the Failure Flag

When choosing the failure flag, note that -f 2 tells your system to perform an immediate
shutdown without flushing any pending data to disk when the limits of your audit system
are exceeded. Because this shutdown is not a clean shutdown, restrict the use of -f 2
to only the most security-conscious environments and use -f 1 (system continues to
run, issues a warning and audit stops) for any other setup to avoid loss of data or data
corruption.

Directory watches produce less verbose output than separate file watches for the files under these directories. To get detailed logging for your system configuration in `/etc/sysconfig`, for example, add watches for each file. Audit does not support globbing, which means you cannot create a rule that says `-w /etc/*` and watches all files and directories below `/etc`.

For better identification in the log file, a key has been added to each of the file and directory watches. Using the key, it is easier to comb the logs for events related to a certain rule. When creating keys, distinguish between mere log file watches and configuration file watches by using an appropriate prefix with the key, in this case `LOG` for a log file watch and `CFG` for a configuration file watch. Using the file name as part of the key also makes it easier for you to identify events of this type in the log file.

Another thing to keep in mind when creating file and directory watches is that audit cannot deal with files that do not exist when the rules are created. Any file that is added to your system while audit is already running is not watched unless you extend the rule set to watch this new file.

For more information about creating custom rules, refer to *Section 31.4, "Passing Parameters to the Audit System"*.

 Important: Changing Audit Rules

> After you change audit rules, always restart the audit daemon with **systemctl restart auditd** to reread the changed rules.

32.5 Configuring Audit Reports

To avoid having to dig through the raw audit logs to get an impression of what your system is currently doing, run custom audit reports at certain intervals. Custom audit reports enable you to focus on areas of interest and get meaningful statistics on the nature and frequency of the events you are monitoring. To analyze individual events in detail, use the ausearch tool.

Before setting up audit reporting, consider the following:

- What types of events do you want to monitor by generating regular reports? Select the appropriate aureport command lines as described in *Section 31.5.2, "Generating Custom Audit Reports"*.

- What do you want to do with the audit reports? Decide whether to create graphical charts from the data accumulated or whether it should be transferred into any sort of spreadsheet or database. Set up the aureport command line and further processing similar to the examples shown in *Section 32.6, "Configuring Log Visualization"* if you want to visualize your reports.

- When and at which intervals should the reports run? Set up appropriate automated reporting using cron.

For this example, assume that you are interested in finding out about any attempts to access your audit, PAM, and system configuration. Proceed as follows to find out about file events on your system:

1. Generate a full summary report of all events and check for any anomalies in the summary report, for example, have a look at the "failed syscalls" record, because these might have failed because of insufficient permissions to access a file or a file not being there:

```
aureport

Summary Report
======================
Range of time in logs: 03/02/09 14:13:38.225 - 17/02/09 16:30:10.352
Selected time for report: 03/02/09 14:13:38 - 17/02/09 16:30:10.352
Number of changes in configuration: 24
Number of changes to accounts, groups, or roles: 0
Number of logins: 9
Number of failed logins: 15
Number of authentications: 19
Number of failed authentications: 578
Number of users: 3
Number of terminals: 15
Number of host names: 4
Number of executables: 20
Number of files: 279
Number of AVC's: 0
Number of MAC events: 0
Number of failed syscalls: 994
Number of anomaly events: 0
Number of responses to anomaly events: 0
```

```
Number of crypto events: 0
Number of keys: 2
Number of process IDs: 1238
Number of events: 5435
```

2. Run a summary report for failed events and check the "files" record for the number of failed file access events:

```
aureport --failed

Failed Summary Report
======================
Range of time in logs: 03/02/09 14:13:38.225 - 17/02/09 16:30:10.352
Selected time for report: 03/02/09 14:13:38 - 17/02/09 16:30:10.352
Number of changes in configuration: 0
Number of changes to accounts, groups, or roles: 0
Number of logins: 0
Number of failed logins: 15
Number of authentications: 0
Number of failed authentications: 578
Number of users: 1
Number of terminals: 7
Number of host names: 4
Number of executables: 12
Number of files: 77
Number of AVC's: 0
Number of MAC events: 0
Number of failed syscalls: 994
Number of anomaly events: 0
Number of responses to anomaly events: 0
Number of crypto events: 0
Number of keys: 2
Number of process IDs: 713
Number of events: 1589
```

3. To list the files that could not be accessed, run a summary report of failed file events:

```
aureport -f -i --failed --summary

Failed File Summary Report
===========================
total  file
===========================
80  /var
80  spool
80  cron
80  lastrun
```

```
46  /usr/lib/locale/en_GB.UTF-8/LC_CTYPE
45  /usr/lib/locale/locale-archive
38  /usr/lib/locale/en_GB.UTF-8/LC_IDENTIFICATION
38  /usr/lib/locale/en_GB.UTF-8/LC_MEASUREMENT
38  /usr/lib/locale/en_GB.UTF-8/LC_TELEPHONE
38  /usr/lib/locale/en_GB.UTF-8/LC_ADDRESS
38  /usr/lib/locale/en_GB.UTF-8/LC_NAME
38  /usr/lib/locale/en_GB.UTF-8/LC_PAPER
38  /usr/lib/locale/en_GB.UTF-8/LC_MESSAGES
38  /usr/lib/locale/en_GB.UTF-8/LC_MONETARY
38  /usr/lib/locale/en_GB.UTF-8/LC_COLLATE
38  /usr/lib/locale/en_GB.UTF-8/LC_TIME
38  /usr/lib/locale/en_GB.UTF-8/LC_NUMERIC
8   /etc/magic.mgc
...
```

To focus this summary report on a few files or directories of interest only, such as `/etc/audit/auditd.conf`, `/etc/pam.d`, and `/etc/sysconfig`, use a command similar to the following:

```
aureport -f -i --failed --summary |grep -e "/etc/audit/auditd.conf" -e "/etc/pam.d/"
 -e "/etc/sysconfig"

1  /etc/sysconfig/displaymanager
```

4. From the summary report, then proceed to isolate these items of interest from the log and find out their event IDs for further analysis:

```
aureport -f -i --failed |grep -e "/etc/audit/auditd.conf" -e "/etc/pam.d/" -e "/etc/sysconfig"

993. 17/02/09 16:47:34 /etc/sysconfig/displaymanager readlink no /bin/vim-normal
 root 7887
994. 17/02/09 16:48:23 /etc/sysconfig/displaymanager getxattr no /bin/vim-normal
 root 7889
```

5. Use the event ID to get a detailed record for each item of interest:

```
ausearch -a 7887 -i
----
time->Tue Feb 17 16:48:23 2009
type=PATH msg=audit(1234885703.090:7889): item=0 name="/etc/sysconfig/
displaymanager" inode=369282 dev=08:06 mode=0100644 ouid=0 ogid=0 rdev=00:00
type=CWD msg=audit(1234885703.090:7889):  cwd="/root"
type=SYSCALL msg=audit(1234885703.090:7889): arch=c000003e syscall=191 success=no
 exit=-61 a0=7e1e20 a1=7f90e4cf9187 a2=7fffed5b57d0 a3=84 items=1 ppid=25548
```

```
pid=23045 auid=0 uid=0 gid=0 euid=0 suid=0 fsuid=0 egid=0 sgid=0 fsgid=0 tty=pts2
ses=1166 comm="vim" exe="/bin/vim-normal" key=(null)
```

 Tip: Focusing on a Certain Time Frame

If you are interested in events during a particular period of time, trim down the reports by using start and end dates and times with your **aureport** commands (`-ts` and `-te`). For more information, refer to *Section 31.5.2, "Generating Custom Audit Reports"*.

All steps (except for the last one) can be run automatically and would easily be scriptable and configured as cron jobs. Any of the `--failed --summary` reports could be transformed easily into a bar chart that plots files versus failed access attempts. For more information about visualizing audit report data, refer to *Section 32.6, "Configuring Log Visualization"*.

32.6 Configuring Log Visualization

Using the scripts **mkbar** and **mkgraph** you can illustrate your audit statistics with various graphs and charts. As with any other **aureport** command, the plotting commands are scriptable and can easily be configured to run as cron jobs.

mkbar and **mkgraph** were created by Steve Grubb at Red Hat. They are available from http://people.redhat.com/sgrubb/audit/visualize/ ↗. Because the current version of audit in SUSE Linux Enterprise Server does not ship with these scripts, proceed as follows to make them available on your system:

 Warning: Downloaded Content Is Dangerous

Use **mkbar** and **mkgraph** at your own risk. Any content downloaded from the Web is potentially dangerous to your system, even more so when run with `root` privileges.

1. Download the scripts to `root`'s `~/bin` directory:

```
wget http://people.redhat.com/sgrubb/audit/visualize/mkbar -O ~/bin/mkbar
wget http://people.redhat.com/sgrubb/audit/visualize/mkgraph -O ~/bin/mkgraph
```

2. Adjust the file permissions to read, write, and execute for `root`:

```
chmod 744 ~/bin/mk{bar,graph}
```

To plot summary reports, such as the ones discussed in *Section 32.5, "Configuring Audit Reports"*, use the script **mkbar**. Some example commands could look like the following:

Create a Summary of Events

```
aureport -e -i --summary | mkbar events
```

Create a Summary of File Events

```
aureport -f -i --summary | mkbar files
```

Create a Summary of Login Events

```
aureport -l -i --summary | mkbar login
```

Create a Summary of User Events

```
aureport -u -i --summary | mkbar users
```

Create a Summary of System Call Events

```
aureport -s -i --summary | mkbar syscalls
```

To create a summary chart of failed events of any of the above event types, add the `--failed` option to the respective **aureport** command. To cover a certain period of time only, use the `-ts` and `-te` options on aureport. Any of these commands can be tweaked further by narrowing down its scope using grep or egrep and regular expressions. See the comments in the **mkbar** script for an example. Any of the above commands produces a PNG file containing a bar chart of the requested data.

To illustrate the relationship between different kinds of audit objects, such as users and system calls, use the script **mkgraph**. Some example commands could look like the following:

Users versus Executables

```
LC_ALL=C aureport -u -i | awk '/^[0-9]/ { print $4" "$7 }' | sort | uniq | mkgraph
 users_vs_exec
```

Users versus Files

```
LC_ALL=C aureport -f -i | awk '/^[0-9]/ { print $8" "$4 }' | sort | uniq | mkgraph
 users_vs_files
```

System Calls versus Commands

```
LC_ALL=C aureport -s -i | awk '/^[0-9]/ { print $4" "$6 }' | sort | uniq | mkgraph
  syscall_vs_com
```

System Calls versus Files

```
LC_ALL=C aureport -s -i | awk '/^[0-9]/ { print $5" "$4 }' | sort | uniq | mkgraph |
  syscall_vs_file
```

Graphs can also be combined to illustrate complex relationships. See the comments in the **mk-graph** script for further information and an example. The graphs produced by this script are created in PostScript format by default, but you can change the output format by changing the EXT variable in the script from ps to png or jpg.

33 Introducing an Audit Rule Set

The following example configuration illustrates how audit can be used to monitor your system. It highlights the most important items that need to be audited to cover the list of auditable events specified by Controlled Access Protection Profile (CAPP).

The example rule set is divided into the following sections:

- Basic audit configuration (see *Section 33.1, "Adding Basic Audit Configuration Parameters"*)

- Watches on audit log files and configuration files (see *Section 33.2, "Adding Watches on Audit Log Files and Configuration Files"*)

- Monitoring operations on file system objects (see *Section 33.3, "Monitoring File System Objects"*)

- Monitoring security databases (see *Section 33.4, "Monitoring Security Configuration Files and Databases"*)

- Monitoring miscellaneous system calls (*Section 33.5, "Monitoring Miscellaneous System Calls"*)

- Filtering system call arguments (see *Section 33.6, "Filtering System Call Arguments"*)

To transform this example into a configuration file to use in your live setup, proceed as follows:

1. Choose the appropriate settings for your setup and adjust them.

2. Adjust the file `/etc/audit/audit.rules` by adding rules from the examples below or by modifying existing rules.

 Note: Adjusting the Level of Audit Logging

Do not copy the example below into your audit setup without adjusting it to your needs. Determine what and to what extent to audit.

The entire `audit.rules` is a collection of **auditctl** commands. Every line in this file expands to a full **auditctl** command line. The syntax used in the rule set is the same as that of the **auditctl** command.

33.1 Adding Basic Audit Configuration Parameters

```
-D ❶
-b 8192 ❷
-f 2 ❸
```

❶ Delete any preexisting rules before starting to define new ones.

❷ Set the number of buffers to take the audit messages. Depending on the level of audit logging on your system, increase or decrease this figure.

❸ Set the failure flag to use when the kernel needs to handle critical errors. Possible values are `0` (silent), `1` (printk, print a failure message), and `2` (panic, halt the system).

By emptying the rule queue with the `-D` option, you make sure that audit does not use any other rule set than what you are offering it by means of this file. Choosing an appropriate buffer number (`-b`) is vital to avoid having your system fail because of too high an audit load. Choosing the panic failure flag `-f 2` ensures that your audit records are complete even if the system is encountering critical errors. By shutting down the system on a critical error, audit makes sure that no process escapes from its control as it otherwise might if level 1 (`printk`) were chosen.

 Important: Choosing the Failure Flag

> Before using your audit rule set on a live system, make sure that the setup has been thoroughly evaluated on test systems using the *worst case production workload*. It is even more critical that you do this when specifying the `-f 2` flag, because this instructs the kernel to panic (perform an immediate halt without flushing pending data to disk) if any thresholds are exceeded. Consider the use of the `-f 2` flag for only the most security-conscious environments.

33.2 Adding Watches on Audit Log Files and Configuration Files

Adding watches on your audit configuration files and the log files themselves ensures that you can track any attempt to tamper with the configuration files or detect any attempted accesses to the log files.

Note: Creating Directory and File Watches

Creating watches on a directory is not necessarily sufficient if you need events for file access. Events on directory access are only triggered when the directory's inode is updated with metadata changes. To trigger events on file access, add watches for each file to monitor.

```
-w /var/log/audit/  ❶
-w /var/log/audit/audit.log

-w /var/log/audit/audit_log.1
-w /var/log/audit/audit_log.2
-w /var/log/audit/audit_log.3
-w /var/log/audit/audit_log.4

-w /etc/audit/auditd.conf -p wa❷
-w /etc/audit/audit.rules -p wa
-w /etc/libaudit.conf -p wa
```

❶ Set a watch on the directory where the audit log is located. Trigger an event for any type of access attempt to this directory. If you are using log rotation, add watches for the rotated logs as well.

❷ Set a watch on an audit configuration file. Log all write and attribute change attempts to this file.

33.3 Monitoring File System Objects

Auditing system calls helps track your system's activity well beyond the application level. By tracking file system–related system calls, get an idea of how your applications are using these system calls and determine whether that use is appropriate. By tracking mount and unmount operations, track the use of external resources (removable media, remote file systems, etc.).

Important: Auditing System Calls

Auditing system calls results in a high logging activity. This activity, in turn, puts a heavy load on the kernel. With a kernel less responsive than usual, the system's backlog and rate limits might be exceeded. Carefully evaluate which system calls to include in your audit rule set and adjust the log settings accordingly. See *Section 31.2, "Configuring the Audit Daemon"* for details on how to tweak the relevant settings.

```
-a entry,always -S chmod -S fchmod -S chown -S chown32 -S fchown -S fchown32 -S lchown -S
  lchown32 ❶

-a entry,always -S creat -S open -S truncate -S truncate64 -S ftruncate -S ftruncate64 ❷

-a entry,always -S mkdir -S rmdir ❸

-a entry,always -S unlink -S rename -S link -S symlink ❹

-a entry,always -S setxattr ❺
-a entry,always -S lsetxattr
-a entry,always -S fsetxattr
-a entry,always -S removexattr
-a entry,always -S lremovexattr
-a entry,always -S fremovexattr

-a entry,always -S mknod ❻

-a entry,always -S mount -S umount -S umount2 ❼
```

❶ Enable an audit context for system calls related to changing file ownership and permissions. Depending on the hardware architecture of your system, enable or disable the *32 rules. 64-bit systems, like AMD64/Intel 64, require the *32 rules to be removed.

❷ Enable an audit context for system calls related to file content modification. Depending on the hardware architecture of your system, enable or disable the *64 rules. 64-bit systems, like AMD64/Intel 64, require the *64 rules to be removed.

❸ Enable an audit context for any directory operation, like creating or removing a directory.

❹ Enable an audit context for any linking operation, such as creating a symbolic link, creating a link, unlinking, or renaming.

❺ Enable an audit context for any operation related to extended file system attributes.

❻ Enable an audit context for the **mknod** system call, which creates special (device) files.

⑦ Enable an audit context for any mount or umount operation. For the x86 architecture, disable the `umount` rule. For the Intel 64 architecture, disable the `umount2` rule.

33.4 Monitoring Security Configuration Files and Databases

To make sure that your system is not made to do undesired things, track any attempts to change the `cron` and `at` configurations or the lists of scheduled jobs. Tracking any write access to the user, group, password and login databases and logs helps you identify any attempts to manipulate your system's user database.

Tracking changes to your system configuration (kernel, services, time, etc.) helps you spot any attempts of others to manipulate essential functionality of your system. Changes to the PAM configuration should also be monitored in a secure environment, because changes in the authentication stack should not be made by anyone other than the administrator, and it should be logged which applications are using PAM and how it is used. The same applies to any other configuration files related to secure authentication and communication.

```
①
-w /var/spool/atspool
-w /etc/at.allow
-w /etc/at.deny

-w /etc/cron.allow -p wa
-w /etc/cron.deny -p wa
-w /etc/cron.d/ -p wa
-w /etc/cron.daily/ -p wa
-w /etc/cron.hourly/ -p wa
-w /etc/cron.monthly/ -p wa
-w /etc/cron.weekly/ -p wa
-w /etc/crontab -p wa
-w /var/spool/cron/root

②
-w /etc/group -p wa
-w /etc/passwd -p wa
-w /etc/shadow

-w /etc/login.defs -p wa
-w /etc/securetty
-w /var/log/lastlog
```

```
❸
-w /etc/hosts -p wa
-w /etc/sysconfig/
w /etc/init.d/
w /etc/ld.so.conf -p wa
w /etc/localtime -p wa
w /etc/sysctl.conf -p wa
w /etc/modprobe.d/
w /etc/modprobe.conf.local -p wa
w /etc/modprobe.conf -p wa
❹
w /etc/pam.d/
❺
-w /etc/aliases -p wa
-w /etc/postfix/ -p wa

❻
-w /etc/ssh/sshd_config

-w /etc/stunnel/stunnel.conf
-w /etc/stunnel/stunnel.pem

-w /etc/vsftpd.ftpusers
-w /etc/vsftpd.conf

❼
-a exit,always -S sethostname
-w /etc/issue -p wa
-w /etc/issue.net -p wa
```

❶ Set watches on the `at` and `cron` configuration and the scheduled jobs and assign labels to these events.

❷ Set watches on the user, group, password, and login databases and logs and set labels to better identify any login-related events, such as failed login attempts.

❸ Set a watch and a label on the static host name configuration in `/etc/hosts`. Track changes to the system configuration directory, `/etc/sysconfig`. Enable per-file watches if you are interested in file events. Set watches and labels for changes to the boot configuration in the `/etc/init.d` directory. Enable per-file watches if you are interested in file events. Set watches and labels for any changes to the linker configuration in `/etc/ld.so.conf`. Set watches and a label for `/etc/localtime`. Set watches and labels for the kernel configuration files `/etc/sysctl.conf`, `/etc/modprobe.d/`, `/etc/modprobe.conf.local`, and `/etc/modprobe.conf`.

④ Set watches on the PAM configuration directory. If you are interested in particular files below the directory level, add explicit watches to these files as well.

⑤ Set watches to the postfix configuration to log any write attempt or attribute change and use labels for better tracking in the logs.

⑥ Set watches and labels on the **SSH**, **stunnel**, and **vsftpd** configuration files.

⑦ Perform an audit of the **sethostname** system call and set watches and labels on the system identification configuration in `/etc/issue` and `/etc/issue.net`.

33.5   Monitoring Miscellaneous System Calls

Apart from auditing file system related system calls, as described in *Section 33.3, "Monitoring File System Objects"*, you can also track various other system calls. Tracking task creation helps you understand your applications' behavior. Auditing the `umask` system call lets you track how processes modify creation mask. Tracking any attempts to change the system time helps you identify anyone or any process trying to manipulate the system time.

```
①
-a entry,always -S clone -S fork -S vfork

②
-a entry,always -S umask

③
-a entry,always -S adjtimex -S settimeofday
```

① Track task creation.

② Add an audit context to the umask system call.

③ Track attempts to change the system time. `adjtimex` can be used to skew the time. `settimeofday` sets the absolute time.

33.6   Filtering System Call Arguments

In addition to the system call auditing introduced in *Section 33.3, "Monitoring File System Objects"* and *Section 33.5, "Monitoring Miscellaneous System Calls"*, you can track application behavior to an even higher degree. Applying filters helps you focus audit on areas of primary interest to you. This section introduces filtering system call arguments for non-multiplexed system calls like access and for multiplexed ones like socketcall or ipc. Whether system calls are multiplexed depends on the hardware architecture used. Both socketcall and ipc are not multiplexed on 64-bit architectures, such as AMD64/Intel 64.

 Important: Auditing System Calls

> Auditing system calls results in high logging activity, which in turn puts a heavy load on the kernel. With a kernel less responsive than usual, the system's backlog and rate limits might well be exceeded. Carefully evaluate which system calls to include in your audit rule set and adjust the log settings accordingly. See *Section 31.2, "Configuring the Audit Daemon"* for details on how to tweak the relevant settings.

The access system call checks whether a process would be allowed to read, write or test for the existence of a file or file system object. Using the `-F` filter flag, build rules matching specific access calls in the format `-F a1=ACCESS_MODE`. Check `/usr/include/fcntl.h` for a list of possible arguments to the access system call.

```
-a entry,always -S access -F a1=4 ①
-a entry,always -S access -F a1=6 ②
-a entry,always -S access -F a1=7 ③
```

①   Audit the access system call, but only if the second argument of the system call (`mode`) is `4` (`R_OK`). This rule filters for all access calls testing for sufficient read permissions to a file or file system object accessed by a user or process.

②   Audit the access system call, but only if the second argument of the system call (`mode`) is `6`, meaning `4 OR 2`, which translates to `R_OK OR W_OK`. This rule filters for access calls testing for sufficient read and write permissions.

③   Audit the access system call, but only if the second argument of the system call (`mode`) is `7`, meaning `4 OR 2 OR 1`, which translates to `R_OK OR W_OK OR X_OK`. This rule filters for access calls testing for sufficient read, write, and execute permissions.

The socketcall system call is a multiplexed system call. Multiplexed means that there is only one system call for all possible calls and that libc passes the actual system call to use as the first argument (`a0`). Check the manual page of socketcall for possible system calls and refer to `/usr/src/linux/include/linux/net.h` for a list of possible argument values and system call names. Audit supports filtering for specific system calls using a `-F a0=SYSCALL_NUMBER`.

```
-a entry,always -S socketcall -F a0=1 -F a1=10 ①
```

```
## Use this line on x86_64, ia64 instead
#-a entry,always -S socket -F a0=10

-a entry,always -S socketcall -F a0=5 ❷
## Use this line on x86_64, ia64 instead
#-a entry, always -S accept
```

❶ Audit the socket(PF_INET6) system call. The `-F a0=1` filter matches all socket system calls and the `-F a1=10` filter narrows the matches down to socket system calls carrying the IPv6 protocol family domain parameter (PF_INET6). Check `/usr/include/linux/net.h` for the first argument (`a0`) and `/usr/src/linux/include/linux/socket.h` for the second parameter (`a1`). 64-bit platforms, like AMD64/Intel 64, do not use multiplexing on socketcall system calls. For these platforms, comment the rule and add the plain system call rules with a filter on PF_INET6.

❷ Audit the socketcall system call. The filter flag is set to filter for `a0=5` as the first argument to socketcall, which translates to the accept system call if you check `/usr/include/linux/net.h`. 64-bit platforms, like AMD64/Intel 64, do not use multiplexing on socketcall system calls. For these platforms, comment the rule and add the plain system call rule without argument filtering.

The ipc system call is another example of multiplexed system calls. The actual call to invoke is determined by the first argument passed to the ipc system call. Filtering for these arguments helps you focus on those IPC calls of interest to you. Check `/usr/include/linux/ipc.h` for possible argument values.

```
❶
## msgctl
-a entry,always -S ipc -F a0=14
## msgget
-a entry,always -S ipc -F a0=13
## Use these lines on x86_64, ia64 instead
#-a entry,always -S msgctl
#-a entry,always -S msgget

❷
## semctl
-a entry,always -S ipc -F a0=3
## semget
-a entry,always -S ipc -F a0=2
## semop
-a entry,always -S ipc -F a0=1
## semtimedop
-a entry,always -S ipc -F a0=4
```

```
## Use these lines on x86_64, ia64 instead
#-a entry,always -S semctl
#-a entry,always -S semget
#-a entry,always -S semop
#-a entry,always -S semtimedop

❸
## shmctl
-a entry,always -S ipc -F a0=24
## shmget
-a entry,always -S ipc -F a0=23
## Use these lines on x86_64, ia64 instead
#-a entry,always -S shmctl
#-a entry,always -S shmget
```

❶ Audit system calls related to IPC SYSV message queues. In this case, the a0 values specify that auditing is added for the msgctl and msgget system calls (14 and 13). 64-bit platforms, like AMD64/Intel 64, do not use multiplexing on ipc system calls. For these platforms, comment the first two rules and add the plain system call rules without argument filtering.

❷ Audit system calls related to IPC SYSV message semaphores. In this case, the a0 values specify that auditing is added for the semctl, semget, semop, and semtimedop system calls (3, 2, 1, and 4). 64-bit platforms, like AMD64/Intel 64, do not use multiplexing on ipc system calls. For these platforms, comment the first four rules and add the plain system call rules without argument filtering.

❸ Audit system calls related to IPC SYSV shared memory. In this case, the a0 values specify that auditing is added for the shmctl and shmget system calls (24, 23). 64-bit platforms, like AMD64/Intel 64, do not use multiplexing on ipc system calls. For these platforms, comment the first two rules and add the plain system call rules without argument filtering.

33.7 Managing Audit Event Records Using Keys

After configuring a few rules generating events and populating the logs, you need to find a way to tell one event from the other. Using the **ausearch** command, you can filter the logs for various criteria. Using **ausearch** -m *MESSAGE_TYPE*, you can at least filter for events of a certain type. However, to be able to filter for events related to a particular rule, you need to add a key to this rule in the /etc/audit/audit.rules file. This key is then added to the event record every time the rule logs an event. To retrieve these log entries, simply run **ausearch** -k *YOUR_KEY* to get a list of records related to the rule carrying this particular key.

As an example, assume you have added the following rule to your rule file:

```
-w /etc/audit/audit.rules -p wa
```

Without a key assigned to it, you would probably need to filter for SYSCALL or PATH events then use grep or similar tools to isolate any events related to the above rule. Now, add a key to the above rule, using the -k option:

```
-w /etc/audit/audit.rules -p wa -k CFG_audit.rules
```

You can specify any text string as key. Distinguish watches related to different types of files (configuration files or log files) from one another using different key prefixes (CFG, LOG, etc.) followed by the file name. Finding any records related to the above rule now comes down to the following:

```
ausearch -k CFG_audit.rules
----
time->Thu Feb 19 09:09:54 2009
type=PATH msg=audit(1235030994.032:8649): item=3 name="audit.rules~" inode=370603
 dev=08:06 mode=0100640 ouid=0 ogid=0 rdev=00:00
type=PATH msg=audit(1235030994.032:8649): item=2 name="audit.rules" inode=370603
 dev=08:06 mode=0100640 ouid=0 ogid=0 rdev=00:00
type=PATH msg=audit(1235030994.032:8649): item=1  name="/etc/audit" inode=368599
 dev=08:06 mode=040750 ouid=0 ogid=0 rdev=00:00
type=PATH msg=audit(1235030994.032:8649): item=0  name="/etc/audit" inode=368599
 dev=08:06 mode=040750 ouid=0 ogid=0 rdev=00:00
type=CWD msg=audit(1235030994.032:8649):  cwd="/etc/audit"
type=SYSCALL msg=audit(1235030994.032:8649): arch=c000003e syscall=82 success=yes exit=0
 a0=7deeb0 a1=883b30 a2=2 a3=ffffffffffffffff items=4 ppid=25400 pid=32619 auid=0 uid=0
 gid=0 euid=0 suid=0 fsuid=0 egid=0 sgid=0 fsgid=0 tty=pts1 ses=1164 comm="vim" exe="/
bin/vim-normal" key="CFG_audit.rules"
```

34 Useful Resources

There are other resources available containing valuable information about the Linux audit framework:

The Audit Manual Pages

There are several man pages installed along with the audit tools that provide valuable and very detailed information:

`auditd(8)`

The Linux audit daemon

`auditd.conf(5)`

The Linux audit daemon configuration file

`auditctl(8)`

A utility to assist controlling the kernel's audit system

`autrace(8)`

A program similar to strace

`ausearch(8)`

A tool to query audit daemon logs

`aureport(8)`

A tool that produces summary reports of audit daemon logs

`audispd.conf(5)`

The audit event dispatcher configuration file

`audispd(8)`

The audit event dispatcher daemon talking to plug-in programs.

http://people.redhat.com/sgrubb/audit/index.html ↗

The home page of the Linux audit project. This site contains several specifications relating to different aspects of Linux audit, and a short FAQ.

`/usr/share/doc/packages/audit`

The audit package itself contains a README with basic design information and sample `.rules` files for different scenarios:

`capp.rules`: Controlled Access Protection Profile (CAPP)

`lspp.rules`: Labeled Security Protection Profile (LSPP)

`nispom.rules`: National Industrial Security Program Operating Manual Chapter 8(NISPOM)

`stig.rules`: Secure Technical Implementation Guide (STIG)

http://www.commoncriteriaportal.org/ ↗

The official Web site of the Common Criteria project. Learn all about the Common Criteria security certification initiative and which role audit plays in this framework.

A Achieving PCI-DSS Compliance

To protect customers and the business itself, companies that handle credit card payments must keep data as safe and secure as possible. Following the Payment Card Industry Data Security Standard helps to secure all areas that are connected to payment processes and to implement security-relevant actions to keep the data and the computing environment safe.

This document aims to provide a basic understanding of how SUSE Linux Enterprise Server can be configured to comply with the Payment Card Industry Data Security Standard.

It is important to understand that protecting systems includes more than configuration. The entire environment and people involved must be taken into account.

An essential part of implementing PCI-DSS is the combination of actions:

1. Create a secure configuration.

2. Track and review all changes made to the configuration: who changed what at which point in time.

A.1 What is the PCI-DSS?

The Payment Card Industry Data Security Standard (PCI-DSS) is a set of requirements to guide a merchant to protect cardholder data. The standard covers 6 main categories with currently 12 requirement topics how to implement, protect, maintain and monitor systems that are involved with credit cardholder data processing.

PCI-DSS was created and is maintained by the PCI Security Standards Council (SSC) that was founded by all five major credit card brands Visa, MasterCard, American Express, Discover, and JCB. In December 2004, PCI-DSS 1.0 was released to address the growing thread of online credit card fraud. The current version, PCI-DSS version 3.2 has been available since April 2016.

BUILD AND MAINTAIN A SECURE NETWORK AND SYSTEMS

1. Install and maintain a firewall configuration to protect cardholder data

2. Do not use vendor-supplied defaults for system passwords and other security parameters

3. Protect stored cardholder data

4. Encrypt transmission of cardholder data across open, public networks

MAINTAIN A VULNERABILITY MANAGEMENT PROGRAM

5. Protect all systems against malware and regularly update anti-virus software or programs

6. Develop and maintain secure systems and applications

IMPLEMENT STRONG ACCESS CONTROL MEASURES

7. Restrict access to cardholder data by business need to know

8. Identify and authenticate access to system components

9. Restrict physical access to cardholder data

REGULARLY MONITOR AND TEST NETWORKS

10. Track and monitor all access to network resources and cardholder data

11. Regularly test security systems and processes

MAINTAIN AN INFORMATION SECURITY POLICY

12. Maintain a policy that addresses information security for all personnel

Most requirements of PCI-DSS are organizational guidelines that help ensure the security of all areas involved with cardholder data. There is usually no specific wording of technical aspects.

This means that it is up to auditors to decide which security settings are valid for a requirement and which are not. Therefore, the recommendations in this document can only provide a starting point for implementing the PCI-DSS and are necessarily subject to discussion.

A.2 Focus of This Document: Areas Relevant to the Operating System

The PCI-DSS covers a wide range of aspects related to cardholder data. Not all of these aspects concern the operating system and this document will not focus on these. Instead, this document focuses on aspects that affect OS configuration, including:

* System security

* Access control

* System maintenance to protect against known vulnerabilities

Topics beyond the scope of this document include data processing applications, database design, and formal processes outside of the OS scope. In particular, requirement 9 (restrict physical access) and requirement 12 (maintain a policy) are not discussed extensively in this document.

A.3 Requirements in Detail

The following section goes through relevant parts of the PCI-DSS in detail, following the ordering of the standard itself.

A.3.1 Requirement 1: Install and Maintain a Firewall Configuration to Protect Cardholder Data

The listed terms in this section are mostly design, documentation and formal process requirements. All changes to the firewalls and routers need to be approved, documented and verified, and all stakeholders need to be involved. The network design includes a DMZ environment, access to the Internet, a protected network for database servers, traffic filtering rules between network segments etc.

In addition to a dedicated firewall and router, SUSE Linux Enterprise Server comes with a host firewall based on iptables. The system can be easily configured to allow only connections on certain inbound ports. With the YaST firewall module it is also possible to define more complex rules. For example, to disable connections not coming from certain network addresses. This allows integrating the local system firewall into an overall firewall design that maximizes network security.

In generalized terms, the technical points in requirement 1 are the following:

- Identify insecure services and protocols.

- Limit traffic to and from the system so that unneeded and unwanted traffic is directly avoided.

1.1.6.b Identify insecure services, protocols, and ports allowed; and verify that security features are documented for each service.

This task is embedded into the requirement to identify, document and justify all services and protocols running on a system. A special interest are services and protocols that could lead to a security risk. If an insecure service or protocol is used, it must be evaluated to understood its potential security impact. Services or protocols that are not necessary for the business to function should be disabled or removed.

1.2.1.b Examine firewall and router configurations to verify that inbound and outbound traffic is limited to that which is necessary for the cardholder data environment.

Inbound traffic filtering rules can be defined from the YaST firewall module. Systems with multiple interfaces can be configured to make the SSH daemon only reachable on the administration interface and not on the general network card. Furthermore, it is possible to define the source addresses that a service allows traffic from.

Usually all outbound system traffic is allowed by the SuSEFirewall2 script. Therefore outbound rules need to be defined manually inside the SuSEFirewall2 custom script. Activate the custom script inside the general SuSEFirewall2 configuration file `/etc/sysconfig/SuSEfirewall2` by uncommenting the `FW_CUSTOMRULES` line.

To add an outbound rule, add an appropriate **iptables** command line inside the `fw_custom_after_chain_creation()` function. This function hook is executed during the firewall setup and allows any customized `iptables` rule.

For example, to allow only outbound DNS requests over the interface `eth0` to server `10.0.0.4`, use:

```
tux > sudo iptables -A OUTPUT -d 10.0.0.4/32 -o eth0 -p udp -m udp --dport 53 -j
  ACCEPT
```

Also see the `deny all OUTPUT` rule described in *1.2.1.c Examine firewall and router configurations to verify that all other inbound and outbound traffic is specifically denied, for example by using an explicit "deny all" or an implicit "deny after allow" statement.* .

1.2.1.c Examine firewall and router configurations to verify that all other inbound and outbound traffic is specifically denied, for example by using an explicit "deny all" or an implicit "deny after allow" statement.

The "deny all" rules of other inbound and outbound traffic can easily be achieved with iptables. The `INPUT` and `FORWARD` table policies are directly set by the SuSEFirewall2 script, so all unwanted traffic is dropped. Forwarding is usually completely disabled by a kernel parameter and should not be enabled for endpoint servers.

The `OUTPUT` policy needs to be defined manually inside the custom SuSEFirewall2 script because in general, all outgoing traffic is allowed. The following two rules need to be added to the `fw_custom_after_chain_creation()` function so that only outbound traffic that is related to an established inbound connection is allowed.

```
tux > sudo iptables -A OUTPUT -m conntrack --ctstate ESTABLISHED -j ACCEPT
```

```
tux > sudo iptables -P OUTPUT DROP
```

In addition, inbound traffic can also be configured for certain services via the tcp wrapper configuration file `/etc/hosts.deny`.

Most of the following tasks are about examine and verifying that the defined inbound and outbound rules are really limiting the traffic between and within all network segments, like the DMZ and the Internet, to a needed minimum for full system operation.

1.3.3 Implement anti-spoofing measures to detect and block forged source IP addresses from entering the network.

There are two ways to implement anti-spoofing measurements in SUSE Linux Enterprise Server:

- `iptables` **rules that only allow input from certain addresses on specified interfaces.** The used address space for communications can be clearly defined in the system setup. Any use of addresses that violate these definitions can be logged and trigger an alarm.

- **Linux Kernel Reverse Path Filtering.** This feature discards packet replies that do not go through the same interface as the initial packet. This feature is enabled by default in SUSE Linux Enterprise Server and can be checked with the following command:

```
tux > cat /proc/sys/net/ipv4/conf/all/rp_filter
```

When enabled, this returns `1`.

1.3.5 Permit only "established" connections into the network.

The SuSEFirewall2 enables connection tracking via `iptables`. Connections to an interface that has been marked as external are dropped by default. Only connections that associated with an established connection are allowed.

It is possible to define certain services that are allowed to connect to the external interface. However, this must be in compliance with the general security policy.

Keep in mind that the first line of defense against malicious connections from the Internet should be a dedicated firewall system that handles all traffic and acts as a gate keeper. Unwanted connections should never reach the DMZ network. However, simple firewall rules on SUSE Linux Enterprise Server systems can help avoid misconfigurations and act as another line of defense.

1.3.7 Do not disclose private IP addresses and routing information to unauthorized parties.

A SUSE Linux Enterprise Server system can also act as a router to forward traffic from one interface to another network on a second interface. It is possible to use Network Address Translation (NAT) on the external interface so that no internal IP address is actually exposed to outside. This is done to mitigate the information an external attacker can gather by simply analyzing the network traffic. NAT can also be used on virtualization hosts or container-based environments that connect to the outside via a specific interface.

A.3.2 Requirement 2: Do Not Use Vendor-Supplied Defaults for System Passwords and Other Security Parameters

During the installation of SUSE Linux Enterprise Server, general system passwords are already set by the administrator. The setup also uses a password checker (**cracklib**) that identifies weak entries against a dictionary. This means that the standard configuration already includes customer-defined security options for most services.

For more information about OS security, see Security Guide and *Book "Security and Hardening Guide"*.

2.1 Always change vendor-supplied defaults and remove or disable unnecessary default accounts before installing a system on the network.

The configuration of any system service must be evaluated to meet the needed security standards. This goes from limiting the used protocols to only allow currently secure versions and to disable legacy implementations, to the definition of access controls and authentication. The default settings of SUSE Linux Enterprise Server already provide good overall security, but they can be tweaked further.

For example, the following security settings might be relevant:

- By default, the SNMP daemon only allows incoming requests to `localhost`. However, the default community string is named `public` and should be changed before accepting general inbound connections.

- By default, certain insecure upstream settings of the `sshd` daemon are listed and commented out inside the `sshd` configuration file `/etc/ssh/sshd_config`. For example, the insecure protocol version 1 and empty passwords (`PermitEmptyPasswords no`) are already disabled.

  To further increase SSH security, if applicable, deny direct `root` access by setting `PermitRootLogin` to `no`.

Default settings can be customized by automating system installation with an AutoYaST profile. This allows rolling out new instances of SUSE Linux Enterprise Server and automatically enabling an evaluated configuration. This setup procedure can also be automated with the SUSE Manager. For more information, see the SUSE Manager documentation at https://www.suse.com/documentation/suse-manager ↗.

By default, SUSE Linux Enterprise Server does not create additional accounts apart from the `root` administrative user. There are system accounts defined in `/etc/passwd`, but they are not activated and therefore not directly reachable. This can be validated by checking the lines inside the `/etc/shadow` file.

In that file, the second column represents the defined password:

- An asterisk (`*`) means that a password was never defined and the account is therefore locked.

- An exclamation mark (`!`) stands for a locked account and can stand all by itself or in front of a password hash.

2.2 Develop configuration standards for all system components. Assure that these standards address all known security vulnerabilities and are consistent with industry-accepted system hardening standards.

As mentioned inside the PCI-DSS document, possible sources for industry-accepted hardening standards are:

1. Center for Internet Security (CIS)

2. International Organization for Standardization (ISO)

3. SysAdmin Audit Network Security (SANS) Institute

4. National Institute of Standards Technology (NIST)

As the PCI-DSS requirements are not specified precisely, there is no direct relationship between hardening standards and specific requirements. However, other hardening resources can also help in complying with these specifications, including Security Guide and *Book "Security and Hardening Guide"*.

2.2.1 Implement only one primary function per server to prevent functions that require different security levels from co-existing on the same server. (For example, web servers, database servers, and DNS should be implemented on separate servers.)

To help separate services, use the variety of virtualization and containerization methods included with SUSE Linux Enterprise Server: KVM, Xen, LXC, and Docker.

You can also run SUSE Linux Enterprise Server on third-party virtualization servers like VMware ESX or Microsoft Hyper-V to achieve service separation.

When using the options built in to SUSE Linux Enterprise Server, see:

- For information about virtualization, see *Book "Virtualization Guide"* .

- For information about containerization, see *Book "Docker Guide"* .

2.2.2 Enable only necessary services, protocols, daemons, etc., as required for the function of the system.

This is directly related to an item of requirement 1: To allow only services that are really needed and are using secure protocols and settings (*1.1.6.b Identify insecure services, protocols, and ports allowed; and verify that security features are documented for each service.*). All parties involved must be aware of the dangers of using insecure communication. Research, clearly document and communicate the risk of using insecure protocols and services.

Enable and disable system services using the following **systemctl** commands:

```
tux > systemctl status SERVICE
```

```
tux > sudo systemctl enable SERVICE
```

```
tux > sudo systemctl disable SERVICE
```

To list all available services that are installed on the system and see their status, use the following command:

```
tux > systemctl list-unit-files --type=service
```

2.2.3.a Inspect configuration settings to verify that security features are documented and implemented for all insecure services, daemons, or protocols.

To add an additional layer of security to insecure services, use VPN tunnels (for example, IPsec). With a VPN tunnel, network traffic of such services can be isolated and all data is protected against eavesdropping, both internally and externally. However, note that the communication is still insecure at the endpoints of the VPN tunnel and that this is only a workaround.

For additional security within SUSE Linux Enterprise Server, use SELinux or AppArmor. However, the setup of these frameworks is beyond the scope of this document:

- For information about SELinux, see *Chapter 30, Configuring SELinux*.

- For information about AppArmor, see *Part IV, "Confining Privileges with AppArmor"*.

2.2.5.a Select a sample of system components and inspect the configurations to verify that all unnecessary functionality (for example, scripts, drivers, features, subsystems, file systems, etc.) is removed.

The Linux kernel is the main system component. It consists of a core image that is extended by kernel modules which are loaded depending on the hardware and system design. For example: Network card drivers are automatically loaded depending on the system's network card. File system modules can be enabled to extend the Linux kernel's file system support.

The list of loaded kernel modules is usually quite long and includes modules that are only used occasionally. The kernel module framework allows blacklisting modules and limiting which functionality is loaded.

To block modules from being loaded, configure them via the directory `/etc/modprobe.d`. For example, the kernel module `floppy` is only necessary for systems that have a floppy drive. On systems that do not have a floppy drive, prevent the module from loading: Create a configuration file `/etc/modprobe.d/00-disable-modules.conf` with the following content:

```
install floppy /bin/true
```

The `floppy` module is usually loaded during the execution of the initial RAM disk. Therefore, propagate this configuration change to the `initrd` file using the **mkinitrd** script.

```
tux > sudo mkinitrd
```

It is harder to remove or restrict application functionality, as functionality is in most cases compiled into the application or library itself. Even cases where deleting a file cleanly removes a functionality are problematic: If the file was installed from an RPM package, it will be reinstalled when the package is updated.

2.3 Encrypt all non-console administrative access using strong cryptography. Use technologies such as SSH, VPN, or TLS for web-based management and other non-console administrative access.

Encrypt all administrative network access: SSH with appropriate configuration settings that fit into the security concept should be the tool of choice.

Administrative access can also be granted via a Web site. In this case, the complete connection chain between the browser and the server system must be encrypted. This is done via TLS and X.509 certificates.

A.3.3   Requirement 3: Protect Stored Cardholder Data

The section explains how to handle cardholder and authentication data securely. The following definitions apply:

- *Cardholder data* includes information such as the cardholder name and the Primary Account Number (PAN).

- *Authentication data* includes the Personal Identification Number (PIN) and the Card Validation Code (CVC2).

The main difference between cardholder data and authentication data is that storing authentication is never allowed. In contrast, data such as the PAN can be stored, but must be encrypted and unreadable in case an attacker gains access to the stored data.

The database design for storing cardholder data is beyond the scope of this document. However, data can be encrypted in different ways:

* The DBMS can use column-level encryption inside the database scheme.

* Alternatively, the database files can be encrypted.

* SUSE Linux Enterprise Server supports full-disk encryption, so that the whole database storage is always encrypted. However, access to an encrypted disk works the same way as to a non-encrypted disk. This is discussed in more detail in requirement 3.4.1.

3.4.1.a If disk encryption is used, inspect the configuration and observe the authentication process to verify that logical access to encrypted file systems is implemented via a mechanism that is separate from the native operating system's authentication mechanism (for example, not using local user account databases or general network login credentials).

The guidance description of the PCI-DSS document says the following about this requirement: "Full disk encryption helps to protect data in the event of physical loss of a disk and therefore may be appropriate for portable devices that store cardholder data."

From an administrator's point of view, a block device encryption with the Linux Unified Key Setup (LUKS)/dm-crypt offers an abstraction layer that allows the usage of encrypted disks in the same way as unencrypted disks.

Therefore, access control can only be limited with the general ACL permissions that the file system offers. To comply with this requirement, the decryption key used must not be associated with any general login credentials or authentication methods.

When using LUKS, this is usually fulfilled: The password needs to be entered separately when booting, inserting portable devices or manually mounting disks.

LUKS in fully integrated into SUSE Linux Enterprise Server and can be used via YaST to create new partitions.

3.4.1.c Examine the configurations and observe the processes to verify that cardholder data on removable media is encrypted wherever stored.

As described in *3.4.1.a If disk encryption is used, inspect the configuration and observe the authentication process to verify that logical access to encrypted file systems is implemented via a mechanism that is separate from the native operating system's authentication mechanism (for example, not using local user account databases or general network login credentials).* , LUKS/dm-crypt provides full-disk encryption that fulfills this requirement. Access to the stored data is only possible via a decryption password that must be entered when the disk is mounted.

A.3.4   Requirement 4: Encrypt Transmission of Cardholder Data Across Open, Public Networks

Cardholder data must be encrypted during transmissions over insecure networks. Ideally, encrypt all traffic, externally and internally. This makes it hard for attackers to gain inside information and privileged access to the cardholder data environment.

4.1 Use strong cryptography and security protocols (for example, TLS, IPSEC, SSH, etc.) to safeguard sensitive cardholder data during transmission over open, public networks, including the following: (1) Only trusted keys and certificates are accepted, (2) The protocol in use only supports secure versions or configurations, (3) The encryption strength is appropriate for the encryption methodology in use.

Any connection that transmits sensitive information must be protected against eavesdropping and tampering.

For incoming client requests, use the HTTPS protocol with a secure TLS connection. The authentication is done with a public X.509 certificate that proves to a certain level that the server is the right endpoint the customer is looking for.

SUSE Linux Enterprise Server comes with a set of services and tools that allow protected HTTPS connections. For example, this can be directly done with the Apache HTTP Server or via **stunnel** that functions as a proxy to offer TLS encryption functionality.

IPsec or other VPN technologies can be used for securing the connection between network segments that are connected via a public network. Such connections can also be secured with a public X.509 certificate. For internal usage, it is possible to use a private Certificate Authority (CA) to sign X.509 certificates and to keep track of trusted keys.

In SUSE Linux Enterprise Server, this can be directly established with strongSwan that is a IPsec-based VPN solution or with OpenVPN that is using a custom security protocol.

To administrate the OS, use SSH. For information about configuring SSH to provide better security, see *Section A.3.1, "Requirement 1: Install and Maintain a Firewall Configuration to Protect Cardholder Data"* **and** *Section A.3.2, "Requirement 2: Do Not Use Vendor-Supplied Defaults for System Passwords and Other Security Parameters"*.

A.3.5 Requirement 5: Protect All Systems Against Malware and Regularly Update Anti-Virus Software or Programs

For PCI-DSS compliance, it is necessary to protect against malicious software. Third-party anti-virus software is available from the major anti-virus software vendors and can be integrated into the Linux environment. SUSE Linux Enterprise Server comes with the open source anti-virus engine ClamAV.

ClamAV has a limited set of scanning capabilities and limited performance compared to third-party products. Hence, expect ClamAV to only provide basic protection.

On the other hand, ClamAV is shipped with SUSE Linux Enterprise Server and it can be included during server installation. This makes it easy to fulfill this requirement, but the drawbacks compared to third-party products need to be clearly understood.

A.3.6 Requirement 6: Develop and maintain secure systems and applications

The major part of this requirement concerns in-house software development, documentation, and design questions that are beyond the scope of this document. However, SUSE Linux Enterprise Server provides tools that help keep your systems safe:

* The software package manager Zypper is a powerful instrument of SUSE Linux Enterprise Server. Among other things, it resolves dependencies of packages, products, patterns, and patches, has a locking mechanism to prevent package installation, and provides a complete update stack to keep the system up-to-date and protected against know security issues.
  `zypper` is part of any SUSE Linux Enterprise Server installation and has direct access to the update repositories after system registration.
  For information about Zypper, see Book *"Administration Guide", Chapter 6 "Managing Software with Command Line Tools", Section 6.1 "Using Zypper"*.

* For system management, SUSE provides SUSE Manager that provides an efficient way to keep systems up-to-date. It offers seamless management of both SUSE Linux Enterprise Server and RedHat Enterprise Linux client systems. This is particularly useful in larger system environments, when you need to check the current update status of each system and to react to known security risks.
  For information about SUSE Manager, see https://www.suse.com/documentation/suse-manager/ ↗.

6.2.a Examine policies and procedures related to security patch installation to verify processes are defined for: (1) Installation of applicable critical vendor-supplied security patches within one month of release, (2) Installation of all applicable vendor-supplied security patches within an appropriate time frame (for example, within three months).

To identify patches that need to be installed to secure your system, do the following:

First, refresh all software repositories, so you have up-to-date information:

```
tux > sudo zypper refresh
```

Then use the patch-related commands of Zypper:

- Search for important security fixes that have not yet been installed:

```
tux > zypper list-patches --category security --severity important
```

- It is also possible to search for CVE or SUSE Bugzilla numbers. By default, only necessary patches are listed by this command. To also show patches that have already been installed, use the parameter `--all`:

```
tux > zypper list-patches --all --cve=CVE-2016-4957
```

- To list details of individual patches, use the **patch-info** subcommand:

```
tux > zypper patch-info SUSE-SLE-SERVER-12-SP1-2016-600
```

- To install only important security patches, use the **patch** subcommand.

```
tux > sudo zypper patch --category security --severity important
```

To perform updates automatically, the parameter `--non-interactive`, that is supported by all Zypper subcommands, is helpful.

For more information about Zypper, see Book *"Administration Guide", Chapter 6 "Managing Software with Command Line Tools", Section 6.1 "Using Zypper"*.

A.3.7 Requirement 7: Restrict access to cardholder data by business need to know

OS access control is a complex topic. Again, this PCI-DSS requirement is not specified precisely and does not specifically state to which degree the restrictions need to be implemented. SUSE Linux Enterprise Server comes with all general Linux tools to limit and restrict access to certain system areas and components:

- Access can be controlled via specific users and groups of users using the traditional Unix permission settings.
  For information about managing permissions, see *Chapter 10, Access Control Lists in Linux*.

- A more flexible mechanism for file systems are Access Control Lists (ACLs) that offer a more granular approach. SELinux can be used for maximum system separation and to protect processes from gaining more resources and access then allowed. SELinux or AppArmor are beyond the scope of this document but should be employed to protect critical systems that are likely to be targeted.

  - For information about SELinux, see *Chapter 30, Configuring SELinux*.

  - For information about AppArmor, see *Part IV, "Confining Privileges with AppArmor"*.

7.1.2 Restrict access to privileged user IDs to least privileges necessary to perform job responsibilities.

The standard Unix permissions allow setting Read, Write, and Execution flags to user and group IDs. A general group called others or world defines the access for users that do not fit into the first two groups. This provides a straightforward way to grant or deny access to file system resources.

ACLs provide an extra level of restrictions. It is possible to set read-write access for one user ID and only read access to a second one. The same goes for group IDs.

The commands **getfacl** and **setfacl** (on SUSE Linux Enterprise Server shipped with the package acl) allow direct modification of file system resources. For example, to check and set ACL restrictions of the file /tmp/test.txt for the user wilber:

```
tux > getfacl /tmp/test.txt
# file: /tmp/test.txt
# owner: tux
# group: users
user::r--
group::r--
```

```
  other::r--

  tux > setfacl -m "u:wilber:rw" /tmp/test.txt

  tux > getfacl /tmp/test.txt
  # file: /tmp/test.txt
  # owner: tux
  # group: users
  user::rw-
  user:wilber:r--
  group::r--
  mask::r--
  other::r--
```

Standard Unix permissions include the so-called Sticky Bit. This allows the execution of certain programs with higher privileges then the user who is executing those programs. The best example of this is the **passwd** tool that needs to modify the /etc/shadow to change the user password.

For a more gradual approach to explicitly allowing certain operations or behaviors to binaries, use extended capabilities. As an example for a command that uses extended capabilities by default, consider **ping** (from the package iputils).

ping sends ICMP IP packets over the network card. For this, it needs the CAP_NET_RAW capability to be Effective and Permitted (+ep):

```
  root # sudo getcap /usr/bin/ping
  /usr/bin/ping = cap_net_raw+ep
```

Login access control to the system can be managed using Pluggable Authentication Modules (PAM). There are several modules available in SUSE Linux Enterprise Server that allow setups such as logging the login time, multiple authentication mechanisms and central databases like NIS, LDAP or Active Directory.

For more information about managing permissions, see *Chapter 10, Access Control Lists in Linux*.

A.3.8 Requirement 8: Identify and authenticate access to system component

Ideally, use a central database with user information and a unique identifier (UID) to grant or deny access to certain system components. This makes it easy to give administrators special access to group of servers or a database engineer permission to a certain DBMS system.

On a stand-alone server, unique identifiers are managed via the standard Linux user and group IDs. These are listed inside `/etc/passwd` and `/etc/group`.

8.1.4 Remove/disable inactive user accounts within 90 days.

In this context, there are many advantages to using a centralized infrastructure for user accounts like NIS, LDAP, or Active Directory:

* It is easy to identify and automatically disable inactive accounts.

* User accounts only need to be disabled in one place. After their access is revoked, the user cannot use any service that relies on the centralized account infrastructure.

However, if you are using local accounts, these can be checked for inactivity when a user is logging in. This module checks the last login time recorded in `/var/log/lastlog` and calculates the number of days since. By default, access is denied when the inactivity reaches 90 days.
To list the local accounts last login time use the command **lastlog**.

8.1.6 Limit repeated access attempts by locking out the user ID after not more than six attempts.

As stated in *8.1.4 Remove/disable inactive user accounts within 90 days.*, a centralized account infrastructure will have this capability. On SUSE Linux Enterprise Server systems, access attempts can be checked and limited with the `pam_tally2` PAM module. The module is executed during login time and checks the recorded failed attempts since the last successful login. To check and reset the account status, use the tool **pam_tally2**.

8.1.7 Set the lockout duration to a minimum of 30 minutes or until an administrator enables the user ID.

The PAM module `pam_tally2` described in *8.1.6 Limit repeated access attempts by locking out the user ID after not more than six attempts.* can be used to lock an account for a given time after a failed login attempt. The parameter `unlock_time=1800` must be specified in the PAM configuration. By default, only the administrator can reactivate a locked account.

8.3.1 Incorporate multi-factor authentication for all non-console access into the CDE for personnel with administrative access.

To authenticate users for administrative access with multiple factors, use the following methods:

* Use Pluggable Authentication Modules (PAM): This increases flexibility when adding new methods to the authentication process and when adjusting it.

For third-party one-time password (OTP) products, there is usually also a Linux PAM module available.

For information about PAM, see *Chapter 2, Authentication with PAM*.

* To add multi-factor authentication for SSH connections, mandate use of public keys in addition to passwords.

  To connect to a system, it is then necessary to prove possession of an appropriate private key. At the second stage, you then enter a password. This means attackers need to acquire a private key before they can even try to brute force a password prompt.

8.3.2 Incorporate multi-factor authentication for all remote network access (both user and administrator, and including third-party access for support or maintenance) originating from outside the entity's network.

For details, see *8.3.1 Incorporate multi-factor authentication for all non-console access into the CDE for personnel with administrative access.* .

A.3.9   Requirement 9: Restrict physical access to cardholder data

Physical access to systems that are involved in processing cardholder data are not within the scope of general operating system security. Appropriate facility entry controls must be in place to allow onside personnel employees and visitors to access systems directly.

A.3.10   Requirement 10: Track and monitor all access to network resources and cardholder data

To track user activities, it is important to have a synchronized time reference. This is done via the NTP protocol that allows servers to keep their local time in synchronization with a central system. The central NTP server inside the cardholder data environment (CDE) should not rely on external connections to the Internet to update the system time. Alternatively, system time can be updated using DCF77 radio transmissions or a GPS receiver.

A synchronized time reference makes it easier to correlate events inside recorded log files. This reference can include general system log entries collected by a central system log server or kernel audit messages by the daemon `audit`.

For information about auditing, see *Part VI, "The Linux Audit Framework"*.

All subsections of this requirement relevant to auditing can be complied with by defining auditing rules that in a central storage.

A.3.11   Requirement 11: Regularly Test Security Systems and Processes

Testing the discussed security mechanisms is also a key requirement for PCI-DSS. Evaluating the configurations and testing logging mechanisms can protect against know security risks and ensure that essential information are available to identify possible security breaches. Testing capabilities should be considered during system design already.

To keep track of system integrity, SUSE Linux Enterprise Server comes with the Advanced Intrusion Detection Environment (AIDE). AIDE creates a hash value database of all relevant OS files. After initialization, it can be used to verify the integrity of all previously saved files. To employ AIDE, it is best to regularly create database snapshots and save them to a central system on which you can evaluate possible modifications.

For more information about AIDE, see *Chapter 13, Intrusion Detection with AIDE*.

A.3.12   Requirement 12: Maintain a Policy That Addresses Information Security for All Personnel

Any organization that handles valuable information should have general security policy. All relevant aspects should be included to make it clear for employees and stakeholders about possible risks and how to avoid them.

All security policies should also be evaluated regularly and adjusted to keep the protection level as high as possible.

B Documentation Updates

This chapter lists content changes for this document.

This manual was updated on the following dates:

B.1 January 2018 (Maintenance Release for SUSE Linux Enterprise Server 12 SP3)

Appendix A, Achieving PCI-DSS Compliance

Added new PCI-DSS appendix. (Fate #314831)

B.2 September 2017 (Initial Release of SUSE Linux Enterprise Server 12 SP3)

General

* Numerous small fixes and additions to the documentation, based on technical feedback.

* Removed all references to the `faillog` package, which is no longer shipped (https://bugzilla.suse.com/show_bug.cgi?id=710788).

- Added documentation on using the YaST *LDAP and Kerberos Client* module to *Chapter 5, LDAP—A Directory Service* and *Chapter 6, Network Authentication with Kerberos* (http:// bugzilla.suse.com/show_bug.cgi?id=1034818 ↗).

- Added note about deprecation of *Unix Attributes* plug-in in Microsoft Windows* Server 2016 in *Chapter 7, Active Directory Support* (Doc Comment #33098).

Chapter 14, SSH: Secure Network Operations

- Added a tip on viewing `sshd` log files to *Section 14.4, "The SSH Daemon (sshd)"*.

Chapter 15, Masquerading and Firewalls

- In *Section 15.3, "Firewalling Basics"*, updated a link to a HOWTO (https://bugzilla.suse.com/show_bug.cgi?id=1053601 ↗).

B.3 November 2016 (Initial Release of SUSE Linux Enterprise Server 12 SP2)

General

- The e-mail address for documentation feedback has changed to `docteam@suse.com`.

- The documentation for Docker has been enhanced and renamed to *Docker Guide.*

- In *Section 4.2, "Configuring an Authentication Client with YaST"*, the command is called **sss_cache** (https://bugzilla.suse.com/show_bug.cgi?id=993377 ⬈).

Chapter 7, Active Directory Support

- Added information about the new YaST module *User Logon Management* to *Section 7.3, "Configuring a Linux Client for Active Directory"* (Fate# 320407).

Chapter 14, SSH: Secure Network Operations

- New section *Section 14.4.2, "Rotating Host Keys"* (Fate #318427).

Chapter 16, Configuring a VPN Server

- openVPN is now set up via wicked, adjusted *Section 16.2.1, "Configuring the VPN Server"* accordingly (Fate #317974).

- Added *Section 16.4, "Setting Up a VPN Server or Client Using YaST"* (Fate #320616).

B.4 March 2016 (Maintenance Release of SUSE Linux Enterprise Server 12 SP1)

Chapter 6, Network Authentication with Kerberos

Fixed wrong service name (sldapd to slapd) (https://bugzilla.suse.com/show_bug.cgi?id=963047 ⬈).

Chapter 16, Configuring a VPN Server

Use larger keys (min. 2048bit) instead of 1024 (https://bugzilla.suse.com/show_bug.cgi?id=959634 ⬈).

B.5 December 2015 (Initial Release of SUSE Linux Enterprise Server 12 SP1)

General

- *Book "Subscription Management Tool for SLES 12 SP3"* is now part of the documentation for SUSE Linux Enterprise Server.

- Add-ons provided by SUSE have been renamed as modules and extensions. The manuals have been updated to reflect this change.

- Numerous small fixes and additions to the documentation, based on technical feedback.

- The registration service has been changed from Novell Customer Center to SUSE Customer Center.

- In YaST, you will now reach *Network Settings* via the *System* group. *Network Devices* is gone (https://bugzilla.suse.com/show_bug.cgi?id=867809 ↗).

Chapter 4, Setting Up Authentication Servers and Clients Using YaST

Updated the chapter to reflect new GUI improvements for Kerberos/LDAP client (Fate #316349).

Chapter 8, Configuring Security Settings with YaST

Updated chapter because of `systemd`-related changes (Fate #318425).

Chapter 15, Masquerading and Firewalls

- Added *Section 15.4.1.2, "Opening Ports"*.

Chapter 30, Configuring SELinux

- Removed references to the source policy files in *Section 30.6.6, "Working with SELinux Modules"* (not available).

- Minimum policy is now part of the distribution in *Section 30.4, "SELinux Policy"*.

- Removed http://software.opensuse.org as a preferred policy download server, and added https://build.opensuse.org instead in *Section 30.4, "SELinux Policy"*.

Bugfixes

- Removed obsolete `acpid.service` (https://bugzilla.suse.com/show_bug.cgi?id=918655 ↗).

- Removed `/etc/sysconfig/auditd` from *Section 31.2, "Configuring the Audit Daemon"*—this configuration file has been removed without replacement (https://bugzilla.suse.com/show_bug.cgi?id=918655 ↗).

- Extend Firewall Documentation to Describe How to Open a Port (https://bugzilla.suse.com/show_bug.cgi?id=914076 ↗).

B.6   February 2015 (Documentation Maintenance Update)

Bugfixes

- Small fix for *Section 5.5, "Manually Configuring an LDAP Server"*:

  - SLES 12 Documentation is missing "Configuring an LDAP Server with YaST" (https://bugzilla.suse.com/show_bug.cgi?id=911409 ↗).

- Numerous small fixes for *Chapter 16, Configuring a VPN Server*:

  - https://bugzilla.suse.com/show_bug.cgi?id=909494 ↗

  - https://bugzilla.suse.com/show_bug.cgi?id=910121 ↗

  - https://bugzilla.suse.com/show_bug.cgi?id=910132 ↗

  - https://bugzilla.suse.com/show_bug.cgi?id=910133 ↗

  - https://bugzilla.suse.com/show_bug.cgi?id=910137 ↗

  - https://bugzilla.suse.com/show_bug.cgi?id=910142 ↗

  - https://bugzilla.suse.com/show_bug.cgi?id=910148 ↗

B.7   October 2014 (Initial Release of SUSE Linux Enterprise Server 12)

General

- Removed all KDE documentation and references because KDE is no longer shipped.

- Removed all references to SuSEconfig, which is no longer supported (Fate #100011).

- Move from System V init to systemd (Fate #310421). Updated affected parts of the documentation.

- YaST Runlevel Editor has changed to Services Manager (Fate #312568). Updated affected parts of the documentation.

- Removed all references to ISDN support, as ISDN support has been removed (Fate #314594).

- Removed all references to the YaST DSL module as it is no longer shipped (Fate #316264).

- Removed all references to the YaST Modem module as it is no longer shipped (Fate #316264).

- Btrfs has become the default file system for the root partition (Fate #315901). Updated affected parts of the documentation.

- The `dmesg` now provides human-readable time stamps in `ctime()`-like format (Fate #316056). Updated affected parts of the documentation.

- syslog and syslog-ng have been replaced by rsyslog (Fate #316175). Updated affected parts of the documentation.

- MariaDB is now shipped as the relational database instead of MySQL (Fate #313595). Updated affected parts of the documentation.

- SUSE-related products are no longer available from http://download.novell.com ⌝ but from http://download.suse.com ⌝. Adjusted links accordingly.

- Novell Customer Center has been replaced with SUSE Customer Center. Updated affected parts of the documentation.

- `/var/run` is mounted as tmpfs (Fate #303793). Updated affected parts of the documentation.

- The following architectures are no longer supported: IA64 and x86. Updated affected parts of the documentation.

- The traditional method for setting up the network with `ifconfig` has been replaced by `wicked`. Updated affected parts of the documentation.

- A lot of networking commands are deprecated and have been replaced by newer commands (usually **ip**). Updated affected parts of the documentation.

```
arp: ip neighbor
ifconfig: ip addr, ip link
iptunnel: ip tunnel
iwconfig: iw
nameif: ip link, ifrename
netstat: ss, ip route, ip -s link, ip maddr
route: ip route
```

- Numerous small fixes and additions to the documentation, based on technical feedback.

Chapter 2, Authentication with PAM

The `pam_pwcheck` module has been replaced with `pam_cracklib` and `pam_pwhistory`. Updated chapter to reflect this change.

Chapter 4, Setting Up Authentication Servers and Clients Using YaST

Added a chapter about the new YaST authentication module for Kerberos and LDAP (Fate #316349). The chapter consists of two parts: *Section 4.2, "Configuring an Authentication Client with YaST"* and *Section 4.2, "Configuring an Authentication Client with YaST"* (Fate #308902).

Chapter 5, LDAP—A Directory Service

Updated chapter to reflect the changes in YaST regarding authentication setup (Fate #316349).

Chapter 6, Network Authentication with Kerberos

Updated chapter to reflect the changes in YaST regarding authentication setup (Fate #316349).

Chapter 9, Authorization with PolKit

Updated chapter to reflect major software updates.

- Mentioned that SSH on SUSE Linux Enterprise Server uses cryptographic hardware acceleration if available (Fate #308239).

- New section *Section 14.3.2, "Setting Permissions for File Uploads"* (Fate #312774).

Chapter 17, Managing X.509 Certification

The YaST CA module now allows to export key and certificate into different files. See *Section 17.2.5, "Changing Default Values"* (Fate #305490).

Part IV, "Confining Privileges with AppArmor"

- Added short description of supported AppArmor profile flags in *Section 21.6.1, "Profile Flags"*.

- Thoroughly explained the syntax and subtle differences in meaning for AppArmor include statements in *Section 21.3, "Include Statements"*.

- Introduced extended ways to map a profile: Added *Section 21.6.3, "Pattern Matching"*, *Section 21.6.4, "Namespaces"* and updated *Section 21.6.6, "Alias Rules"*.

- Added description for new optional `allow` and `file` keywords for AppArmor profiles in *Section 21.7.7, "Optional allow and file Rules"*.

- Added description for new `safe` and `unsafe` keywords for AppArmor profiles to *Section 21.8.10, "safe and unsafe Keywords"*.

- New `PUx/pux` and `CUx/cux` profile transitions added in *Section 21.8.8, "Fallback Modes for Profile Transitions"*.

- Added new section *Section 21.6.3, "Pattern Matching"*.

- Restructured and completely rewrote *Chapter 25, Profiling Your Web Applications Using ChangeHat*.

- Removed old content describing the YaST method.

- Introduced a command line example on creating a hat for the Adminer application.

Part VI, "The Linux Audit Framework"

Numerous small fixes and additions, based on technical feedback.

Obsolete Content

- Section *Adding a Profile Using the Wizard* has been removed from *Chapter 23, Building and Managing Profiles with YaST* (Fate #308684).

- Section *Updating Profiles from Log Entries* has been removed from *Chapter 23, Building and Managing Profiles with YaST* (Fate #308683).

- Chapter *Using the Fingerprint Reader* has been removed from *Part I, "Authentication"* (Fate #313128).

Bugfixes

- Updated the AppArmor documentation to version 2.8 AppArmor (http://bugzilla.suse.com/show_bug.cgi?id=722915 ↗).

C   GNU Licenses

This appendix contains the GNU Free Documentation License version 1.2.

GNU Free Documentation License

Copyright (C) 2000, 2001, 2002 Free Software Foundation, Inc. 51 Franklin St, Fifth Floor, Boston, MA 02110-1301 USA. Everyone is permitted to copy and distribute verbatim copies of this license document, but changing it is not allowed.

0. PREAMBLE

The purpose of this License is to make a manual, textbook, or other functional and useful document "free" in the sense of freedom: to assure everyone the effective freedom to copy and redistribute it, with or without modifying it, either commercially or non-commercially. Secondarily, this License preserves for the author and publisher a way to get credit for their work, while not being considered responsible for modifications made by others.

This License is a kind of "copyleft", which means that derivative works of the document must themselves be free in the same sense. It complements the GNU General Public License, which is a copyleft license designed for free software.

We have designed this License to use it for manuals for free software, because free software needs free documentation: a free program should come with manuals providing the same freedoms that the software does. But this License is not limited to software manuals; it can be used for any textual work, regardless of subject matter or whether it is published as a printed book. We recommend this License principally for works whose purpose is instruction or reference.

1. APPLICABILITY AND DEFINITIONS

This License applies to any manual or other work, in any medium, that contains a notice placed by the copyright holder saying it can be distributed under the terms of this License. Such a notice grants a world-wide, royalty-free license, unlimited in duration, to use that work under the conditions stated herein. The "Document", below, refers to any such manual or work. Any member of the public is a licensee, and is addressed as "you". You accept the license if you copy, modify or distribute the work in a way requiring permission under copyright law.

A "Modified Version" of the Document means any work containing the Document or a portion of it, either copied verbatim, or with modifications and/or translated into another language.

A "Secondary Section" is a named appendix or a front-matter section of the Document that deals exclusively with the relationship of the publishers or authors of the Document to the Document's overall subject (or to related matters) and contains nothing that could fall directly within that overall subject. (Thus, if the Document is in part a textbook of mathematics, a Secondary Section may not explain any mathematics.) The relationship could be a matter of historical connection with the subject or with related matters, or of legal, commercial, philosophical, ethical or political position regarding them.

The "Invariant Sections" are certain Secondary Sections whose titles are designated, as being those of Invariant Sections, in the notice that says that the Document is released under this License. If a section does not fit the above definition of Secondary then it is not allowed to be designated as Invariant. The Document may contain zero Invariant Sections. If the Document does not identify any Invariant Sections then there are none.

The "Cover Texts" are certain short passages of text that are listed, as Front-Cover Texts or Back-Cover Texts, in the notice that says that the Document is released under this License. A Front-Cover Text may be at most 5 words, and a Back-Cover Text may be at most 25 words.

A "Transparent" copy of the Document means a machine-readable copy, represented in a format whose specification is available to the general public, that is suitable for revising the document straightforwardly with generic text editors or (for images composed of pixels) generic paint programs or (for drawings) some widely available drawing editor, and that is suitable for input to text formatters or for automatic translation to a variety of formats suitable for input to text formatters. A copy made in an otherwise Transparent file format whose markup, or absence of markup, has been arranged to thwart or discourage subsequent modification by readers is not Transparent. An image format is not Transparent if used for any substantial amount of text. A copy that is not "Transparent" is called "Opaque".

Examples of suitable formats for Transparent copies include plain ASCII without markup, Texinfo input format, LaTeX input format, SGML or XML using a publicly available DTD, and standard-conforming simple HTML, PostScript or PDF designed for human modification. Examples of transparent image formats include PNG, XCF and JPG. Opaque formats include proprietary formats that can be read and edited only by proprietary word processors, SGML or XML for which the DTD and/or processing tools are not generally available, and the machine-generated HTML, PostScript or PDF produced by some word processors for output purposes only.

The "Title Page" means, for a printed book, the title page itself, plus such following pages as are needed to hold, legibly, the material this License requires to appear in the title page. For works in formats which do not have any title page as such, "Title Page" means the text near the most prominent appearance of the work's title, preceding the beginning of the body of the text.

A section "Entitled XYZ" means a named subunit of the Document whose title either is precisely XYZ or contains XYZ in parentheses following text that translates XYZ in another language. (Here XYZ stands for a specific section name mentioned below, such as "Acknowledgements", "Dedications", "Endorsements", or "History".) To "Preserve the Title" of such a section when you modify the Document means that it remains a section "Entitled XYZ" according to this definition.

The Document may include Warranty Disclaimers next to the notice which states that this License applies to the Document. These Warranty Disclaimers are considered to be included by reference in this License, but only as regards disclaiming warranties: any other implication that these Warranty Disclaimers may have is void and has no effect on the meaning of this License.

2. VERBATIM COPYING

You may copy and distribute the Document in any medium, either commercially or non-commercially, provided that this License, the copyright notices, and the license notice saying this License applies to the Document are reproduced in all copies, and that you add no other conditions whatsoever to those of this License. You may not use technical measures to obstruct or control the reading or further copying of the copies you make or distribute. However, you may accept compensation in exchange for copies. If you distribute a large enough number of copies you must also follow the conditions in section 3.

You may also lend copies, under the same conditions stated above, and you may publicly display copies.

3. COPYING IN QUANTITY

If you publish printed copies (or copies in media that commonly have printed covers) of the Document, numbering more than 100, and the Document's license notice requires Cover Texts, you must enclose the copies in covers that carry, clearly and legibly, all these Cover Texts: Front-Cover Texts on the front cover, and Back-Cover Texts on the back cover. Both covers must also clearly and legibly identify you as the publisher of these copies. The front cover must present the full title with all words of the title equally prominent and visible. You may add other material on the covers in addition. Copying with changes limited to the covers, as long as they preserve the title of the Document and satisfy these conditions, can be treated as verbatim copying in other respects.

If the required texts for either cover are too voluminous to fit legibly, you should put the first ones listed (as many as fit reasonably) on the actual cover, and continue the rest onto adjacent pages.

If you publish or distribute Opaque copies of the Document numbering more than 100, you must either include a machine-readable Transparent copy along with each Opaque copy, or state in or with each Opaque copy a computer-network location from which the general network-using public has access to download using public-standard network protocols a complete Transparent copy of the Document, free of added material. If you use the latter option, you must take reasonably prudent steps, when you begin distribution of Opaque copies in quantity, to ensure that this Transparent copy will remain thus accessible at the stated location until at least one year after the last time you distribute an Opaque copy (directly or through your agents or retailers) of that edition to the public.

It is requested, but not required, that you contact the authors of the Document well before redistributing any large number of copies, to give them a chance to provide you with an updated version of the Document.

4. MODIFICATIONS

You may copy and distribute a Modified Version of the Document under the conditions of sections 2 and 3 above, provided that you release the Modified Version under precisely this License, with the Modified Version filling the role of the Document, thus licensing distribution and modification of the Modified Version to whoever possesses a copy of it. In addition, you must do these things in the Modified Version:

A. Use in the Title Page (and on the covers, if any) a title distinct from that of the Document, and from those of previous versions (which should, if there were any, be listed in the History section of the Document). You may use the same title as a previous version if the original publisher of that version gives permission.

B. List on the Title Page, as authors, one or more persons or entities responsible for authorship of the modifications in the Modified Version, together with at least five of the principal authors of the Document (all of its principal authors, if it has fewer than five), unless they release you from this requirement.

C. State on the Title page the name of the publisher of the Modified Version, as the publisher.

D. Preserve all the copyright notices of the Document.

E. Add an appropriate copyright notice for your modifications adjacent to the other copyright notices.

F. Include, immediately after the copyright notices, a license notice giving the public permission to use the Modified Version under the terms of this License, in the form shown in the Addendum below.

G. Preserve in that license notice the full lists of Invariant Sections and required Cover Texts given in the Document's license notice.

H. Include an unaltered copy of this License.

I. Preserve the section Entitled "History", Preserve its Title, and add to it an item stating at least the title, year, new authors, and publisher of the Modified Version as given on the Title Page. If there is no section Entitled "History" in the Document, create one stating the title, year, authors, and publisher of the Document as given on its Title Page, then add an item describing the Modified Version as stated in the previous sentence.

J. Preserve the network location, if any, given in the Document for public access to a Transparent copy of the Document, and likewise the network locations given in the Document for previous versions it was based on. These may be placed in the "History" section. You may omit a network location for a work that was published at least four years before the Document itself, or if the original publisher of the version it refers to gives permission.

K. For any section Entitled "Acknowledgements" or "Dedications", Preserve the Title of the section, and preserve in the section all the substance and tone of each of the contributor acknowledgements and/or dedications given therein.

L. Preserve all the Invariant Sections of the Document, unaltered in their text and in their titles. Section numbers or the equivalent are not considered part of the section titles.

M. Delete any section Entitled "Endorsements". Such a section may not be included in the Modified Version.

N. Do not retitle any existing section to be Entitled "Endorsements" or to conflict in title with any Invariant Section.

O. Preserve any Warranty Disclaimers.

If the Modified Version includes new front-matter sections or appendices that qualify as Secondary Sections and contain no material copied from the Document, you may at your option designate some or all of these sections as invariant. To do this, add their titles to the list of Invariant Sections in the Modified Version's license notice. These titles must be distinct from any other section titles.

You may add a section Entitled "Endorsements", provided it contains nothing but endorsements of your Modified Version by various parties--for example, statements of peer review or that the text has been approved by an organization as the authoritative definition of a standard.

You may add a passage of up to five words as a Front-Cover Text, and a passage of up to 25 words as a Back-Cover Text, to the end of the list of Cover Texts in the Modified Version. Only one passage of Front-Cover Text and one of Back-Cover Text may be added by (or through arrangements made by) any one entity. If the Document already includes a cover text for the same cover, previously added by you or by arrangement made by the same entity you are acting on behalf of, you may not add another; but you may replace the old one, on explicit permission from the previous publisher that added the old one.

The author(s) and publisher(s) of the Document do not by this License give permission to use their names for publicity for or to assert or imply endorsement of any Modified Version.

5. COMBINING DOCUMENTS

You may combine the Document with other documents released under this License, under the terms defined in section 4 above for modified versions, provided that you include in the combination all of the Invariant Sections of all of the original documents, unmodified, and list them all as Invariant Sections of your combined work in its license notice, and that you preserve all their Warranty Disclaimers.

The combined work need only contain one copy of this License, and multiple identical Invariant Sections may be replaced with a single copy. If there are multiple Invariant Sections with the same name but different contents, make the title of each such section unique by adding at the end of it, in parentheses, the name of the original author or publisher of that section if known, or else a unique number. Make the same adjustment to the section titles in the list of Invariant Sections in the license notice of the combined work.

In the combination, you must combine any sections Entitled "History" in the various original documents, forming one section Entitled "History"; likewise combine any sections Entitled "Acknowledgements", and any sections Entitled "Dedications". You must delete all sections Entitled "Endorsements".

6. COLLECTIONS OF DOCUMENTS

You may make a collection consisting of the Document and other documents released under this License, and replace the individual copies of this License in the various documents with a single copy that is included in the collection, provided that you follow the rules of this License for verbatim copying of each of the documents in all other respects.

You may extract a single document from such a collection, and distribute it individually under this License, provided you insert a copy of this License into the extracted document, and follow this License in all other respects regarding verbatim copying of that document.

7. AGGREGATION WITH INDEPENDENT WORKS

A compilation of the Document or its derivatives with other separate and independent documents or works, in or on a volume of a storage or distribution medium, is called an "aggregate" if the copyright resulting from the compilation is not used to limit the legal rights of the compilation's users beyond what the individual works permit. When the Document is included in an aggregate, this License does not apply to the other works in the aggregate which are not themselves derivative works of the Document.

If the Cover Text requirement of section 3 is applicable to these copies of the Document, then if the Document is less than one half of the entire aggregate, the Document's Cover Texts may be placed on covers that bracket the Document within the aggregate, or the electronic equivalent of covers if the Document is in electronic form. Otherwise they must appear on printed covers that bracket the whole aggregate.

8. TRANSLATION

Translation is considered a kind of modification, so you may distribute translations of the Document under the terms of section 4. Replacing Invariant Sections with translations requires special permission from their copyright holders, but you may include translations of some or all Invariant Sections in addition to the original versions of these Invariant Sections. You may include a translation of this License, and all the license notices in the Document, and any Warranty Disclaimers, provided that you also include the original English version of this License and the original versions of those notices and disclaimers. In case of a disagreement between the translation and the original version of this License or a notice or disclaimer, the original version will prevail.

If a section in the Document is Entitled "Acknowledgements", "Dedications", or "History", the requirement (section 4) to Preserve its Title (section 1) will typically require changing the actual title.

9. TERMINATION

You may not copy, modify, sublicense, or distribute the Document except as expressly provided for under this License. Any other attempt to copy, modify, sublicense or distribute the Document is void, and will automatically terminate your rights under this License. However, parties who have received copies, or rights, from you under this License will not have their licenses terminated so long as such parties remain in full compliance.

10. FUTURE REVISIONS OF THIS LICENSE

The Free Software Foundation may publish new, revised versions of the GNU Free Documentation License from time to time. Such new versions will be similar in spirit to the present version, but may differ in detail to address new problems or concerns. See http://www.gnu.org/copyleft/ ↗.

Each version of the License is given a distinguishing version number. If the Document specifies that a particular numbered version of this License "or any later version" applies to it, you have the option of following the terms and conditions either of that specified version or of any later version that has been published (not as a draft) by the Free Software Foundation. If the Document does not specify a version number of this License, you may choose any version ever published (not as a draft) by the Free Software Foundation.

ADDENDUM: How to use this License for your documents

```
Copyright (c) YEAR YOUR NAME.
Permission is granted to copy, distribute and/or modify this document
under the terms of the GNU Free Documentation License, Version 1.2
or any later version published by the Free Software Foundation;
with no Invariant Sections, no Front-Cover Texts, and no Back-Cover Texts.
A copy of the license is included in the section entitled "GNU
Free Documentation License".
```

If you have Invariant Sections, Front-Cover Texts and Back-Cover Texts, replace the "with...Texts." line with this:

```
with the Invariant Sections being LIST THEIR TITLES, with the
Front-Cover Texts being LIST, and with the Back-Cover Texts being LIST.
```

If you have Invariant Sections without Cover Texts, or some other combination of the three, merge those two alternatives to suit the situation.

If your document contains nontrivial examples of program code, we recommend releasing these examples in parallel under your choice of free software license, such as the GNU General Public License, to permit their use in free software.

www.ingramcontent.com/pod-product-compliance
Lightning Source LLC
Chambersburg PA
CBHW060921060326
40690CB00041B/2852